WHAZZAT?
CAN I TRANSFORM
INTO OTHER THINGS
BESIDES A FOX?

I MEAN,
I GUESS.
BUT I WON'T.
'CAUSE IT'S A
PAIN.

Four
Knights of
the Apocalypse

Nakaba Suzuki Presents

7

Contents

Four Knights Of The Apocalypse

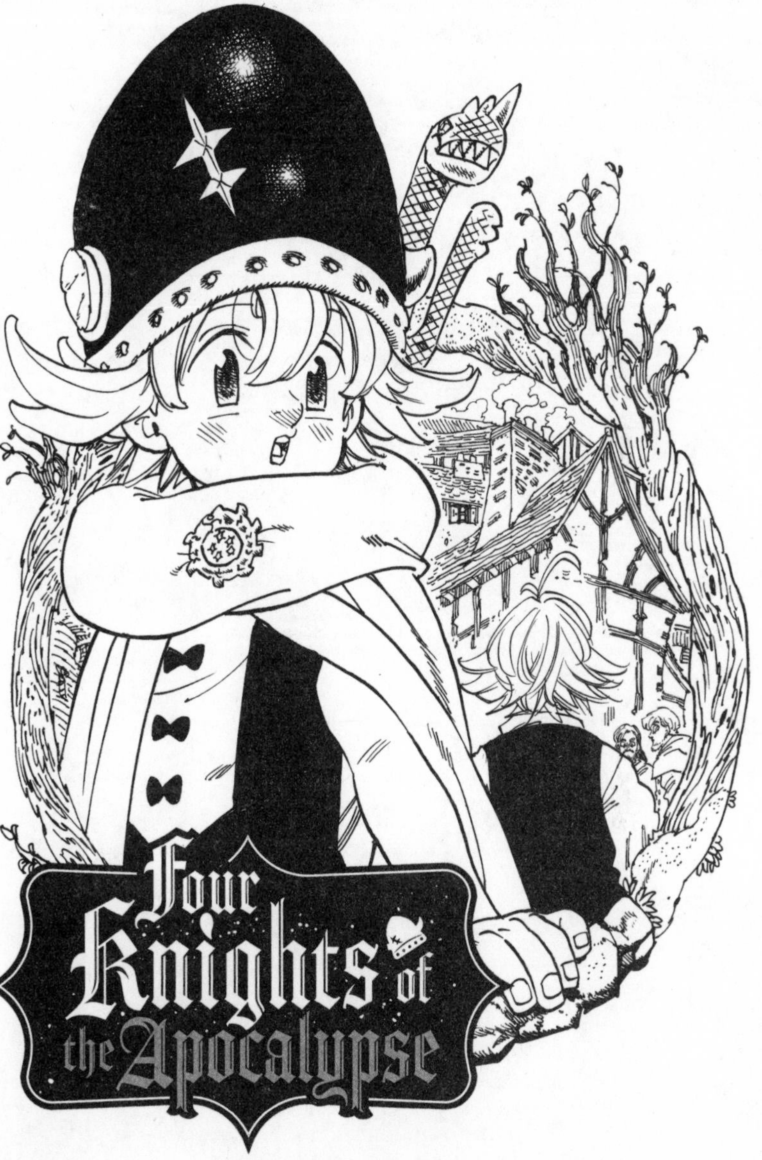
Four Knights of the Apocalypse

CHAPTER 51: THE KING OF LIONES

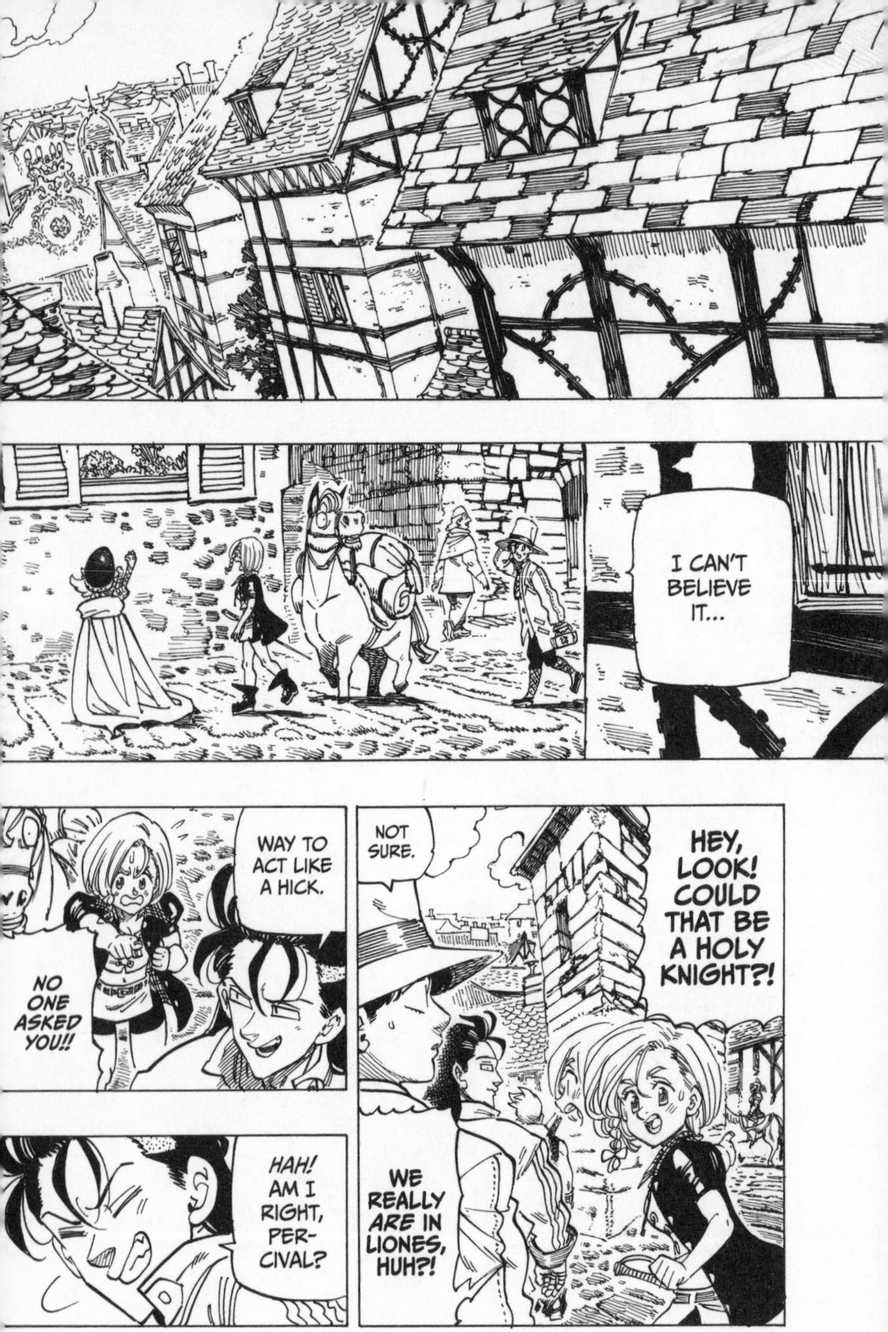
I CAN'T BELIEVE IT...
HEY, LOOK! COULD THAT BE A HOLY KNIGHT?!
NOT SURE.
WE REALLY *ARE* IN LIONES, HUH?!
WAY TO ACT LIKE A HICK.
NO ONE ASKED YOU!!
HAH! AM I RIGHT, PERCIVAL?

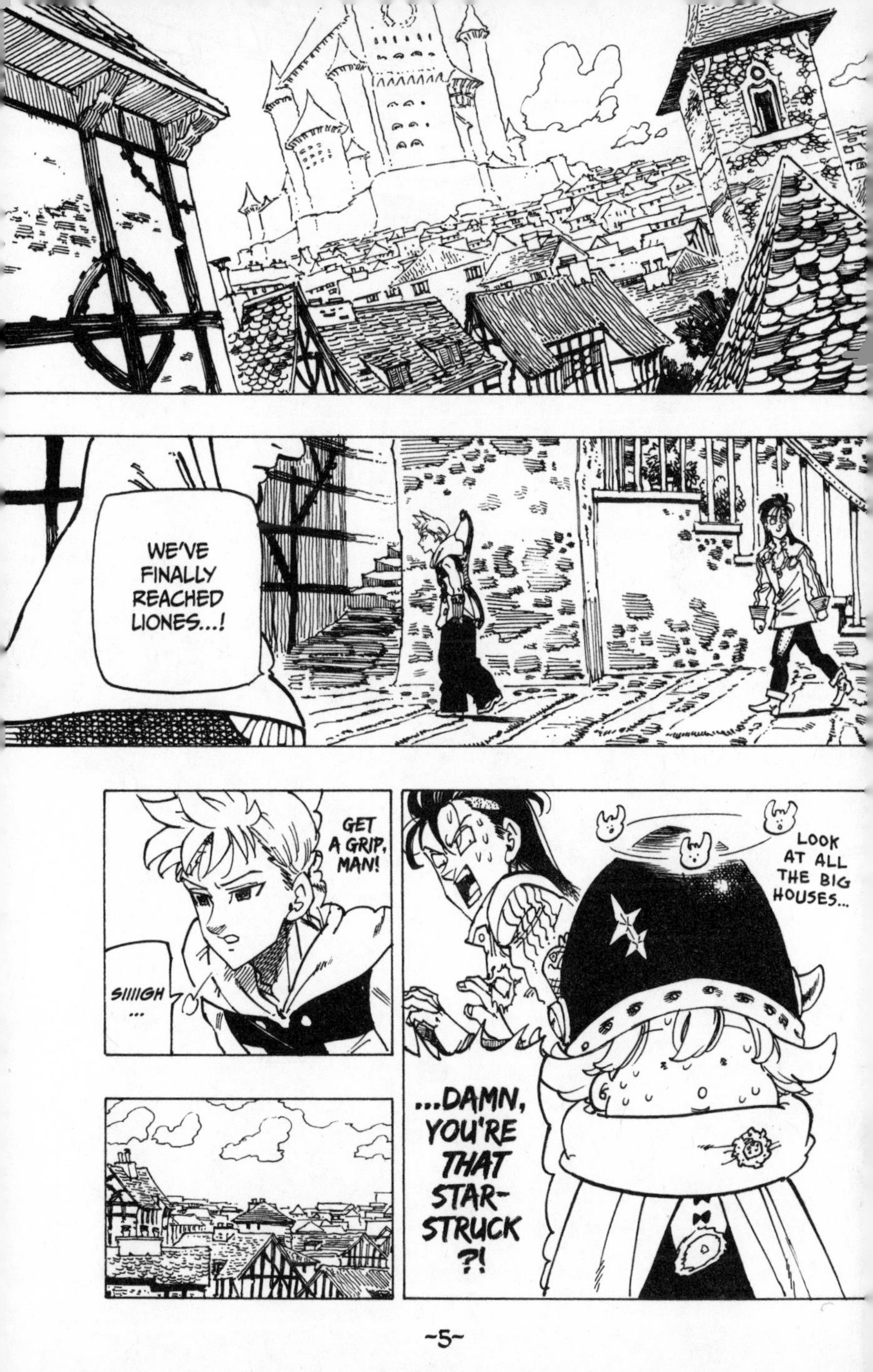
WE'VE FINALLY REACHED LIONES...!
LOOK AT ALL THE BIG HOUSES...
...DAMN, YOU'RE THAT STAR-STRUCK?!
GET A GRIP, MAN!
SIIIIGH ...

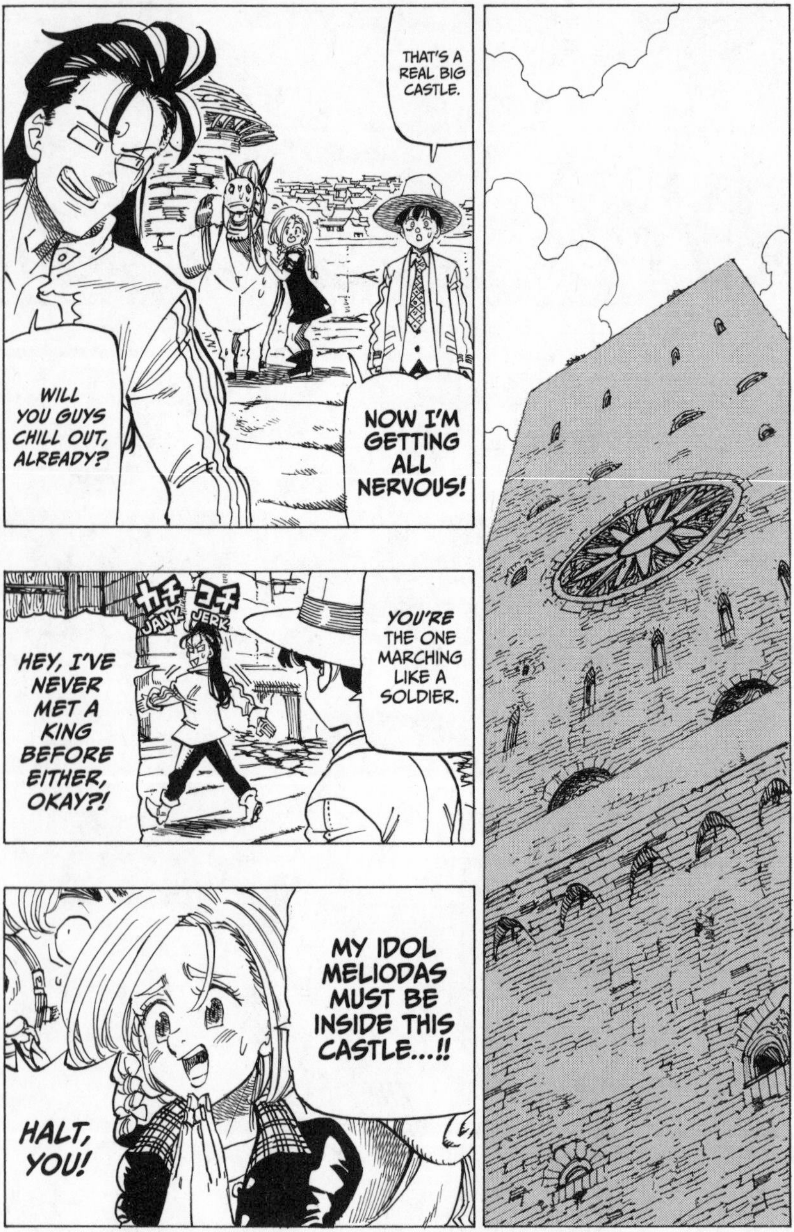

THAT'S A REAL BIG CASTLE.
NOW I'M GETTING ALL NERVOUS!
WILL YOU GUYS CHILL OUT, ALREADY?
YOU'RE THE ONE MARCHING LIKE A SOLDIER.
カチ コチ
JANK JERK
HEY, I'VE NEVER MET A KING BEFORE EITHER, OKAY?!
MY IDOL MELIODAS MUST BE INSIDE THIS CASTLE...!!
HALT, YOU!

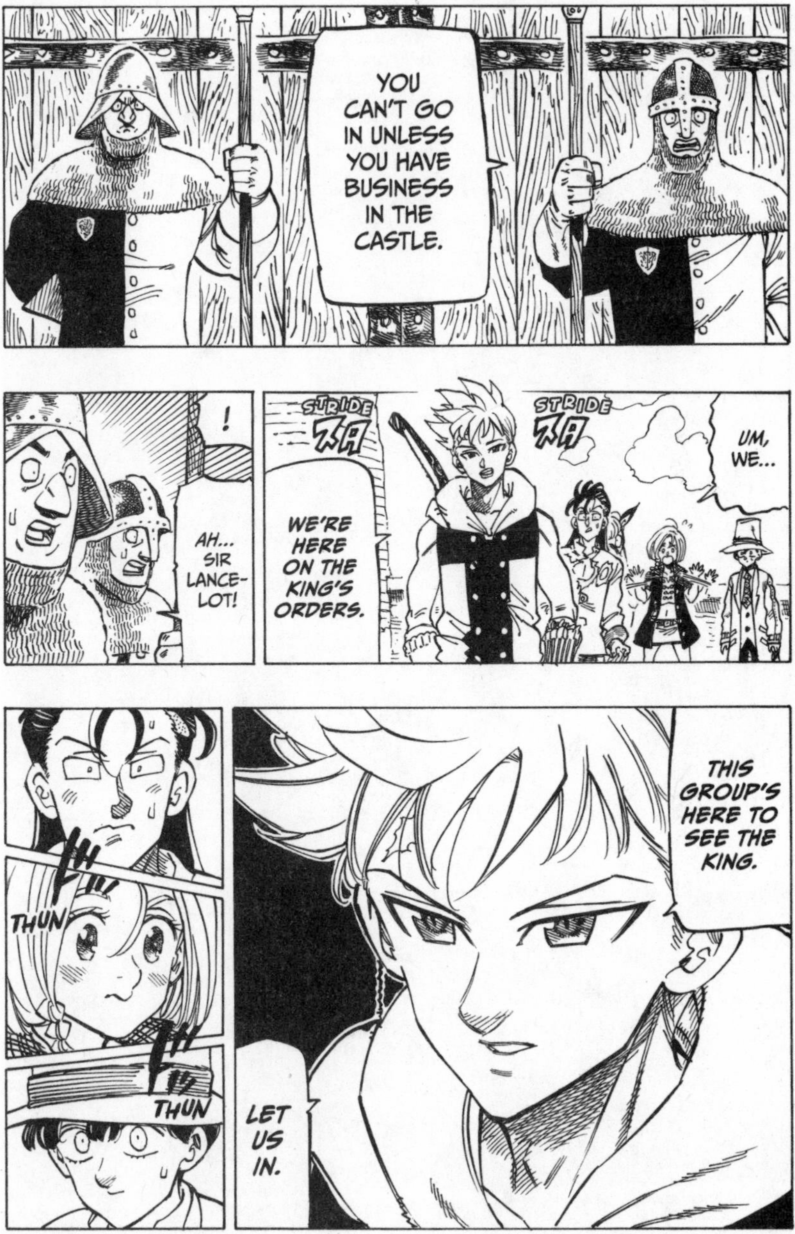

YOU CAN'T GO IN UNLESS YOU HAVE BUSINESS IN THE CASTLE.
UM, WE...
STRIDE
STRIDE
WE'RE HERE ON THE KING'S ORDERS.
!
AH... SIR LANCE-LOT!
THIS GROUP'S HERE TO SEE THE KING.
LET US IN.
THUN
THUN

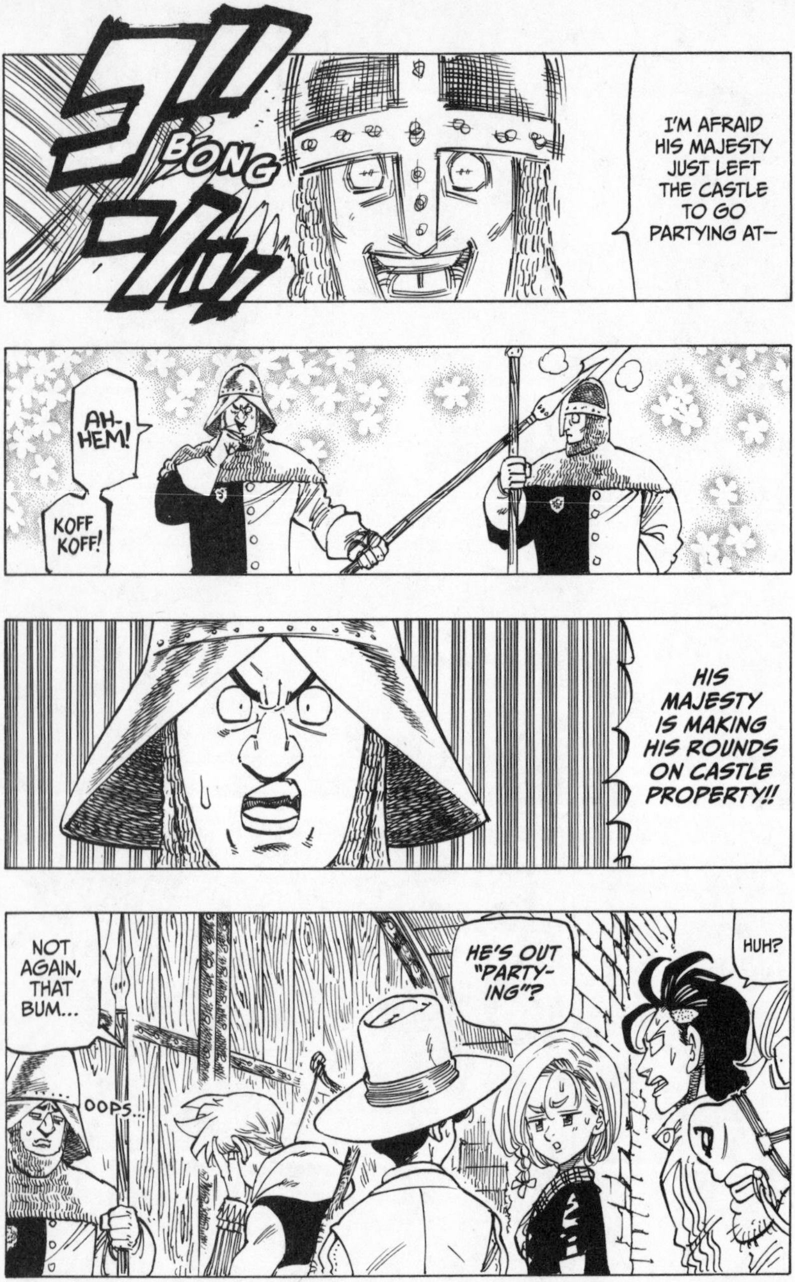
I'M AFRAID HIS MAJESTY JUST LEFT THE CASTLE TO GO PARTYING AT—
BONG
AH-HEM!
KOFF KOFF!
HIS MAJESTY IS MAKING HIS ROUNDS ON CASTLE PROPERTY!!
HUH?
HE'S OUT "PARTY-ING"?
NOT AGAIN, THAT BUM...
OOPS...

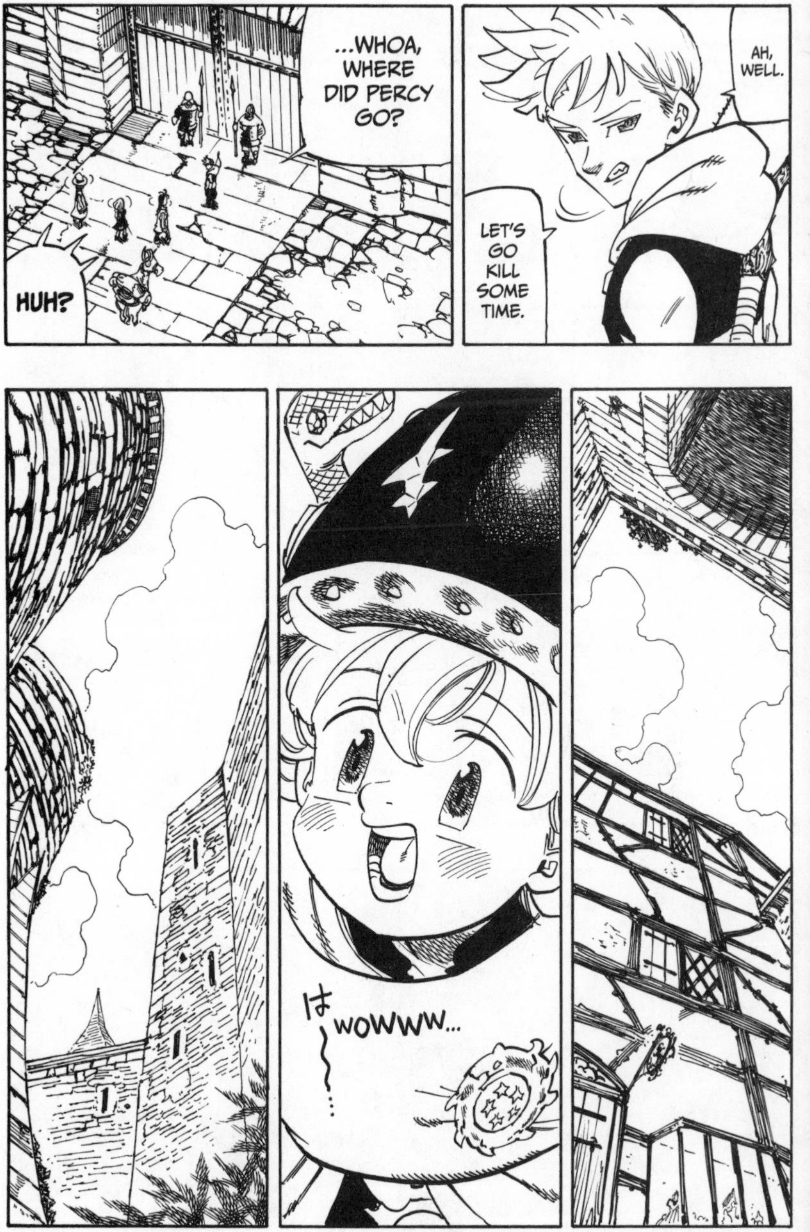
AH, WELL.
LET'S GO KILL SOME TIME.
...WHOA, WHERE DID PERCY GO?
HUH?
は~~...
WOWWW...

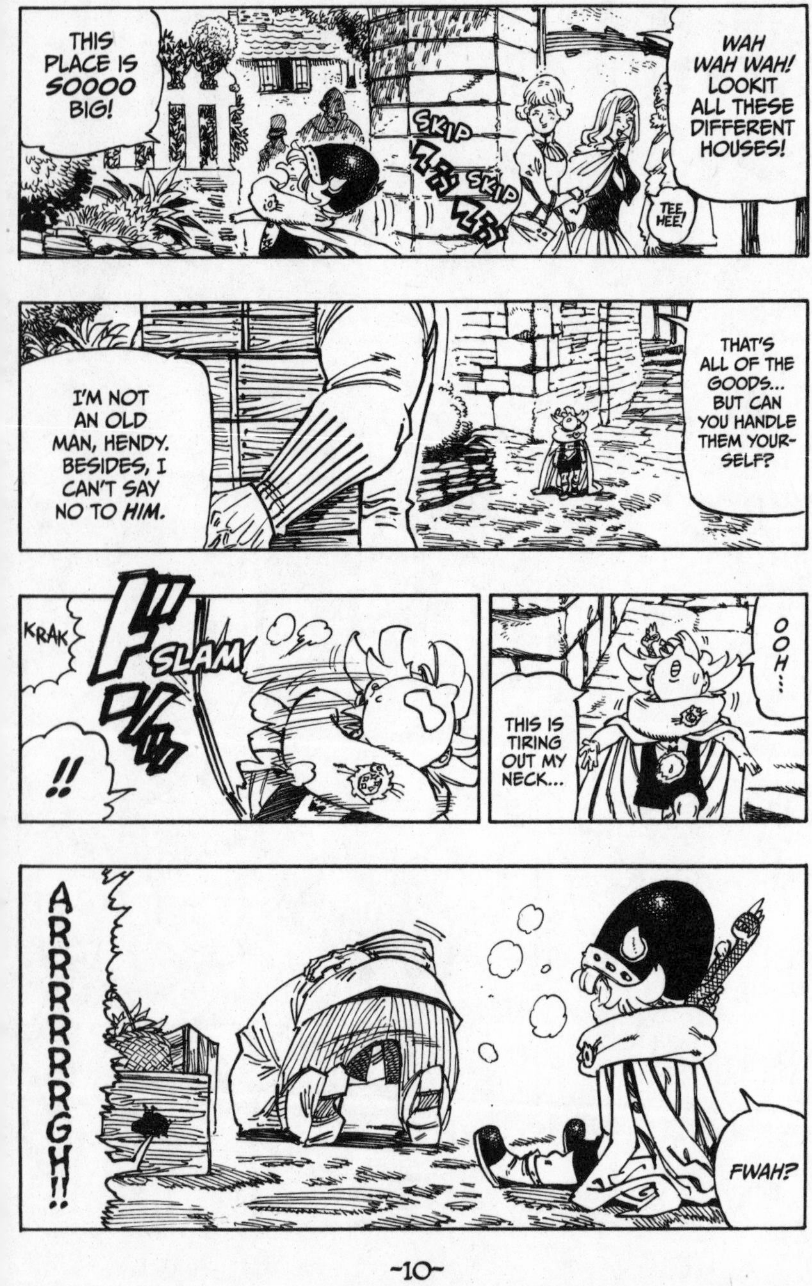
WAH WAH WAH! LOOKIT ALL THESE DIFFERENT HOUSES!
TEE HEE!
SKIP
SKIP
THIS PLACE IS SOOOO BIG!
THAT'S ALL OF THE GOODS... BUT CAN YOU HANDLE THEM YOURSELF?
I'M NOT AN OLD MAN, HENDY. BESIDES, I CAN'T SAY NO TO *HIM*.
OOH...
THIS IS TIRING OUT MY NECK...
SLAM
KRAK
!!
FWAH?
ARRRRRRGH!!

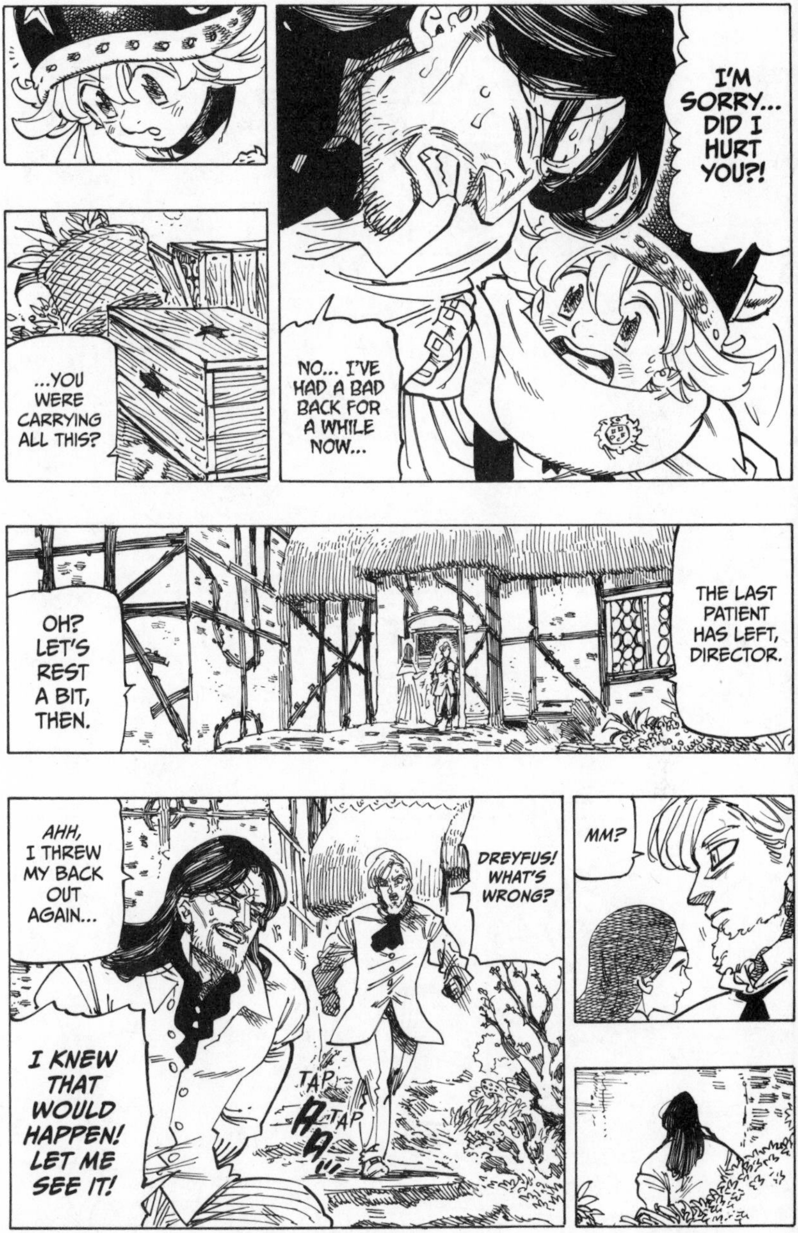
I'M SORRY... DID I HURT YOU?!
NO... I'VE HAD A BAD BACK FOR A WHILE NOW...
...YOU WERE CARRYING ALL THIS?
THE LAST PATIENT HAS LEFT, DIRECTOR.
OH? LET'S REST A BIT, THEN.
MM?
DREYFUS! WHAT'S WRONG?
AHH, I THREW MY BACK OUT AGAIN...
TAP TAP
I KNEW THAT WOULD HAPPEN! LET ME SEE IT!

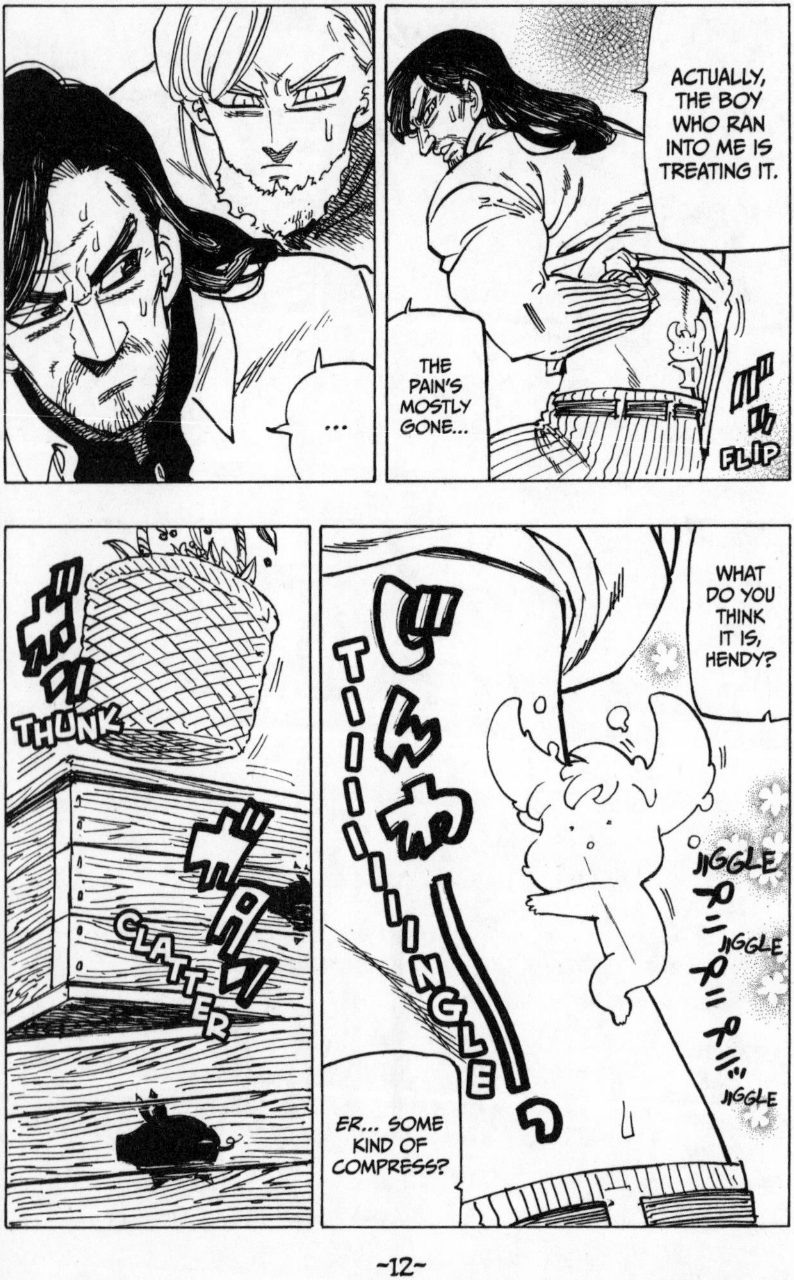
ACTUALLY, THE BOY WHO RAN INTO ME IS TREATING IT.
THE PAIN'S MOSTLY GONE...
FLIP
...
WHAT DO YOU THINK IT IS, HENDY?
TIIIIIIINGLE
JIGGLE
JIGGLE
JIGGLE
ER... SOME KIND OF COMPRESS?
THUNK
CLATTER

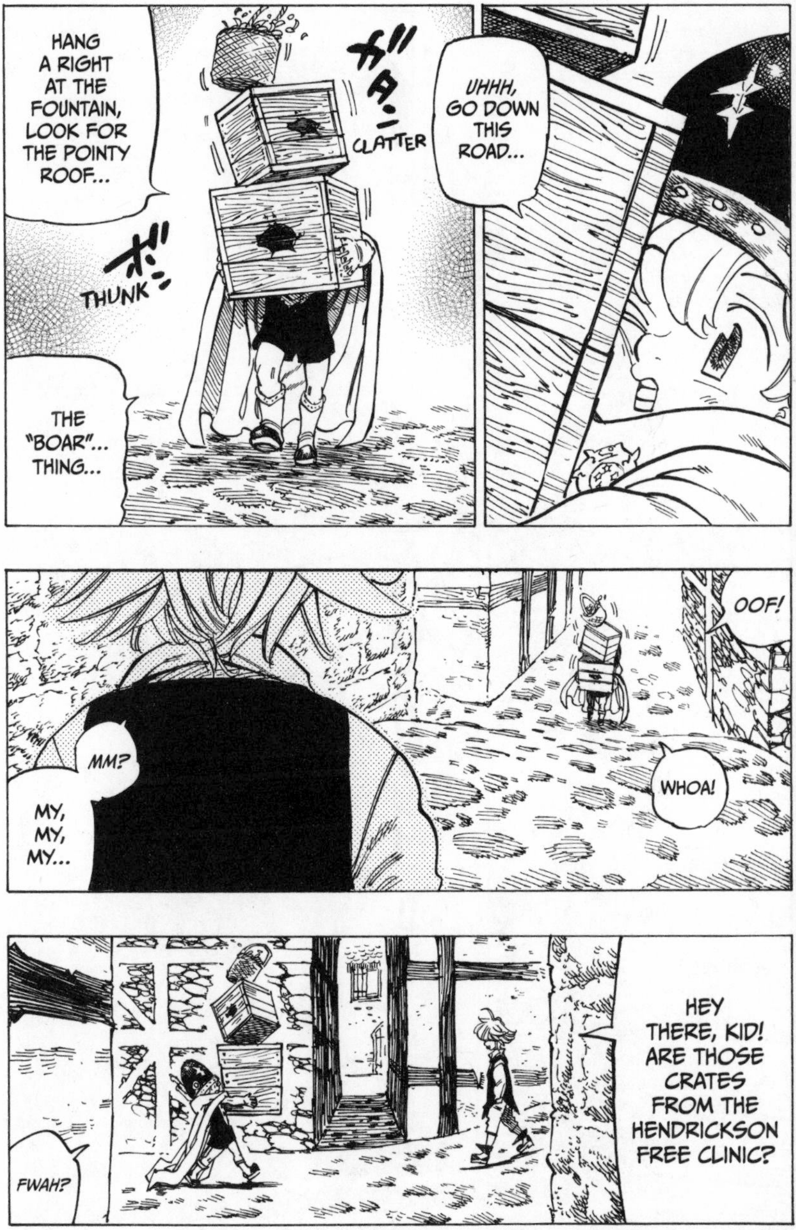
UHHH, GO DOWN THIS ROAD...
HANG A RIGHT AT THE FOUNTAIN, LOOK FOR THE POINTY ROOF...
CLATTER
THUNK
THE "BOAR"... THING...
OOF!
WHOA!
MM?
MY, MY, MY...
HEY THERE, KID! ARE THOSE CRATES FROM THE HENDRICKSON FREE CLINIC?
FWAH?

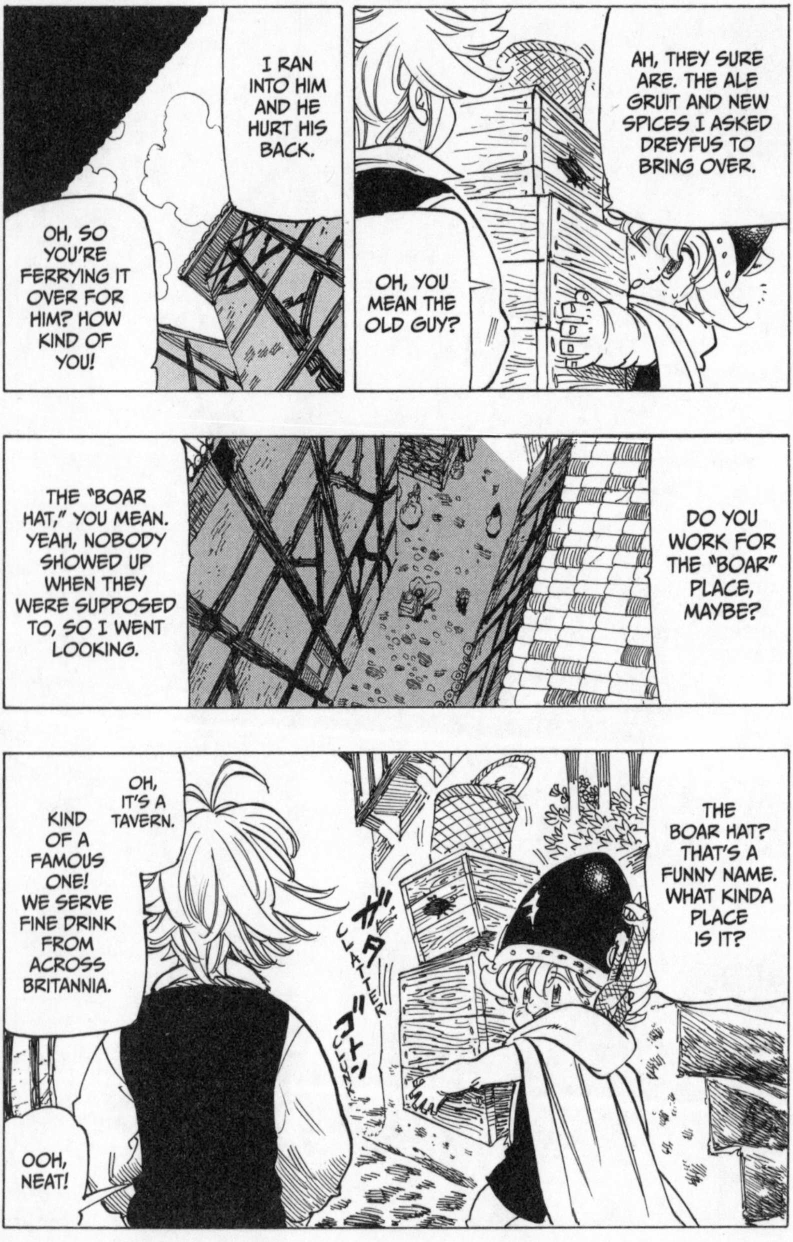

AH, THEY SURE ARE. THE ALE GRUIT AND NEW SPICES I ASKED DREYFUS TO BRING OVER.
OH, YOU MEAN THE OLD GUY?
I RAN INTO HIM AND HE HURT HIS BACK.
OH, SO YOU'RE FERRYING IT OVER FOR HIM? HOW KIND OF YOU!
DO YOU WORK FOR THE "BOAR" PLACE, MAYBE?
THE "BOAR HAT," YOU MEAN. YEAH, NOBODY SHOWED UP WHEN THEY WERE SUPPOSED TO, SO I WENT LOOKING.
THE BOAR HAT? THAT'S A FUNNY NAME. WHAT KINDA PLACE IS IT?
CLATTER
CLUNK
OH, IT'S A TAVERN.
KIND OF A FAMOUS ONE! WE SERVE FINE DRINK FROM ACROSS BRITANNIA.
OOH, NEAT!

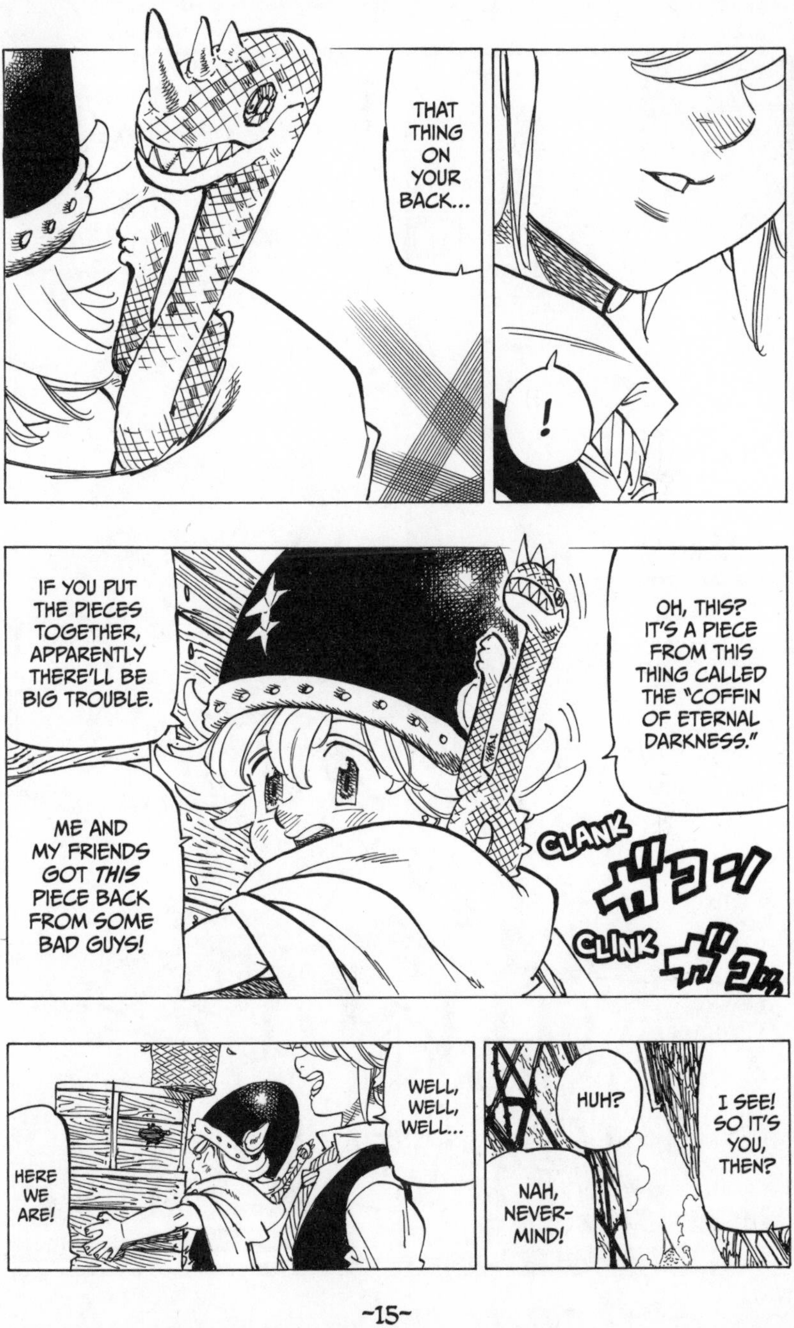
!
THAT THING ON YOUR BACK...
OH, THIS? IT'S A PIECE FROM THIS THING CALLED THE "COFFIN OF ETERNAL DARKNESS."
CLANK
CLINK
IF YOU PUT THE PIECES TOGETHER, APPARENTLY THERE'LL BE BIG TROUBLE.
ME AND MY FRIENDS GOT *THIS* PIECE BACK FROM SOME BAD GUYS!
I SEE! SO IT'S YOU, THEN?
HUH?
NAH, NEVER-MIND!
WELL, WELL, WELL...
HERE WE ARE!

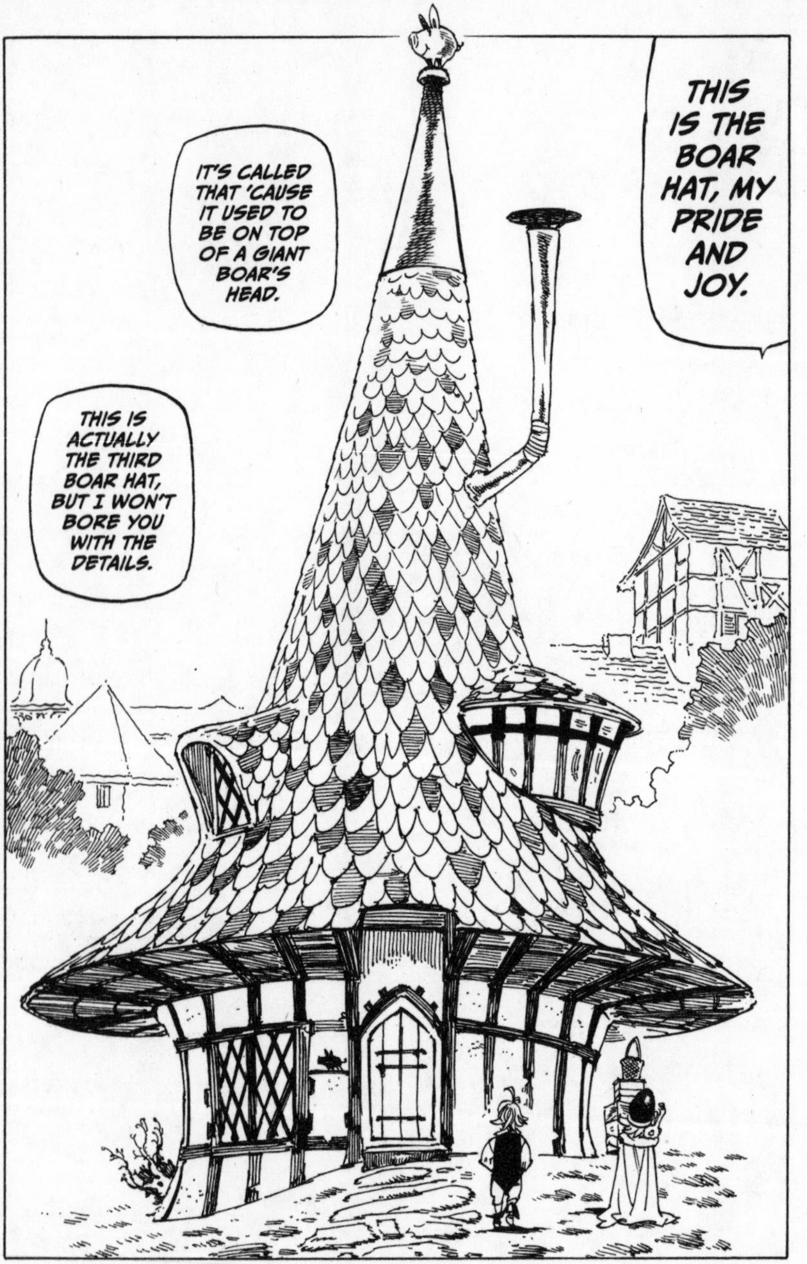
THIS IS THE BOAR HAT, MY PRIDE AND JOY.
IT'S CALLED THAT 'CAUSE IT USED TO BE ON TOP OF A GIANT BOAR'S HEAD.
THIS IS ACTUALLY THE THIRD BOAR HAT, BUT I WON'T BORE YOU WITH THE DETAILS.

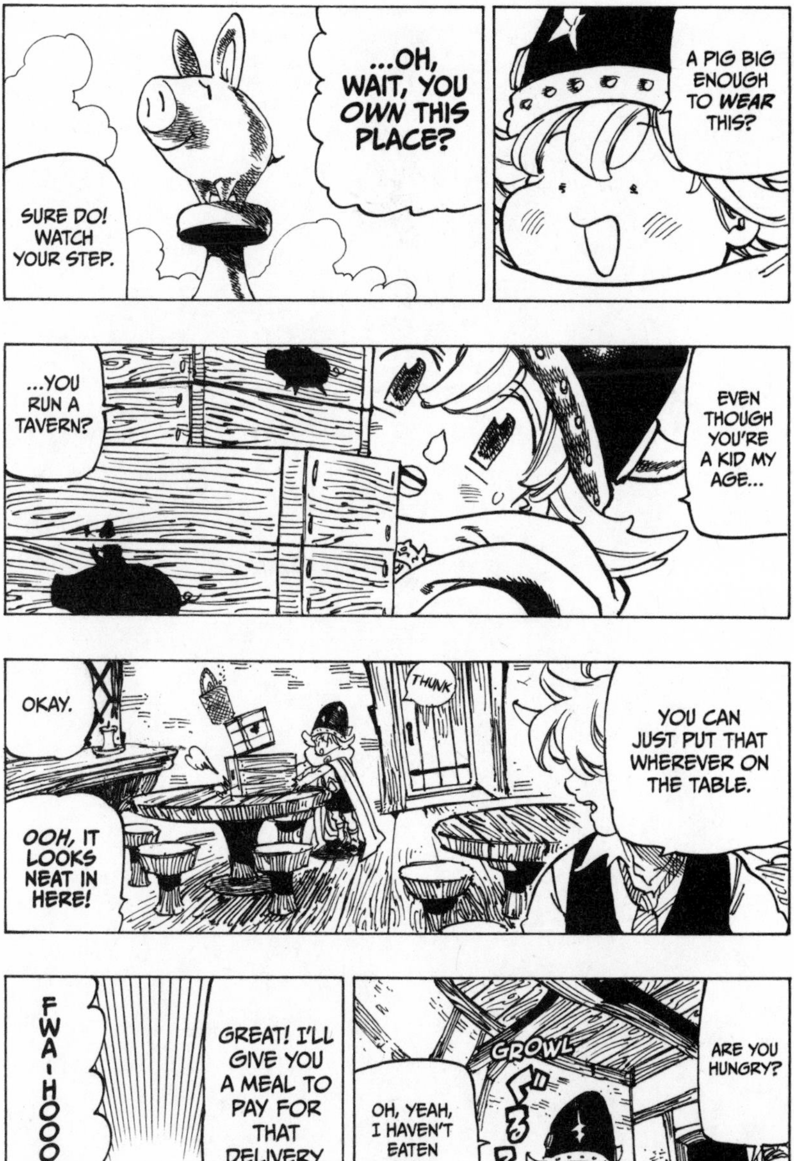
A PIG BIG ENOUGH TO WEAR THIS?
...OH, WAIT, YOU OWN THIS PLACE?
SURE DO! WATCH YOUR STEP.
EVEN THOUGH YOU'RE A KID MY AGE...
...YOU RUN A TAVERN?
YOU CAN JUST PUT THAT WHEREVER ON THE TABLE.
THUNK
OKAY.
OOH, IT LOOKS NEAT IN HERE!
ARE YOU HUNGRY?
GROWL
OH, YEAH, I HAVEN'T EATEN SINCE MORNING.
GREAT! I'LL GIVE YOU A MEAL TO PAY FOR THAT DELIVERY.
FWA-HOOO!♬

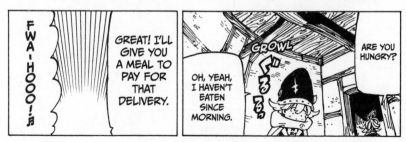

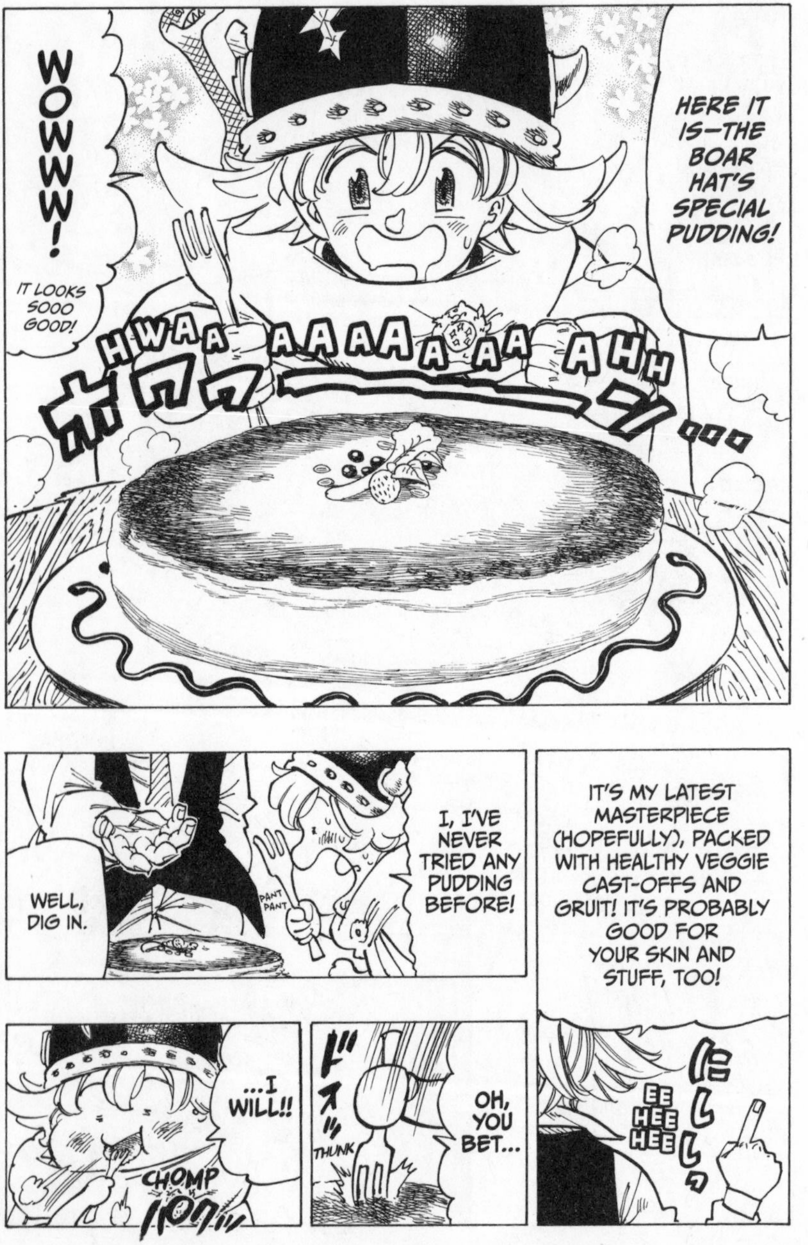
HERE IT IS—THE BOAR HAT'S SPECIAL PUDDING!
WOWWW!
IT LOOKS SOOO GOOD!
HWAAAAAAAAAAAHH
IT'S MY LATEST MASTERPIECE (HOPEFULLY), PACKED WITH HEALTHY VEGGIE CAST-OFFS AND GRUIT! IT'S PROBABLY GOOD FOR YOUR SKIN AND STUFF, TOO!
EE HEE HEE
I, I'VE NEVER TRIED ANY PUDDING BEFORE!
PANT PANT
WELL, DIG IN.
OH, YOU BET...
THUNK
...I WILL!!
CHOMP

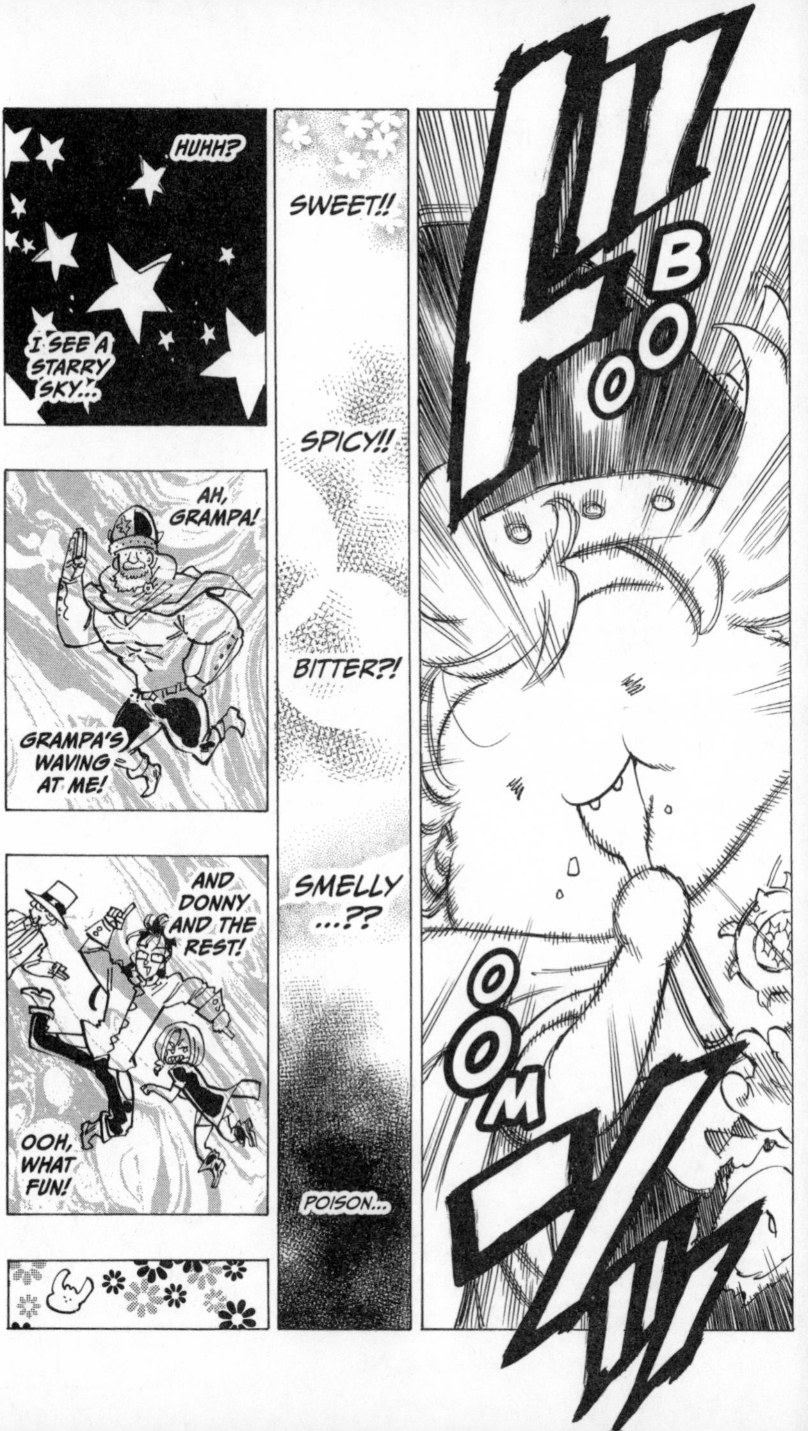
BOO
OOM
SWEET!!
SPICY!!
BITTER?!
SMELLY ...??
POISON...
HUHH?
I SEE A STARRY SKY...
AH, GRAMPA!
GRAMPA'S WAVING AT ME!
AND DONNY AND THE REST!
OOH, WHAT FUN!

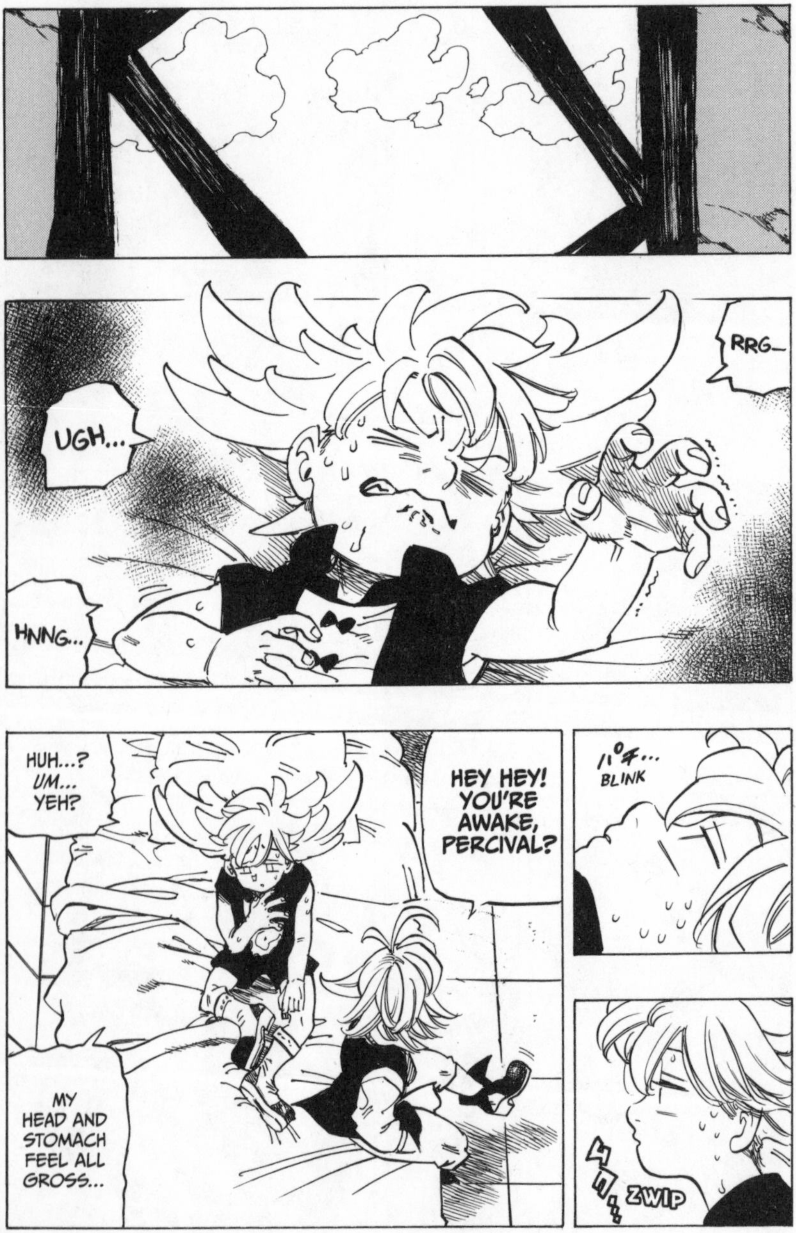
RRG—
UGH...
HNNG...
パチ...
BLINK
ZWIP
HEY HEY! YOU'RE AWAKE, PERCIVAL?
HUH...? UM... YEH?
MY HEAD AND STOMACH FEEL ALL GROSS...

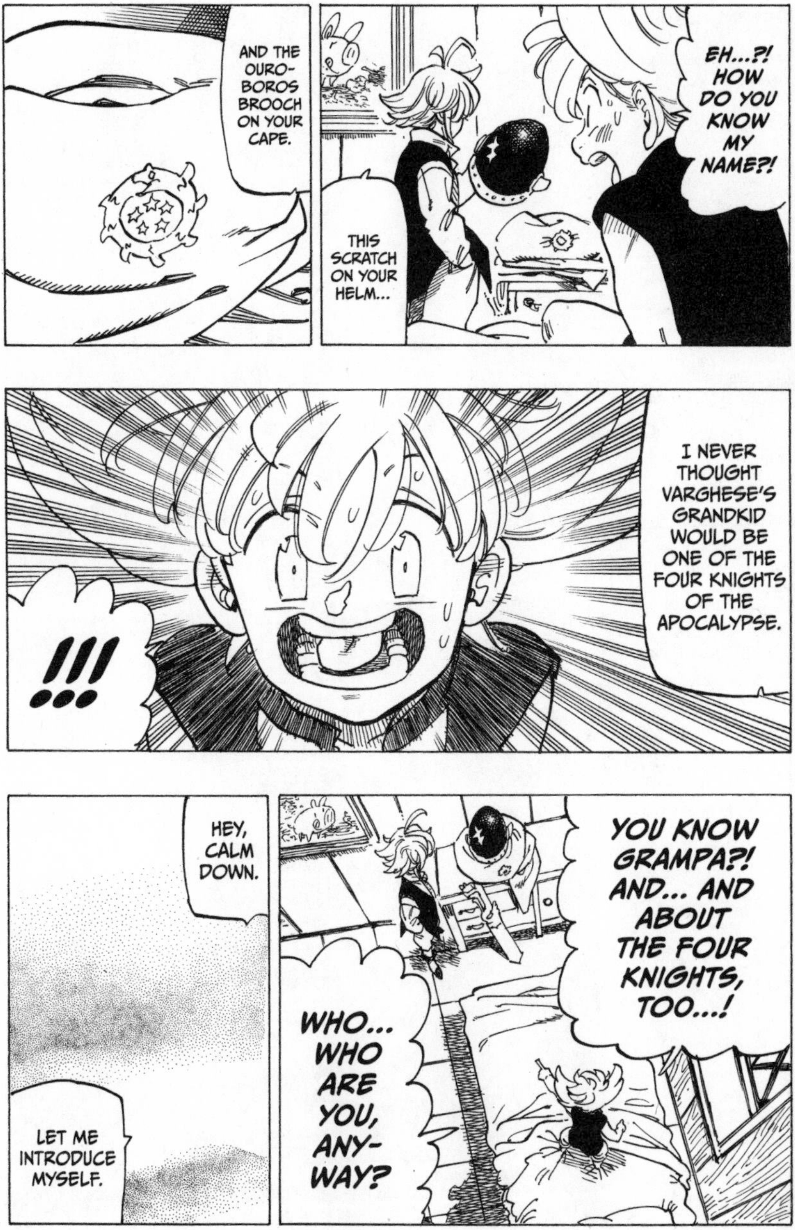
EH...?! HOW DO YOU KNOW MY NAME?!
THIS SCRATCH ON YOUR HELM...
AND THE OURO-BOROS BROOCH ON YOUR CAPE.
I NEVER THOUGHT VARGHESE'S GRANDKID WOULD BE ONE OF THE FOUR KNIGHTS OF THE APOCALYPSE.
!!!...
YOU KNOW GRAMPA?! AND... AND ABOUT THE FOUR KNIGHTS, TOO...!
WHO... WHO ARE YOU, ANY-WAY?
HEY, CALM DOWN.
LET ME INTRODUCE MYSELF.

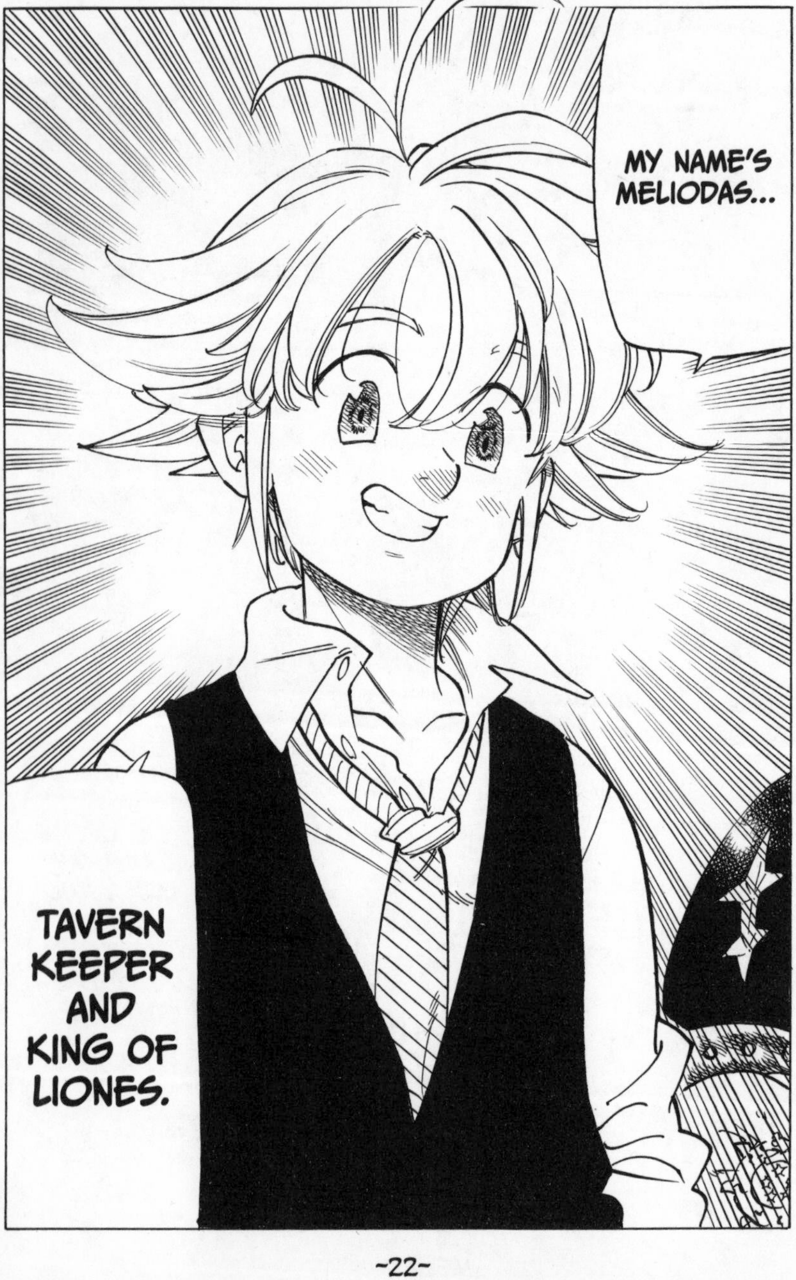
MY NAME'S MELIODAS...
TAVERN KEEPER AND KING OF LIONES.

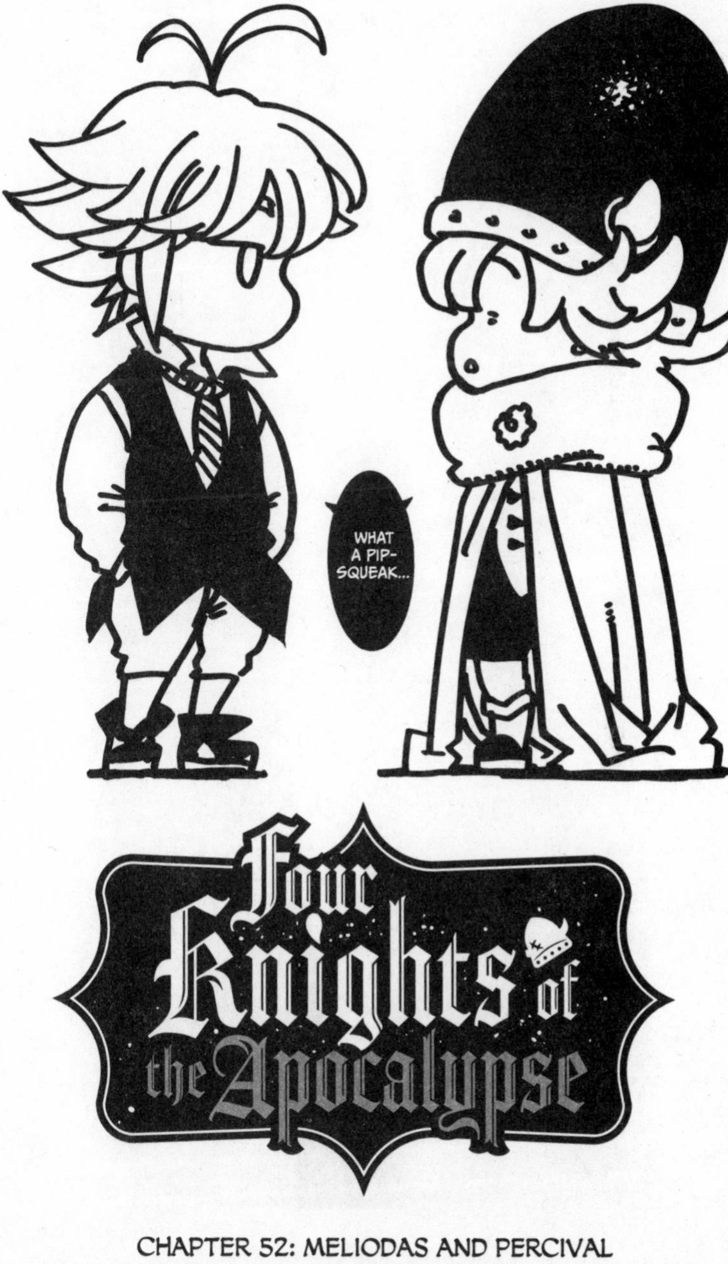
WHAT A PIP-SQUEAK...

Four Knights of the Apocalypse

CHAPTER 52: MELIODAS AND PERCIVAL

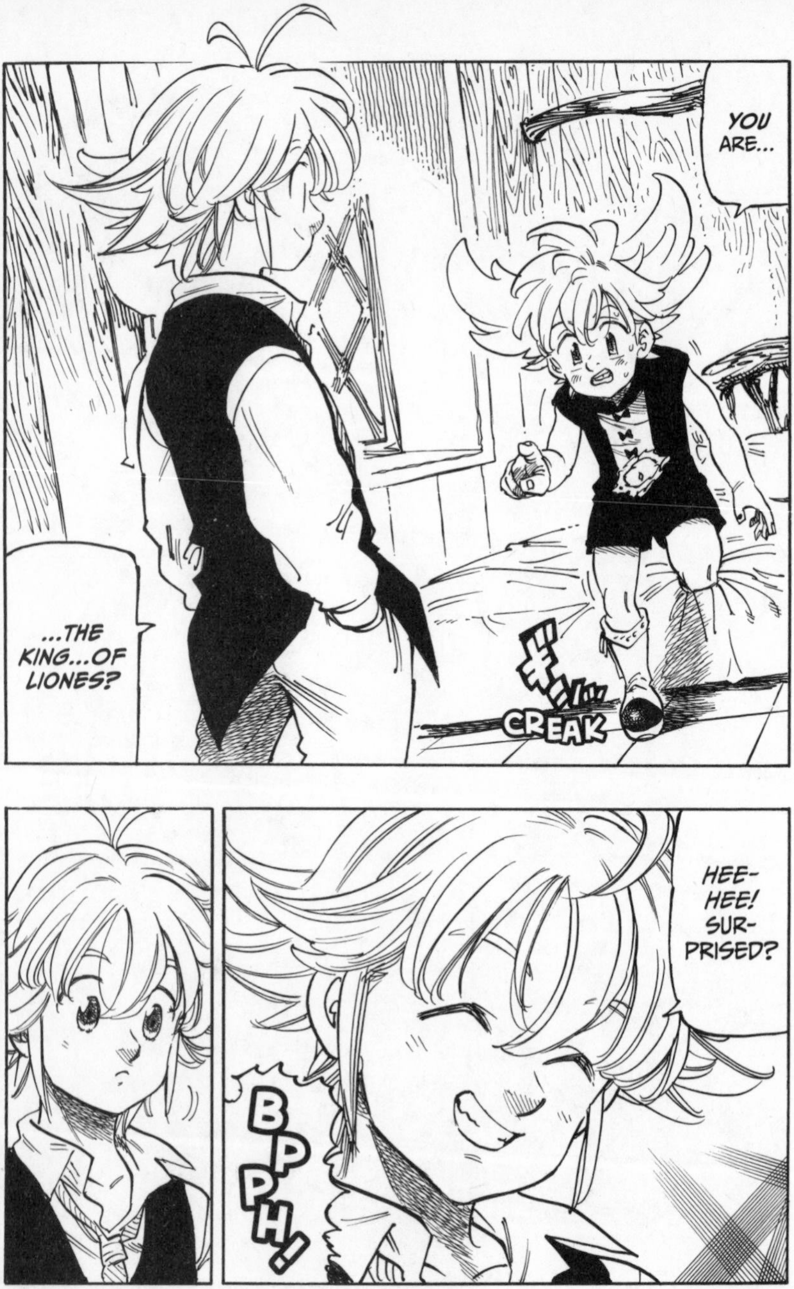
YOU ARE...
CREAK
...THE KING...OF LIONES?
HEE-HEE! SUR-PRISED?
BPPH!

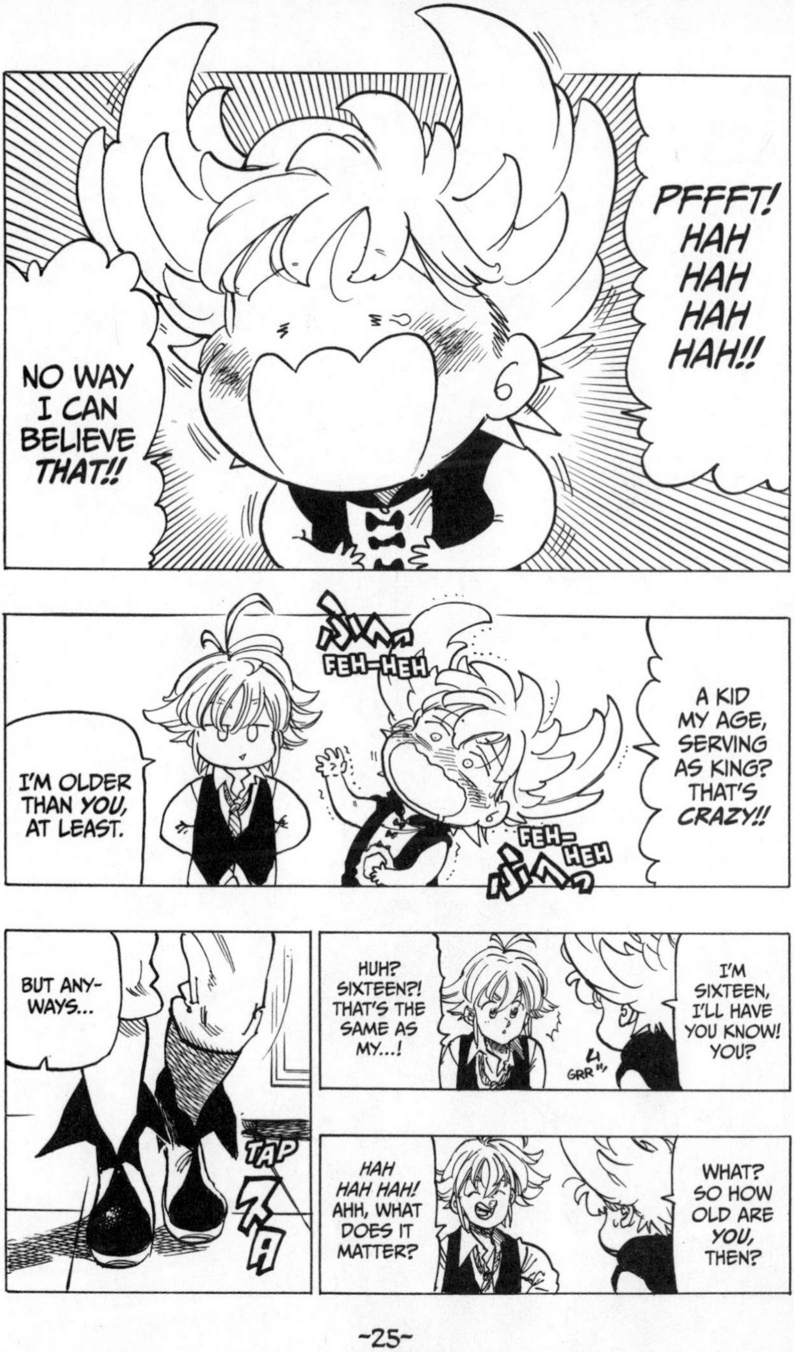
PFFFT! HAH HAH HAH HAH!!
NO WAY I CAN BELIEVE THAT!!
A KID MY AGE, SERVING AS KING? THAT'S CRAZY!!
FEH-HEH
FEH-HEH
I'M OLDER THAN YOU, AT LEAST.
I'M SIXTEEN, I'LL HAVE YOU KNOW! YOU?
GRR
HUH? SIXTEEN?! THAT'S THE SAME AS MY...!
WHAT? SO HOW OLD ARE YOU, THEN?
HAH HAH HAH! AHH, WHAT DOES IT MATTER?
TAP
BUT ANY-WAYS...

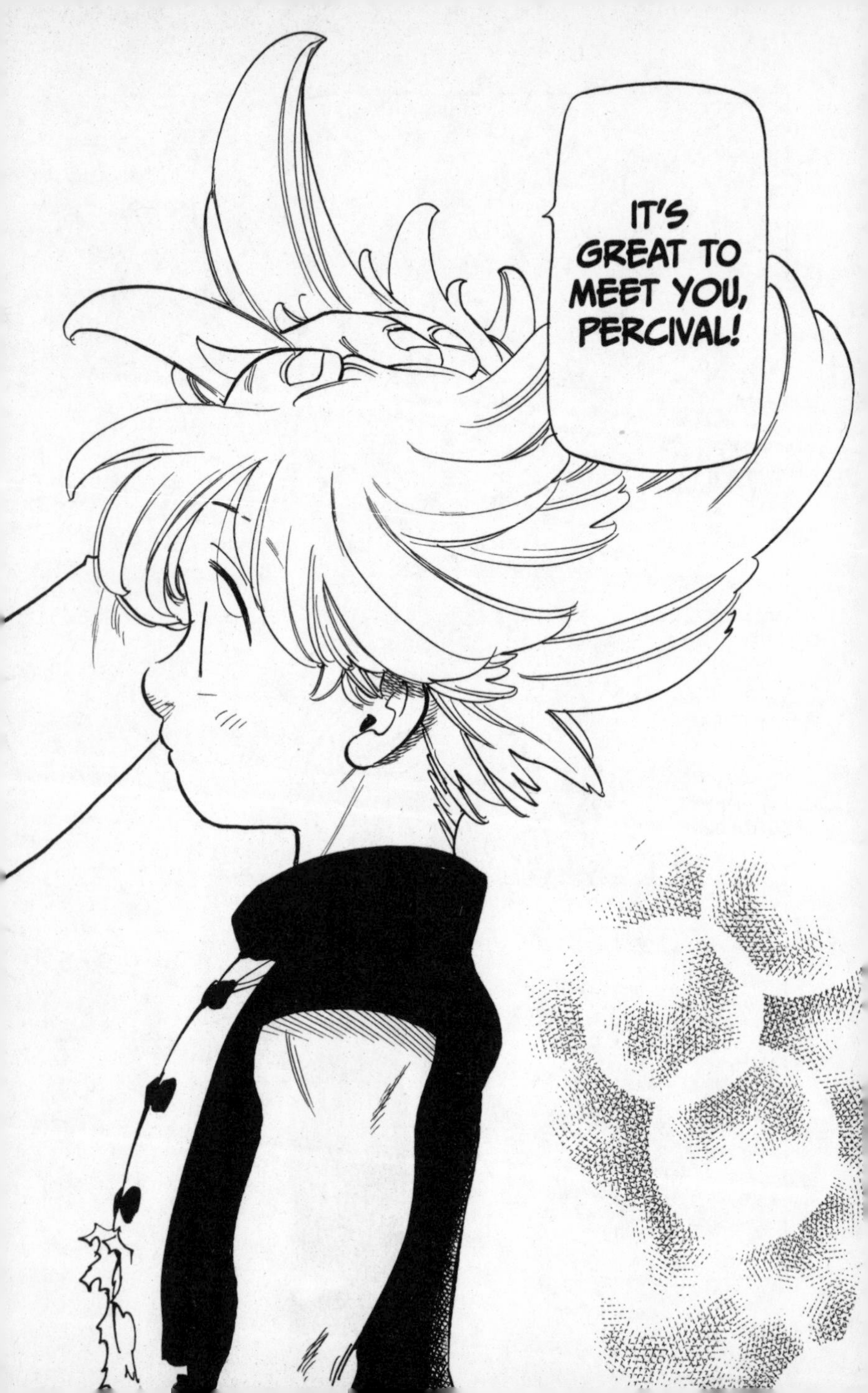
IT'S GREAT TO MEET YOU, PERCIVAL!

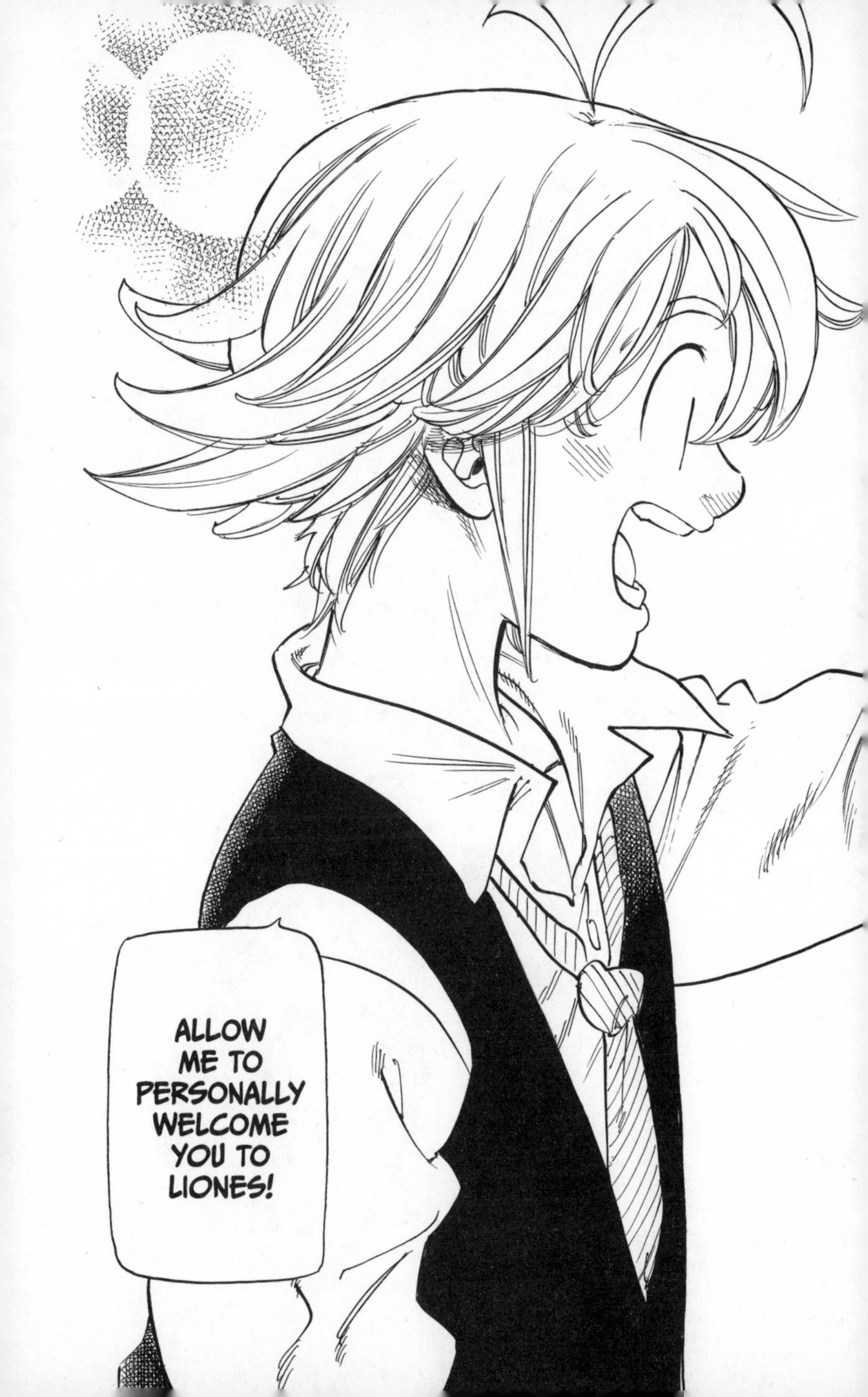
ALLOW ME TO PERSONALLY WELCOME YOU TO LIONES!

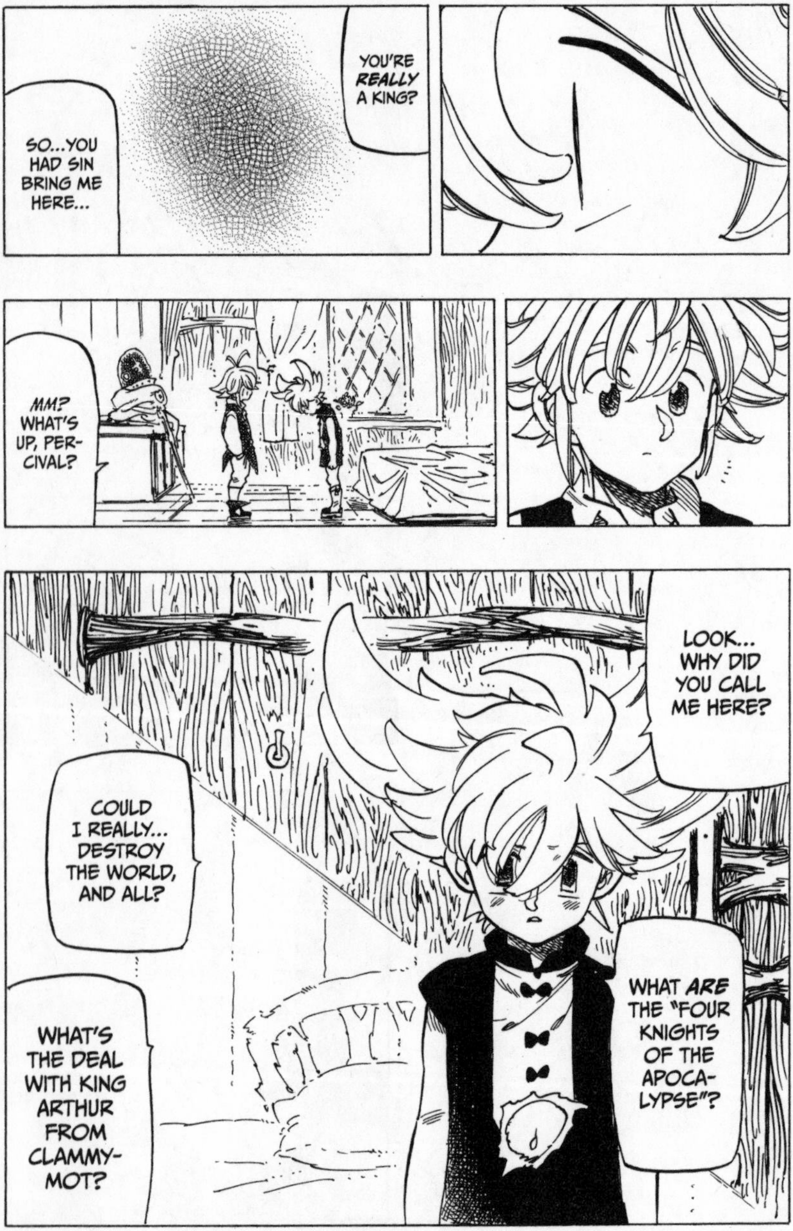
YOU'RE *REALLY* A KING?
SO...YOU HAD SIN BRING ME HERE...
MM? WHAT'S UP, PER-CIVAL?
LOOK... WHY DID YOU CALL ME HERE?
WHAT *ARE* THE "FOUR KNIGHTS OF THE APOCA-LYPSE"?
COULD I REALLY... DESTROY THE WORLD, AND ALL?
WHAT'S THE DEAL WITH KING ARTHUR FROM CLAMMY-MOT?

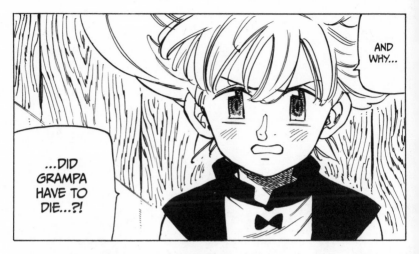

AND WHY...
...DID GRAMPA HAVE TO DIE...?!
...OH.
VARGHESE IS...?
I PLAN TO DISCUSS ALL THAT ONCE EVERYONE IS HERE.
RIGHT NOW, THOUGH, WANNA JOIN ME ON A WALK?
WITH YOU, KING?
JUST CALL ME "MELIO-DAS!"

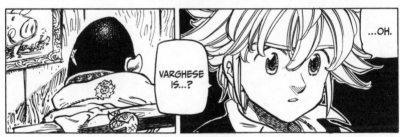

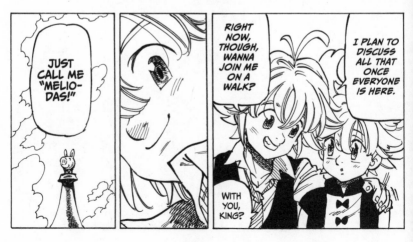

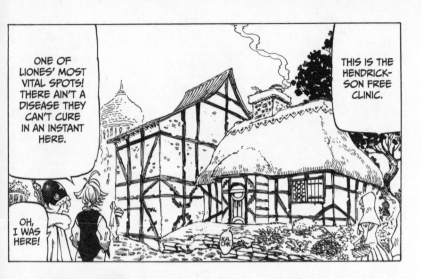

THIS IS THE HENDRICKSON FREE CLINIC.
ONE OF LIONES' MOST VITAL SPOTS! THERE AIN'T A DISEASE THEY CAN'T CURE IN AN INSTANT HERE.
KA-CHK
OH, I WAS HERE!
HEY! THE GEEZER WITH THE BAD BACK!
YO!
YOUR MAJESTY! AND THE BOY'S BACK AGAIN?
MY BACK'S GOOD AS NEW AGAIN, THANKS TO YOU—
OOF!
PUSH
OH... IT'S YOU!
YOU'RE LOOKIN' AT DREYFUS AND HENDRICKSON. THEY'RE BOTH FORMER HOLY KNIGHT CAPTAINS.
DANG, THEY MUST BE STRONG!

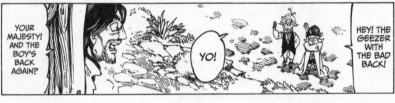

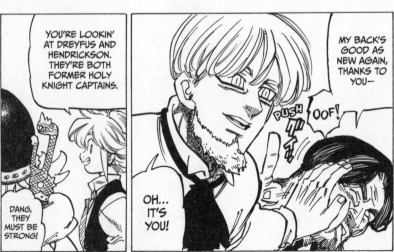

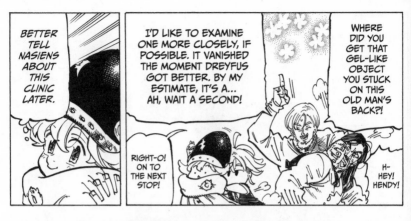

WHERE DID YOU GET THAT GEL-LIKE OBJECT YOU STUCK ON THIS OLD MAN'S BACK?!
I'D LIKE TO EXAMINE ONE MORE CLOSELY, IF POSSIBLE. IT VANISHED THE MOMENT DREYFUS GOT BETTER. BY MY ESTIMATE, IT'S A... AH, WAIT A SECOND!
H-HEY! HENDY!
RIGHT-O! ON TO THE NEXT STOP!
BETTER TELL NASIENS ABOUT THIS CLINIC LATER.
AND THIS IS THE BEST FORGE IN LIONES!
IT'S THE HOME OF OUR HOLY KNIGHT CAPTAIN, ALTHOUGH HE NEVER TOOK OVER THE BUSINESS.
THIS IS HOWZER'S HOUSE?!
HECK, YOU KNOW HIM?
SHEEK
HOWZER'S THE GUY WHO STUCK A BLADE ON THIS DRAGON HANDLE!
YOU DON'T SAY?
AH, YOUR MAJESTY!
ZSH
WHAT BRINGS YOU HERE TODAY?

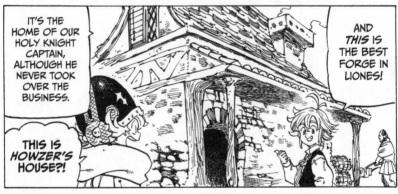

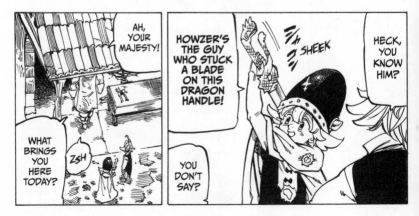

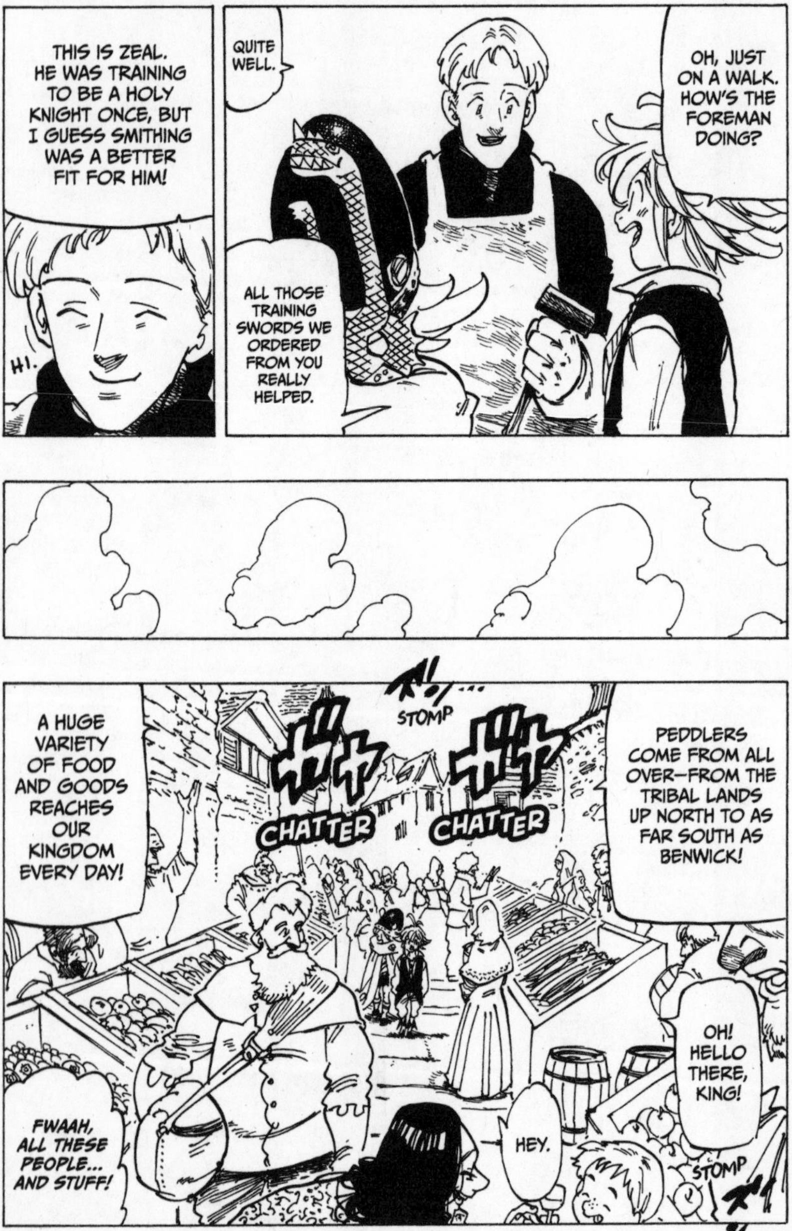
OH, JUST ON A WALK. HOW'S THE FOREMAN DOING?
QUITE WELL.
ALL THOSE TRAINING SWORDS WE ORDERED FROM YOU REALLY HELPED.
THIS IS ZEAL. HE WAS TRAINING TO BE A HOLY KNIGHT ONCE, BUT I GUESS SMITHING WAS A BETTER FIT FOR HIM!
HI.
STOMP
PEDDLERS COME FROM ALL OVER—FROM THE TRIBAL LANDS UP NORTH TO AS FAR SOUTH AS BENWICK!
CHATTER
CHATTER
A HUGE VARIETY OF FOOD AND GOODS REACHES OUR KINGDOM EVERY DAY!
OH! HELLO THERE, KING!
STOMP
HEY.
FWAAH, ALL THESE PEOPLE... AND STUFF!

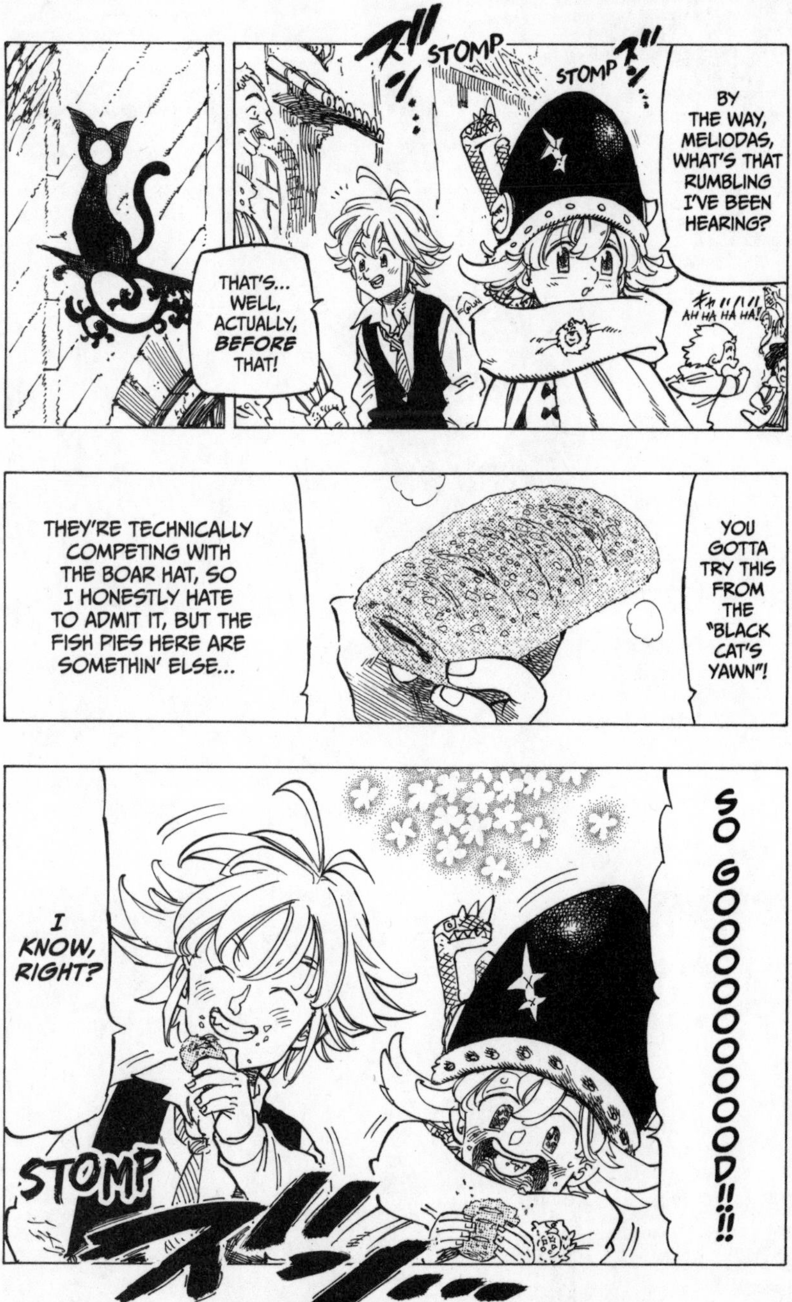
STOMP
STOMP
BY THE WAY, MELIODAS, WHAT'S THAT RUMBLING I'VE BEEN HEARING?
AH HA HA HA!
THAT'S... WELL, ACTUALLY, *BEFORE* THAT!
YOU GOTTA TRY THIS FROM THE "BLACK CAT'S YAWN"!
THEY'RE TECHNICALLY COMPETING WITH THE BOAR HAT, SO I HONESTLY HATE TO ADMIT IT, BUT THE FISH PIES HERE ARE SOMETHIN' ELSE...
SO GOOOOOOOOOD!!
I KNOW, RIGHT?
STOMP

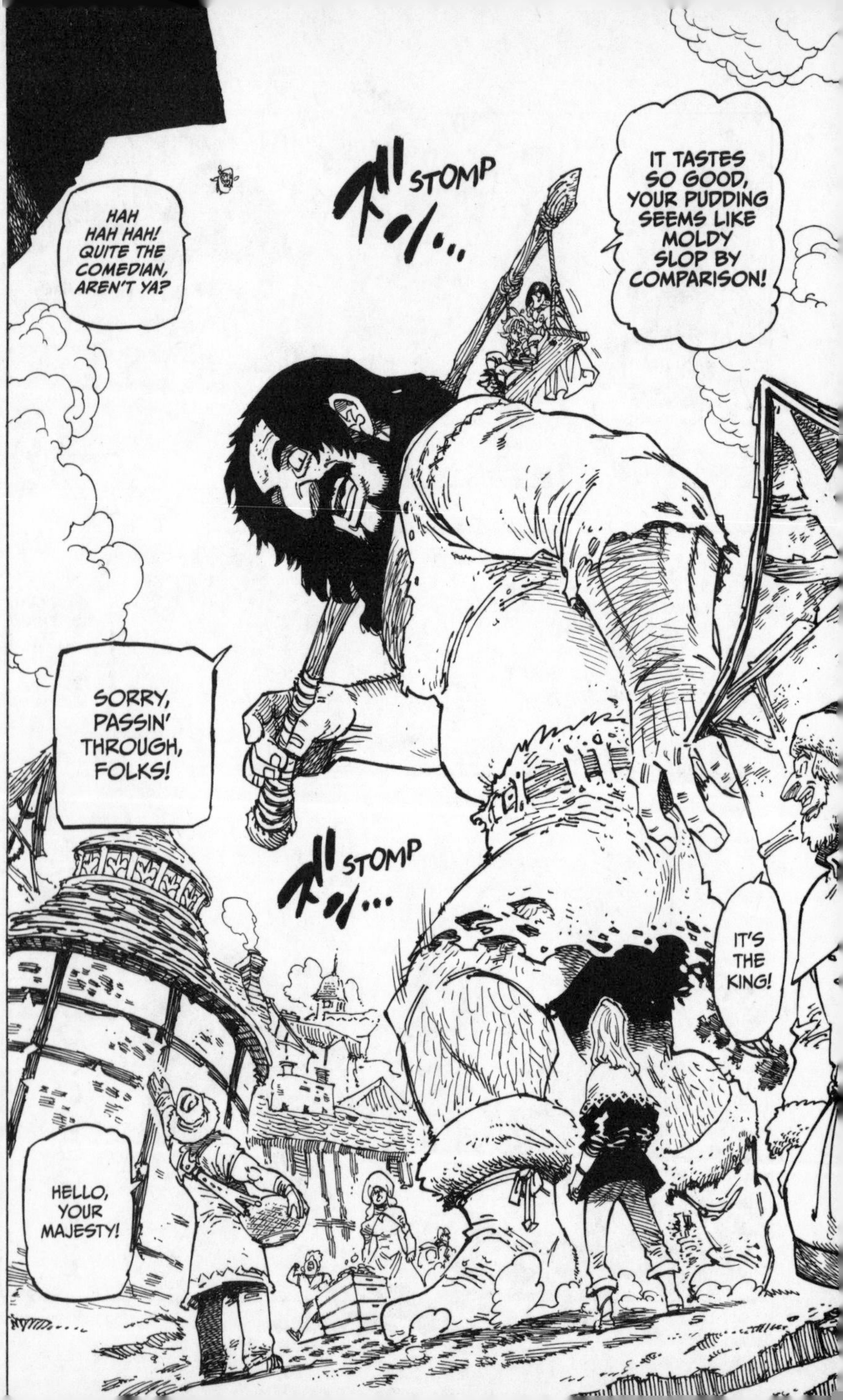
IT TASTES SO GOOD, YOUR PUDDING SEEMS LIKE MOLDY SLOP BY COMPARISON!
STOMP
HAH HAH HAH! QUITE THE COMEDIAN, AREN'T YA?
SORRY, PASSIN' THROUGH, FOLKS!
STOMP
IT'S THE KING!
HELLO, YOUR MAJESTY!

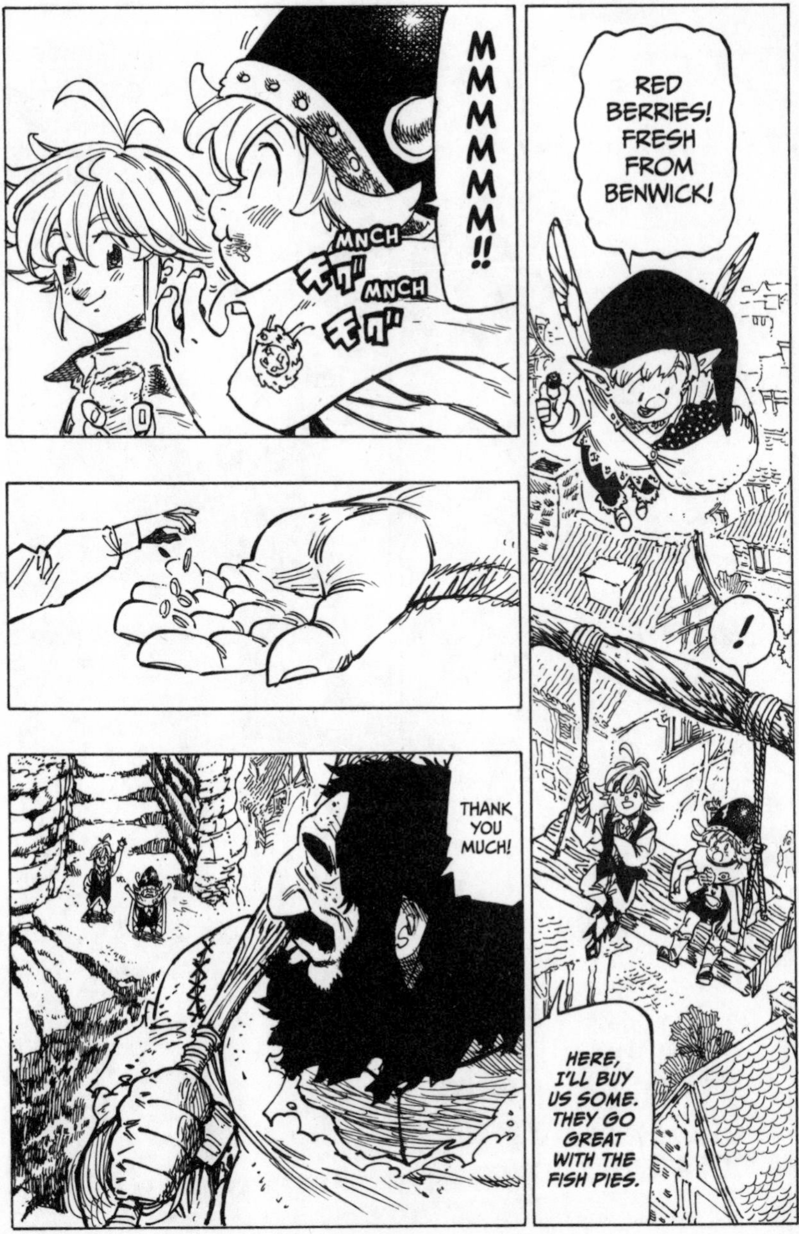
RED BERRIES! FRESH FROM BENWICK!
!
HERE, I'LL BUY US SOME. THEY GO GREAT WITH THE FISH PIES.
MMMMMMM!!
MNCH
モグ
MNCH
モグ
THANK YOU MUCH!

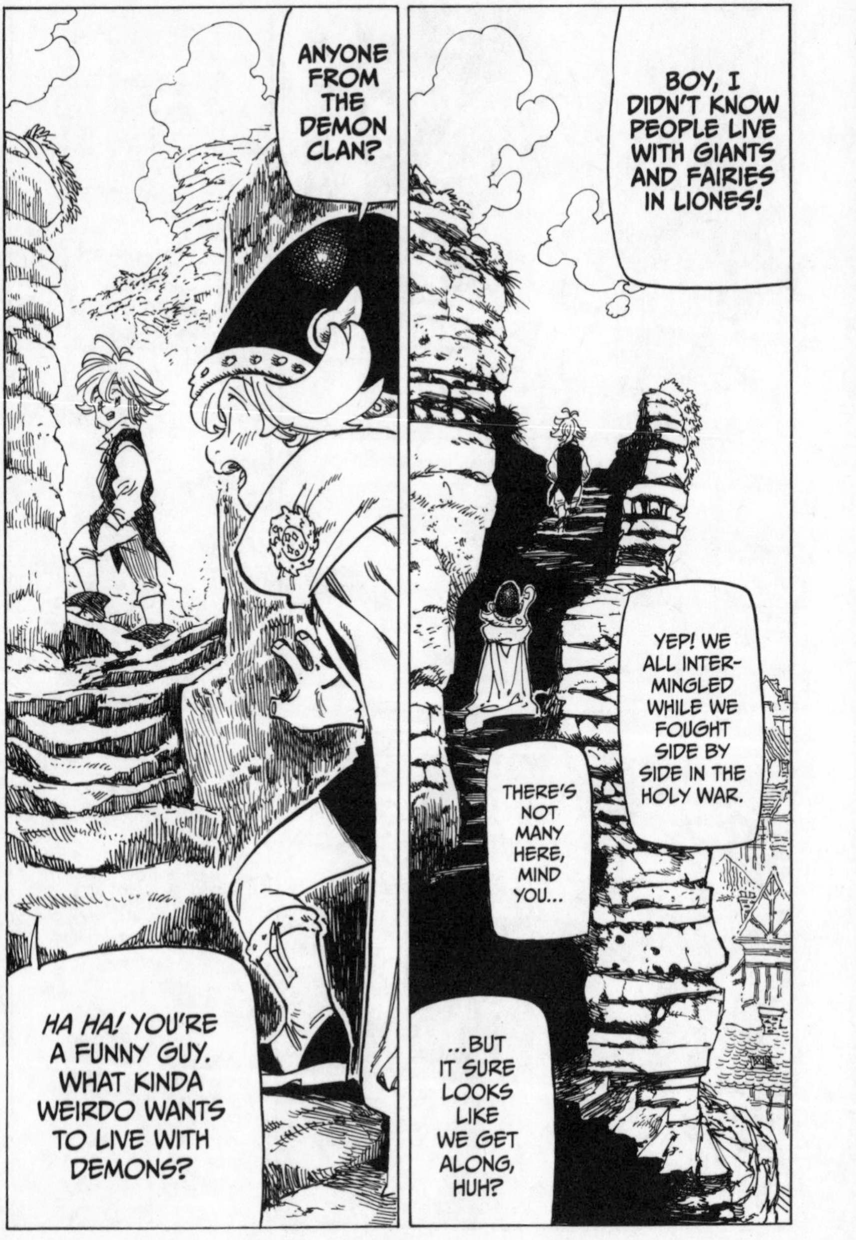
BOY, I DIDN'T KNOW PEOPLE LIVE WITH GIANTS AND FAIRIES IN LIONES!
YEP! WE ALL INTER-MINGLED WHILE WE FOUGHT SIDE BY SIDE IN THE HOLY WAR.
THERE'S NOT MANY HERE, MIND YOU...
...BUT IT SURE LOOKS LIKE WE GET ALONG, HUH?
ANYONE FROM THE DEMON CLAN?
HA HA! YOU'RE A FUNNY GUY. WHAT KINDA WEIRDO WANTS TO LIVE WITH DEMONS?

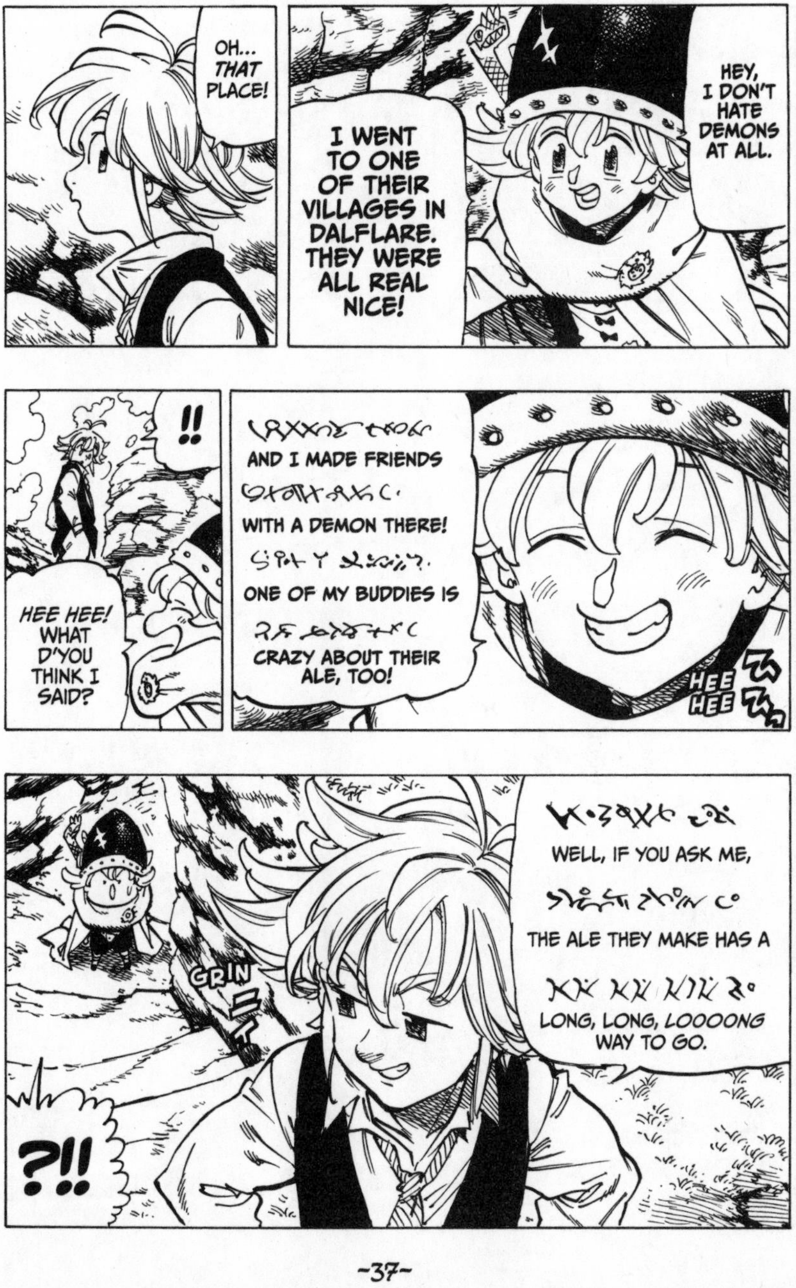
HEY, I DON'T HATE DEMONS AT ALL.
I WENT TO ONE OF THEIR VILLAGES IN DALFLARE. THEY WERE ALL REAL NICE!
OH... THAT PLACE!
AND I MADE FRIENDS
WITH A DEMON THERE!
ONE OF MY BUDDIES IS
CRAZY ABOUT THEIR ALE, TOO!
HEE HEE
!!
HEE HEE! WHAT D'YOU THINK I SAID?
WELL, IF YOU ASK ME,
THE ALE THEY MAKE HAS A
LONG, LONG, LOOOONG WAY TO GO.
GRIN
?!!

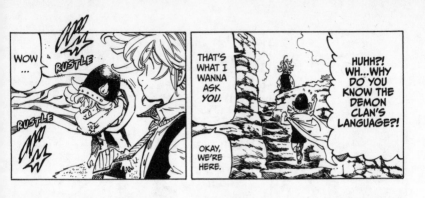

HUHH?! WH...WHY DO YOU KNOW THE DEMON CLAN'S LANGUAGE?!
THAT'S WHAT I WANNA ASK YOU.
OKAY, WE'RE HERE.
WOW ...
RUSTLE
RUSTLE
PRETTY NICE VIEW, HUH?
FWA-WAH...! I CAN EVEN SEE LITTLE TOWNS AND VILLAGES PAST LIONES!

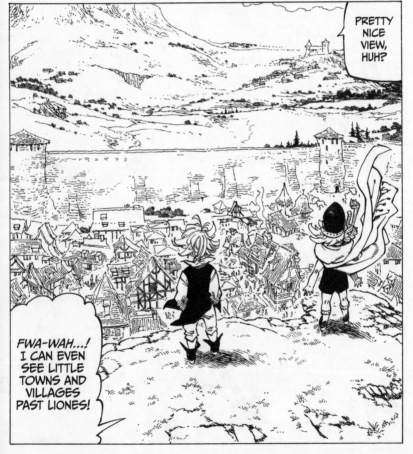

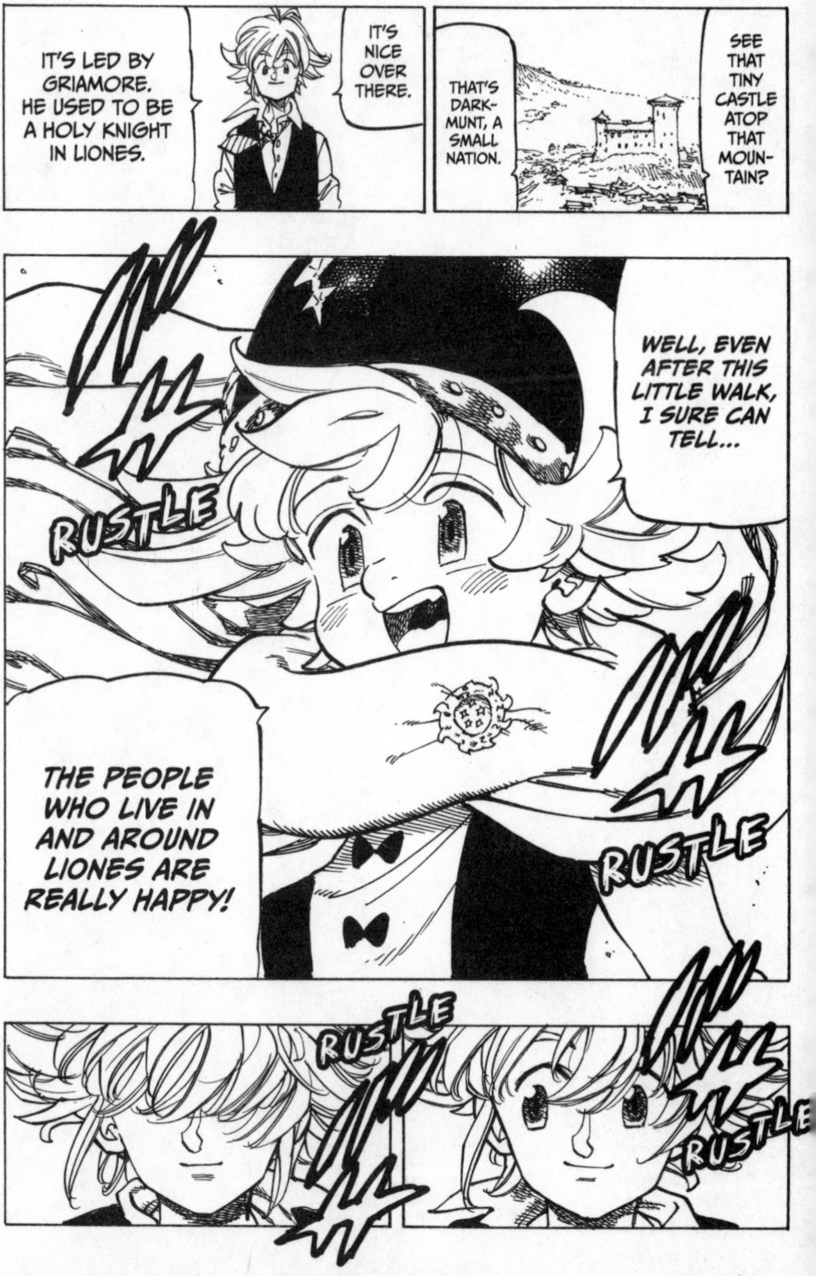
SEE THAT TINY CASTLE ATOP THAT MOUN-TAIN?
THAT'S DARK-MUNT, A SMALL NATION.
IT'S NICE OVER THERE.
IT'S LED BY GRIAMORE. HE USED TO BE A HOLY KNIGHT IN LIONES.
WELL, EVEN AFTER THIS LITTLE WALK, I SURE CAN TELL...
RUSTLE
RUSTLE
THE PEOPLE WHO LIVE IN AND AROUND LIONES ARE REALLY HAPPY!
RUSTLE
RUSTLE

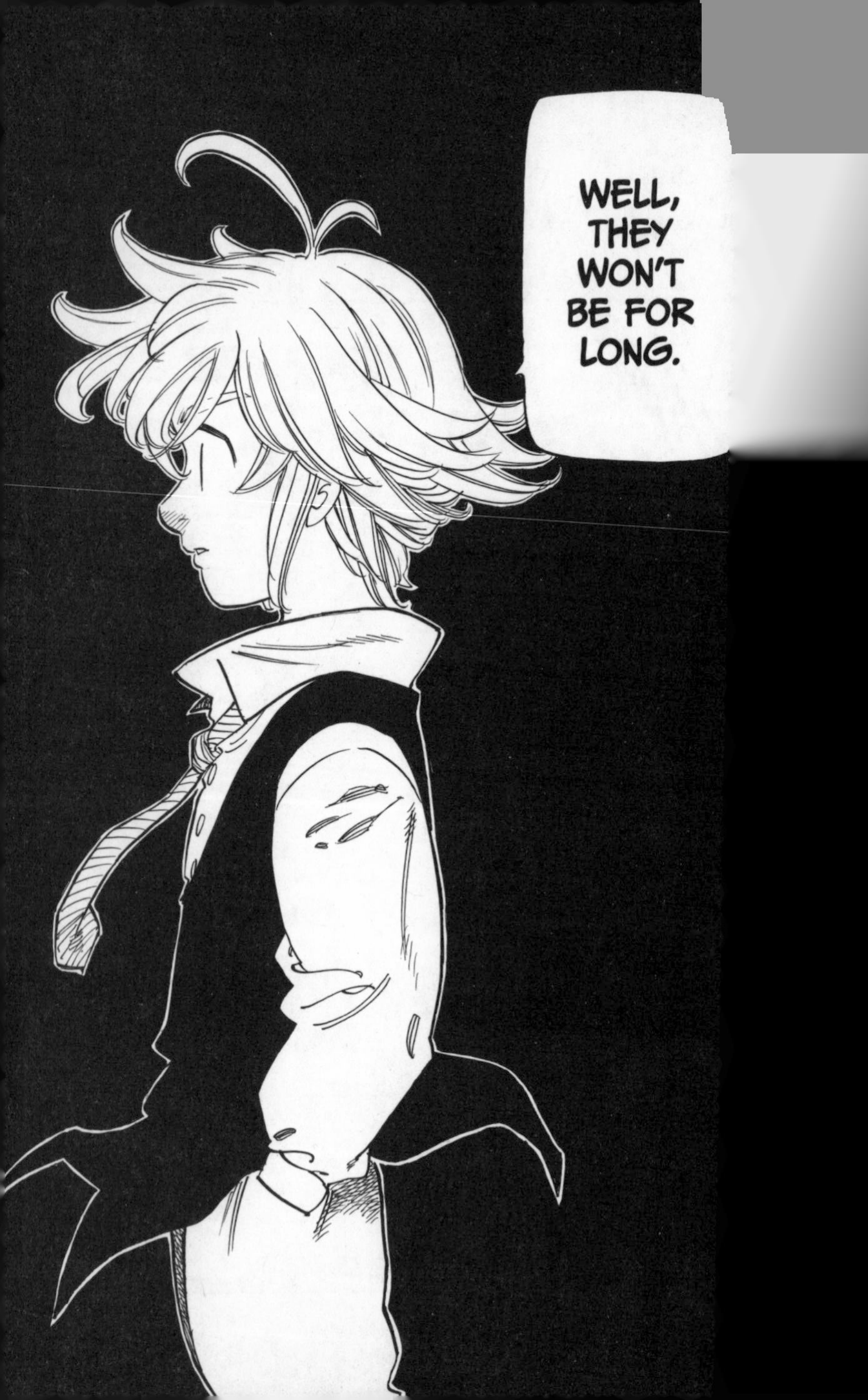
WELL, THEY WON'T BE FOR LONG.

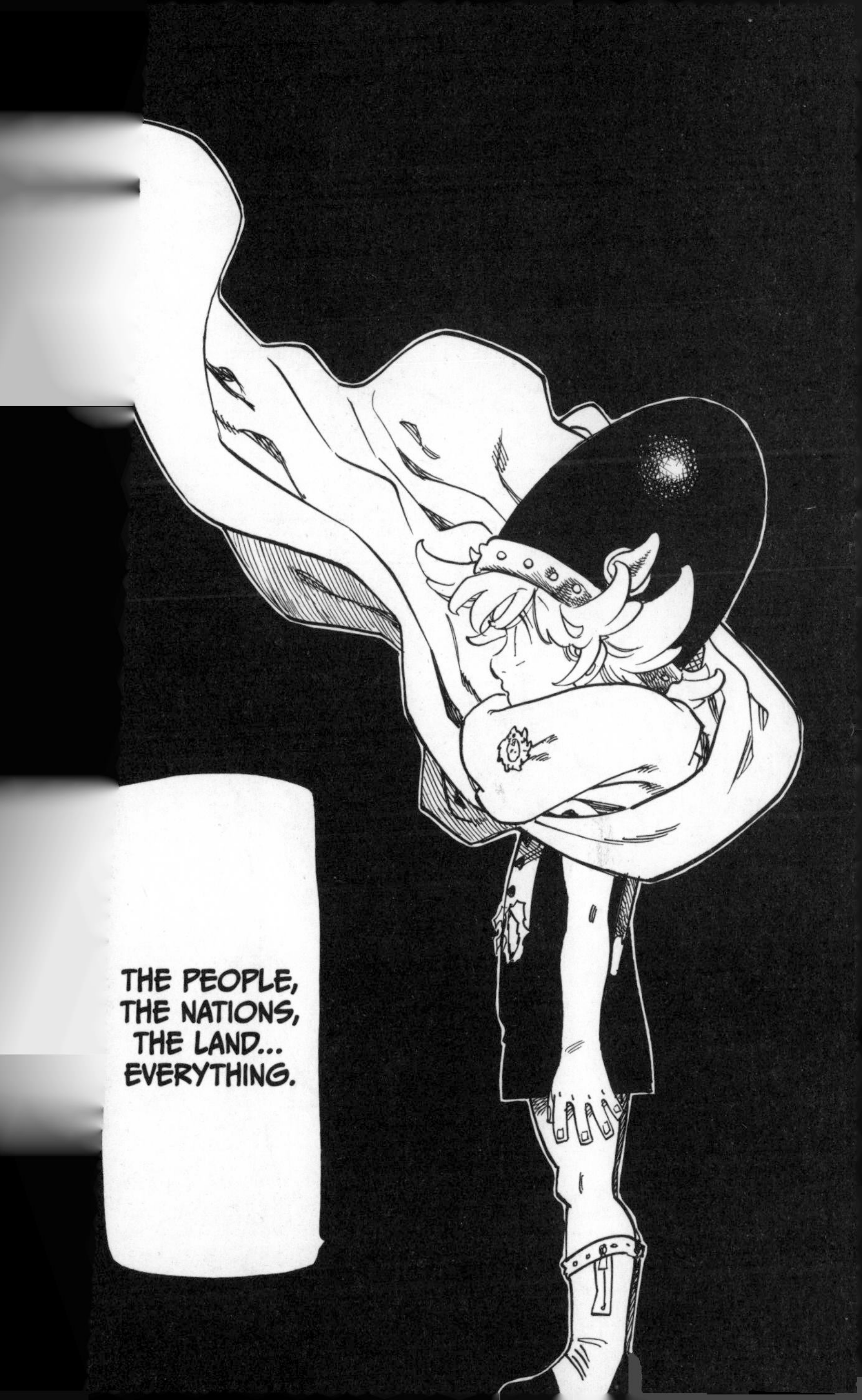
THE PEOPLE, THE NATIONS, THE LAND... EVERYTHING.

PER-CIVAL...

YOU HAVE TO HELP US.

Four Knights of the Apocalypse

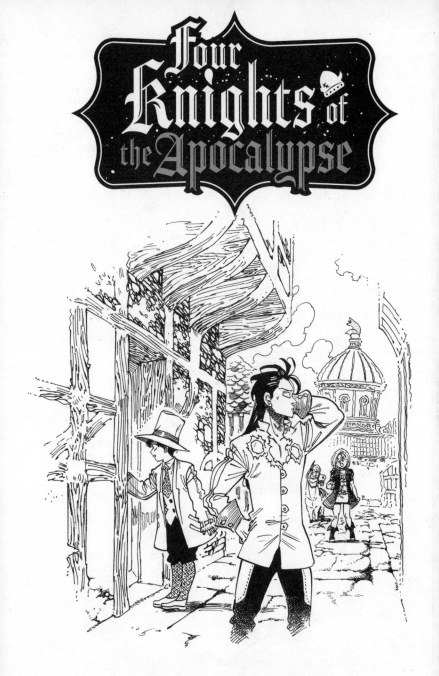

CHAPTER 53: TRIPLE TROUBLE

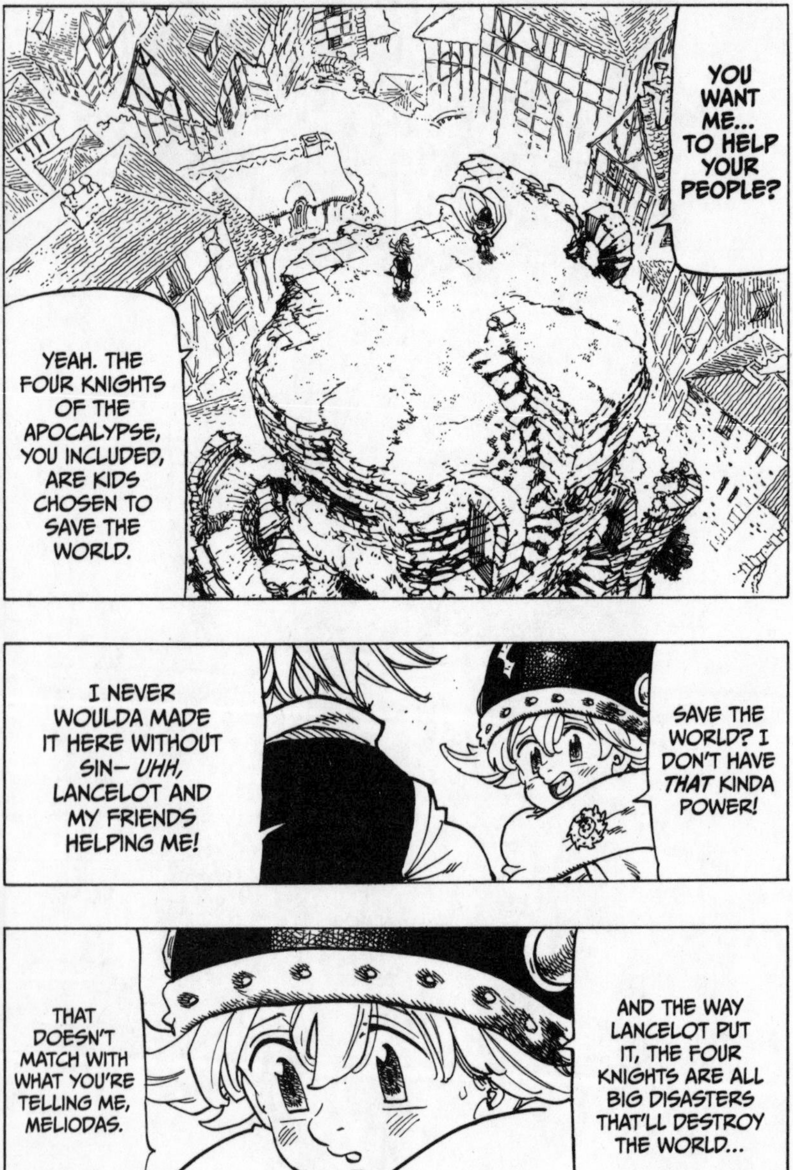
YOU WANT ME... TO HELP YOUR PEOPLE?
YEAH. THE FOUR KNIGHTS OF THE APOCALYPSE, YOU INCLUDED, ARE KIDS CHOSEN TO SAVE THE WORLD.
SAVE THE WORLD? I DON'T HAVE *THAT* KINDA POWER!
I NEVER WOULDA MADE IT HERE WITHOUT SIN— *UHH,* LANCELOT AND MY FRIENDS HELPING ME!
AND THE WAY LANCELOT PUT IT, THE FOUR KNIGHTS ARE ALL BIG DISASTERS THAT'LL DESTROY THE WORLD...
THAT DOESN'T MATCH WITH WHAT YOU'RE TELLING ME, MELIODAS.

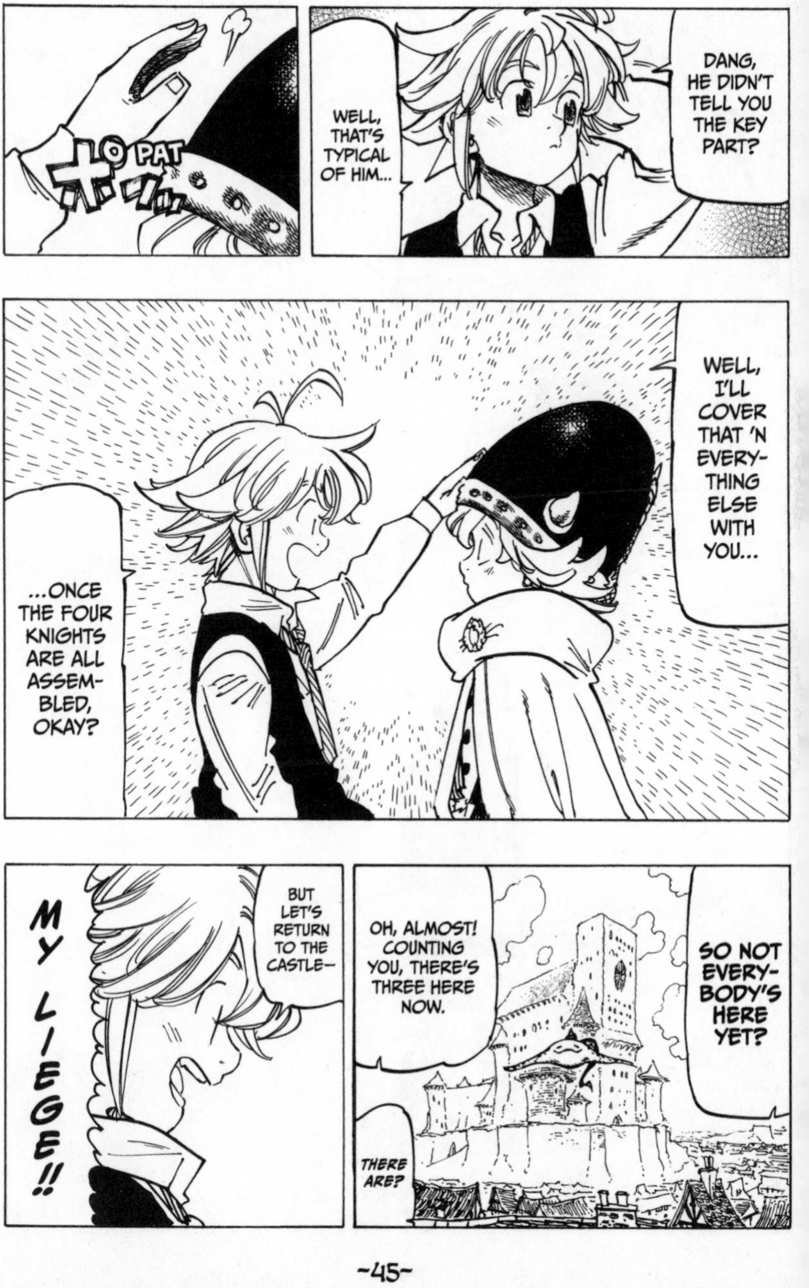
DANG, HE DIDN'T TELL YOU THE KEY PART?
WELL, THAT'S TYPICAL OF HIM...
PAT
WELL, I'LL COVER THAT 'N EVERY-THING ELSE WITH YOU...
...ONCE THE FOUR KNIGHTS ARE ALL ASSEM-BLED, OKAY?
SO NOT EVERY-BODY'S HERE YET?
OH, ALMOST! COUNTING YOU, THERE'S THREE HERE NOW.
THERE ARE?
BUT LET'S RETURN TO THE CASTLE—
MY LIEGE!!

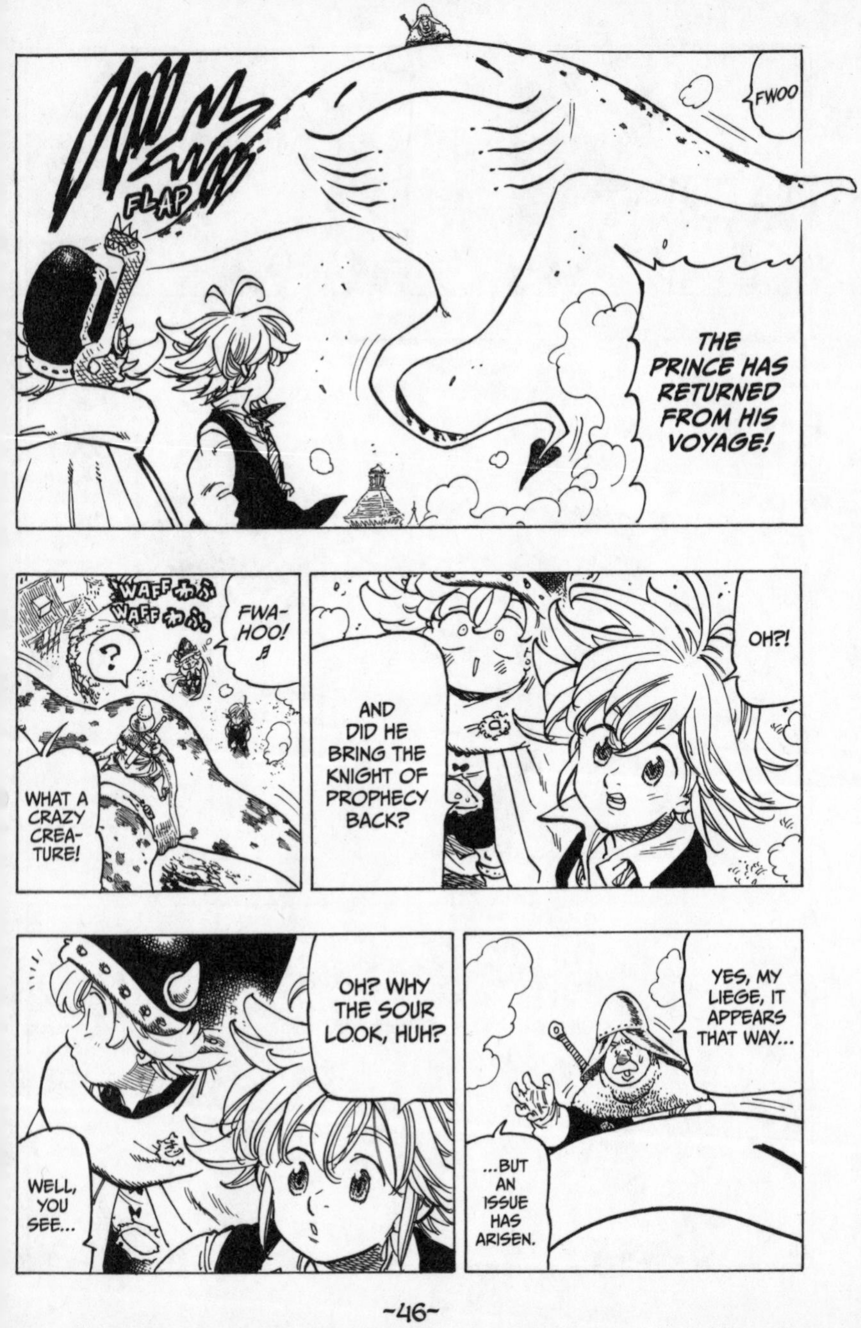
FWOO
THE PRINCE HAS RETURNED FROM HIS VOYAGE!
FLAP
OH?!
AND DID HE BRING THE KNIGHT OF PROPHECY BACK?
FWA-HOO! ♪
WAFF わふ
WAFF わふ
?
WHAT A CRAZY CREA-TURE!
YES, MY LIEGE, IT APPEARS THAT WAY...
...BUT AN ISSUE HAS ARISEN.
OH? WHY THE SOUR LOOK, HUH?
WELL, YOU SEE...

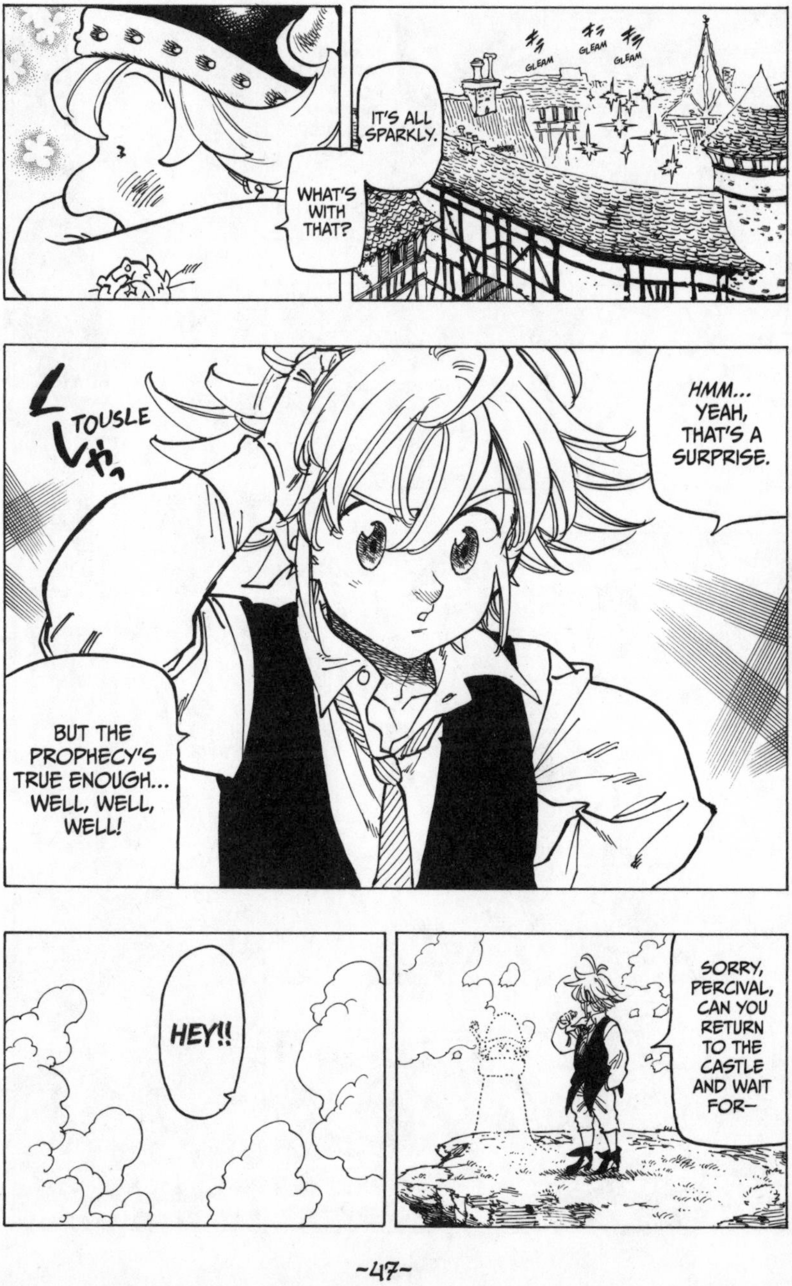
GLEAM
GLEAM
GLEAM
IT'S ALL SPARKLY.
WHAT'S WITH THAT?
HMM... YEAH, THAT'S A SURPRISE.
TOUSLE
BUT THE PROPHECY'S TRUE ENOUGH... WELL, WELL, WELL!
SORRY, PERCIVAL, CAN YOU RETURN TO THE CASTLE AND WAIT FOR–
HEY!!

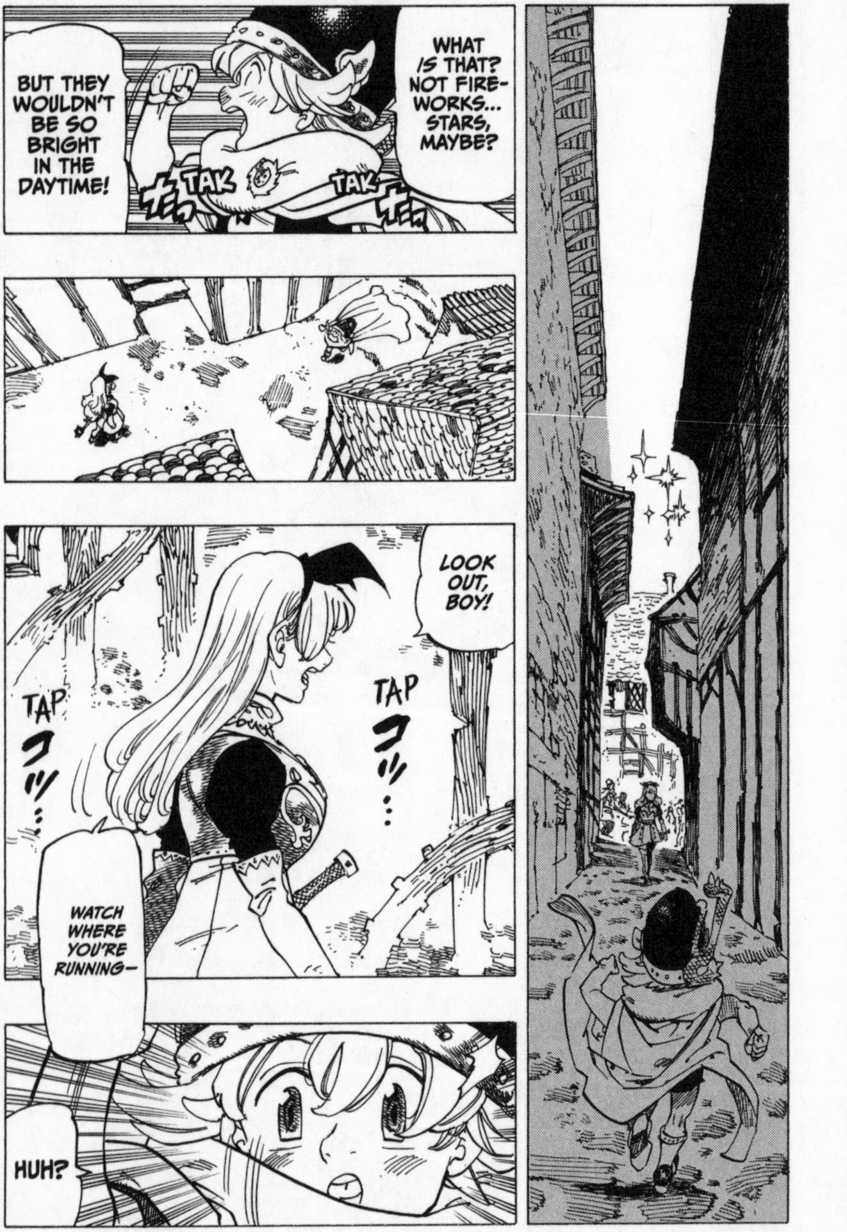
WHAT IS THAT? NOT FIRE-WORKS... STARS, MAYBE?
TAK
TAK
BUT THEY WOULDN'T BE SO BRIGHT IN THE DAYTIME!
LOOK OUT, BOY!
TAP
コッ...
TAP
コッ...
WATCH WHERE YOU'RE RUNNING—
HUH?

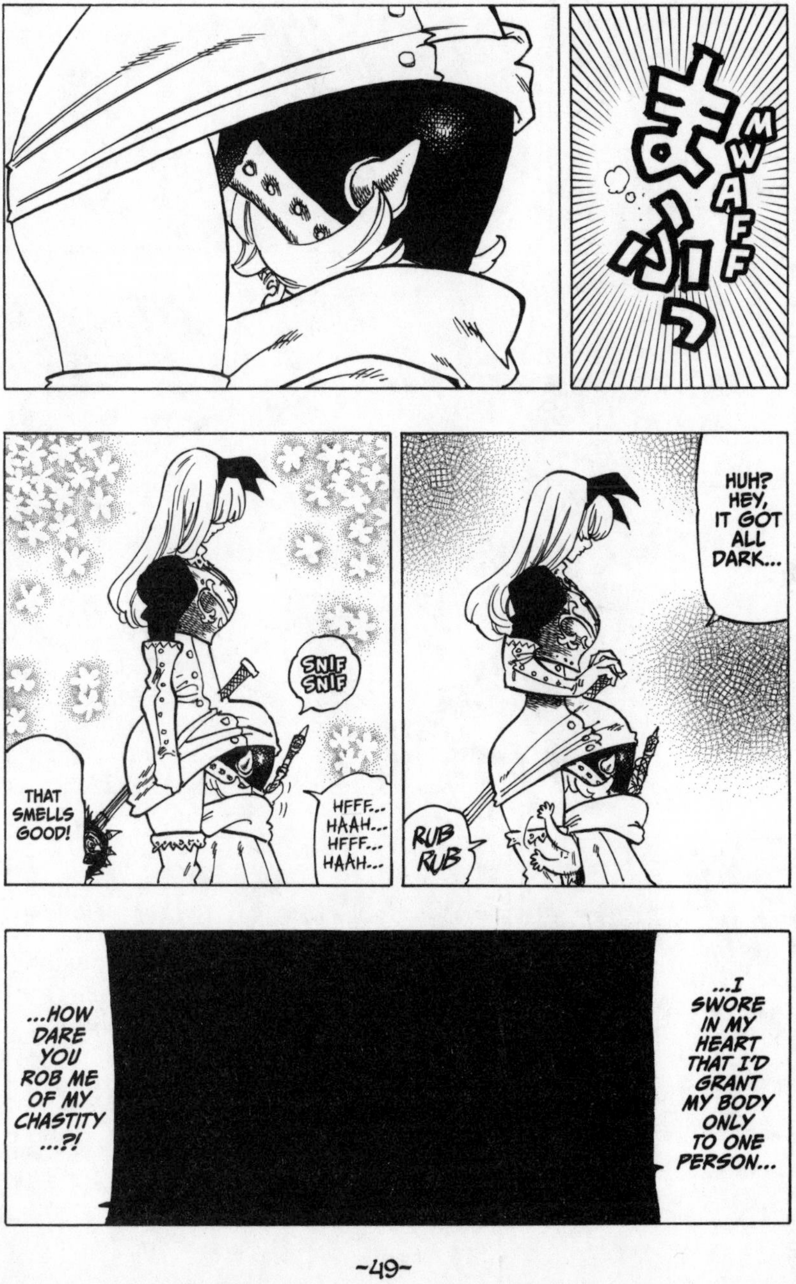
MWAFF
まふっ
HUH? HEY, IT GOT ALL DARK...
RUB RUB
SNIF SNIF
HFFF... HAAH... HFFF... HAAH...
THAT SMELLS GOOD!
...I SWORE IN MY HEART THAT I'D GRANT MY BODY ONLY TO ONE PERSON...
...HOW DARE YOU ROB ME OF MY CHASTITY ...?!

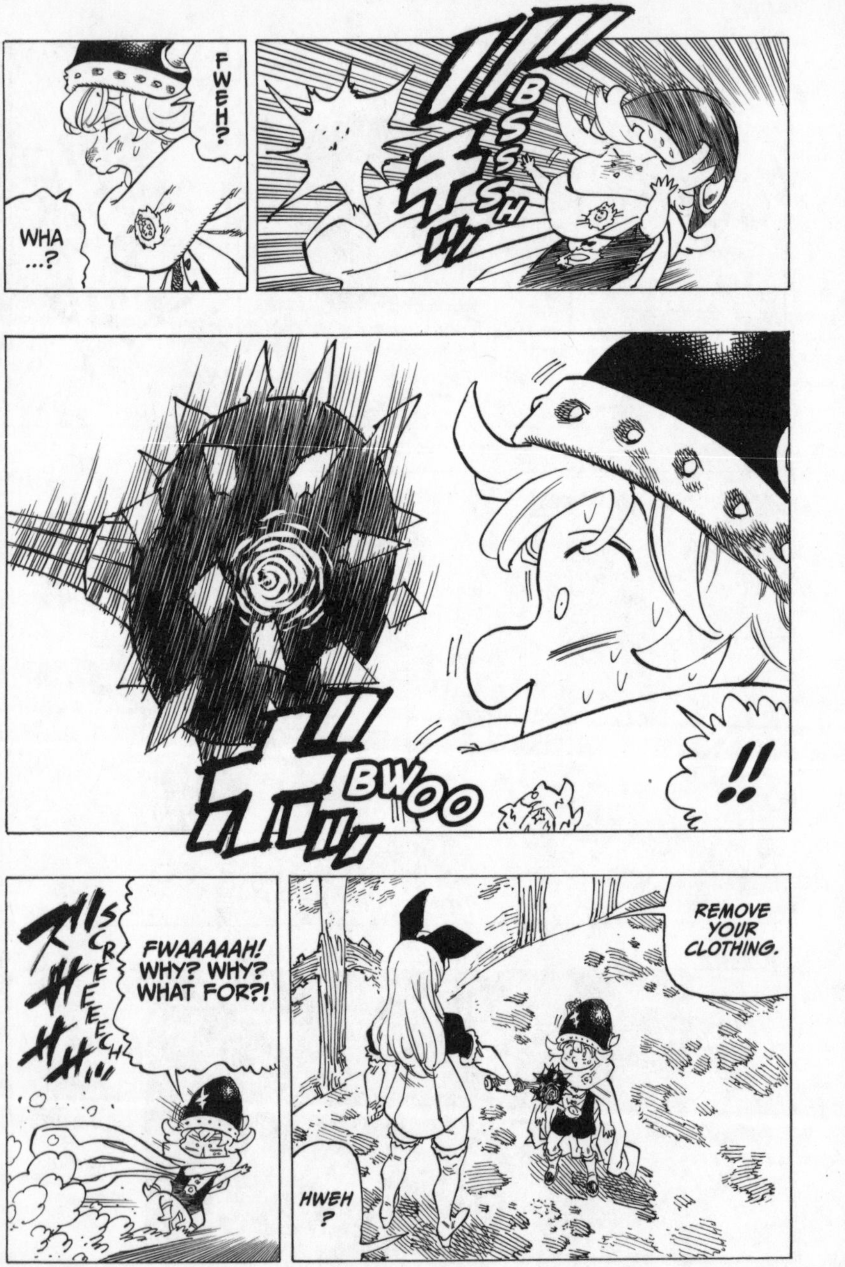
BSSSH
FWEH?
WHA ...?
BWOO
!!
REMOVE YOUR CLOTHING.
HWEH ?
SCREEECH
FWAAAAAH! WHY? WHY? WHAT FOR?!

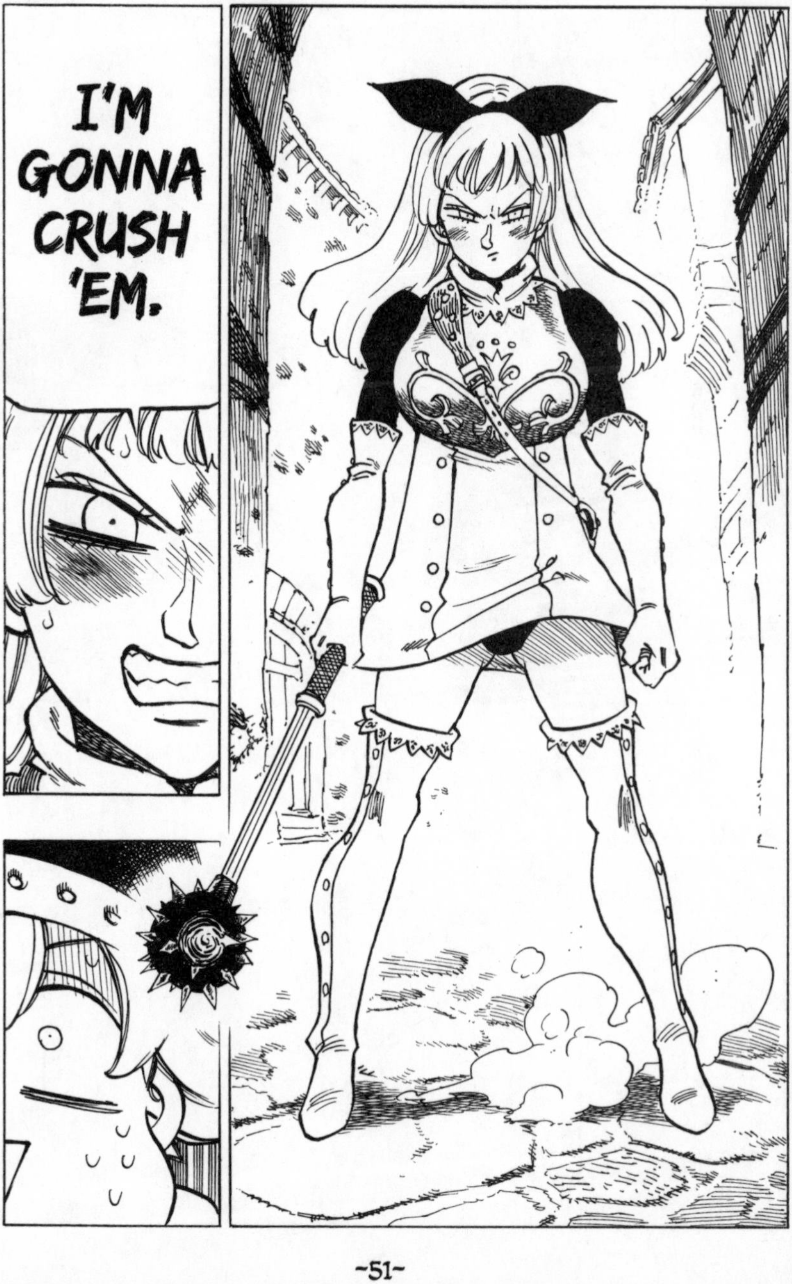
I'M GONNA CRUSH 'EM.

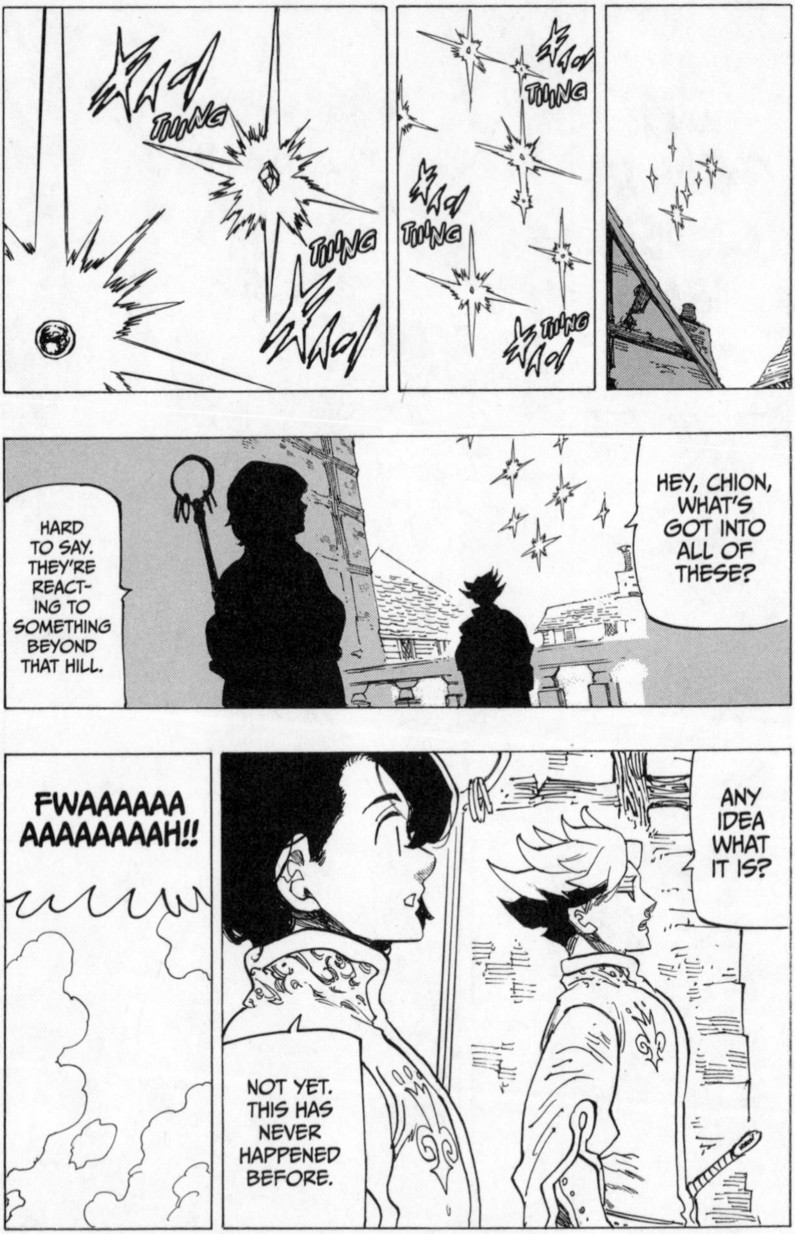
TIIING
TIIING
TIIING
TIIING
TIIING
HEY, CHION, WHAT'S GOT INTO ALL OF THESE?
HARD TO SAY. THEY'RE REACT-ING TO SOMETHING BEYOND THAT HILL.
ANY IDEA WHAT IT IS?
NOT YET. THIS HAS NEVER HAPPENED BEFORE.
FWAAAAAAA AAAAAAAAH!!

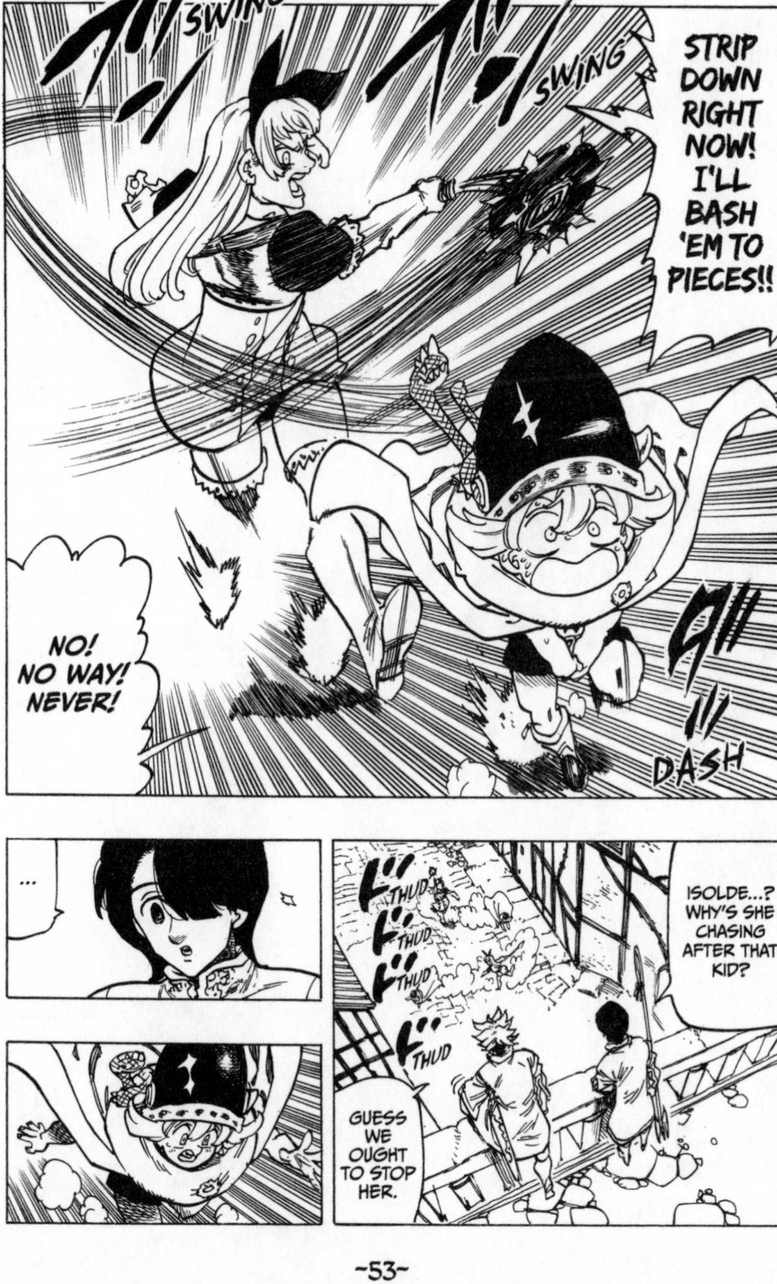
STRIP DOWN RIGHT NOW! I'LL BASH 'EM TO PIECES!!
SWING
SWING
DASH
NO! NO WAY! NEVER!
ISOLDE...? WHY'S SHE CHASING AFTER THAT KID?
THUD
THUD
THUD
THUD
GUESS WE OUGHT TO STOP HER.
...

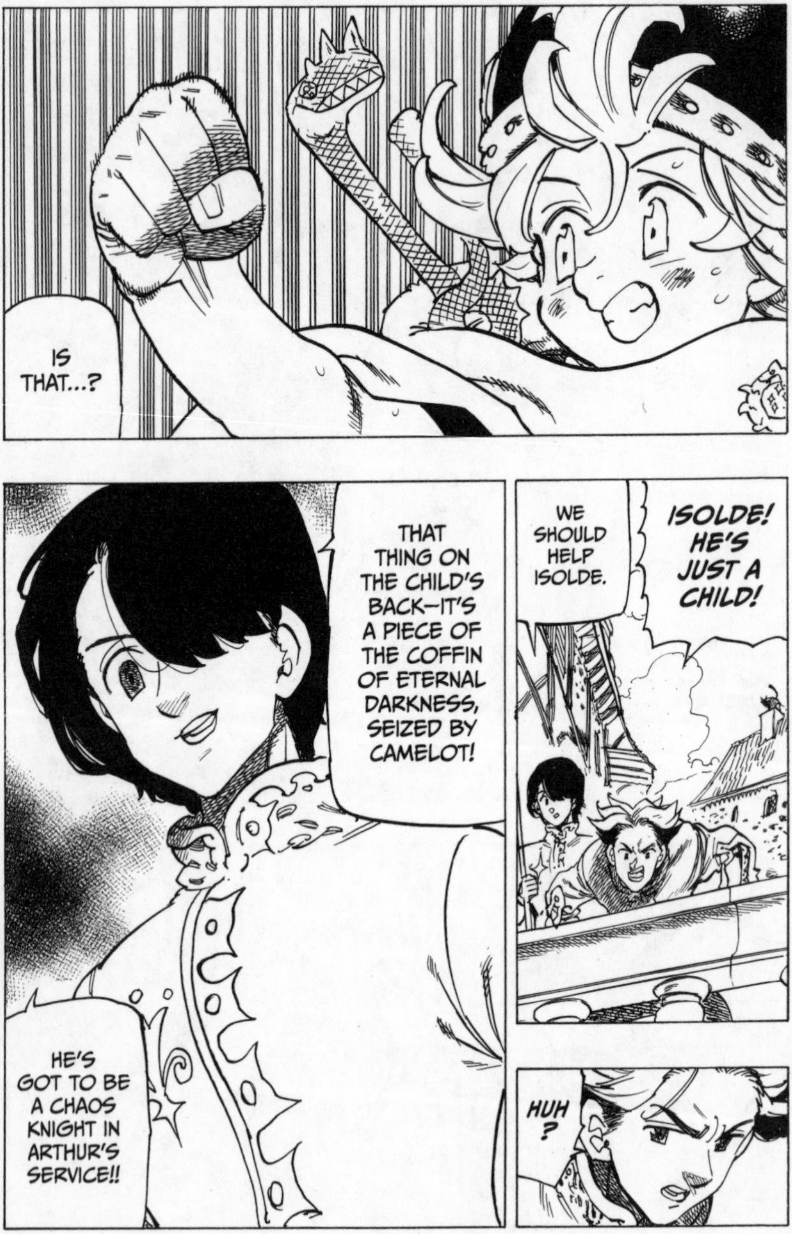
IS THAT...?
ISOLDE! HE'S JUST A CHILD!
WE SHOULD HELP ISOLDE.
HUH?
THAT THING ON THE CHILD'S BACK—IT'S A PIECE OF THE COFFIN OF ETERNAL DARKNESS, SEIZED BY CAMELOT!
HE'S GOT TO BE A CHAOS KNIGHT IN ARTHUR'S SERVICE!!

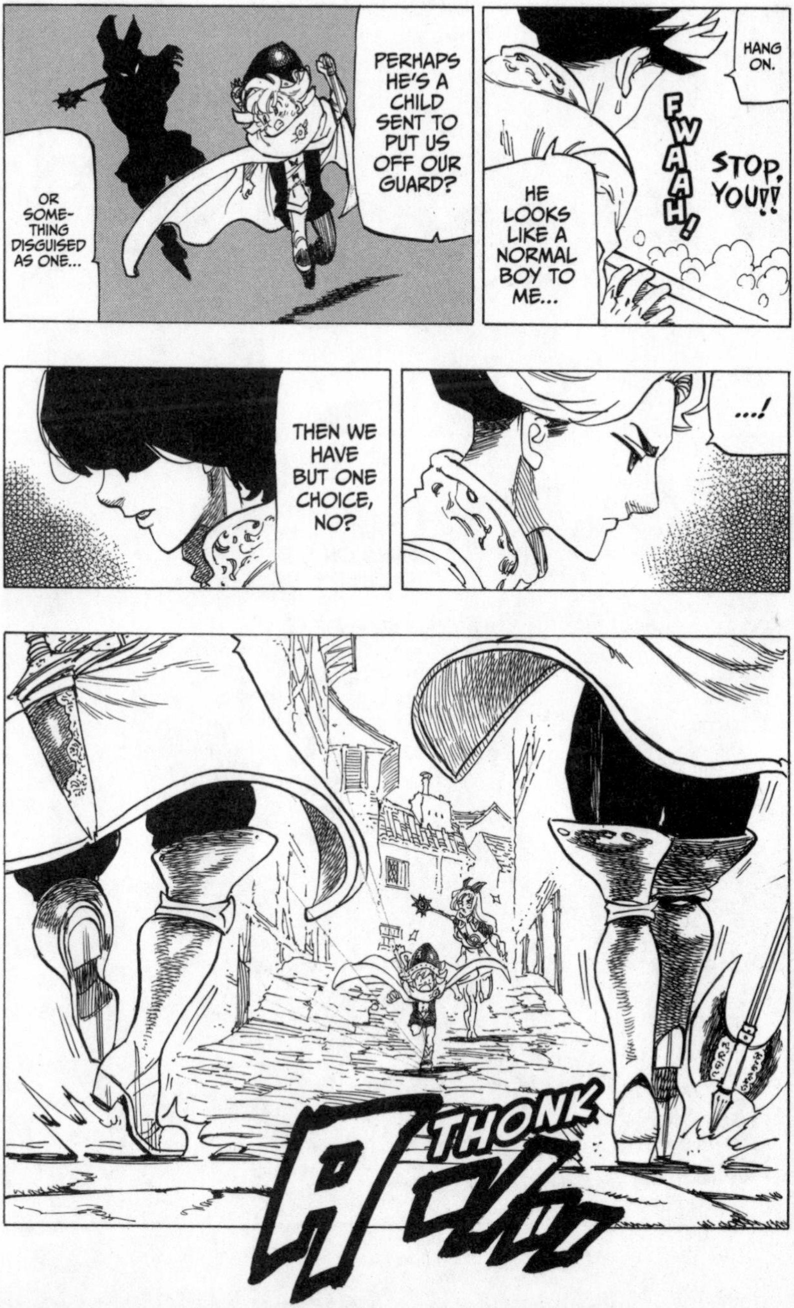
HANG ON.
FWAAAH!
STOP, YOU!!
HE LOOKS LIKE A NORMAL BOY TO ME...
PERHAPS HE'S A CHILD SENT TO PUT US OFF OUR GUARD?
OR SOMETHING DISGUISED AS ONE...
...!
THEN WE HAVE BUT ONE CHOICE, NO?
THONK

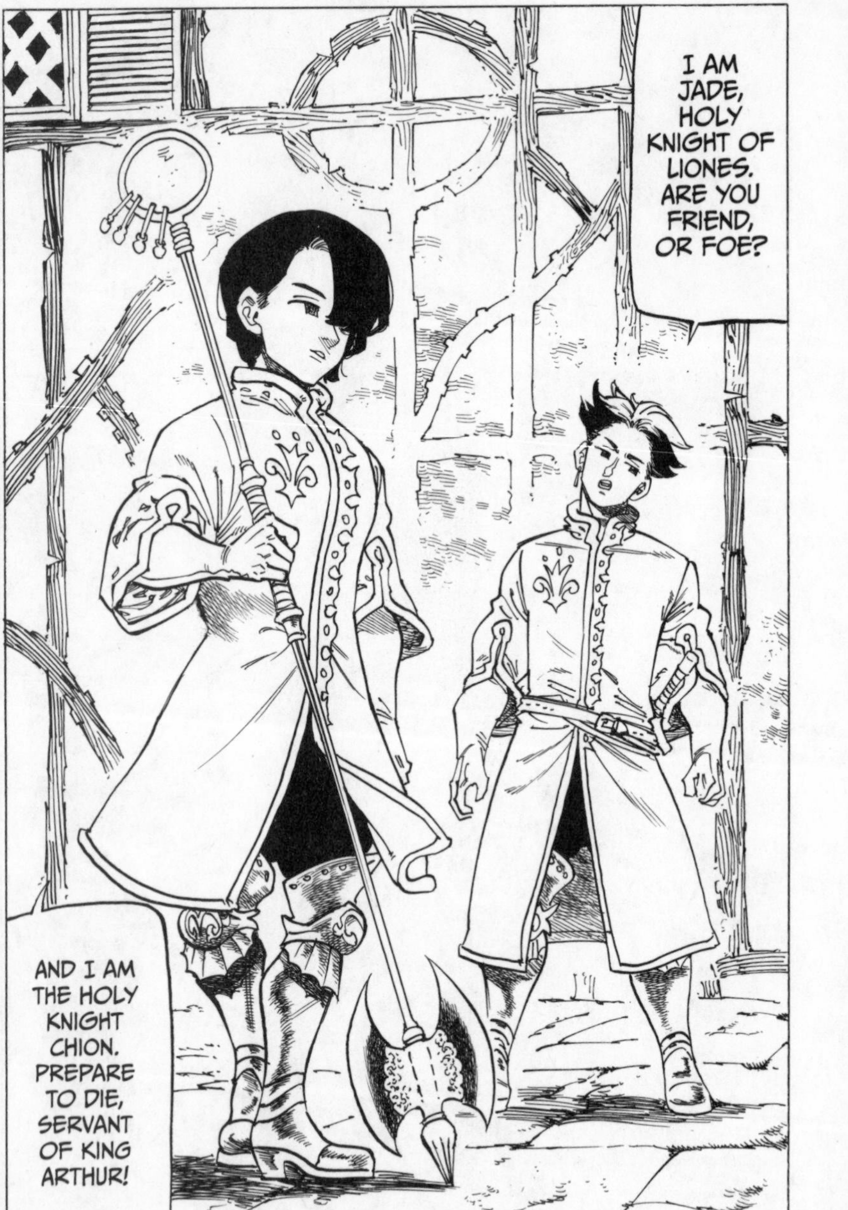
I AM JADE, HOLY KNIGHT OF LIONES. ARE YOU FRIEND, OR FOE?
AND I AM THE HOLY KNIGHT CHION. PREPARE TO DIE, SERVANT OF KING ARTHUR!

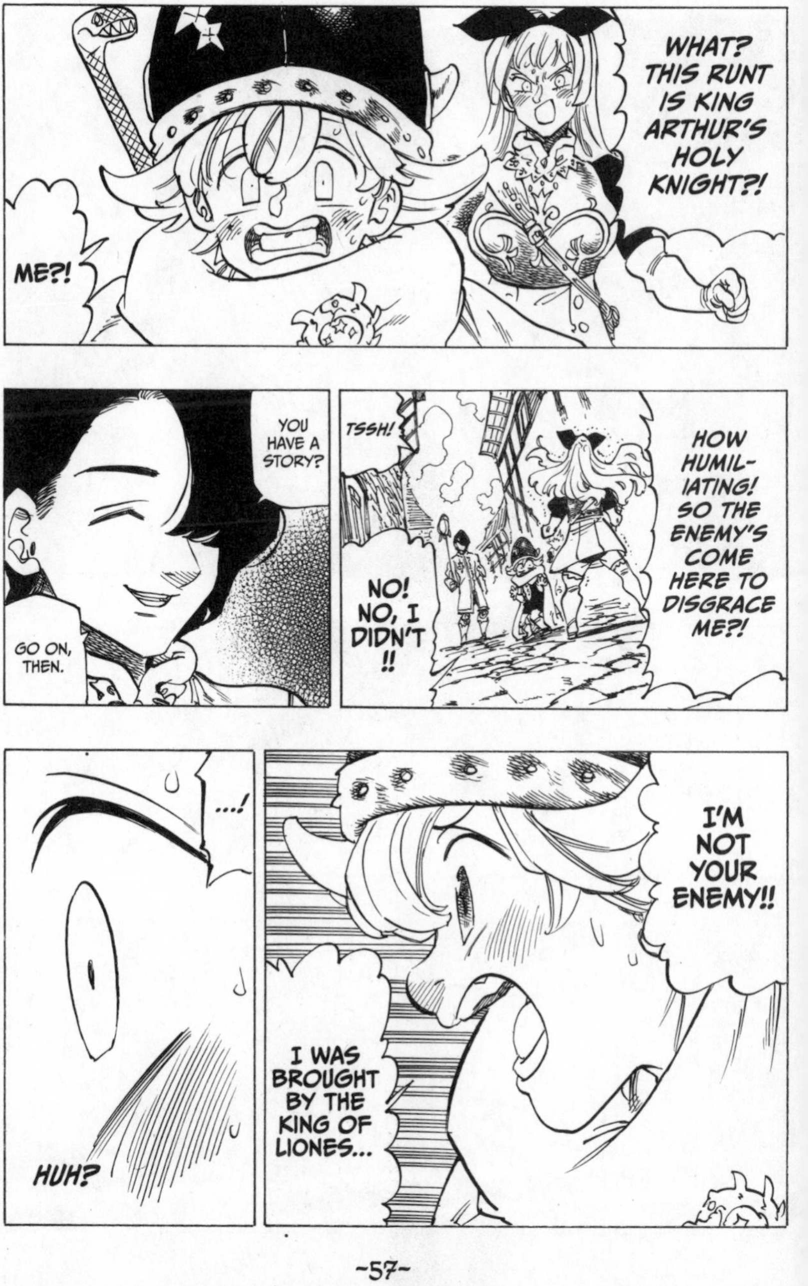
WHAT? THIS RUNT IS KING ARTHUR'S HOLY KNIGHT?!
ME?!
HOW HUMIL-IATING! SO THE ENEMY'S COME HERE TO DISGRACE ME?!
TSSH!
NO! NO, I DIDN'T !!
YOU HAVE A STORY?
GO ON, THEN.
I'M NOT YOUR ENEMY!!
I WAS BROUGHT BY THE KING OF LIONES...
...!
HUH?

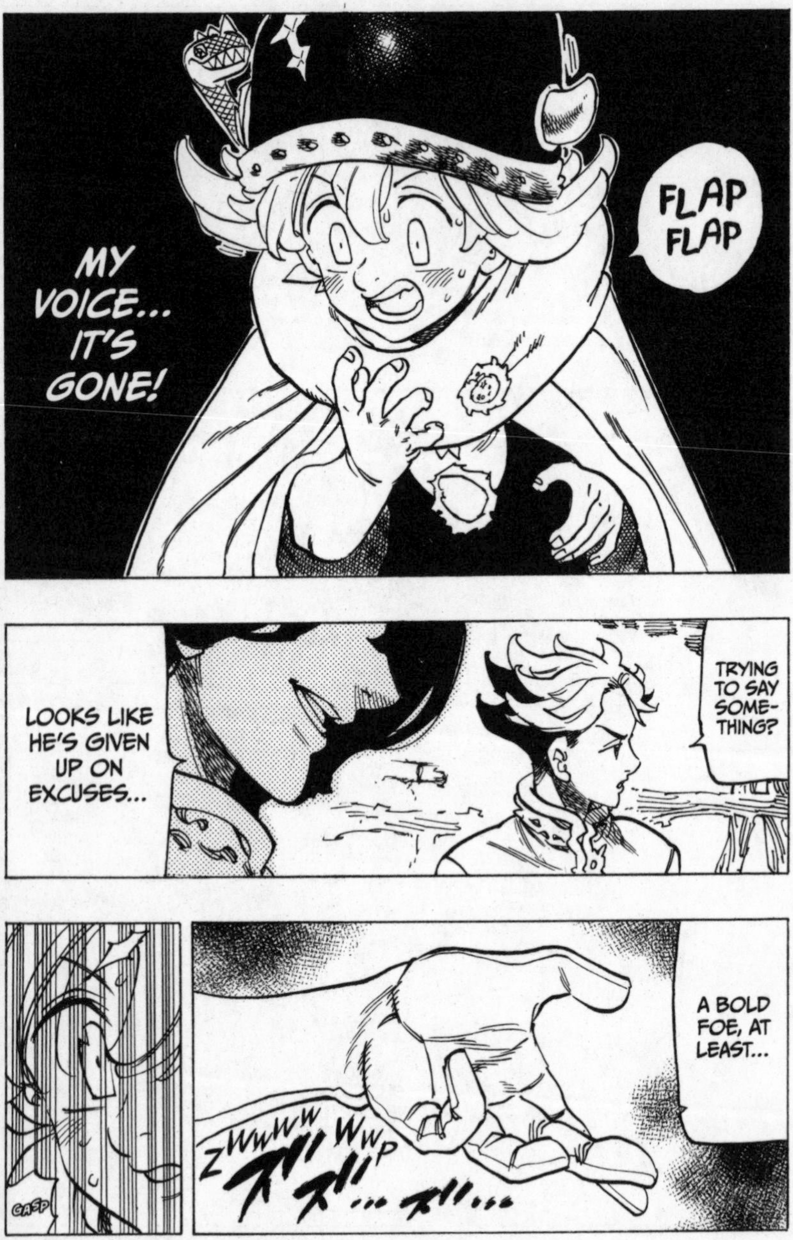
FLAP FLAP
MY VOICE... IT'S GONE!
TRYING TO SAY SOME-THING?
LOOKS LIKE HE'S GIVEN UP ON EXCUSES...
A BOLD FOE, AT LEAST...
ZWWWWWWWP
GASP

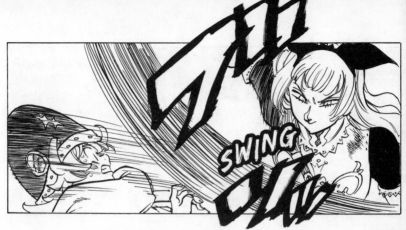

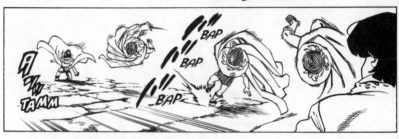

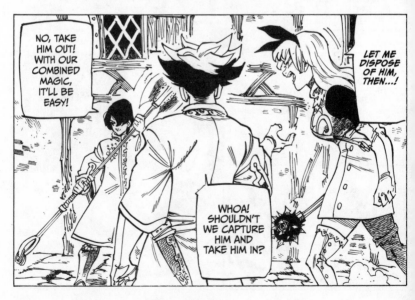

SWING
BAP
BAP
BAP
TAMM
LET ME DISPOSE OF HIM, THEN...!
WHOA! SHOULDN'T WE CAPTURE HIM AND TAKE HIM IN?
NO, TAKE HIM OUT! WITH OUR COMBINED MAGIC, IT'LL BE EASY!

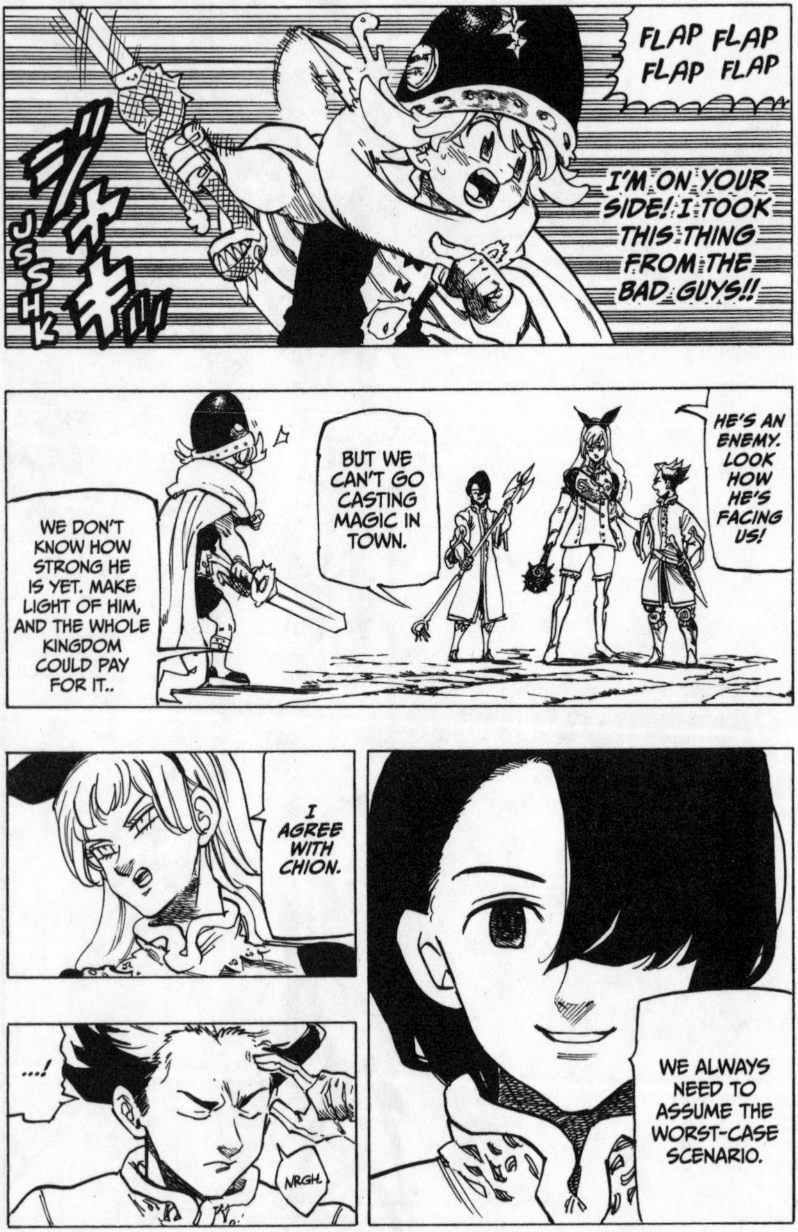
FLAP FLAP
FLAP FLAP
I'M ON YOUR SIDE! I TOOK THIS THING FROM THE BAD GUYS!!
JSSHK
HE'S AN ENEMY. LOOK HOW HE'S FACING US!
BUT WE CAN'T GO CASTING MAGIC IN TOWN.
WE DON'T KNOW HOW STRONG HE IS YET. MAKE LIGHT OF HIM, AND THE WHOLE KINGDOM COULD PAY FOR IT..
WE ALWAYS NEED TO ASSUME THE WORST-CASE SCENARIO.
I AGREE WITH CHION.
...!
NRGH.

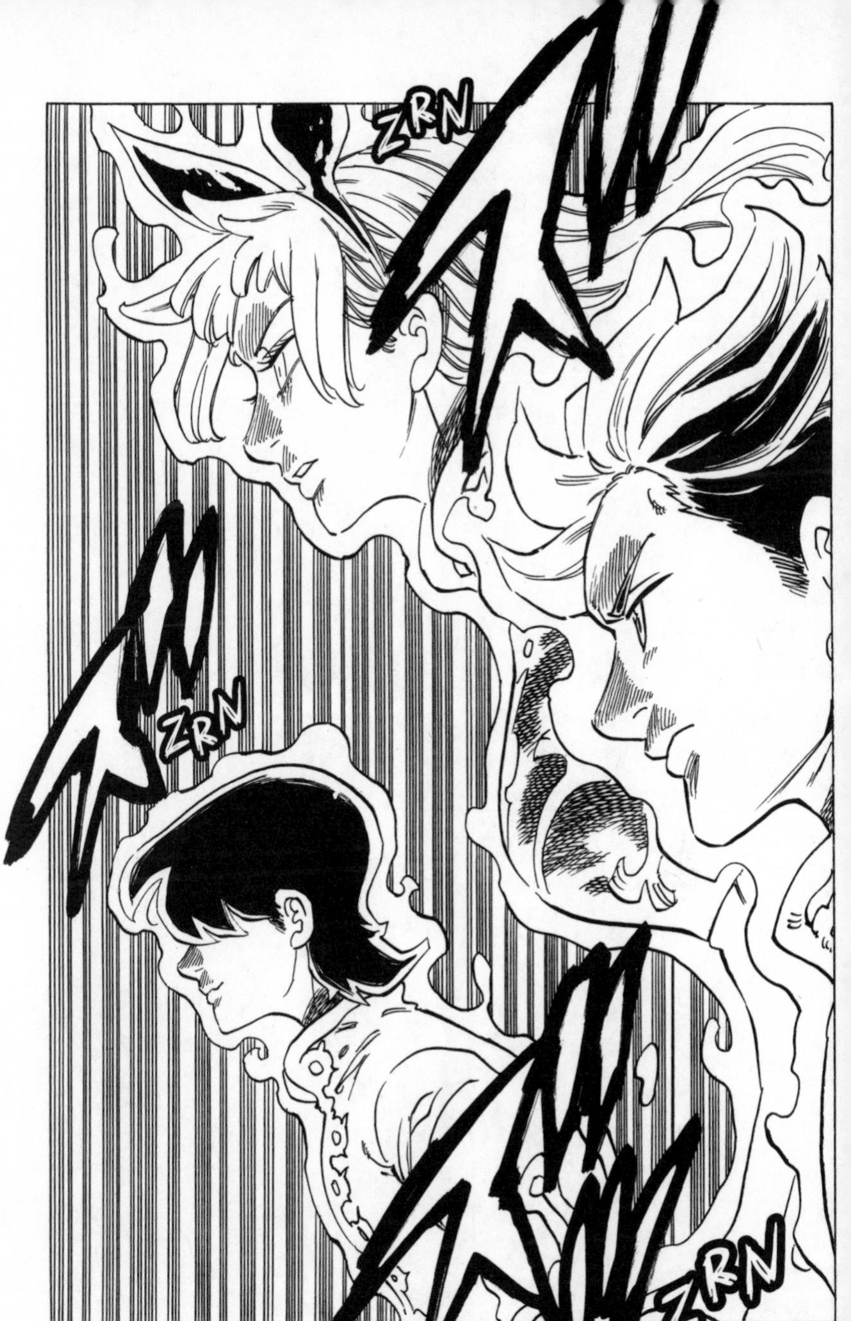
ZRN
ZRN
ZRN

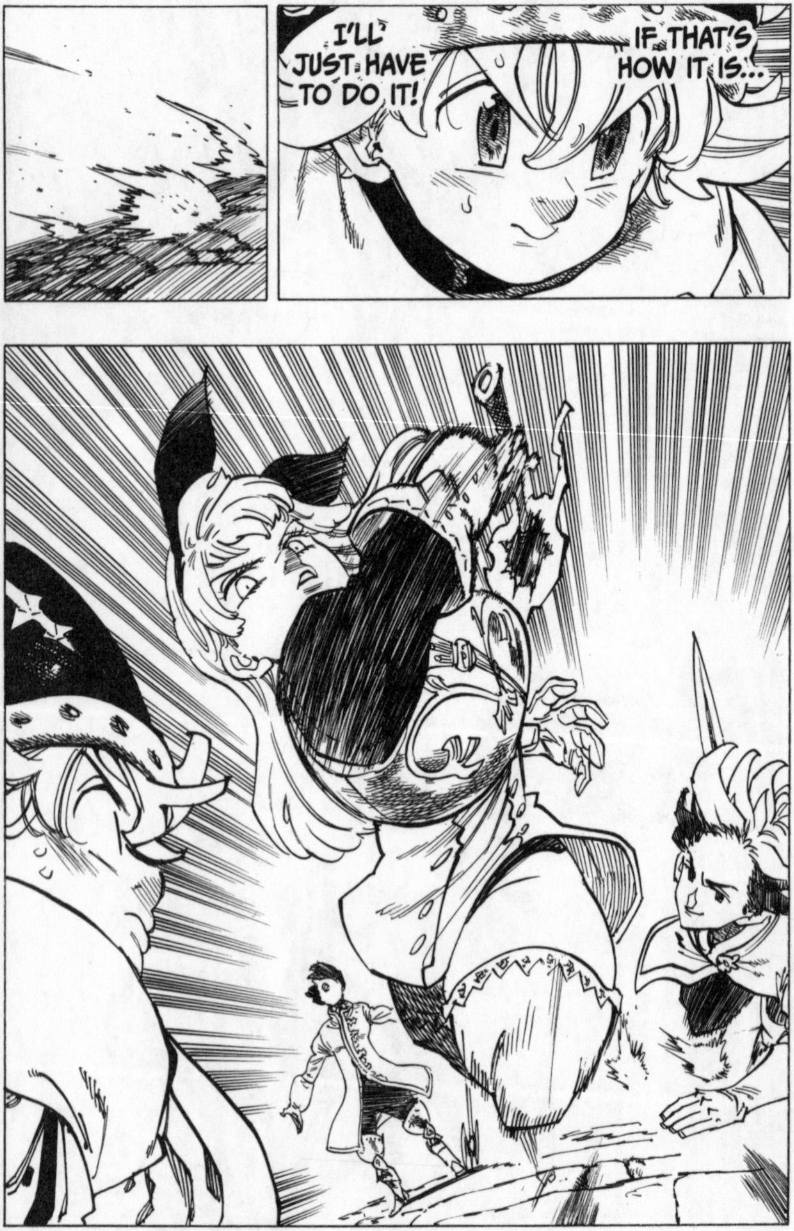
IF THAT'S HOW IT IS...
I'LL JUST HAVE TO DO IT!

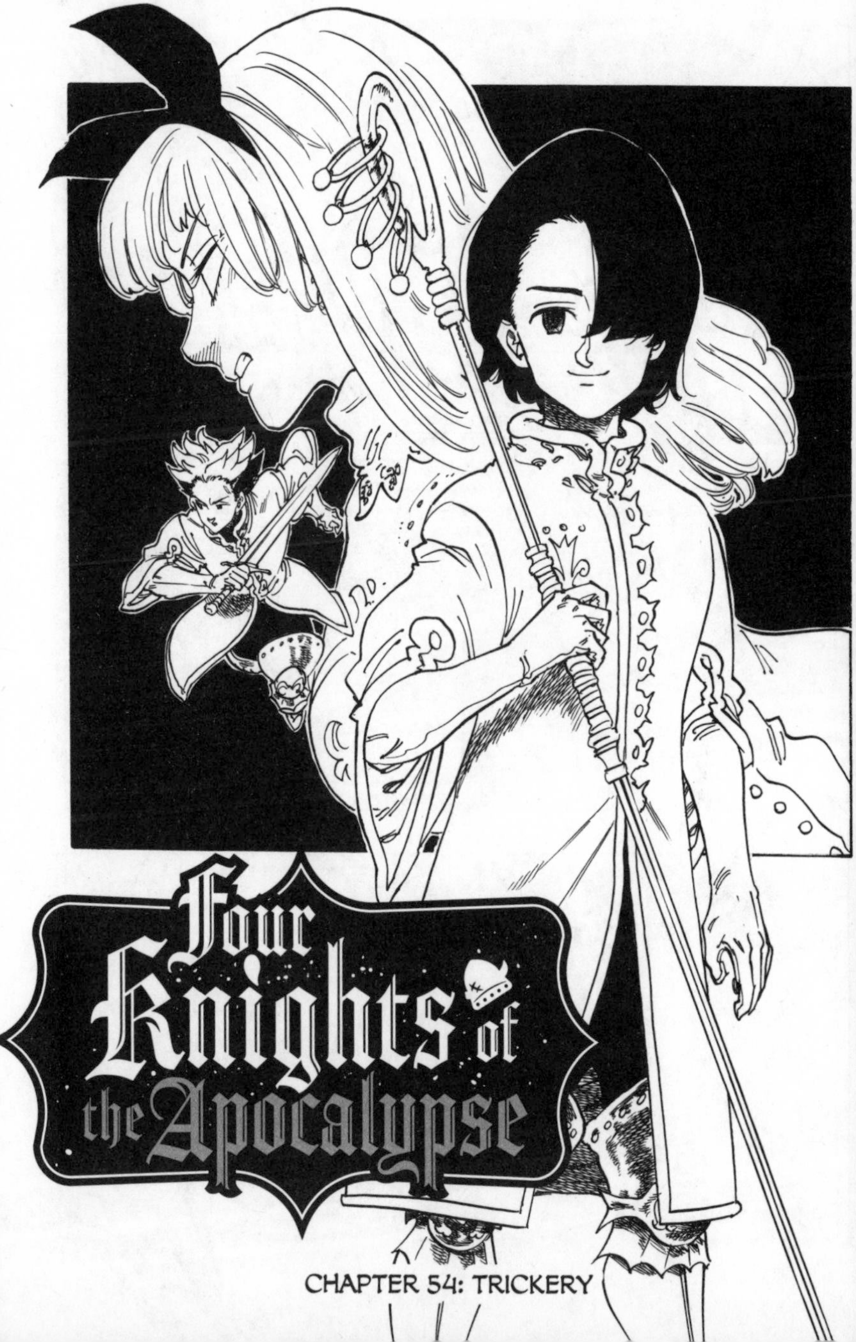

Four Knights of the Apocalypse
CHAPTER 54: TRICKERY

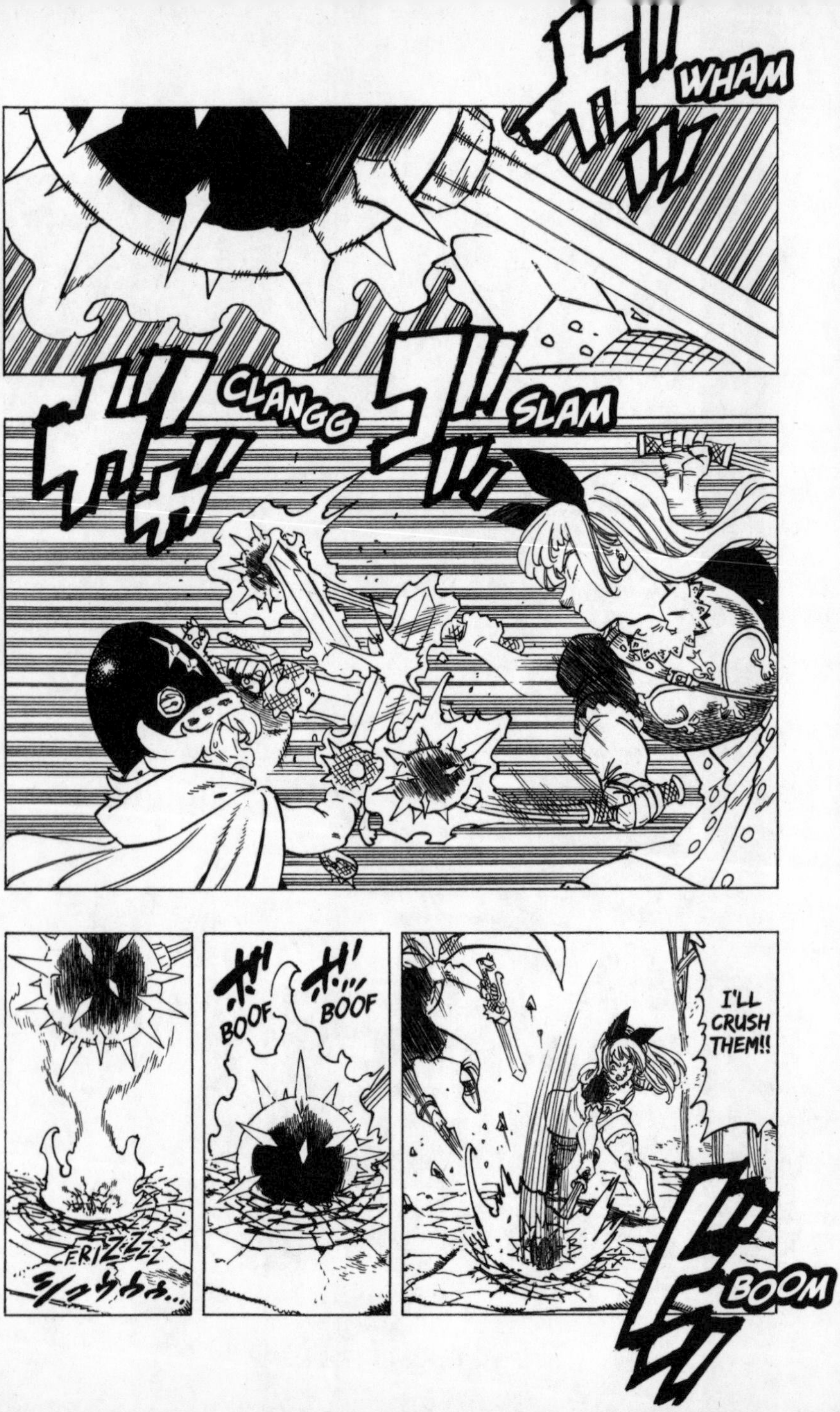
WHAM
SLAM
CLANGG
I'LL CRUSH THEM!!
BOOM
BOOF
BOOF
FRIZZZZ
シュウウウ...

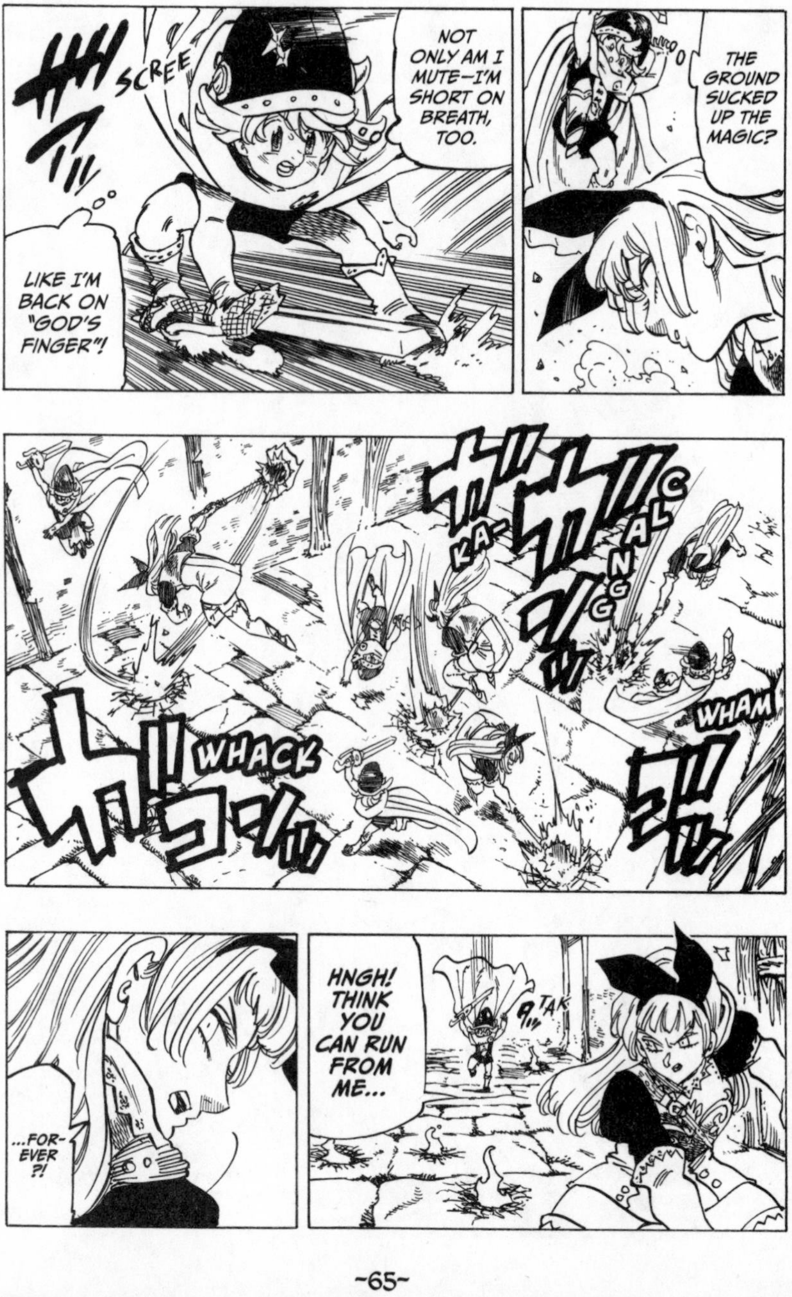
THE GROUND SUCKED UP THE MAGIC?
NOT ONLY AM I MUTE—I'M SHORT ON BREATH, TOO.
SCREE
LIKE I'M BACK ON "GOD'S FINGER"!
KA-CLANGG
WHAM
WHACK
HNGH! THINK YOU CAN RUN FROM ME...
TAK
...FOR-EVER?!

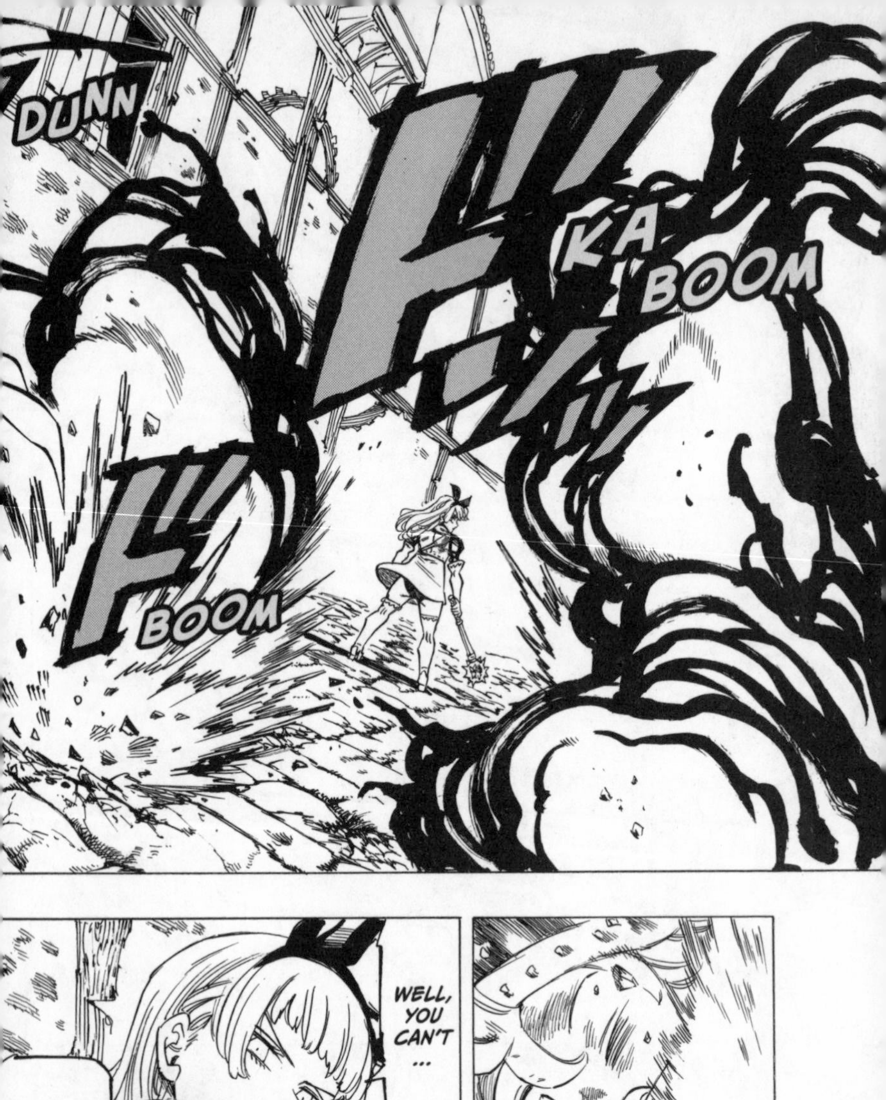
KA BOOM
DUNN
BOOM
THE GROUND EXPLODED?!
WELL, YOU CAN'T ...
...YOU PERVY LITTLE CAMELOT KNIGHT!!

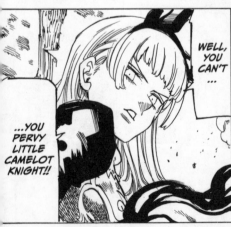

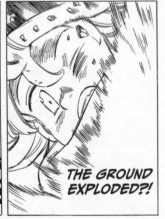

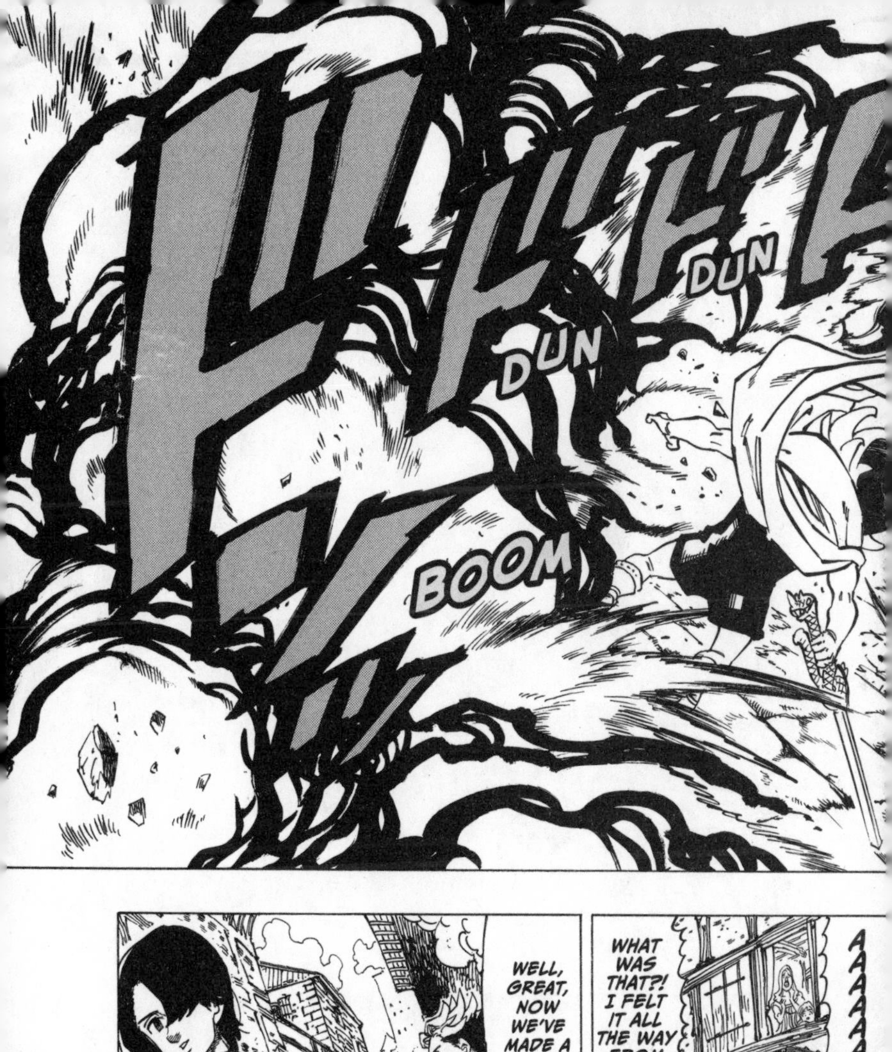
DUN
DUN
BOOM

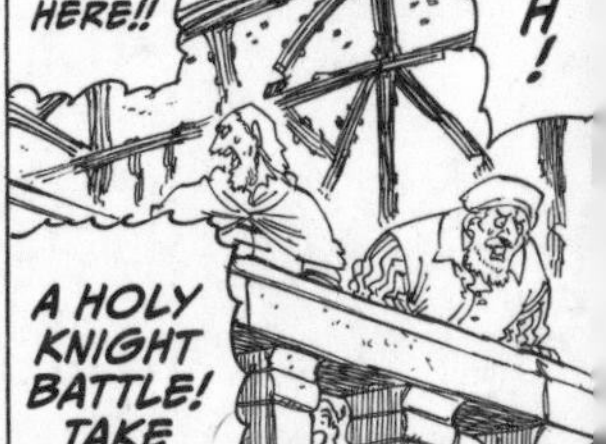
AAAAAAAH!
WHAT WAS THAT?! I FELT IT ALL THE WAY FROM HERE!!
A HOLY KNIGHT BATTLE! TAKE COVER!

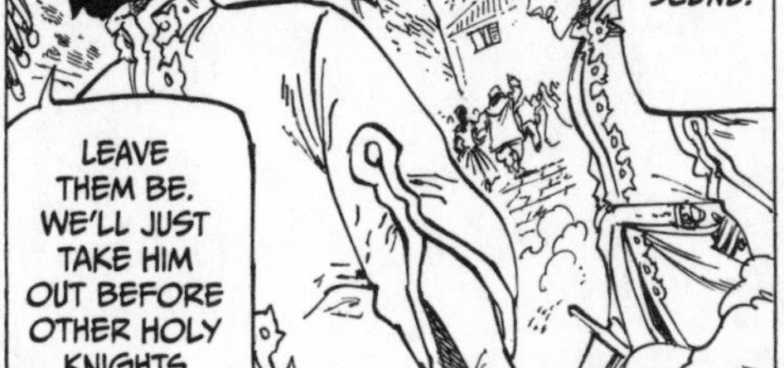
WELL, GREAT, NOW WE'VE MADE A SCENE.
LEAVE THEM BE. WE'LL JUST TAKE HIM OUT BEFORE OTHER HOLY KNIGHTS ARRIVE.

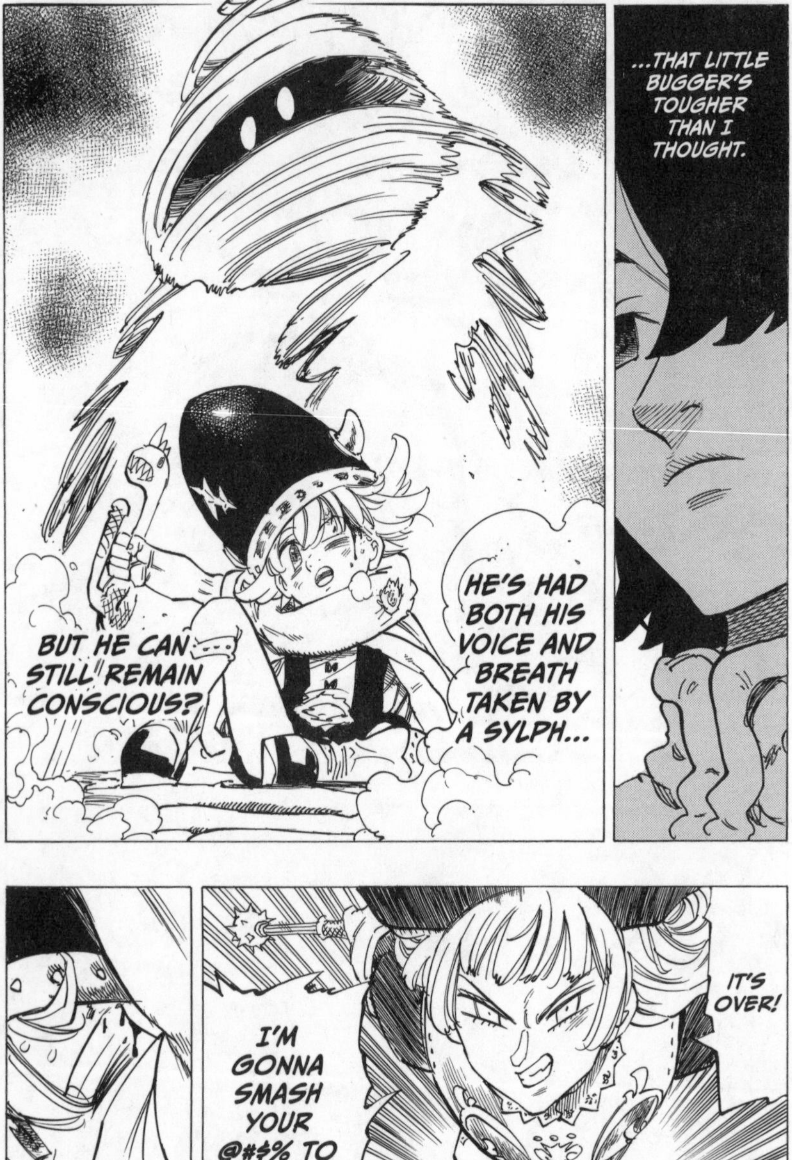
...THAT LITTLE BUGGER'S TOUGHER THAN I THOUGHT.
HE'S HAD BOTH HIS VOICE AND BREATH TAKEN BY A SYLPH...
BUT HE CAN STILL REMAIN CONSCIOUS?
IT'S OVER!
I'M GONNA SMASH YOUR @#$% TO PIECES!!

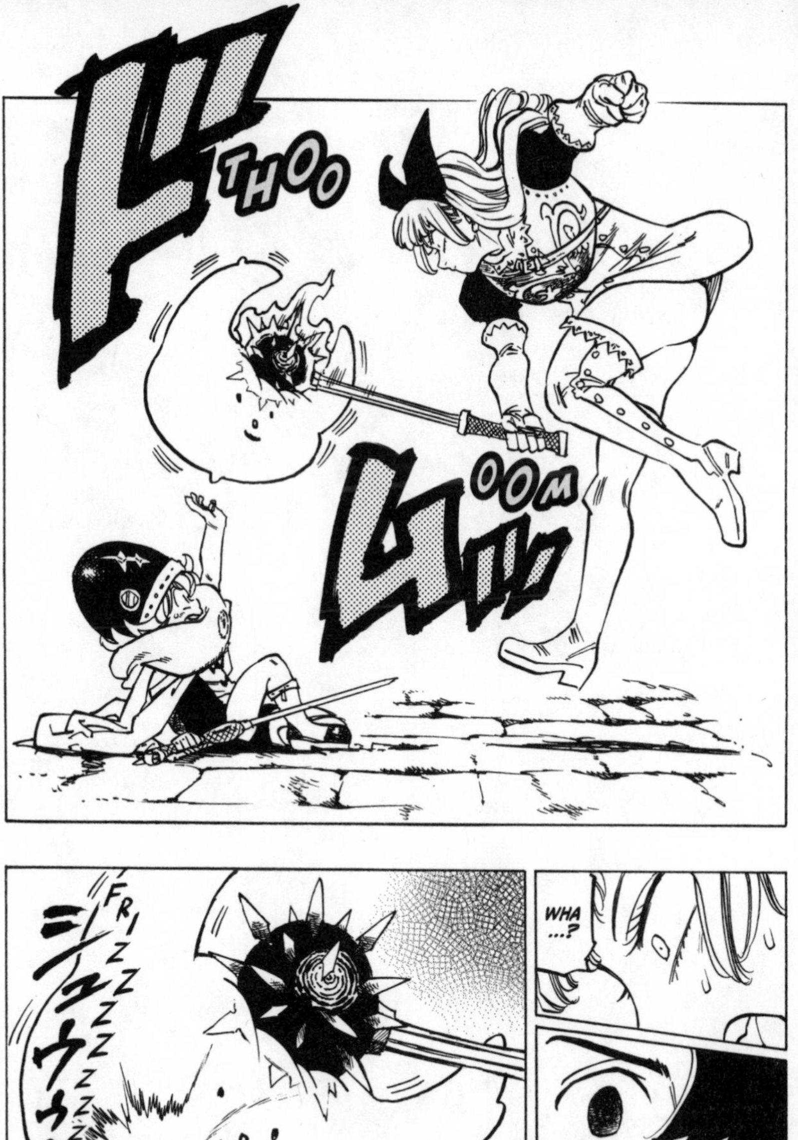
THOO
OOM
WHA ...?
FRIZZZZZZZZZZZ
シュウウウ…
JIGGLE
WHAT IS THIS?

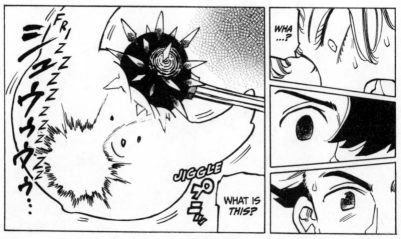

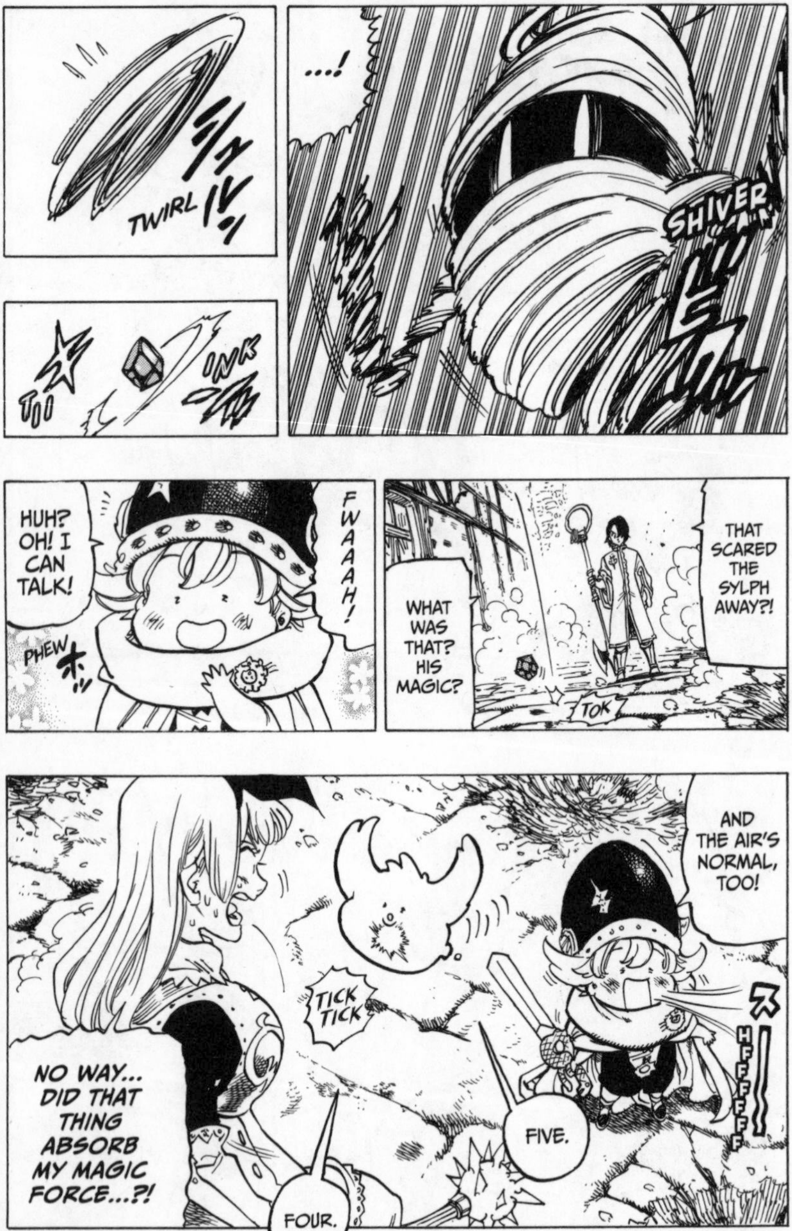
...!
SHIVER
TWIRL
TINK
THAT SCARED THE SYLPH AWAY?!
WHAT WAS THAT? HIS MAGIC?
TOK
FWAAAAH!
HUH? OH! I CAN TALK!
PHEW
AND THE AIR'S NORMAL, TOO!
HFFFFFF
FIVE.
TICK TICK
FOUR.
NO WAY... DID THAT THING ABSORB MY MAGIC FORCE...?!

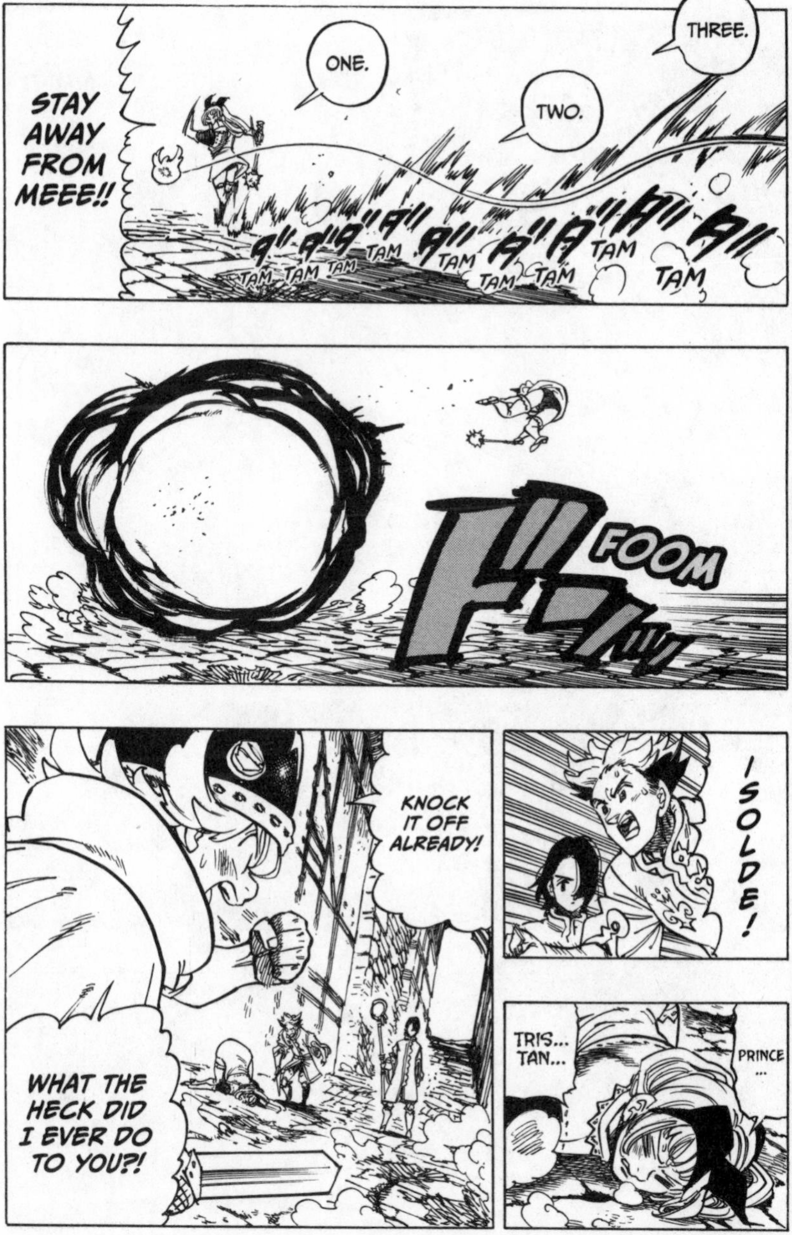
STAY AWAY FROM MEEE!!
ONE.
TWO.
THREE.
TAM TAM TAM TAM TAM TAM TAM TAM TAM
FOOM
ISOLDE!
PRINCE ...
TRIS... TAN...
KNOCK IT OFF ALREADY!
WHAT THE HECK DID I EVER DO TO YOU?!

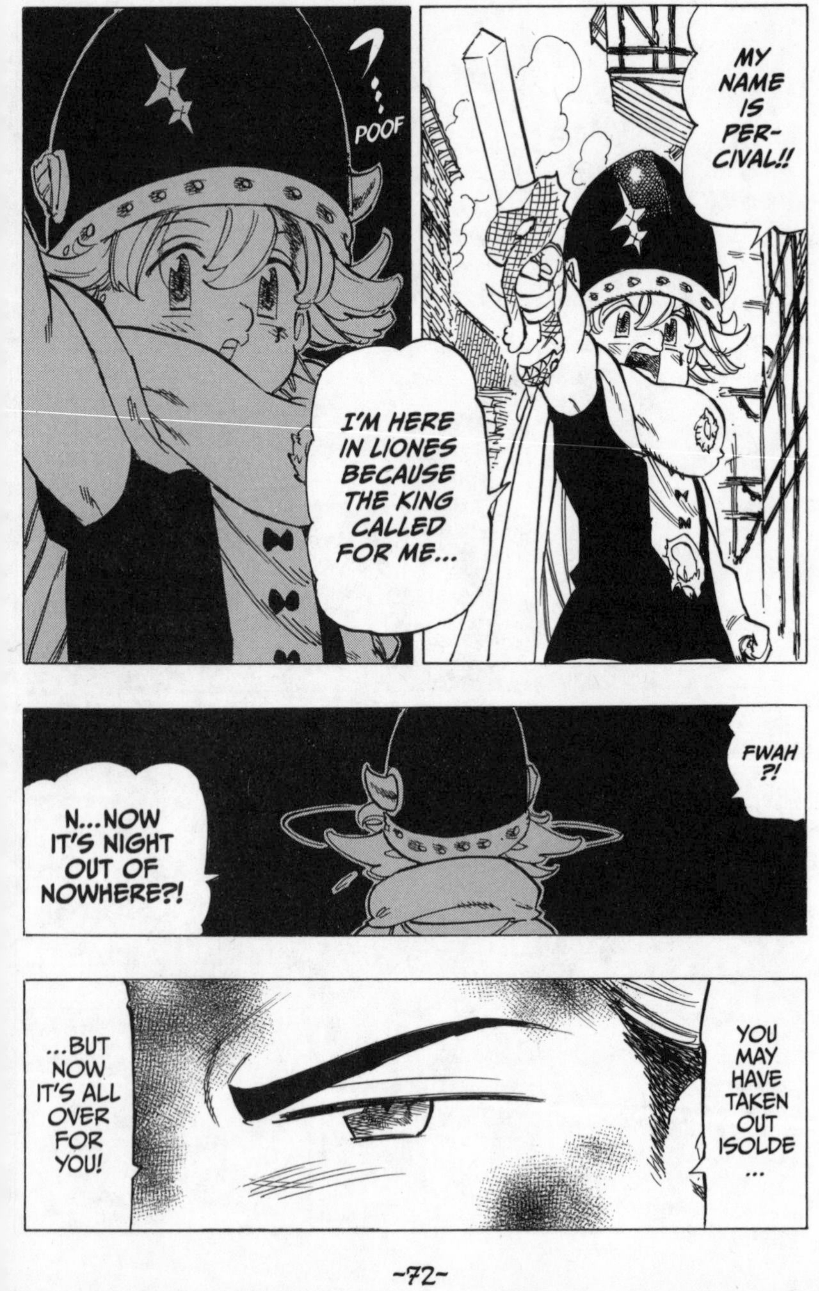
MY NAME IS PER-CIVAL!!
I'M HERE IN LIONES BECAUSE THE KING CALLED FOR ME...
?...
POOF
FWAH ?!
N...NOW IT'S NIGHT OUT OF NOWHERE?!
YOU MAY HAVE TAKEN OUT ISOLDE ...
...BUT NOW IT'S ALL OVER FOR YOU!

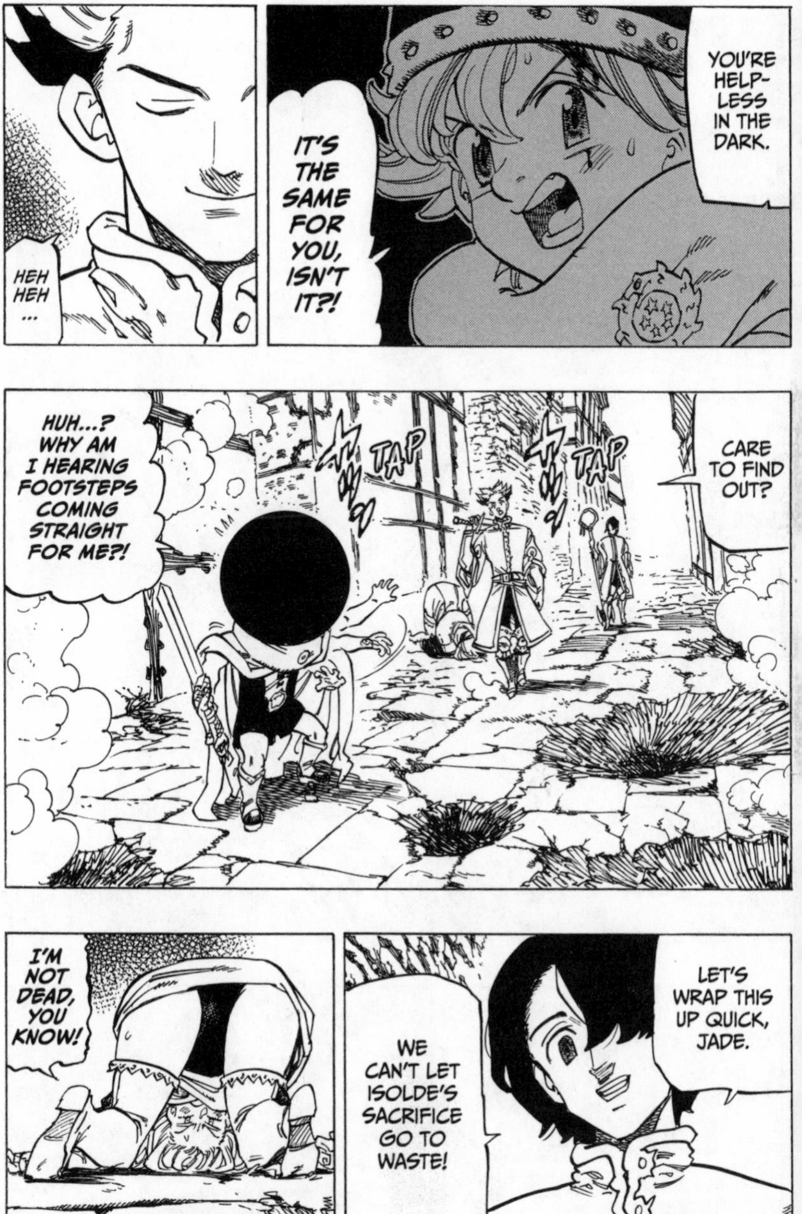
YOU'RE HELP-LESS IN THE DARK.
IT'S THE SAME FOR YOU, ISN'T IT?!
HEH HEH ...
CARE TO FIND OUT?
TAP
TAP
HUH...? WHY AM I HEARING FOOTSTEPS COMING STRAIGHT FOR ME?!
LET'S WRAP THIS UP QUICK, JADE.
WE CAN'T LET ISOLDE'S SACRIFICE GO TO WASTE!
I'M NOT DEAD, YOU KNOW!

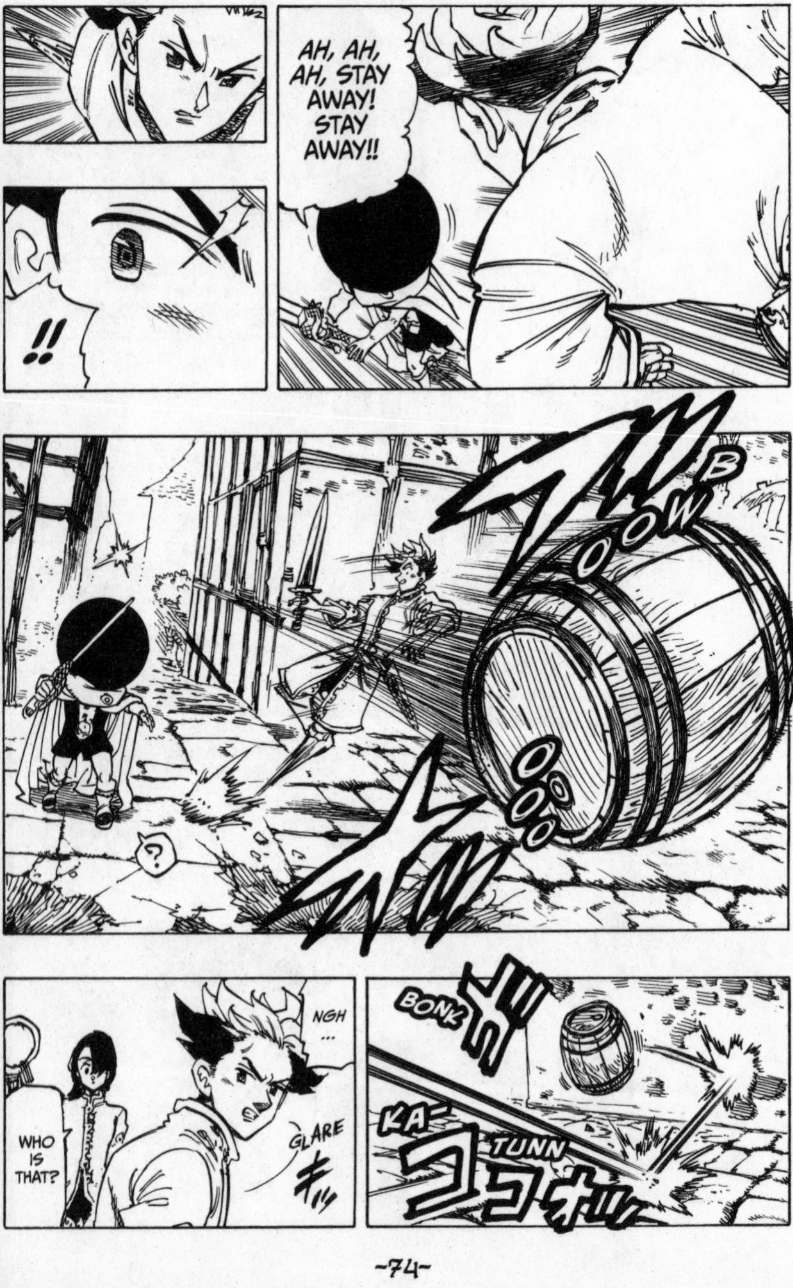
AH, AH, AH, STAY AWAY! STAY AWAY!!
!!
BOOOOW
?
BONK
KA-TUNN
NGH ...
GLARE
WHO IS THAT?

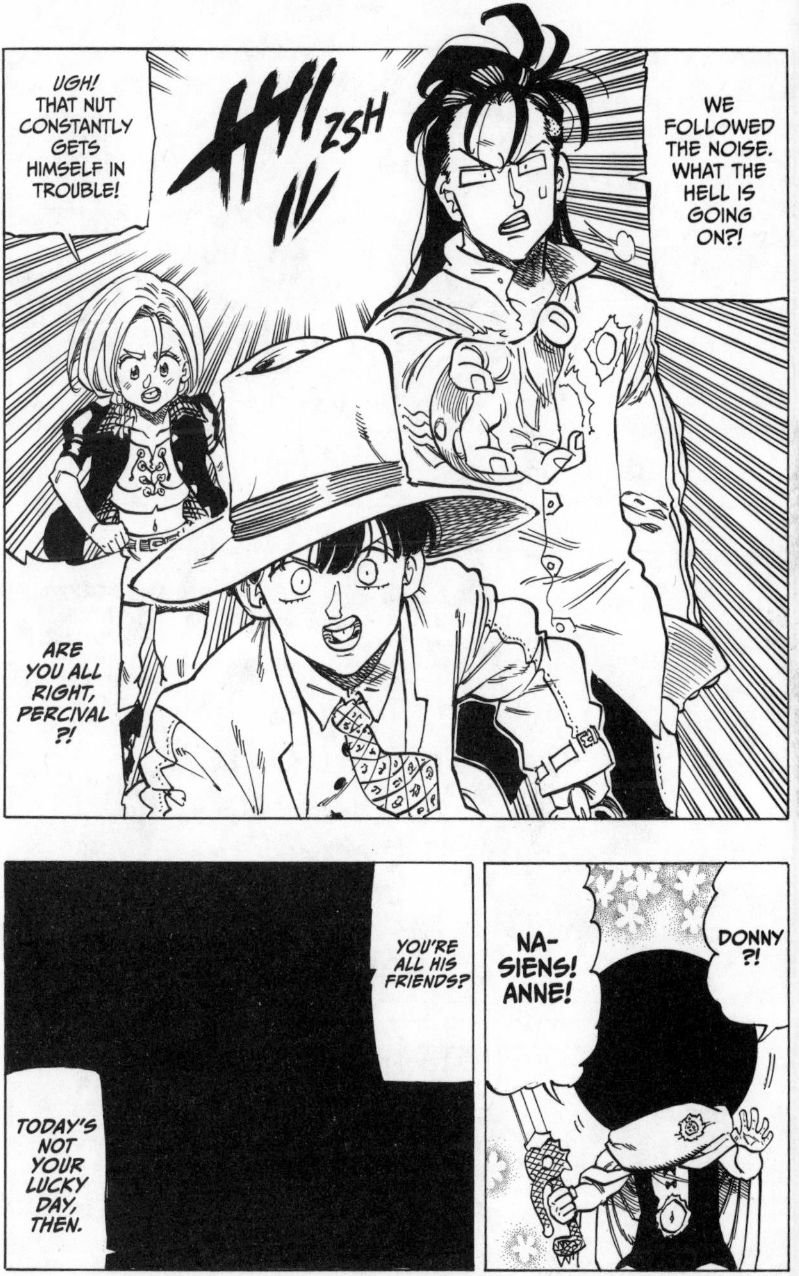
WE FOLLOWED THE NOISE. WHAT THE HELL IS GOING ON?!
ZSH
UGH! THAT NUT CONSTANTLY GETS HIMSELF IN TROUBLE!
ARE YOU ALL RIGHT, PERCIVAL?!
DONNY?!
NA-SIENS! ANNE!
YOU'RE ALL HIS FRIENDS?
TODAY'S NOT YOUR LUCKY DAY, THEN.

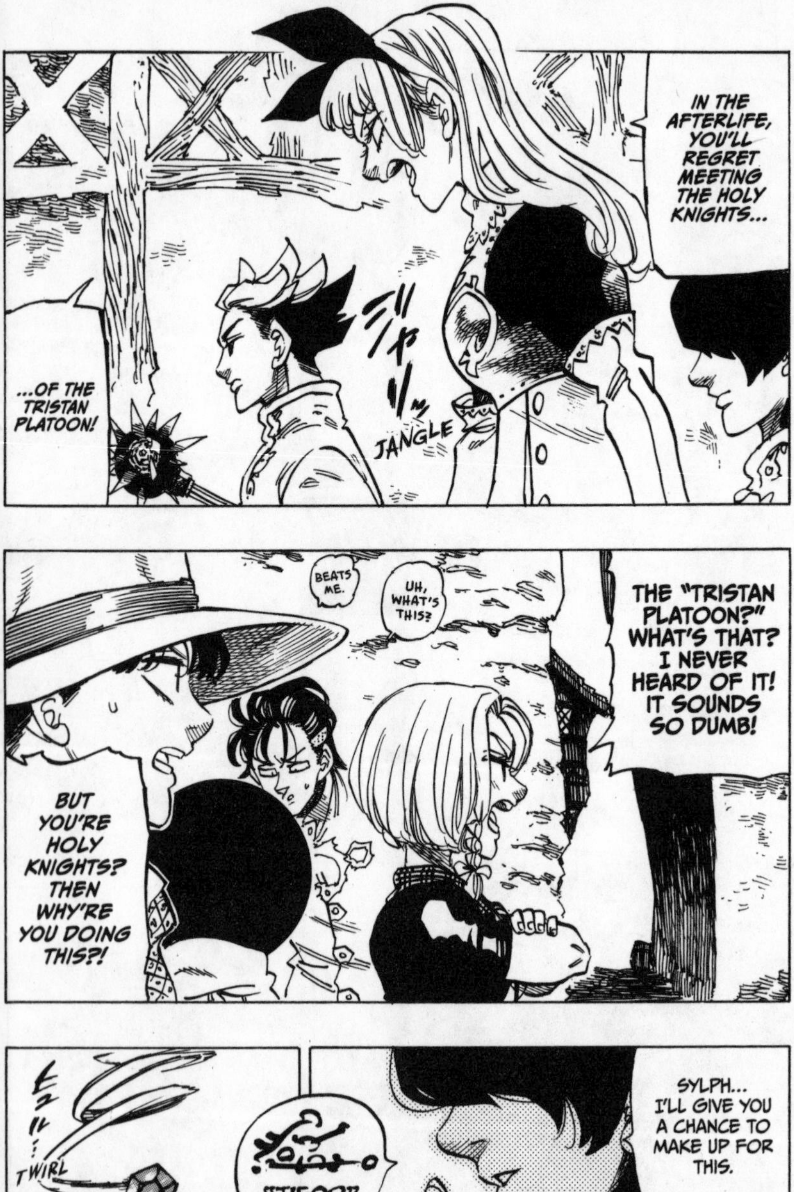
IN THE AFTERLIFE, YOU'LL REGRET MEETING THE HOLY KNIGHTS...
JANGLE
...OF THE TRISTAN PLATOON!
THE "TRISTAN PLATOON?" WHAT'S THAT? I NEVER HEARD OF IT! IT SOUNDS SO DUMB!
UH, WHAT'S THIS?
BEATS ME.
BUT YOU'RE HOLY KNIGHTS? THEN WHY'RE YOU DOING THIS?!
SYLPH... I'LL GIVE YOU A CHANCE TO MAKE UP FOR THIS.
"TIFOS"
TWIRL

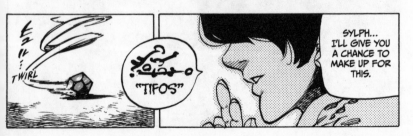

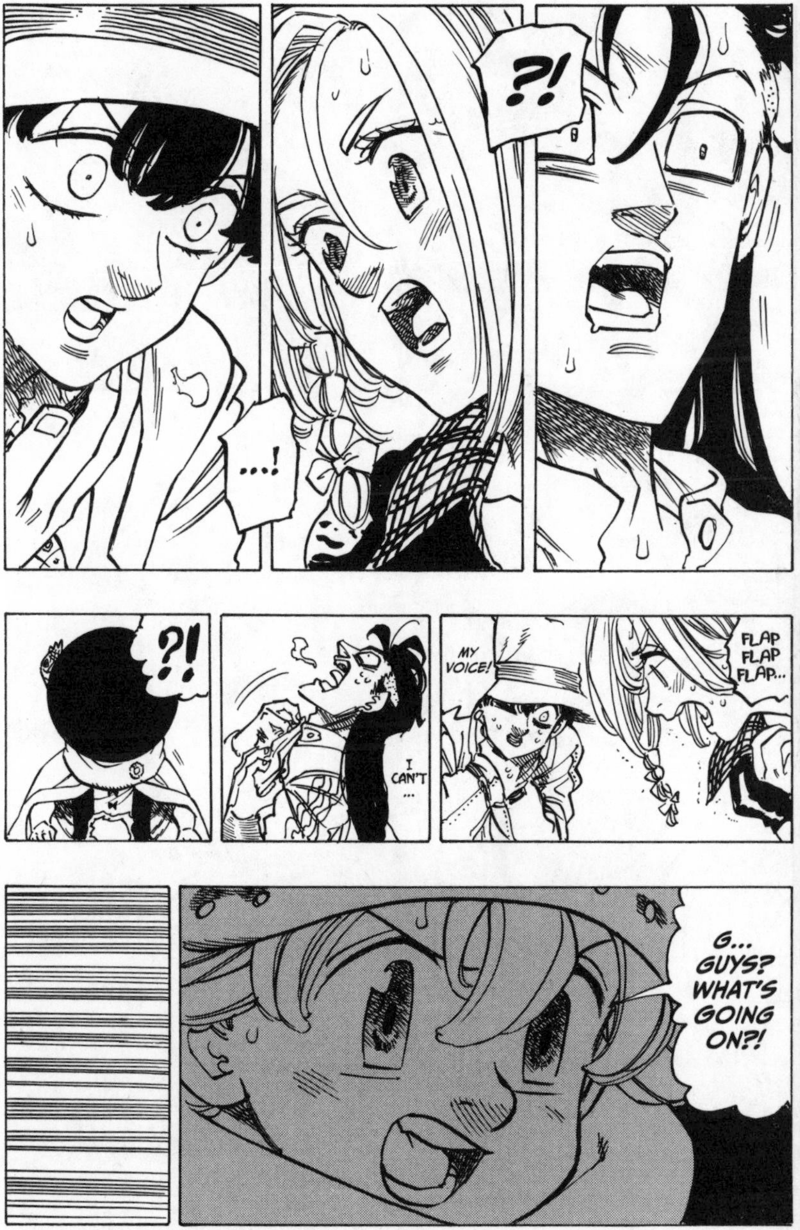
?!
...!
FLAP FLAP FLAP...
MY VOICE!
I CAN'T ...
?!
G... GUYS? WHAT'S GOING ON?!

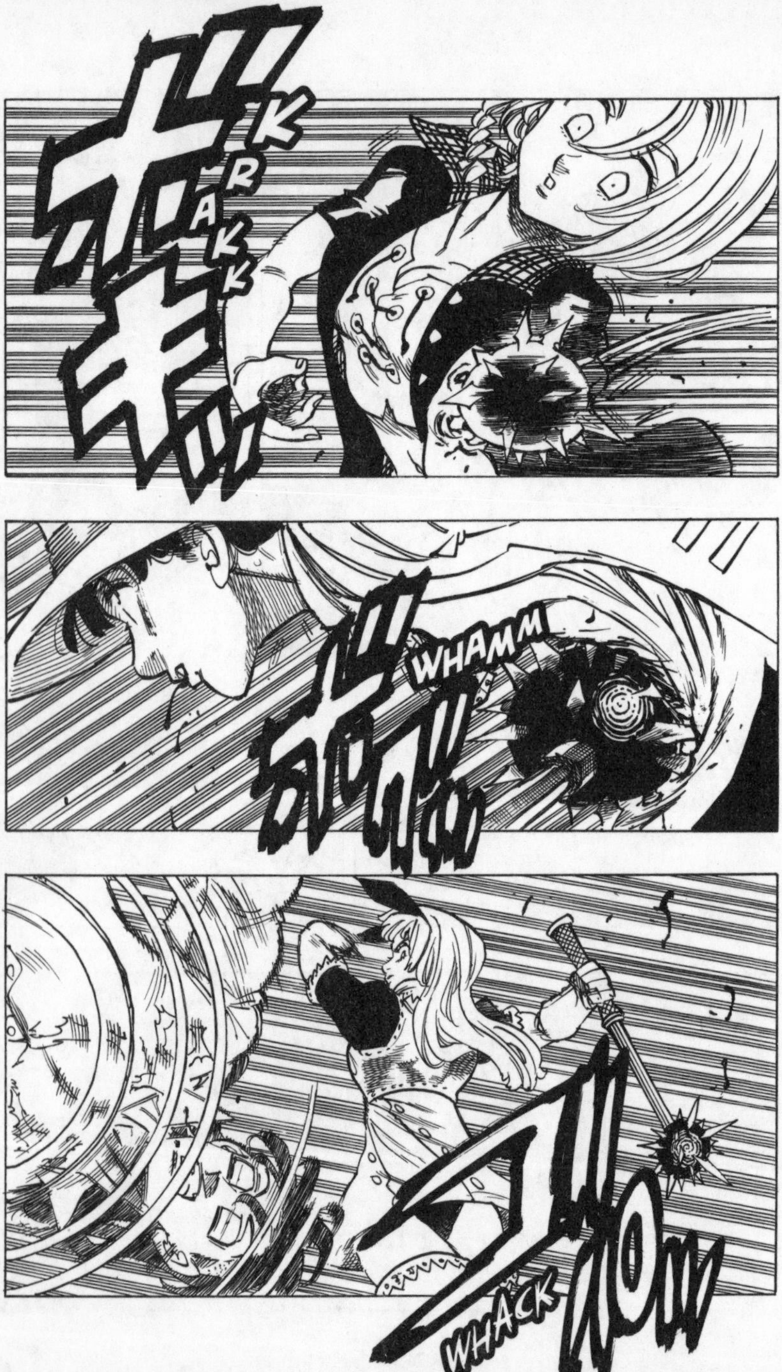
KRAKK
WHAMM
WHACK

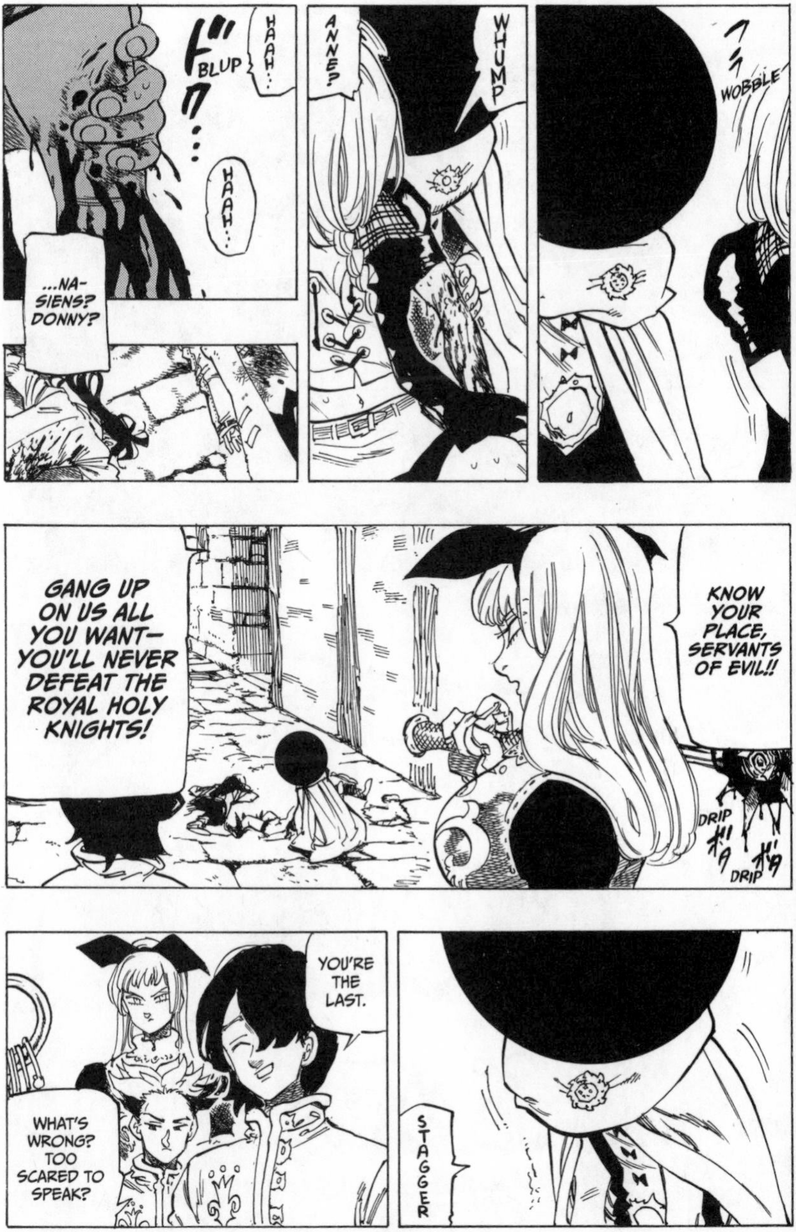
WOBBLE
WHUMP
ANNE?
HAAH...
HAAH...
BLUP
...NA-SIENS? DONNY?
KNOW YOUR PLACE, SERVANTS OF EVIL!!
DRIP
DRIP
GANG UP ON US ALL YOU WANT—YOU'LL NEVER DEFEAT THE ROYAL HOLY KNIGHTS!
STAGGER
YOU'RE THE LAST.
WHAT'S WRONG? TOO SCARED TO SPEAK?

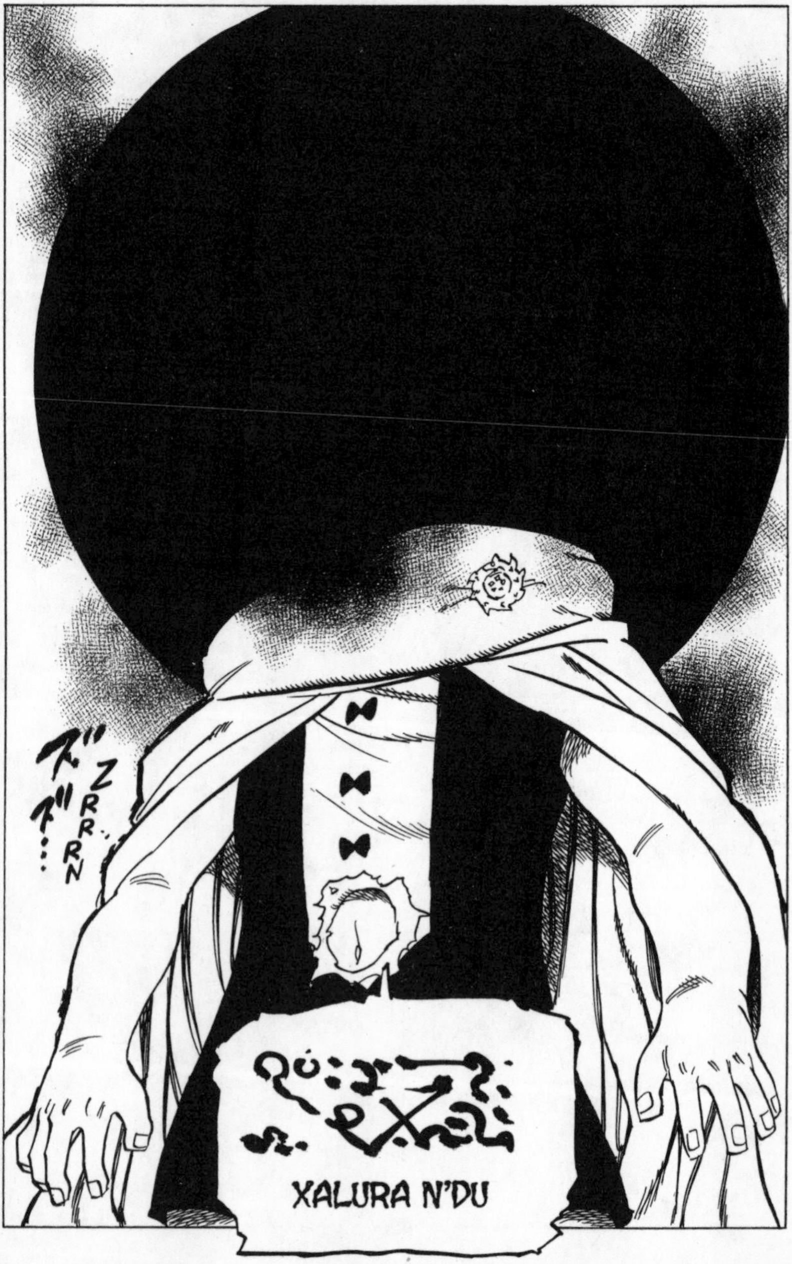
ズズ…
ZRRRN…
XALURA N'DU

ENOUGH! ALL OF YOU...!!

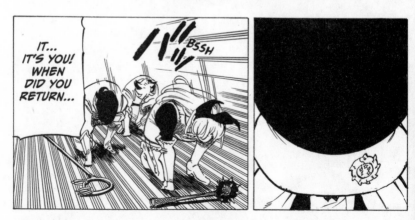

IT... IT'S YOU! WHEN DID YOU RETURN...

BSSH

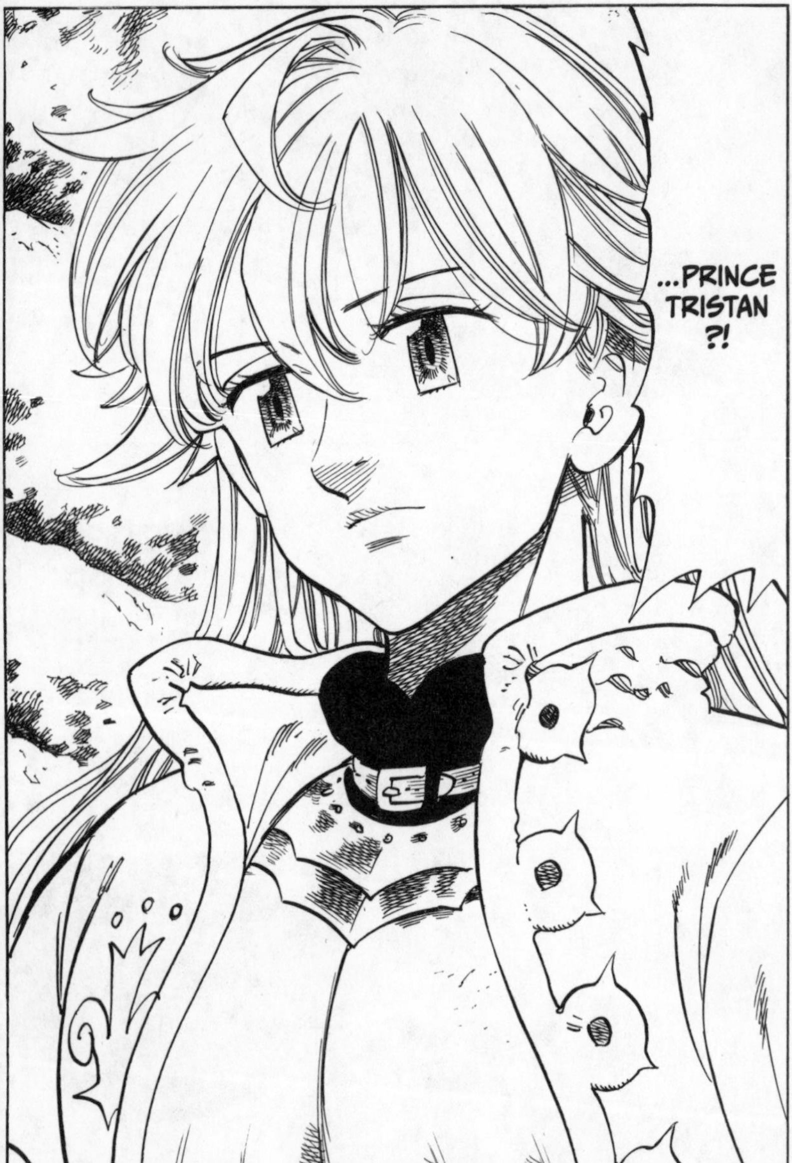
...PRINCE TRISTAN ?!

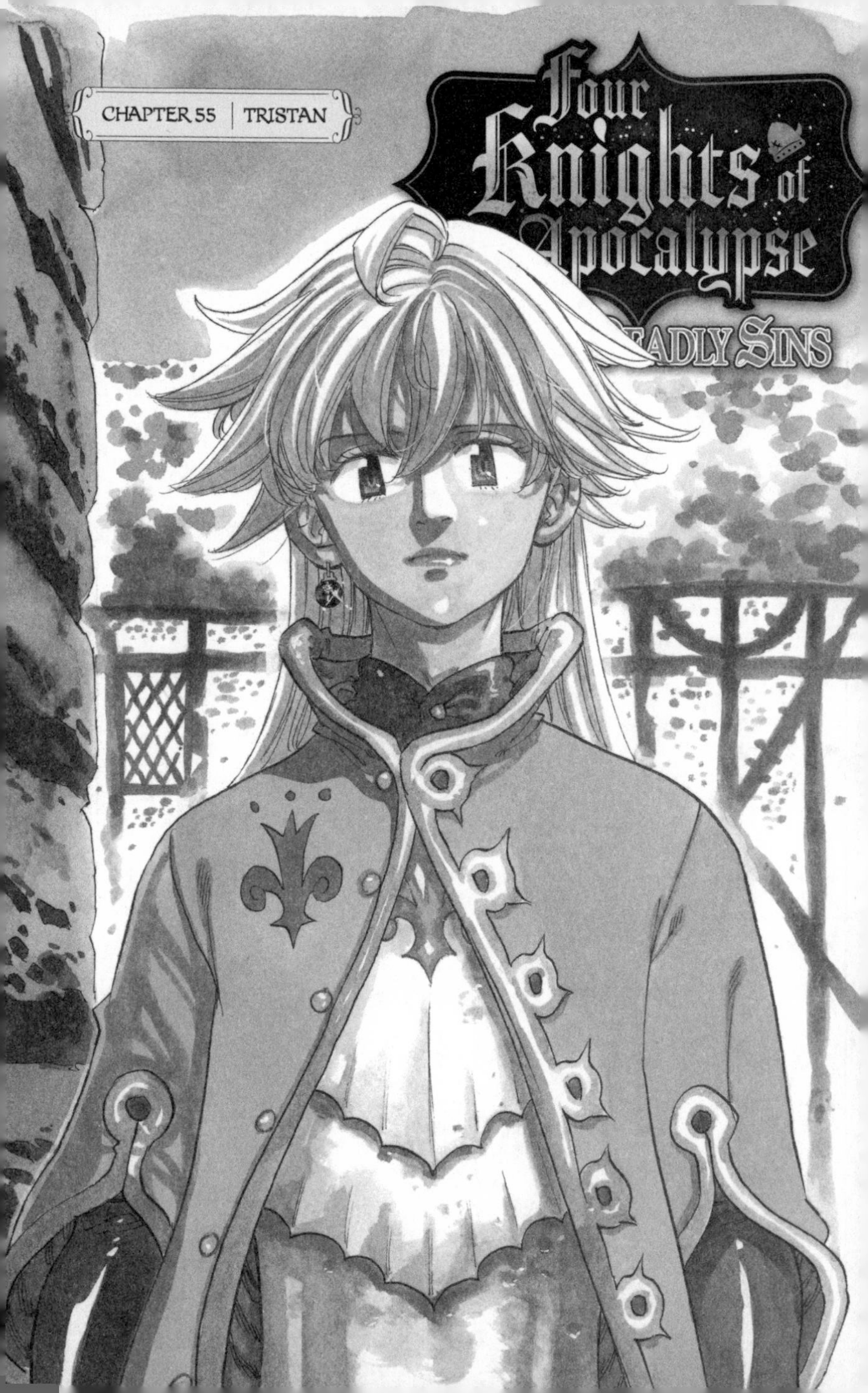
CHAPTER 55 | TRISTAN
Four Knights of Apocalypse
DEADLY SINS

LANCELOT AND THE RED FOX (1)

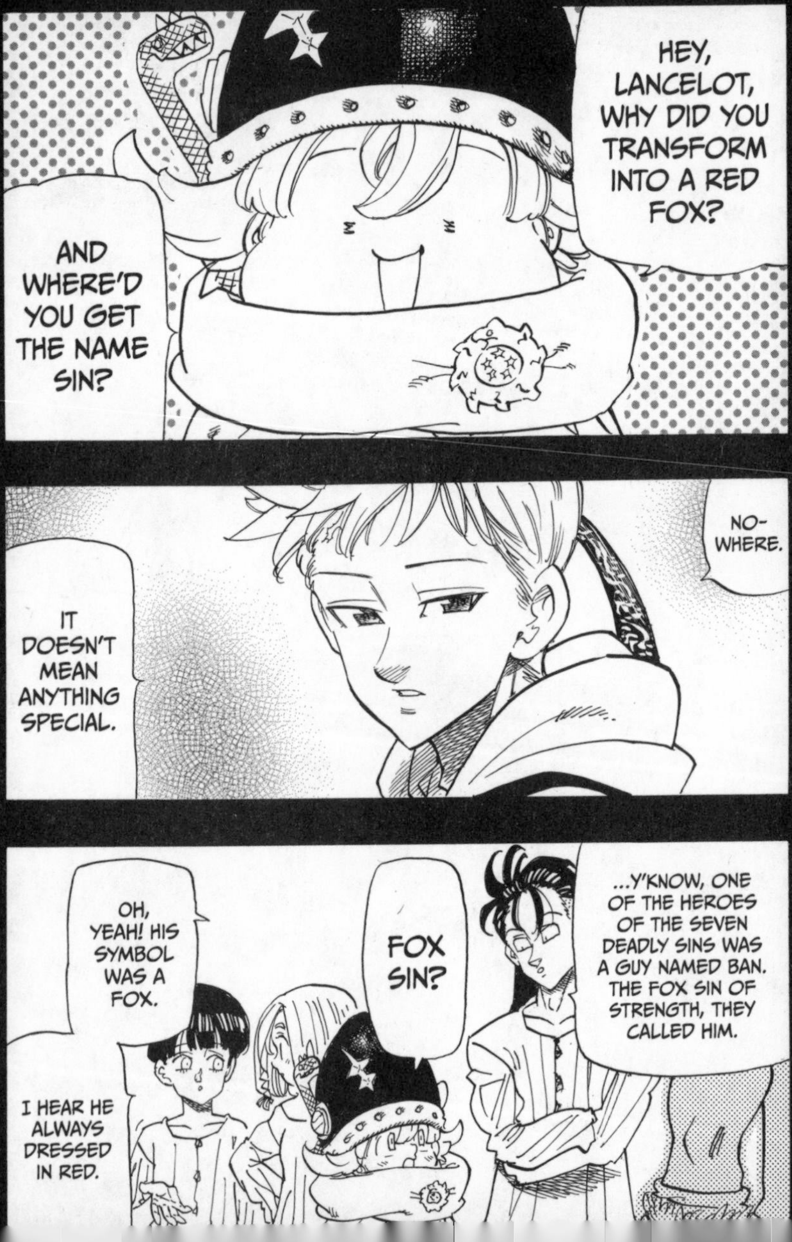
HEY, LANCELOT, WHY DID YOU TRANSFORM INTO A RED FOX?
AND WHERE'D YOU GET THE NAME SIN?
NO-WHERE.
IT DOESN'T MEAN ANYTHING SPECIAL.
...Y'KNOW, ONE OF THE HEROES OF THE SEVEN DEADLY SINS WAS A GUY NAMED BAN. THE FOX SIN OF STRENGTH, THEY CALLED HIM.
FOX SIN?
OH, YEAH! HIS SYMBOL WAS A FOX.
I HEAR HE ALWAYS DRESSED IN RED.

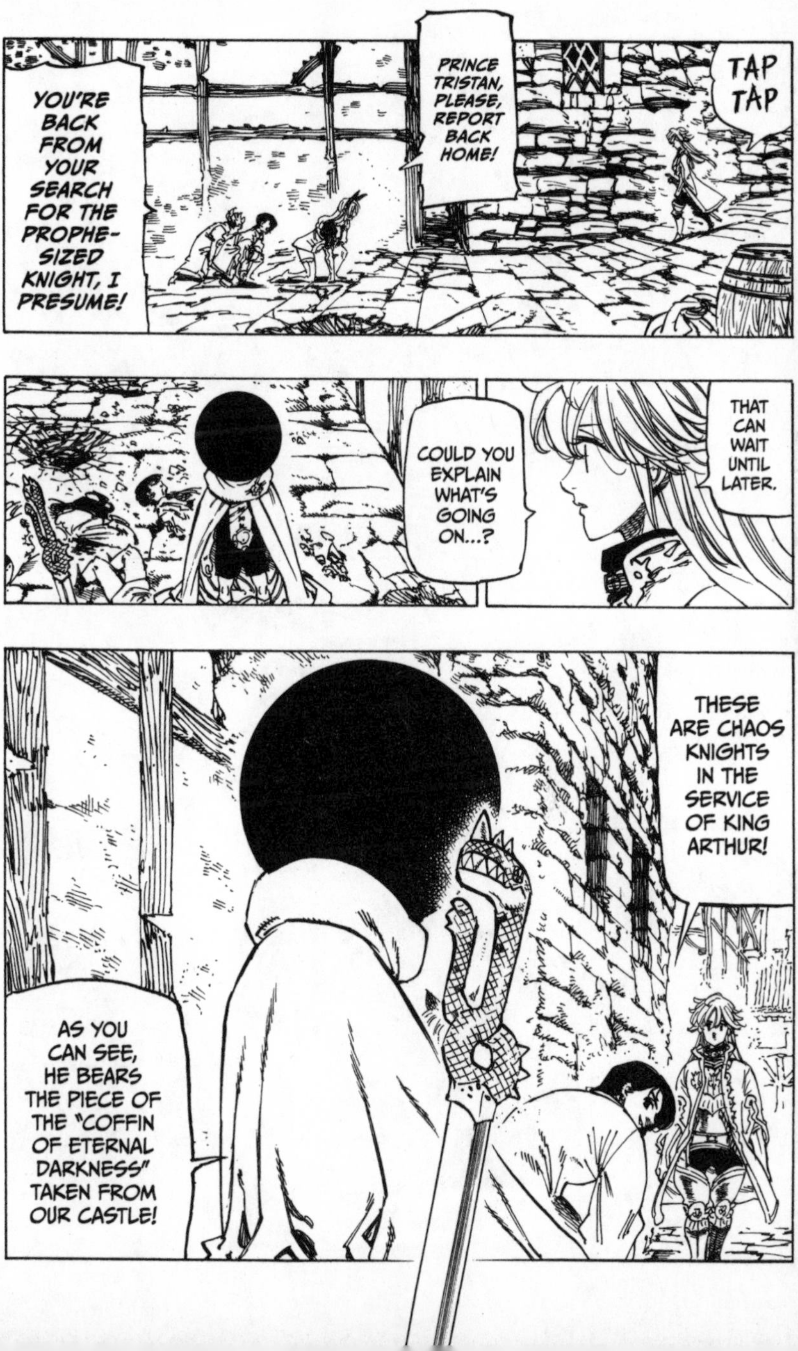
TAP TAP
PRINCE TRISTAN, PLEASE, REPORT BACK HOME!
YOU'RE BACK FROM YOUR SEARCH FOR THE PROPHE-SIZED KNIGHT, I PRESUME!
THAT CAN WAIT UNTIL LATER.
COULD YOU EXPLAIN WHAT'S GOING ON...?
THESE ARE CHAOS KNIGHTS IN THE SERVICE OF KING ARTHUR!
AS YOU CAN SEE, HE BEARS THE PIECE OF THE "COFFIN OF ETERNAL DARKNESS" TAKEN FROM OUR CASTLE!

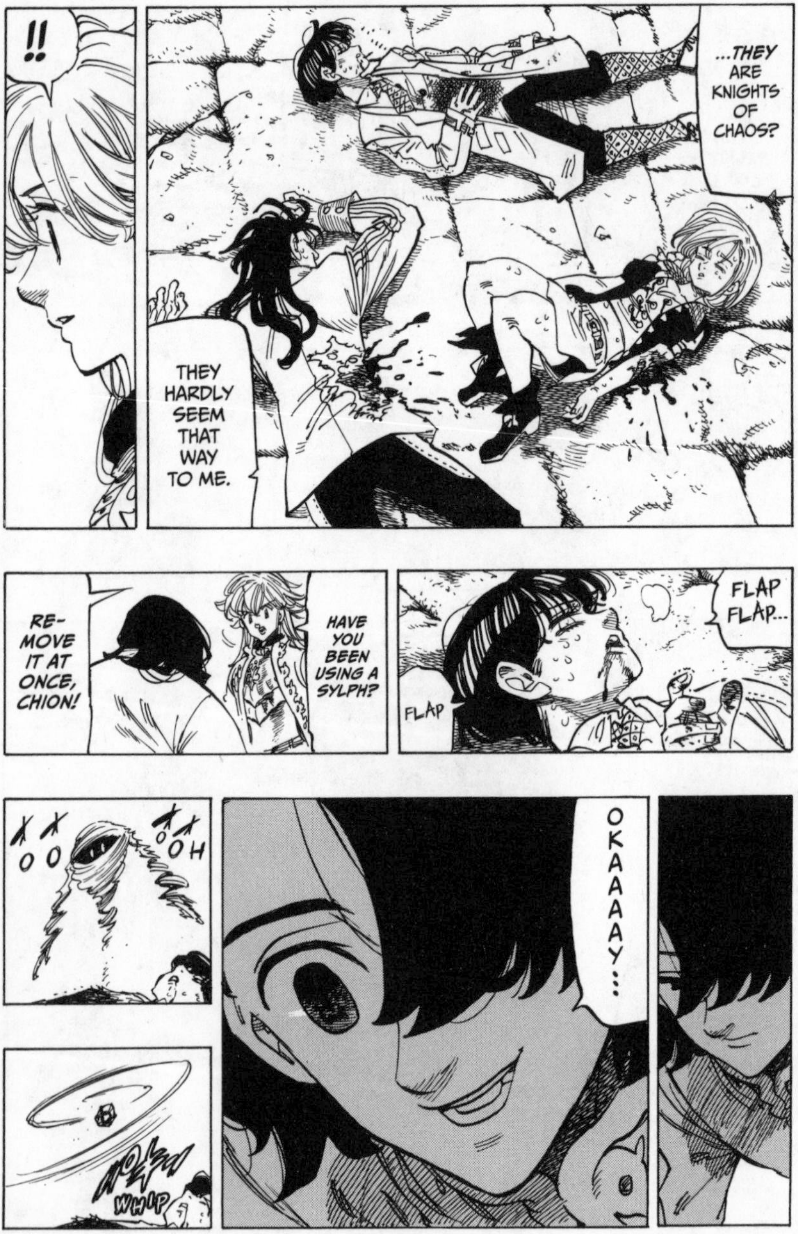
...THEY ARE KNIGHTS OF CHAOS?
THEY HARDLY SEEM THAT WAY TO ME.
!!
FLAP FLAP...
FLAP
HAVE YOU BEEN USING A SYLPH?
RE-MOVE IT AT ONCE, CHION!
OKAAAAY...
OOH
WHIP

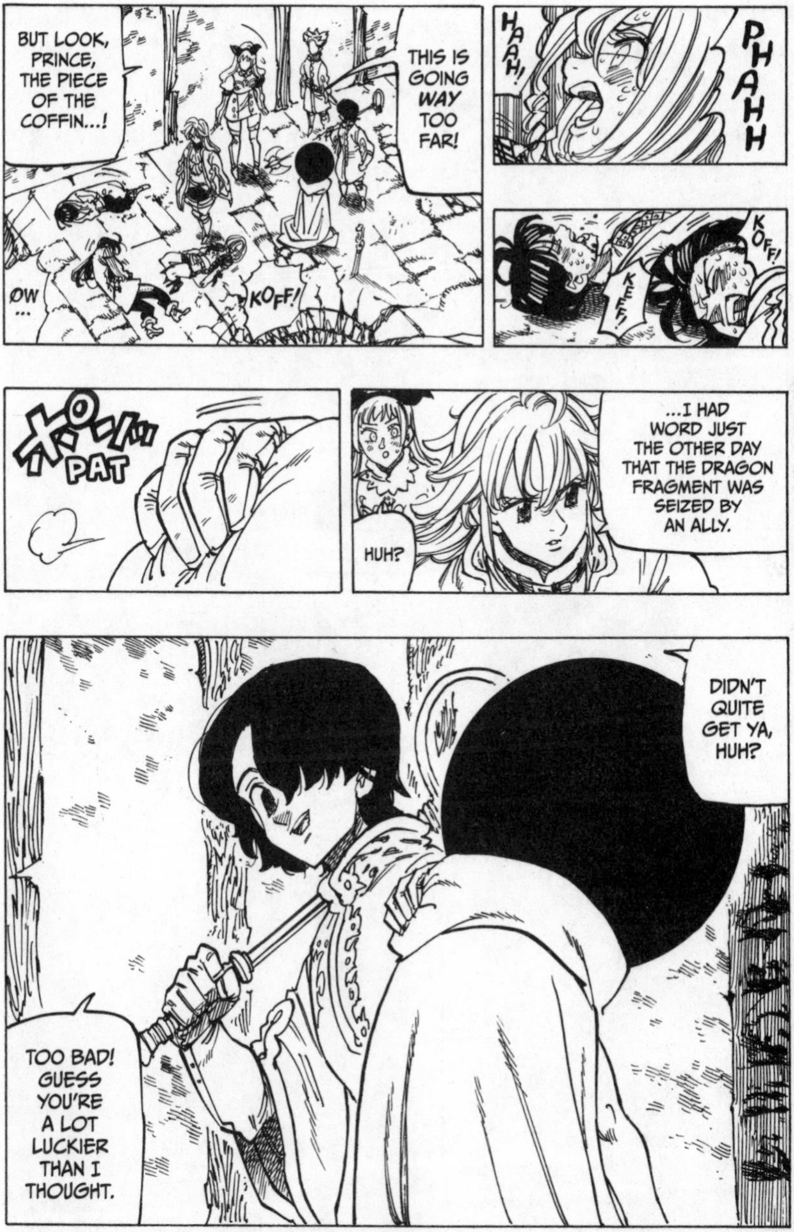
PHAHH
HAAH!
KOFF!
KEFF!
THIS IS GOING WAY TOO FAR!
BUT LOOK, PRINCE, THE PIECE OF THE COFFIN...!
KOFF!
OW...
...I HAD WORD JUST THE OTHER DAY THAT THE DRAGON FRAGMENT WAS SEIZED BY AN ALLY.
HUH?
PAT
DIDN'T QUITE GET YA, HUH?
TOO BAD! GUESS YOU'RE A LOT LUCKIER THAN I THOUGHT.

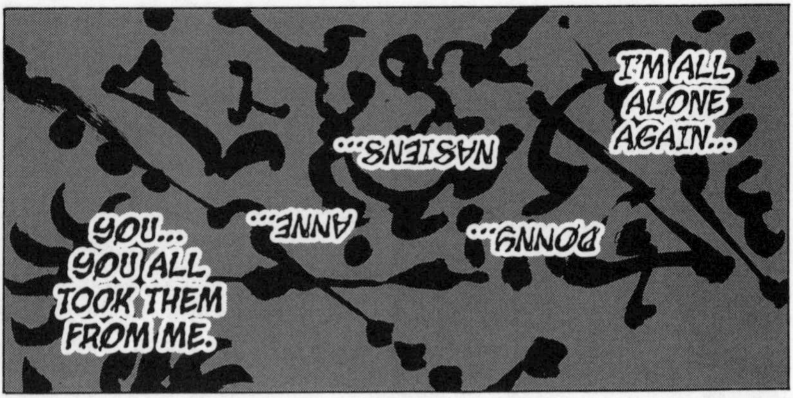
I'M ALL ALONE AGAIN...
NASIENS...
DONNY...
ANNE...
YOU... YOU ALL TOOK THEM FROM ME.

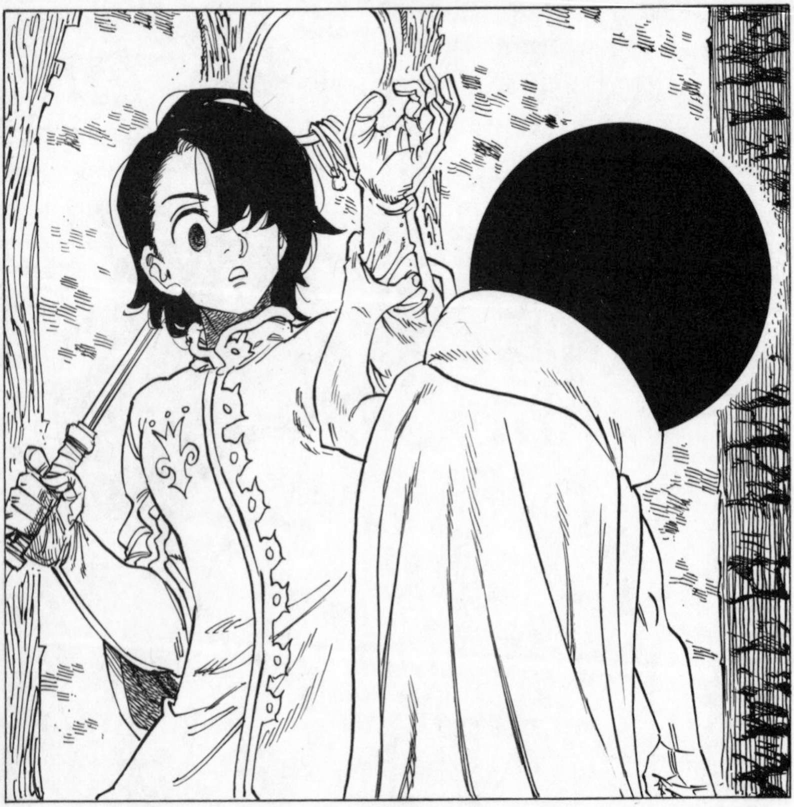

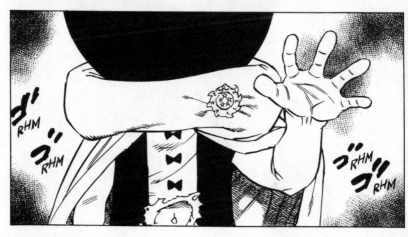

RHM

RHM

RHM

RHM

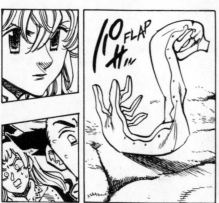

FLAP

MY ARM...

CHION! WHAT IS IT?!

BOOM

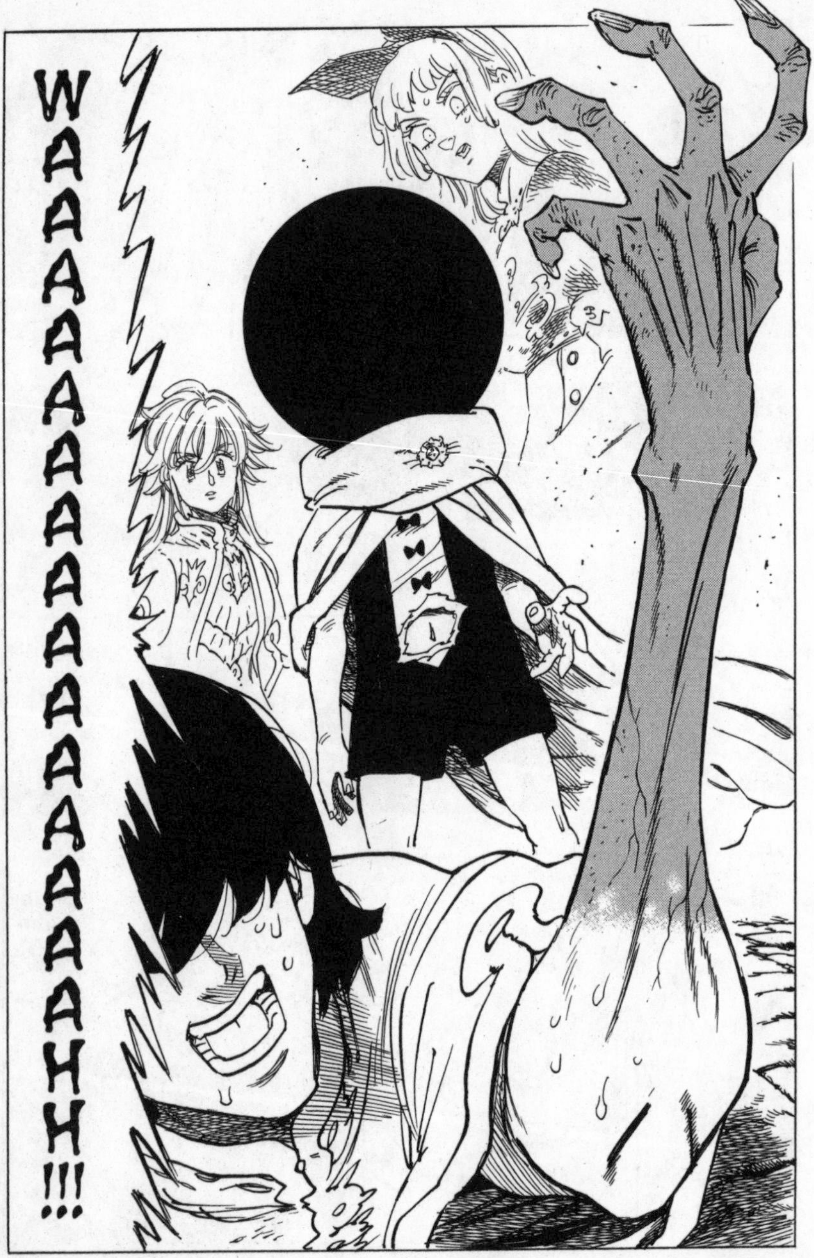
WAAAAAAAAAAAAAAAH!!!

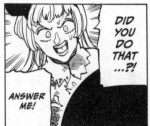

SHAKE
SHAKE
IT'S LIKE HIS ARM'S BEEN MUMMI-FIED...
DID YOU DO THAT ...?!
ANSWER ME!
JADE! REMOVE THE DARK-NESS AT ONCE!
SHOW THIS BOY WHAT HE'S DONE!
YES! RIGHT...
AWAY—
FWIP

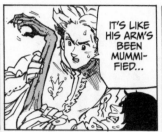

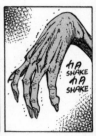

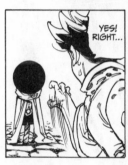

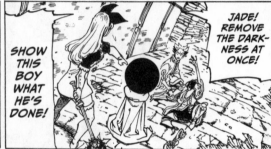

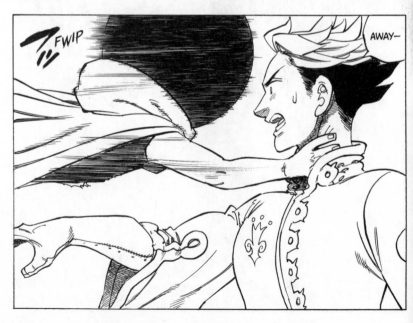

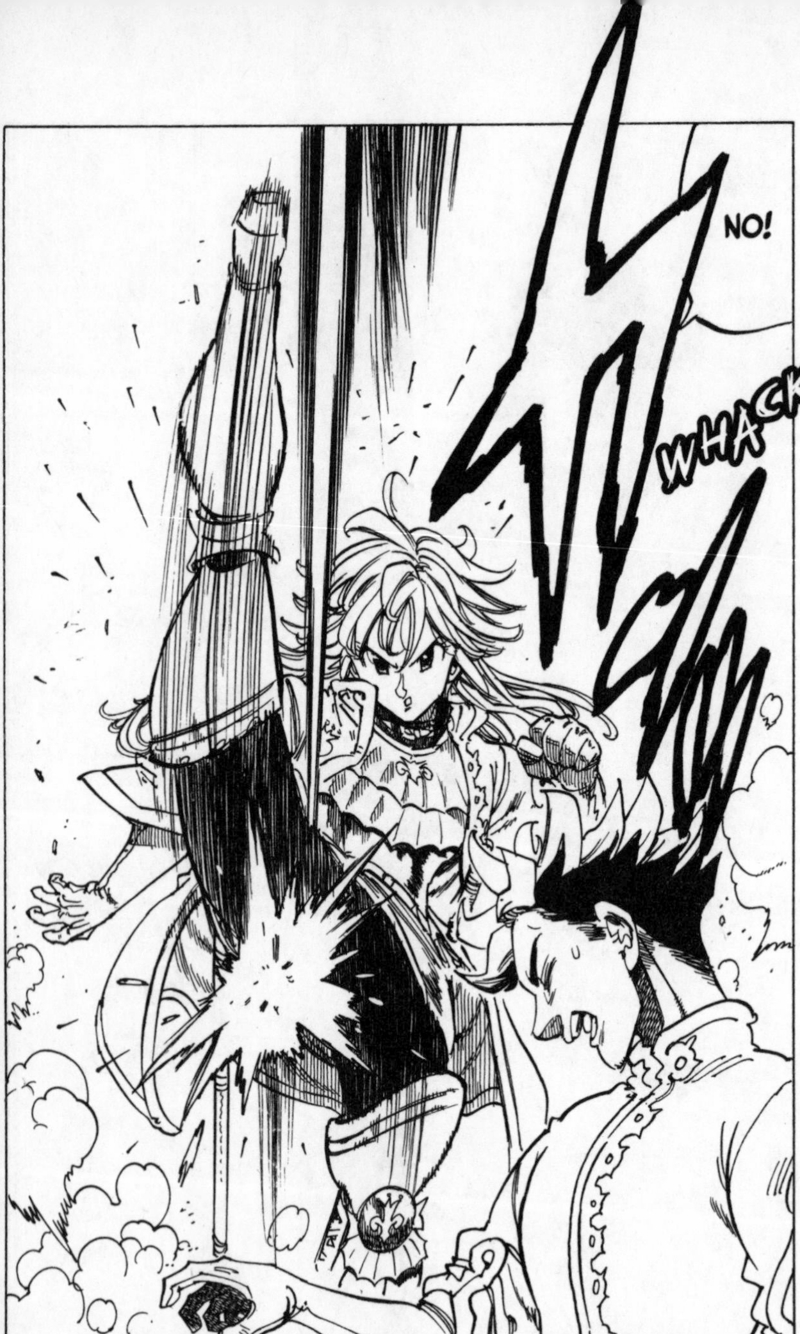
NO!
WHACK

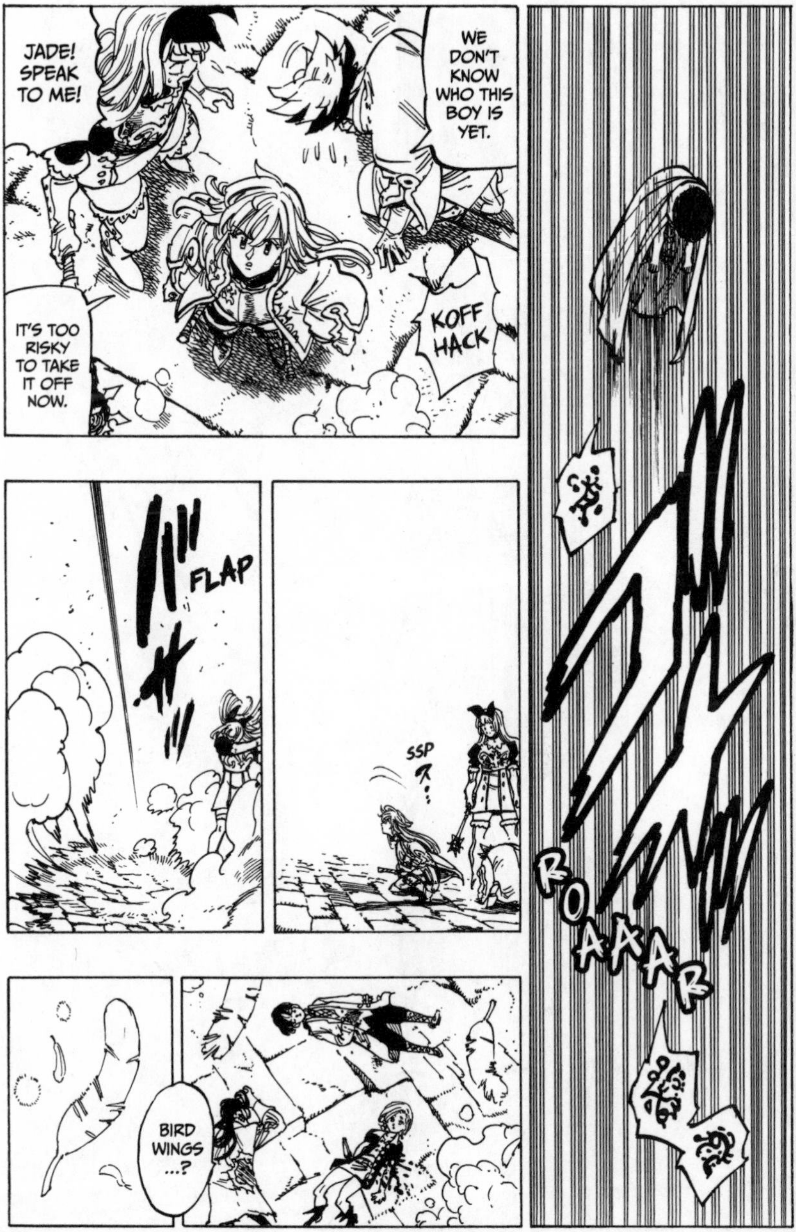
ROAAAR
WE DON'T KNOW WHO THIS BOY IS YET.
JADE! SPEAK TO ME!
KOFF HACK
IT'S TOO RISKY TO TAKE IT OFF NOW.
SSP
FLAP
BIRD WINGS ...?

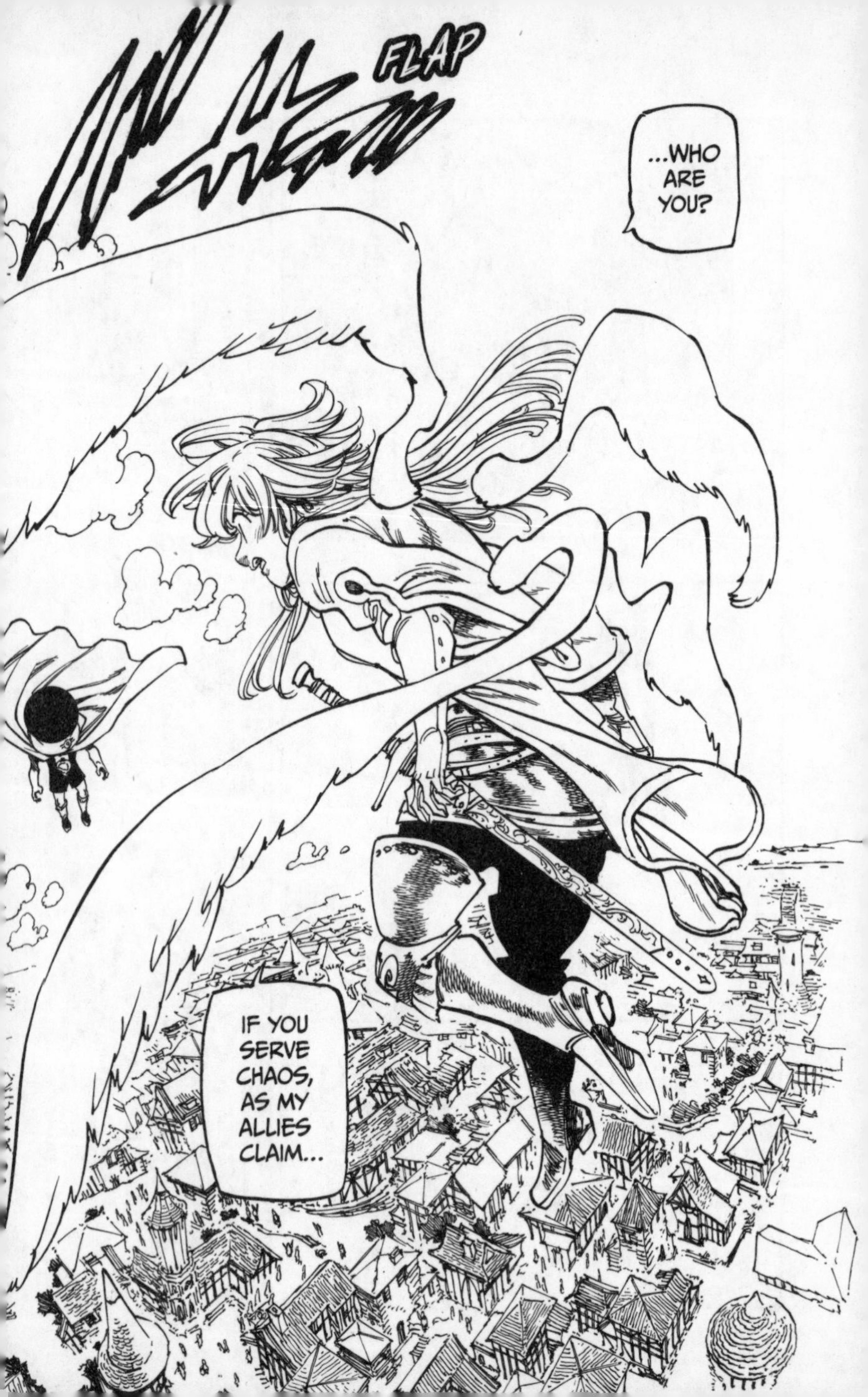
...WHO ARE YOU?
FLAP
IF YOU SERVE CHAOS, AS MY ALLIES CLAIM...

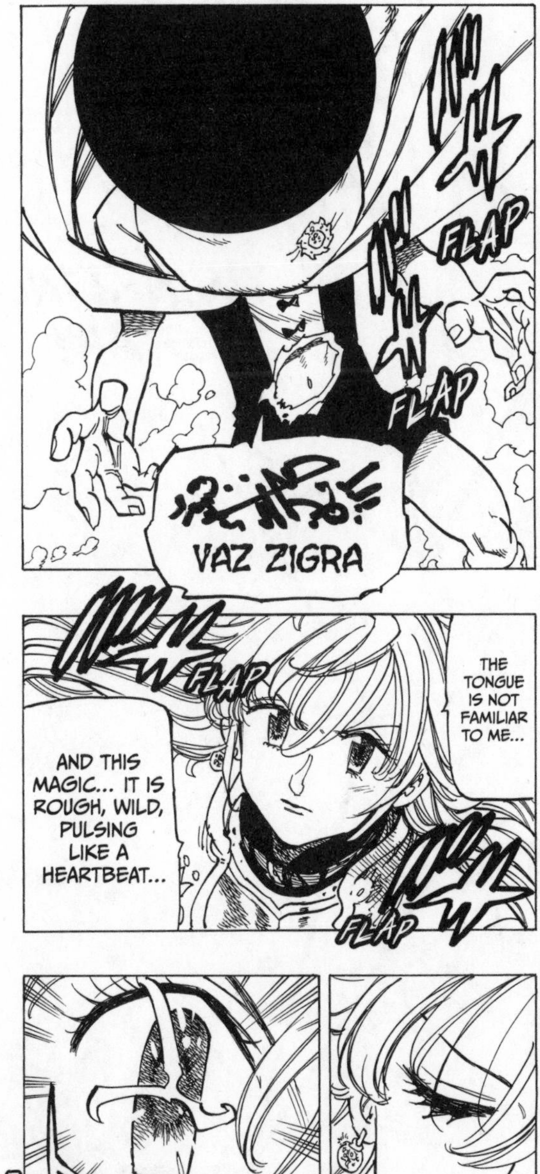
FLAP
FLAP
VAZ ZIGRA
FLAP
THE TONGUE IS NOT FAMILIAR TO ME...
AND THIS MAGIC... IT IS ROUGH, WILD, PULSING LIKE A HEARTBEAT...
FLAP
FWEEE
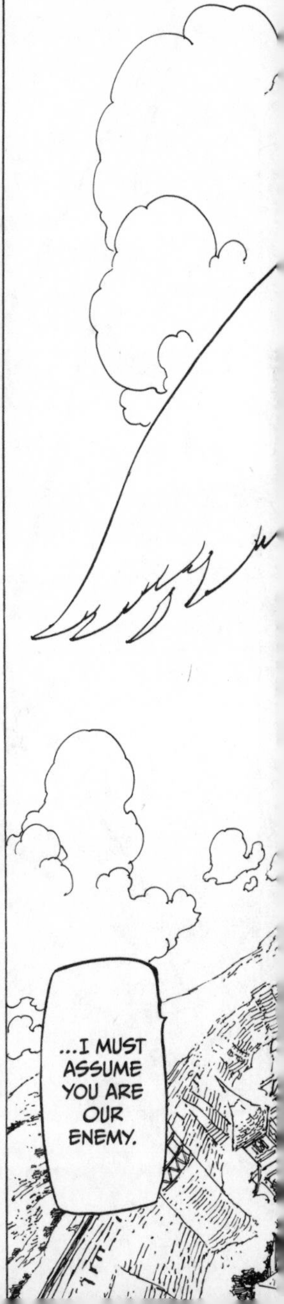
...I MUST ASSUME YOU ARE OUR ENEMY.

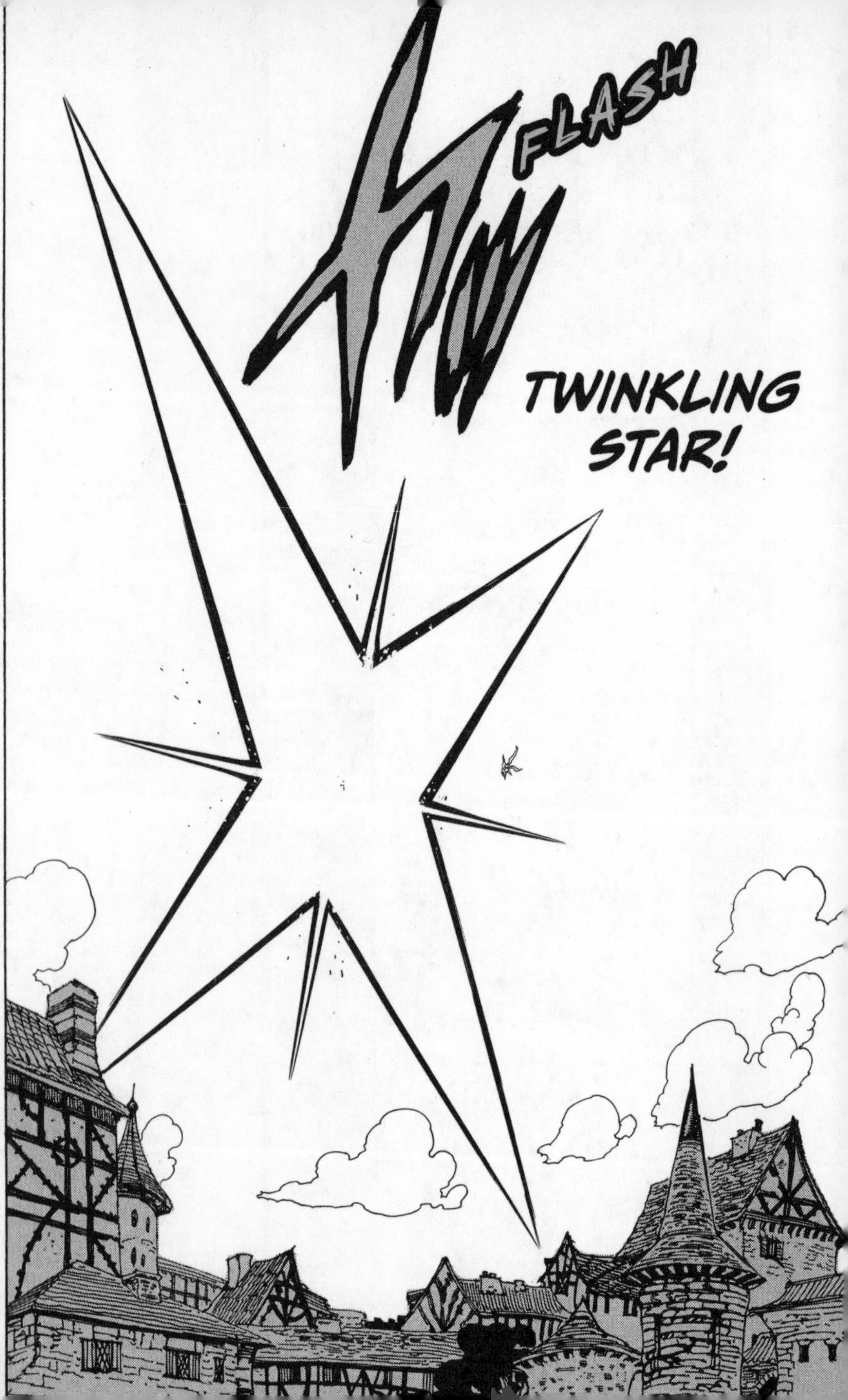
FLASH
TWINKLING STAR!

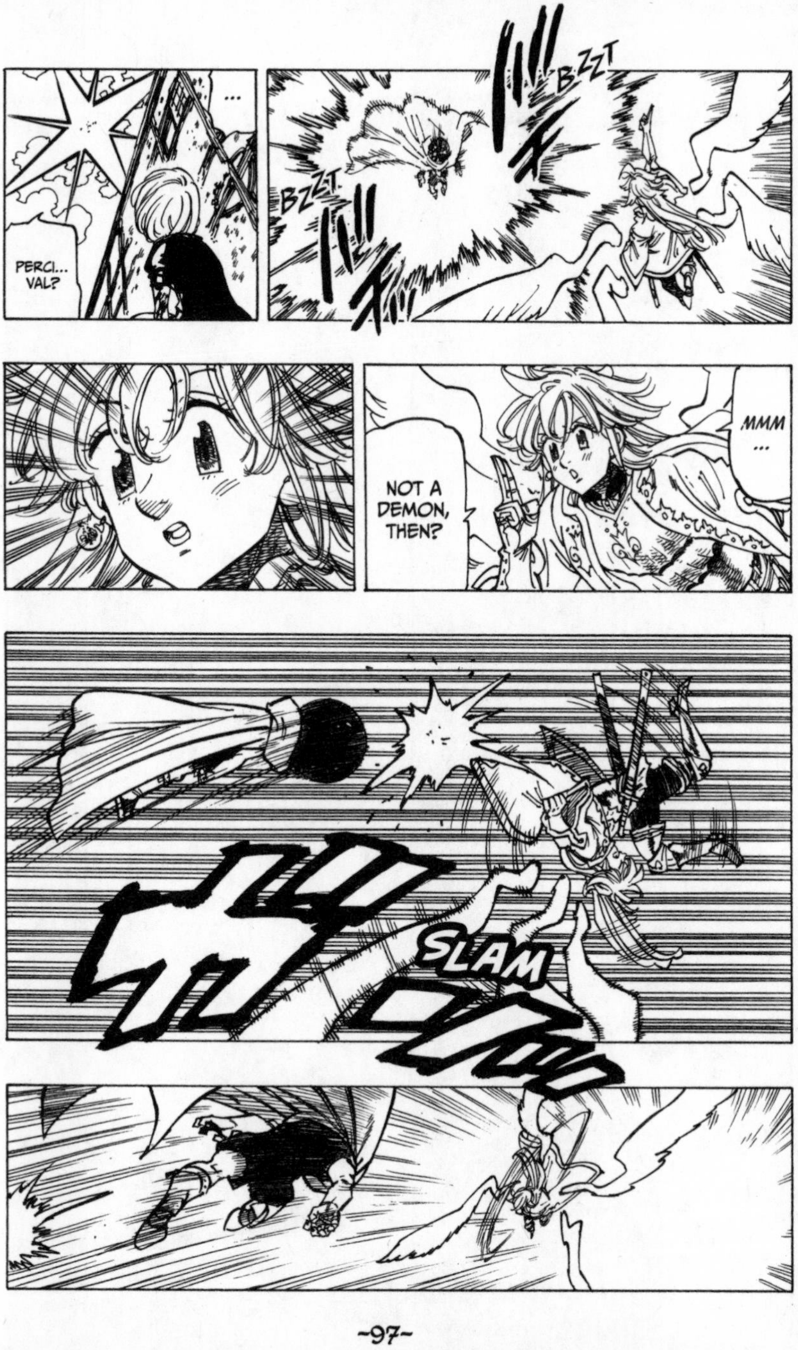
BZZT
BZZT
...
PERCI... VAL?
MMM ...
NOT A DEMON, THEN?
SLAM

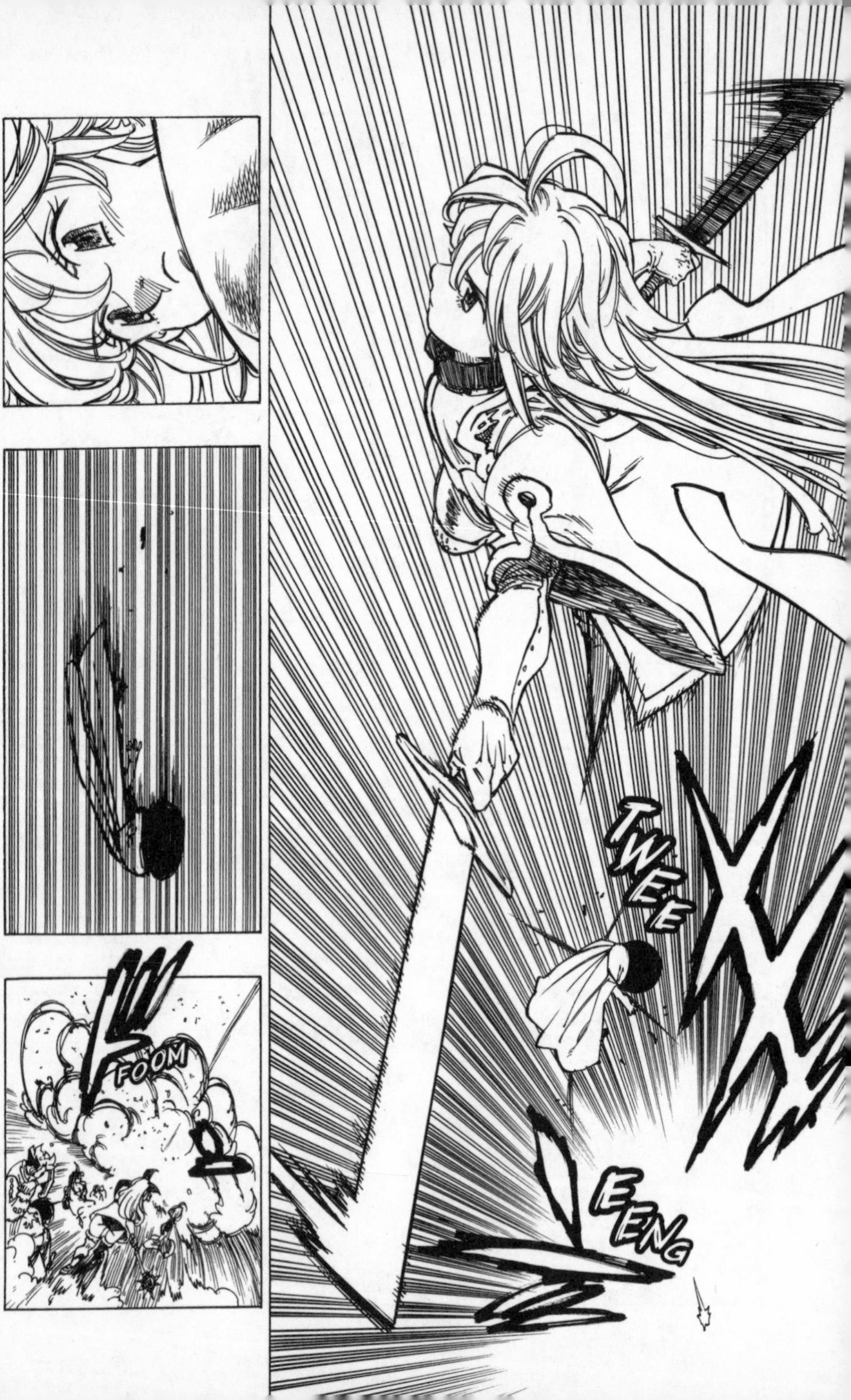
TWEEE
EEENG
FOOM

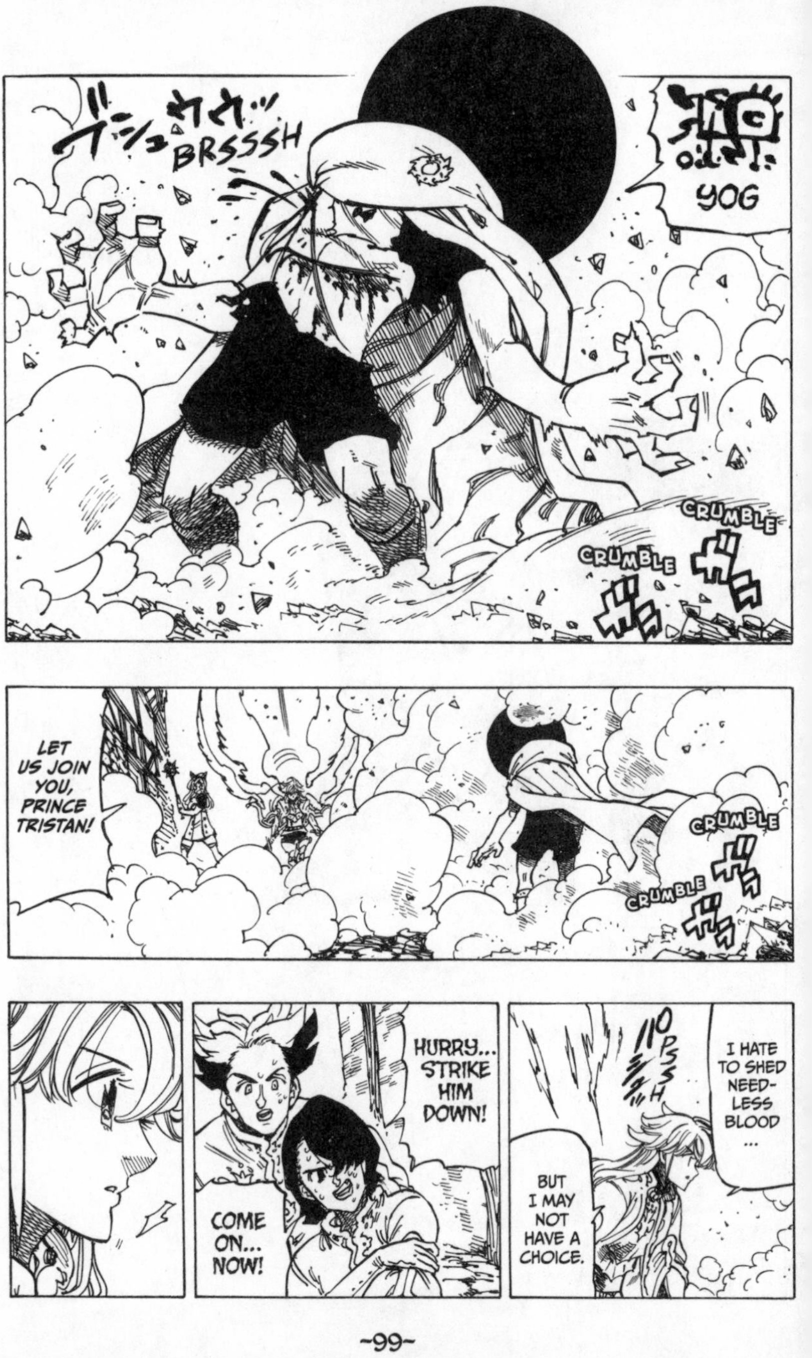
YOG
BRSSSH
CRUMBLE
CRUMBLE
CRUMBLE
CRUMBLE
LET US JOIN YOU, PRINCE TRISTAN!
I HATE TO SHED NEEDLESS BLOOD...
PSSSH
BUT I MAY NOT HAVE A CHOICE.
HURRY... STRIKE HIM DOWN!
COME ON... NOW!

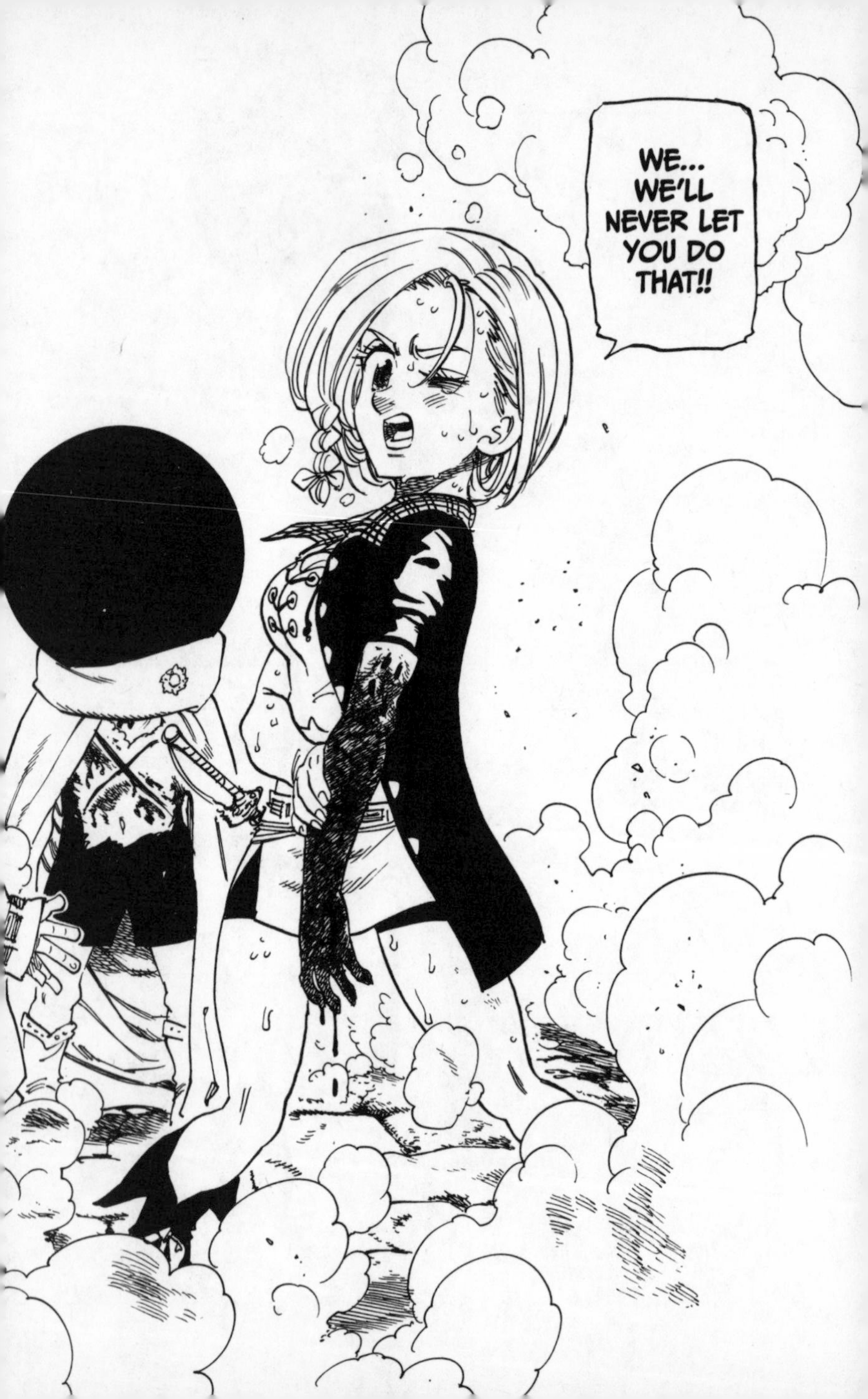
WE... WE'LL NEVER LET YOU DO THAT!!

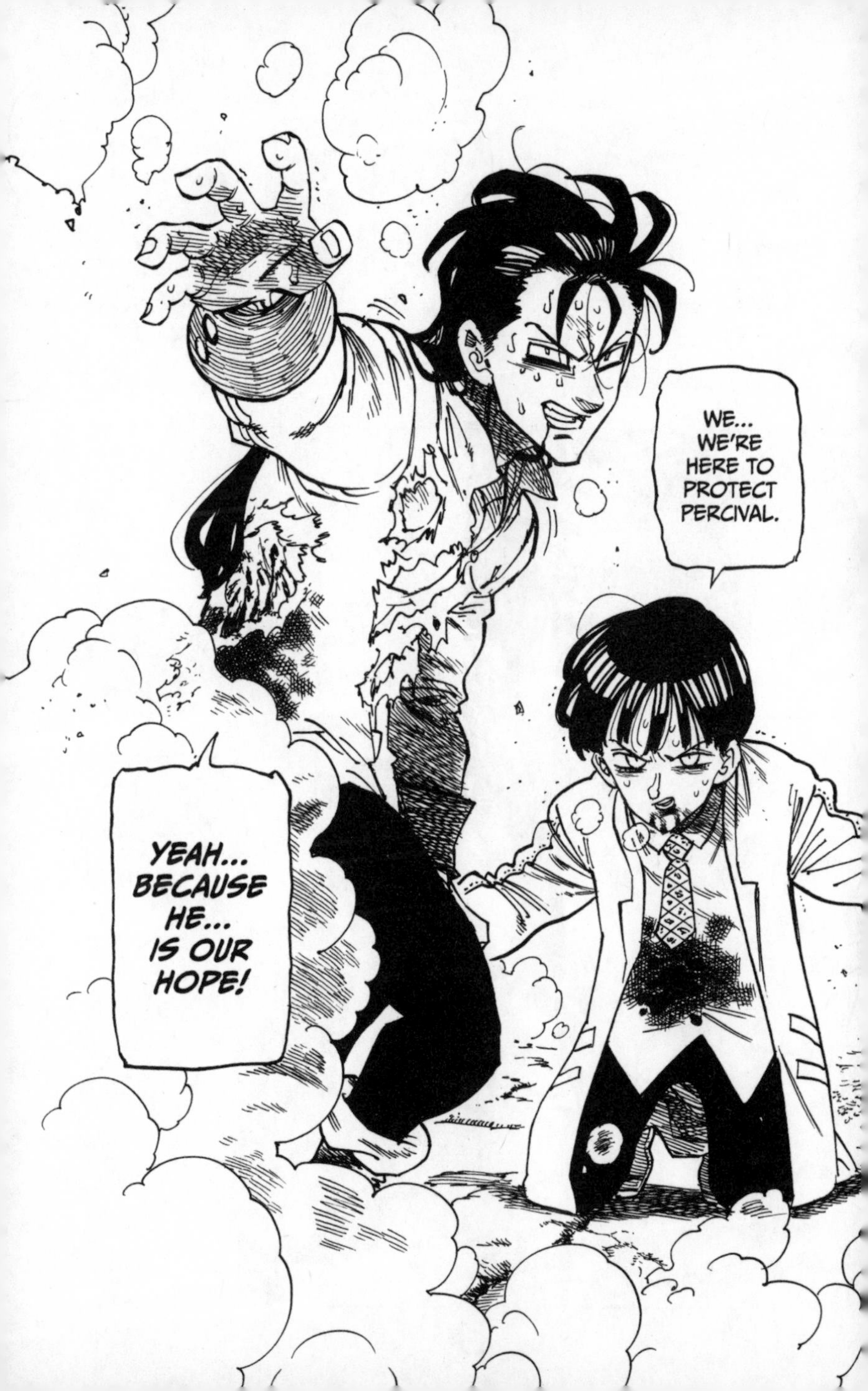
WE... WE'RE HERE TO PROTECT PERCIVAL.
YEAH... BECAUSE HE... IS OUR HOPE!

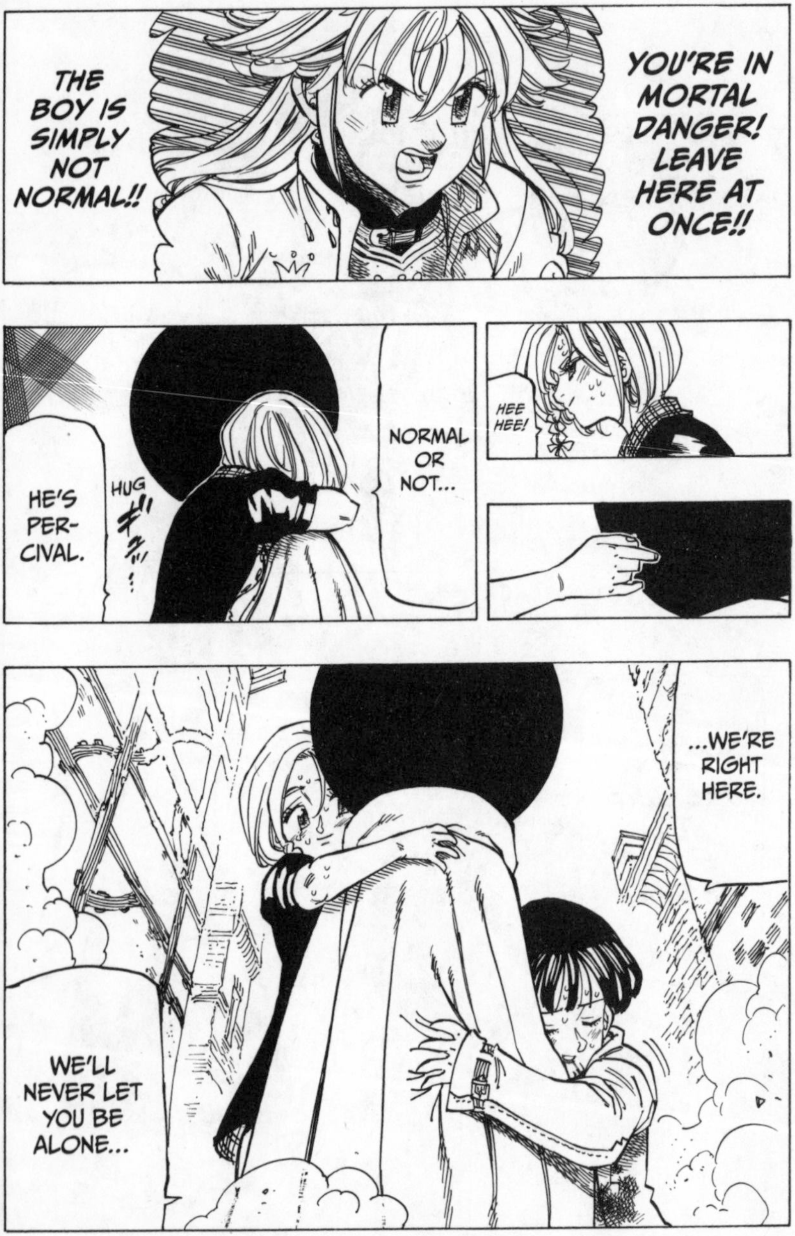
YOU'RE IN MORTAL DANGER! LEAVE HERE AT ONCE!!
THE BOY IS SIMPLY NOT NORMAL!!
HEE HEE!
NORMAL OR NOT...
HUG
HE'S PER-CIVAL.
...WE'RE RIGHT HERE.
WE'LL NEVER LET YOU BE ALONE...

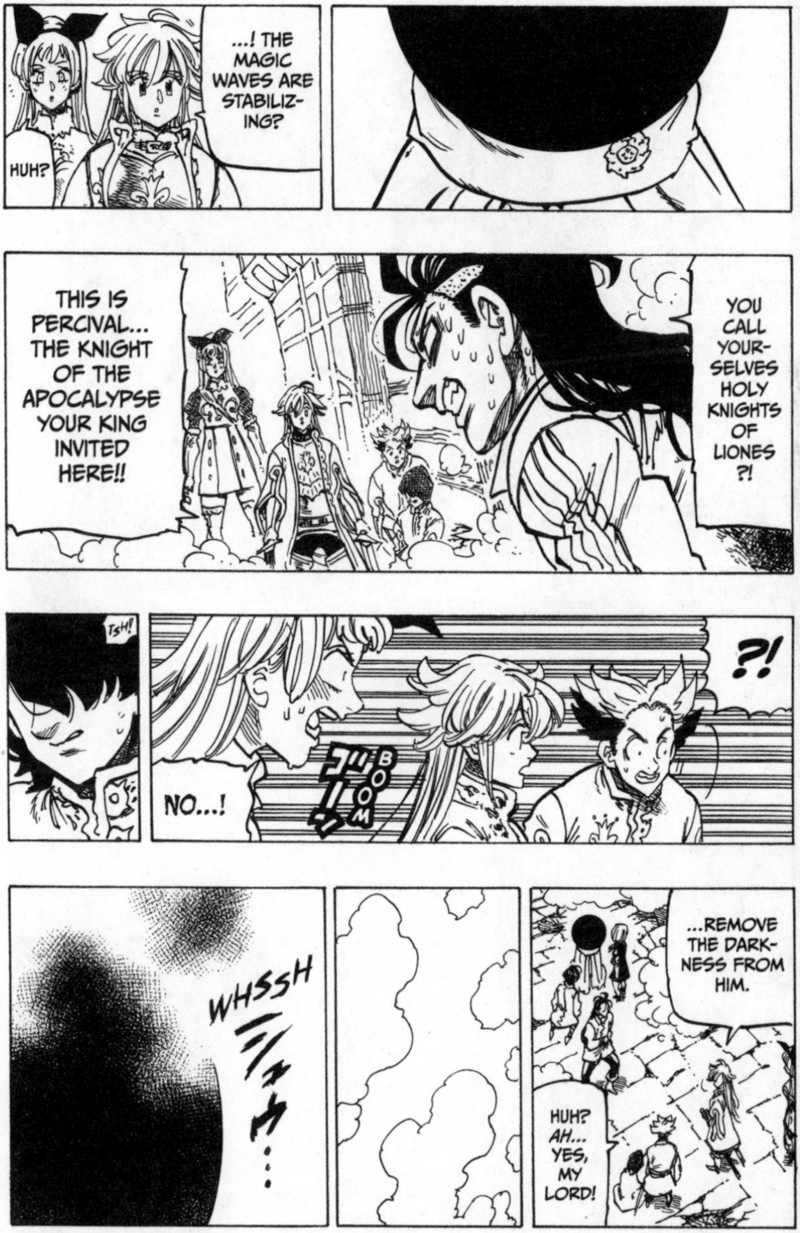
...! THE MAGIC WAVES ARE STABILIZ-ING?
HUH?
YOU CALL YOUR-SELVES HOLY KNIGHTS OF LIONES ?!
THIS IS PERCIVAL... THE KNIGHT OF THE APOCALYPSE YOUR KING INVITED HERE!!
?!
BOOM
NO...!
TSH!
...REMOVE THE DARK-NESS FROM HIM.
HUH? AH... YES, MY LORD!
WHSSH

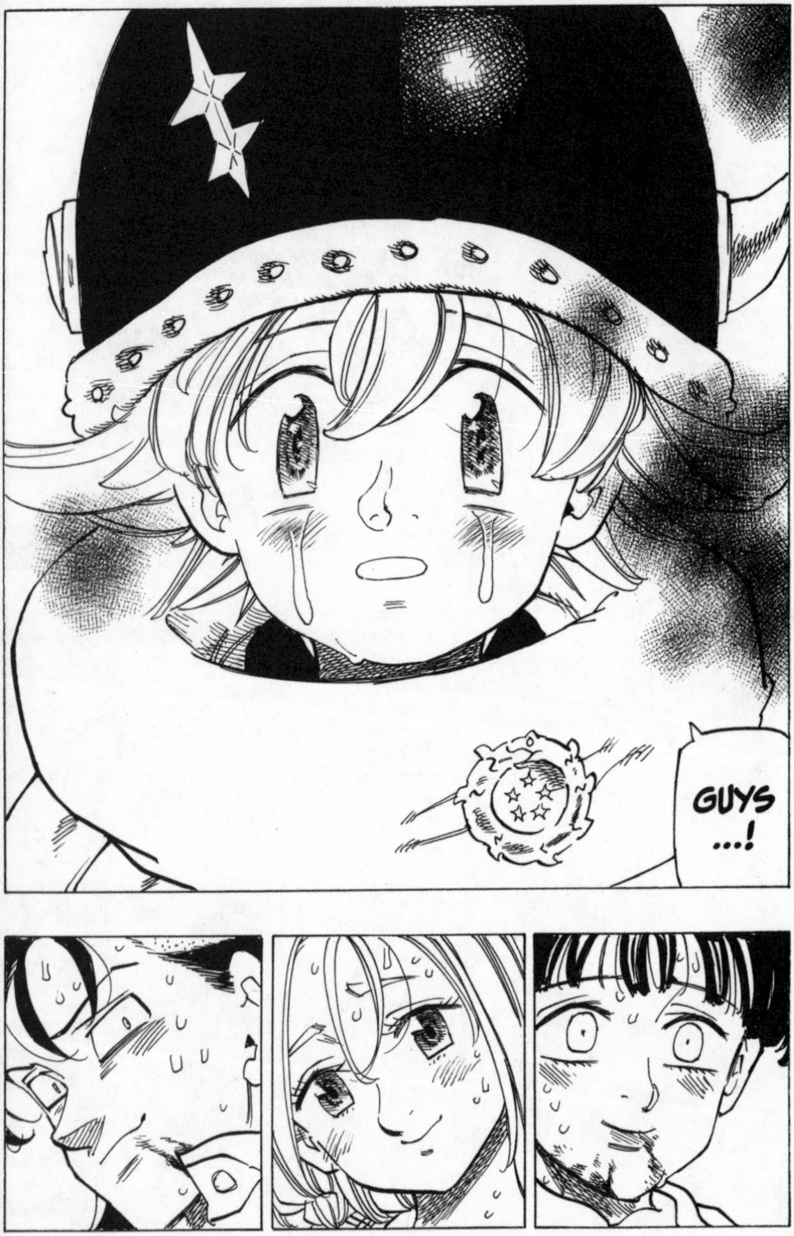
GUYS ...!

Four Knights of the Apocalypse

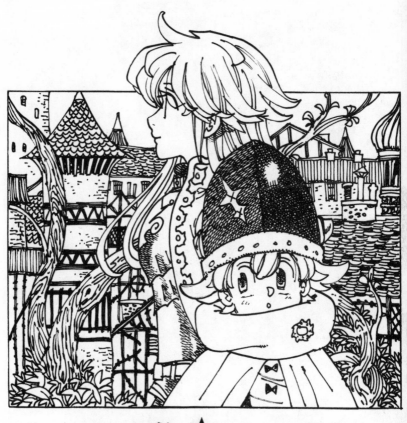

CHAPTER 56: KNIGHTS OF PROPHECY MEET

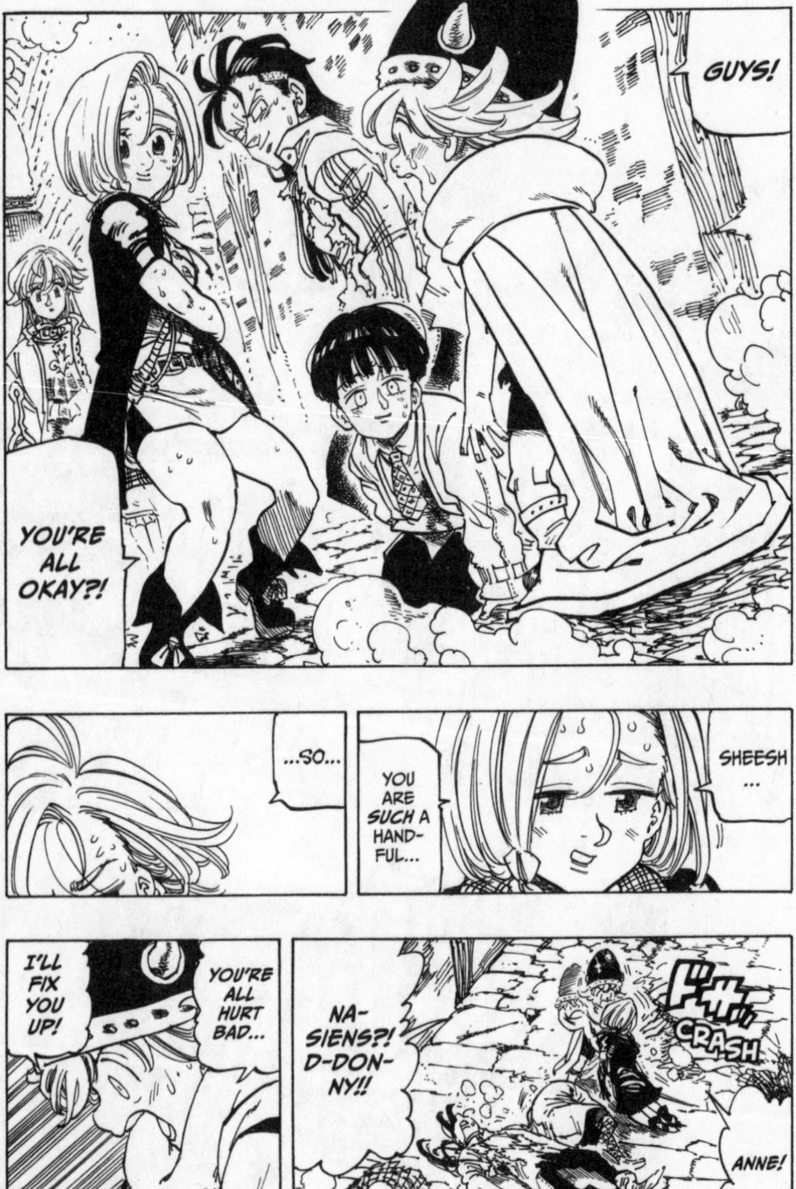
GUYS!
YOU'RE ALL OKAY?!
SHEESH ...
YOU ARE SUCH A HANDFUL...
...SO...
ドサッ
CRASH
NASIENS?! D-DONNY!!
ANNE!
YOU'RE ALL HURT BAD...
I'LL FIX YOU UP!

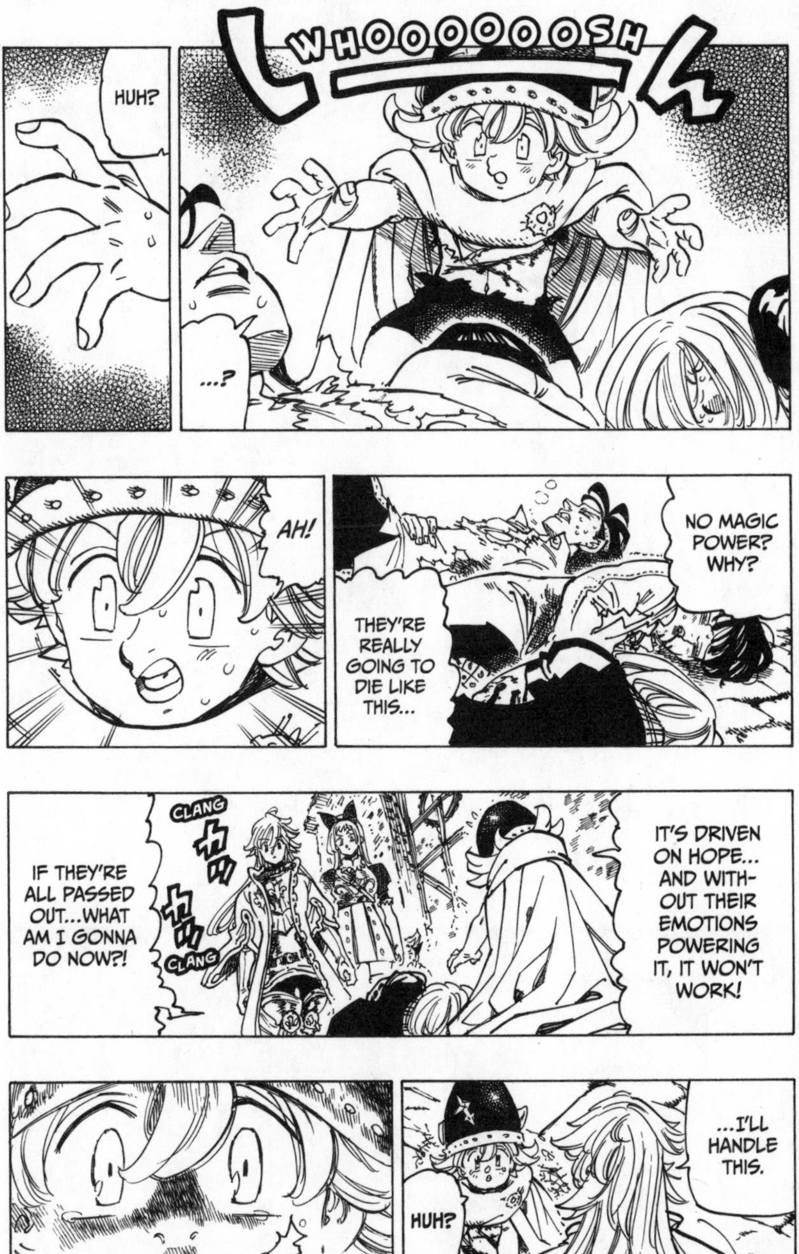

WHOOOOOOOSH
...?
HUH?
NO MAGIC POWER? WHY?
THEY'RE REALLY GOING TO DIE LIKE THIS...
AH!
IT'S DRIVEN ON HOPE... AND WITHOUT THEIR EMOTIONS POWERING IT, IT WON'T WORK!
CLANG
CLANG
IF THEY'RE ALL PASSED OUT...WHAT AM I GONNA DO NOW?!
...I'LL HANDLE THIS.
HUH?

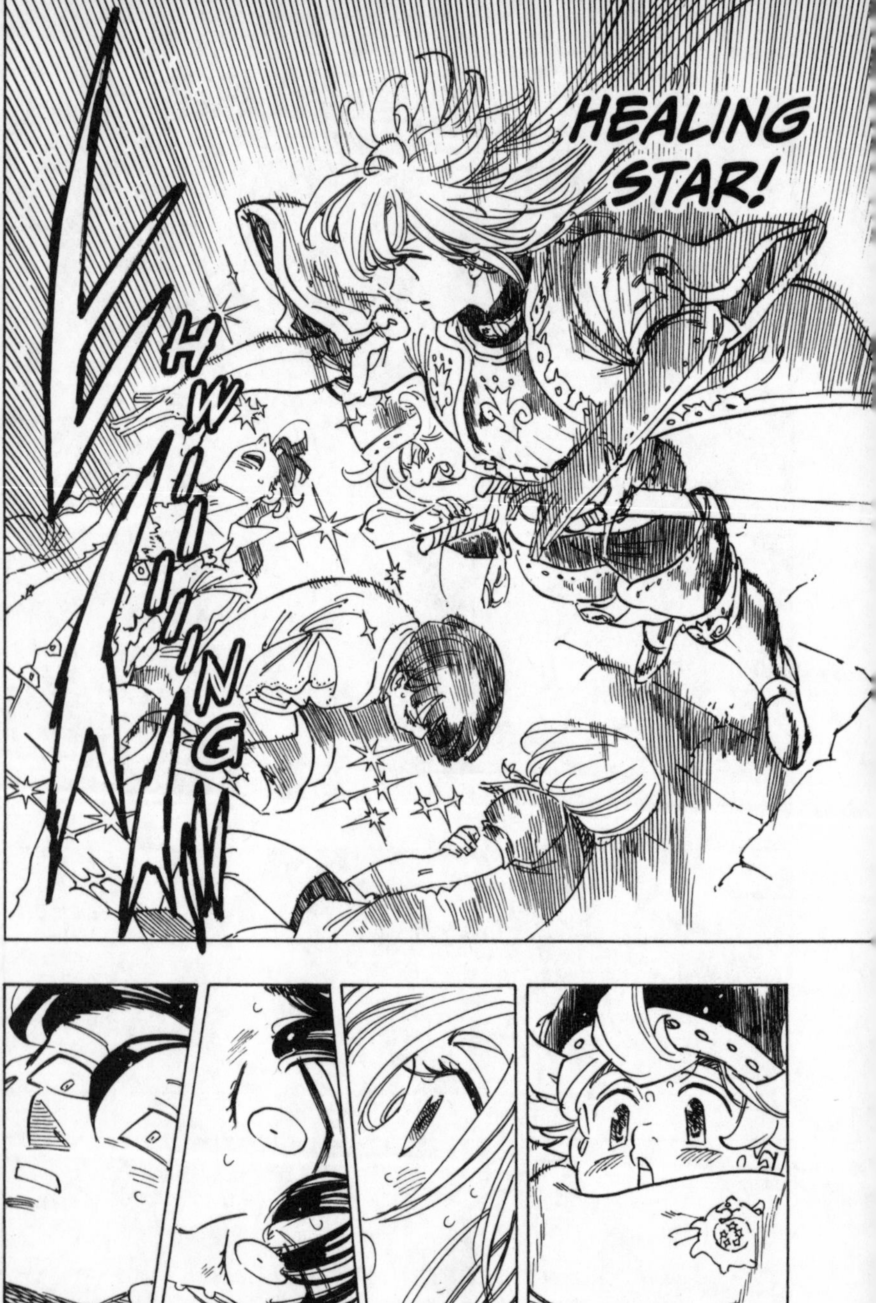
HEALING STAR!
SHWIIIIING

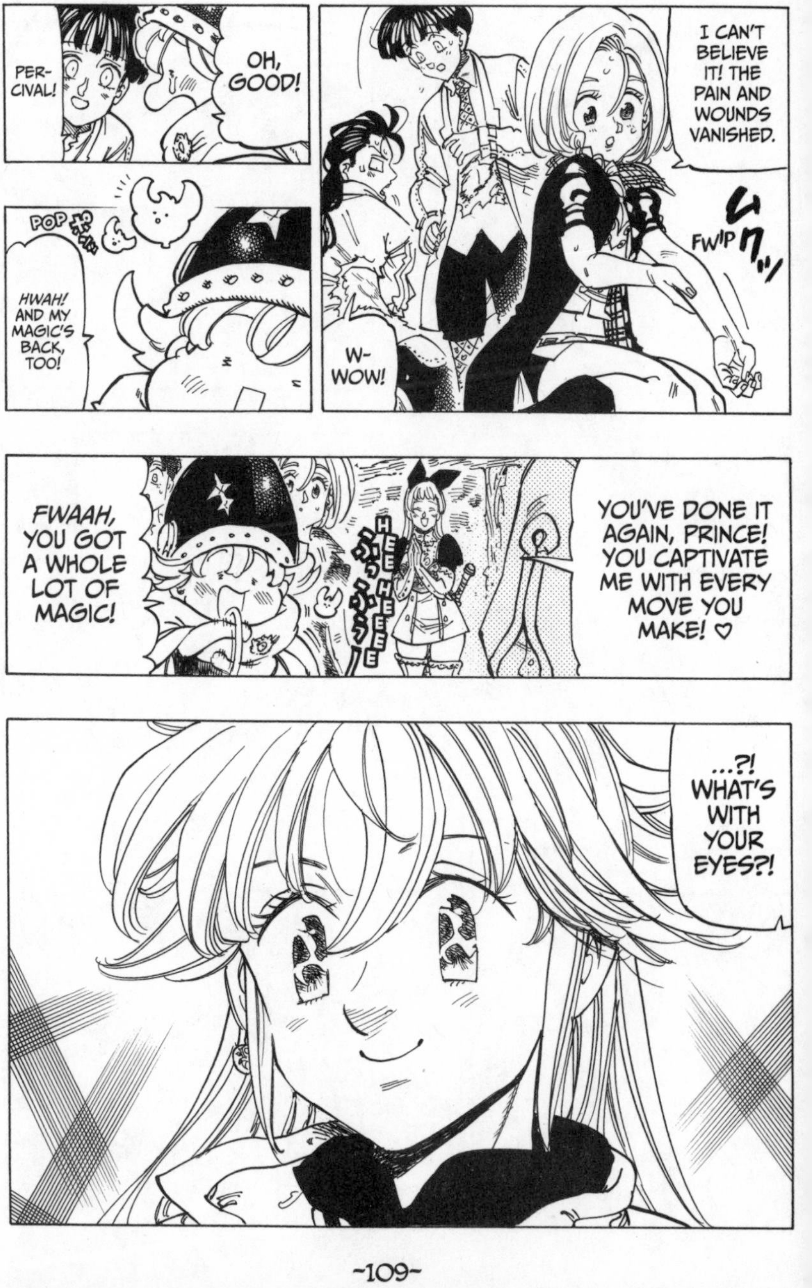

I CAN'T BELIEVE IT! THE PAIN AND WOUNDS VANISHED.
FWIP
W-WOW!
OH, GOOD!
PER-CIVAL!
POP
HWAH! AND MY MAGIC'S BACK, TOO!
YOU'VE DONE IT AGAIN, PRINCE! YOU CAPTIVATE ME WITH EVERY MOVE YOU MAKE! ♡
HEE HEE HEE
FWAAH, YOU GOT A WHOLE LOT OF MAGIC!
...?! WHAT'S WITH YOUR EYES?!

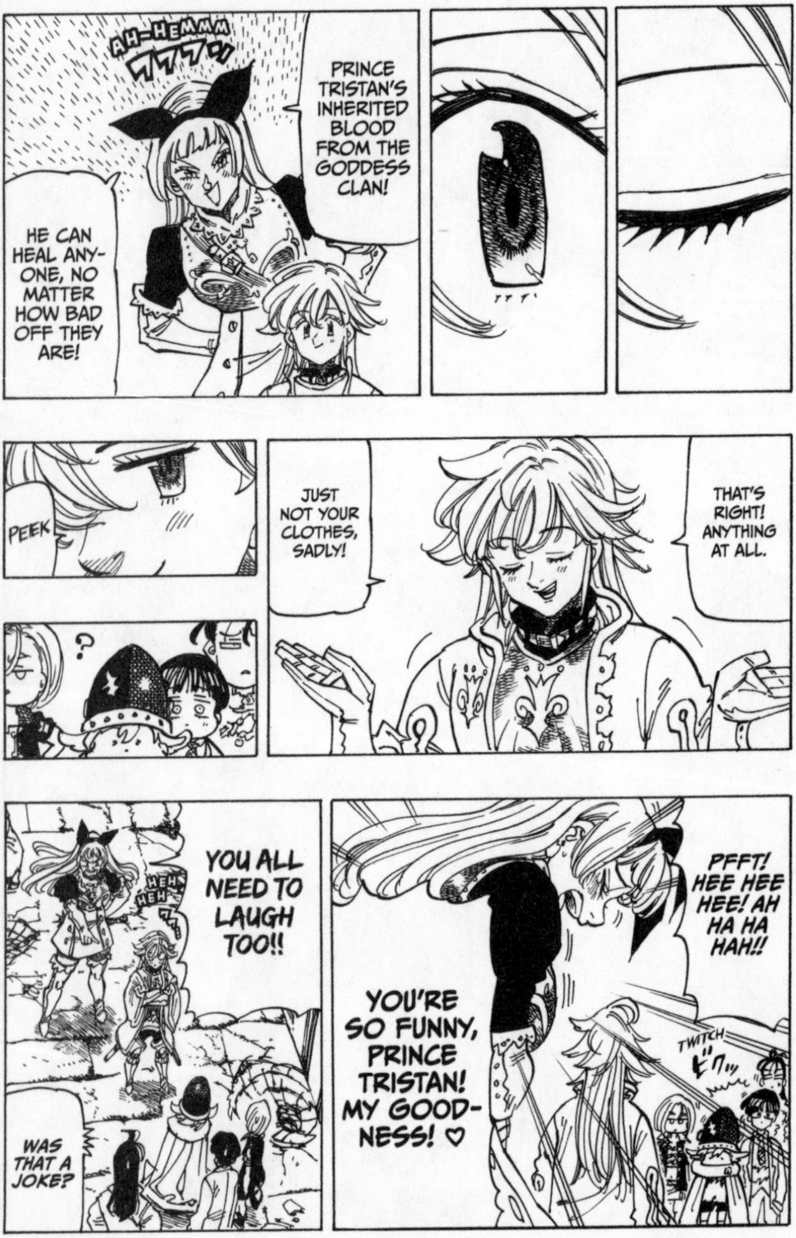
PRINCE TRISTAN'S INHERITED BLOOD FROM THE GODDESS CLAN!
AH-HEMMM
HE CAN HEAL ANYONE, NO MATTER HOW BAD OFF THEY ARE!
THAT'S RIGHT! ANYTHING AT ALL.
JUST NOT YOUR CLOTHES, SADLY!
PEEK
?
PFFT! HEE HEE HEE! AH HA HA HAH!!
YOU'RE SO FUNNY, PRINCE TRISTAN! MY GOODNESS! ♡
TWITCH
YOU ALL NEED TO LAUGH TOO!!
HEH HEH
WAS THAT A JOKE?

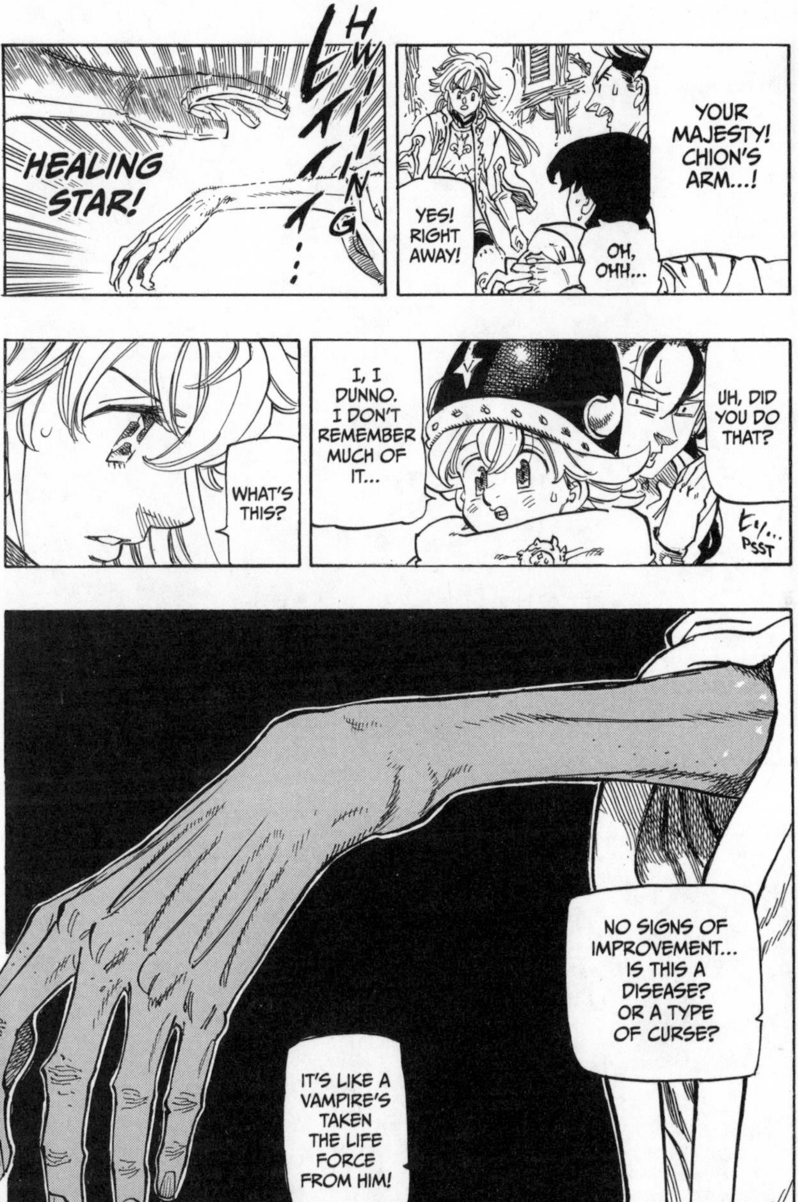
YOUR MAJESTY! CHION'S ARM...!
YES! RIGHT AWAY!
OH, OHH...
HWIIING
HEALING STAR!
UH, DID YOU DO THAT?
PSST
I, I DUNNO. I DON'T REMEMBER MUCH OF IT...
WHAT'S THIS?
NO SIGNS OF IMPROVEMENT... IS THIS A DISEASE? OR A TYPE OF CURSE?
IT'S LIKE A VAMPIRE'S TAKEN THE LIFE FORCE FROM HIM!

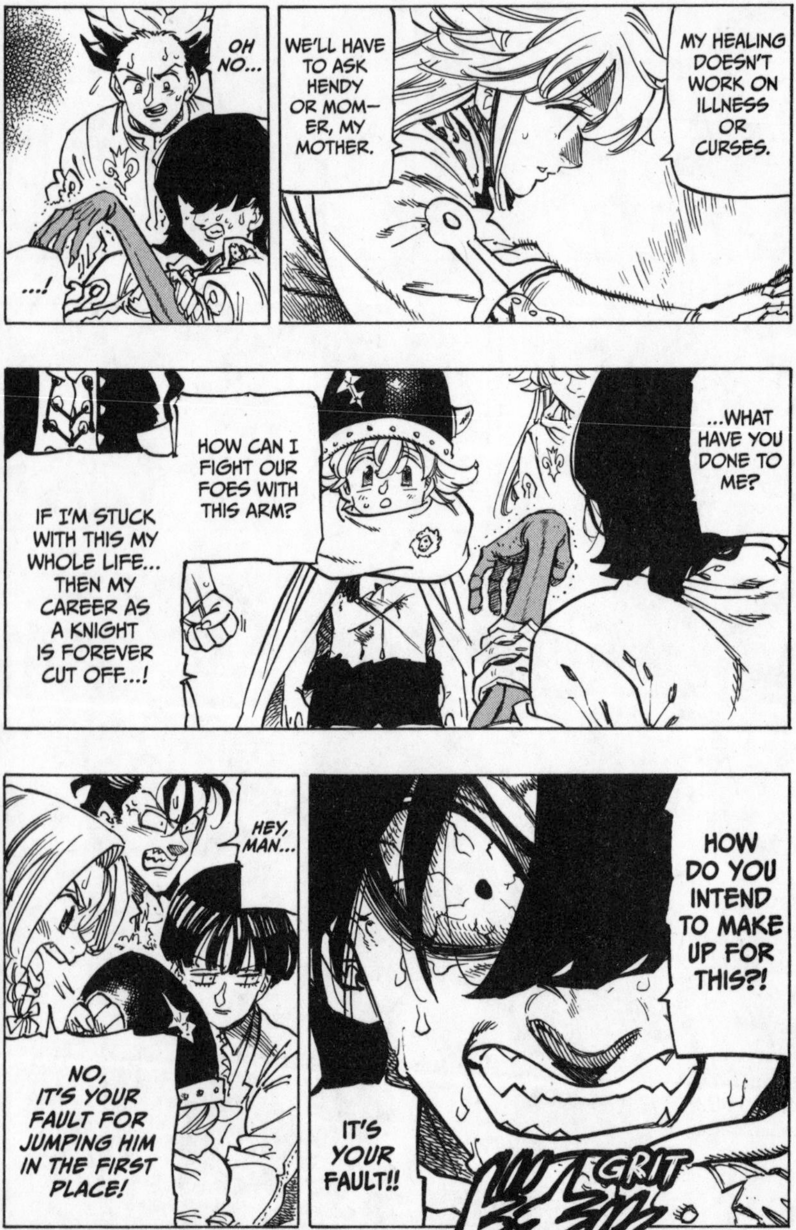
MY HEALING DOESN'T WORK ON ILLNESS OR CURSES.
WE'LL HAVE TO ASK HENDY OR MOM—ER, MY MOTHER.
OH NO...
...!
...WHAT HAVE YOU DONE TO ME?
HOW CAN I FIGHT OUR FOES WITH THIS ARM?
IF I'M STUCK WITH THIS MY WHOLE LIFE... THEN MY CAREER AS A KNIGHT IS FOREVER CUT OFF...!
HOW DO YOU INTEND TO MAKE UP FOR THIS?!
IT'S YOUR FAULT!!
GRIT
HEY, MAN...
NO, IT'S YOUR FAULT FOR JUMPING HIM IN THE FIRST PLACE!

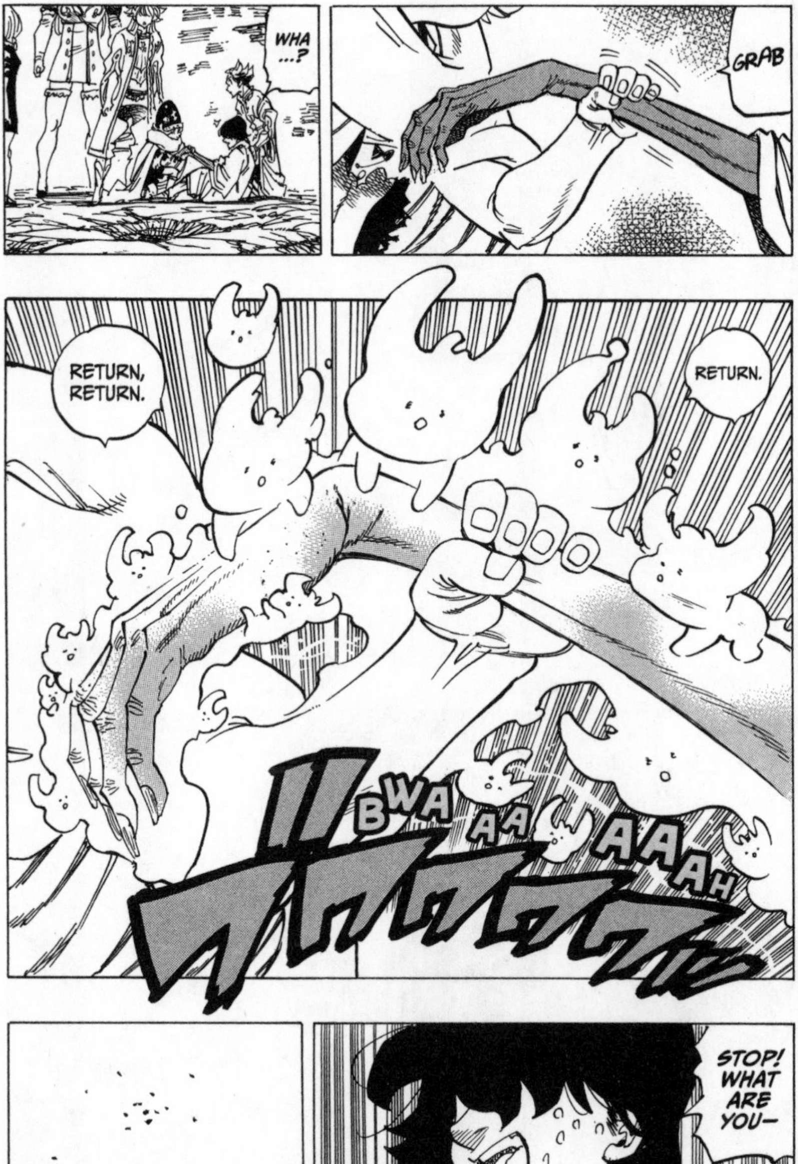
GRAB
WHA ...?
RETURN.
RETURN, RETURN.
BWAAAAAAAH
STOP! WHAT ARE YOU—

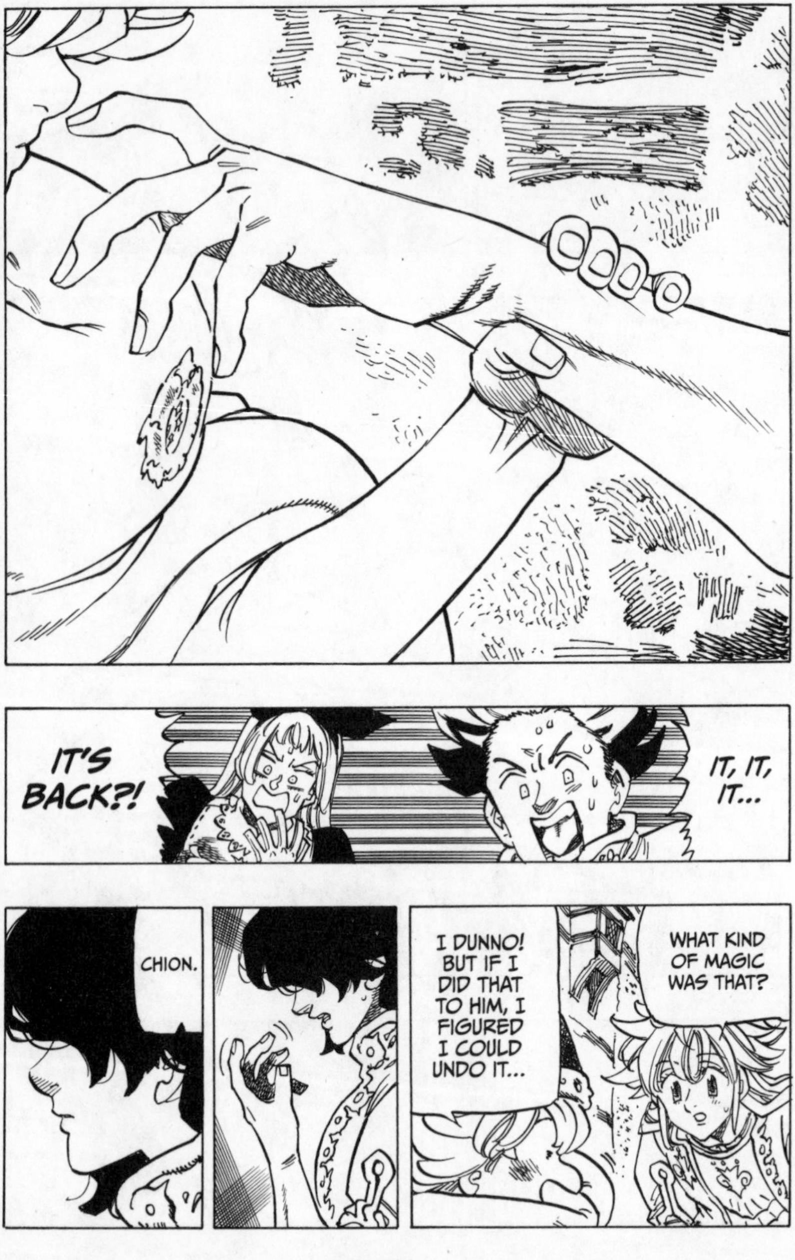
IT, IT, IT...
IT'S BACK?!
WHAT KIND OF MAGIC WAS THAT?
I DUNNO! BUT IF I DID THAT TO HIM, I FIGURED I COULD UNDO IT...
CHION.

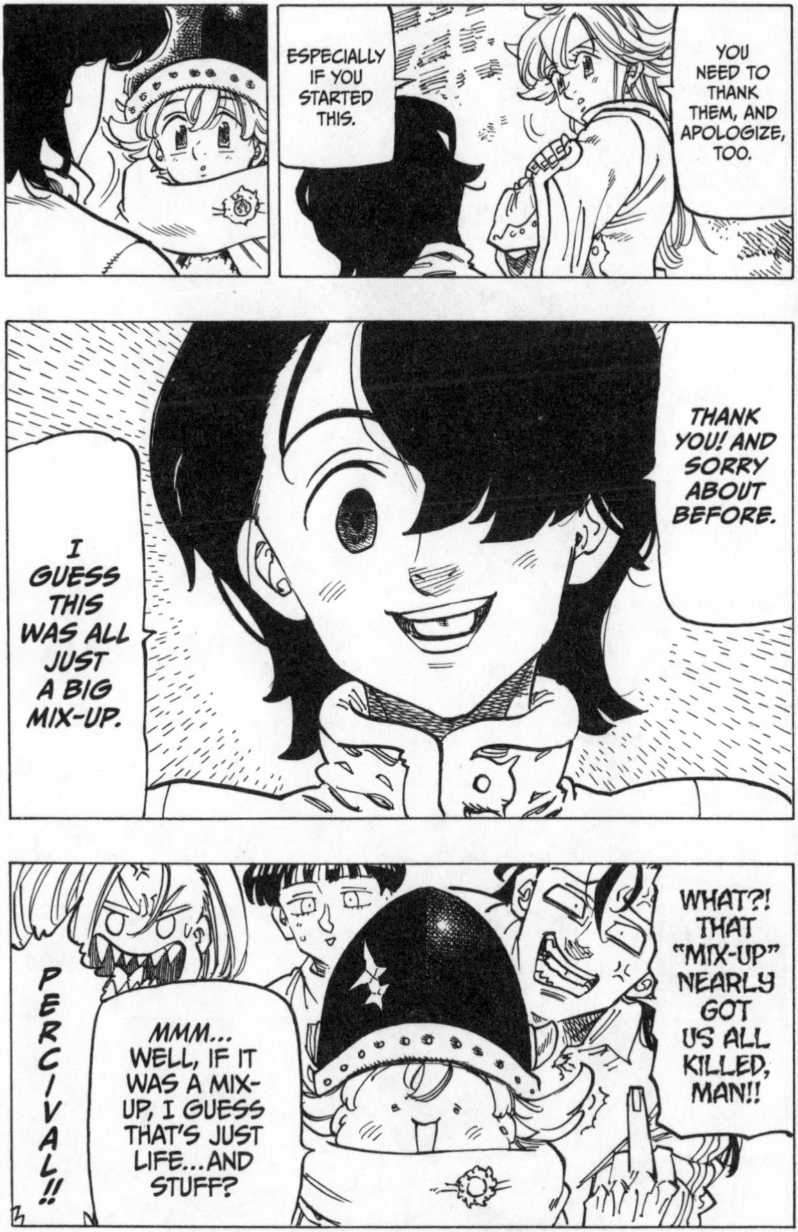

YOU NEED TO THANK THEM, AND APOLOGIZE, TOO.
ESPECIALLY IF YOU STARTED THIS.
THANK YOU! AND SORRY ABOUT BEFORE.
I GUESS THIS WAS ALL JUST A BIG MIX-UP.
WHAT?! THAT "MIX-UP" NEARLY GOT US ALL KILLED, MAN!!
MMM... WELL, IF IT WAS A MIX-UP, I GUESS THAT'S JUST LIFE...AND STUFF?
PERCIVAL!!

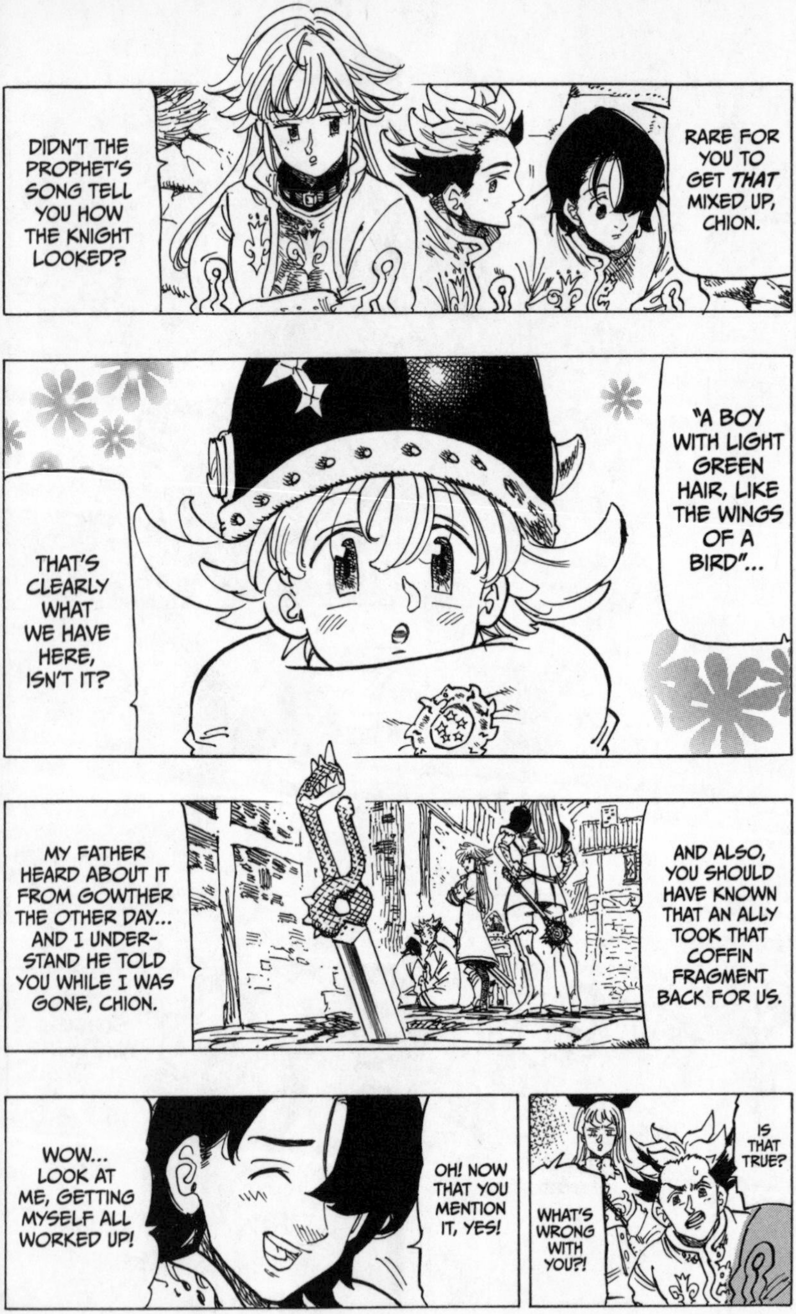
RARE FOR YOU TO GET *THAT* MIXED UP, CHION.
DIDN'T THE PROPHET'S SONG TELL YOU HOW THE KNIGHT LOOKED?
"A BOY WITH LIGHT GREEN HAIR, LIKE THE WINGS OF A BIRD"...
THAT'S CLEARLY WHAT WE HAVE HERE, ISN'T IT?
AND ALSO, YOU SHOULD HAVE KNOWN THAT AN ALLY TOOK THAT COFFIN FRAGMENT BACK FOR US.
MY FATHER HEARD ABOUT IT FROM GOWTHER THE OTHER DAY... AND I UNDER-STAND HE TOLD YOU WHILE I WAS GONE, CHION.
IS THAT TRUE?
WHAT'S WRONG WITH YOU?!
OH! NOW THAT YOU MENTION IT, YES!
WOW... LOOK AT ME, GETTING MYSELF ALL WORKED UP!

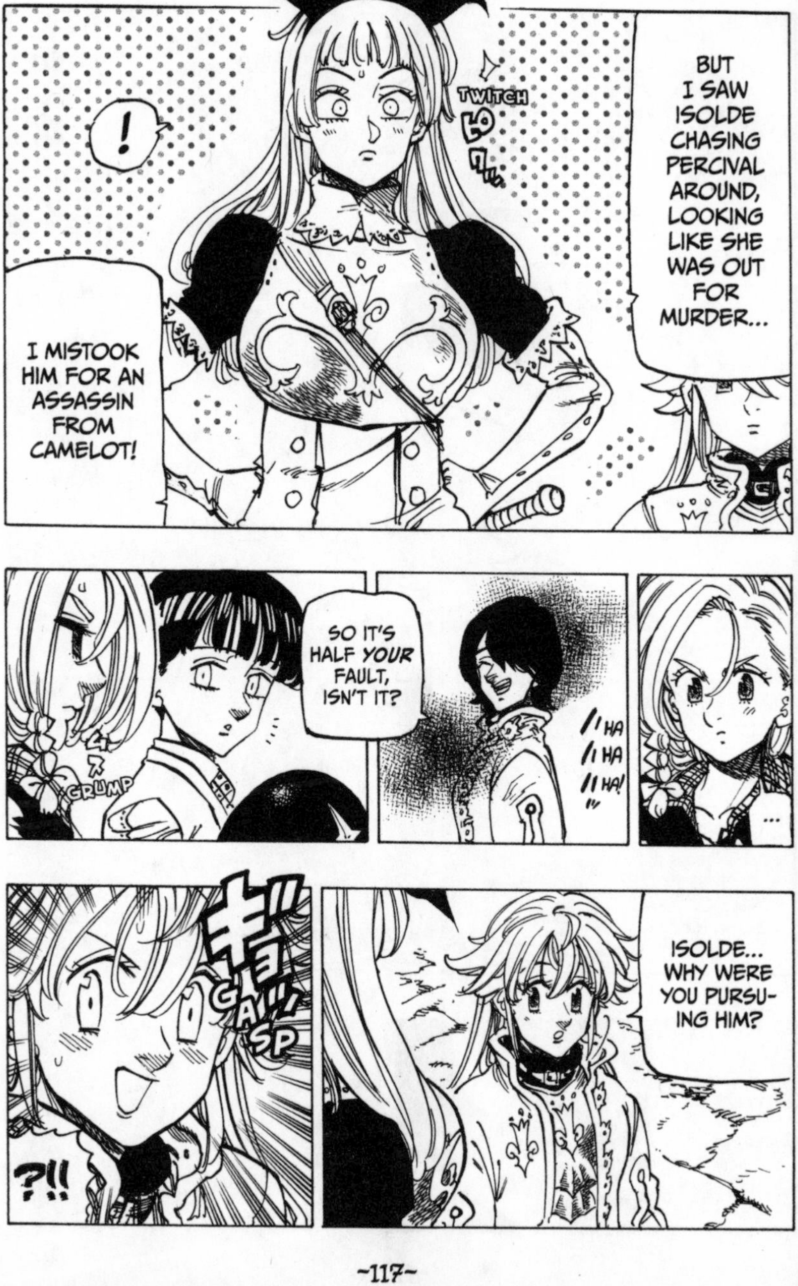
BUT I SAW ISOLDE CHASING PERCIVAL AROUND, LOOKING LIKE SHE WAS OUT FOR MURDER...
TWITCH
!
I MISTOOK HIM FOR AN ASSASSIN FROM CAMELOT!
...
SO IT'S HALF *YOUR* FAULT, ISN'T IT?
HA HA HA!
GRUMP
ISOLDE... WHY WERE YOU PURSU-ING HIM?
GASP
?!!

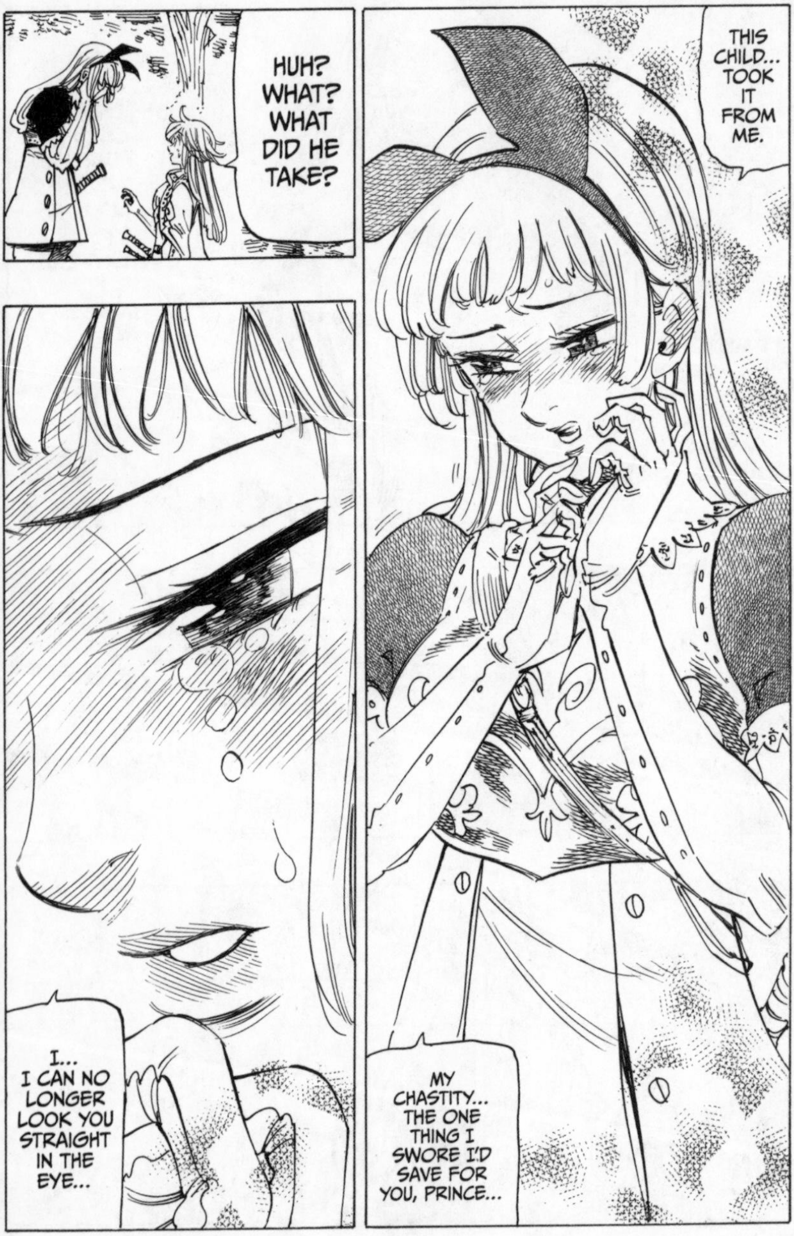

THIS CHILD... TOOK IT FROM ME.
MY CHASTITY... THE ONE THING I SWORE I'D SAVE FOR YOU, PRINCE...
HUH? WHAT? WHAT DID HE TAKE?
I... I CAN NO LONGER LOOK YOU STRAIGHT IN THE EYE...

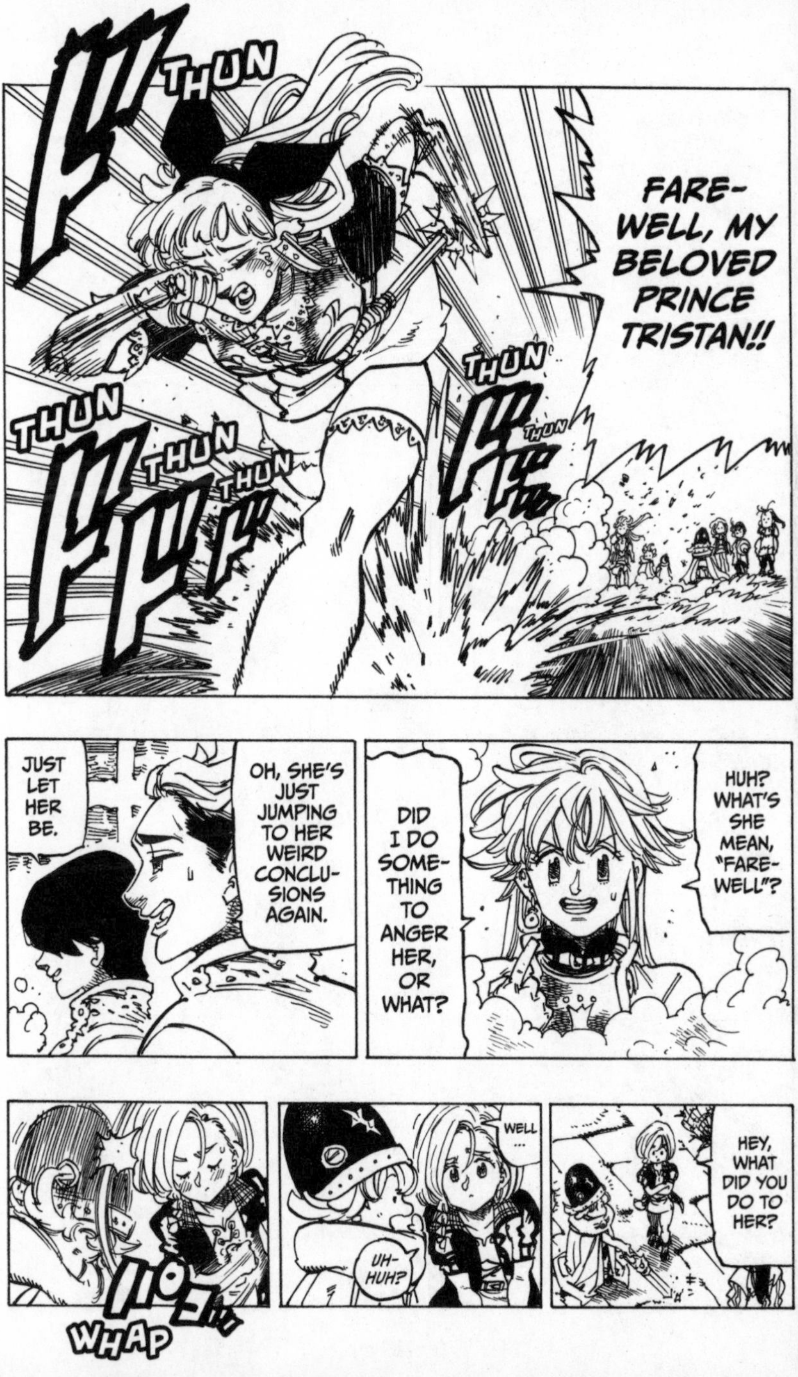
THUN
FARE-WELL, MY BELOVED PRINCE TRISTAN!!
THUN
THUN
THUN
THUN
THUN
HUH? WHAT'S SHE MEAN, "FARE-WELL"?
DID I DO SOME-THING TO ANGER HER, OR WHAT?
OH, SHE'S JUST JUMPING TO HER WEIRD CONCLU-SIONS AGAIN.
JUST LET HER BE.
HEY, WHAT DID YOU DO TO HER?
WELL ...
UH-HUH?
WHAP

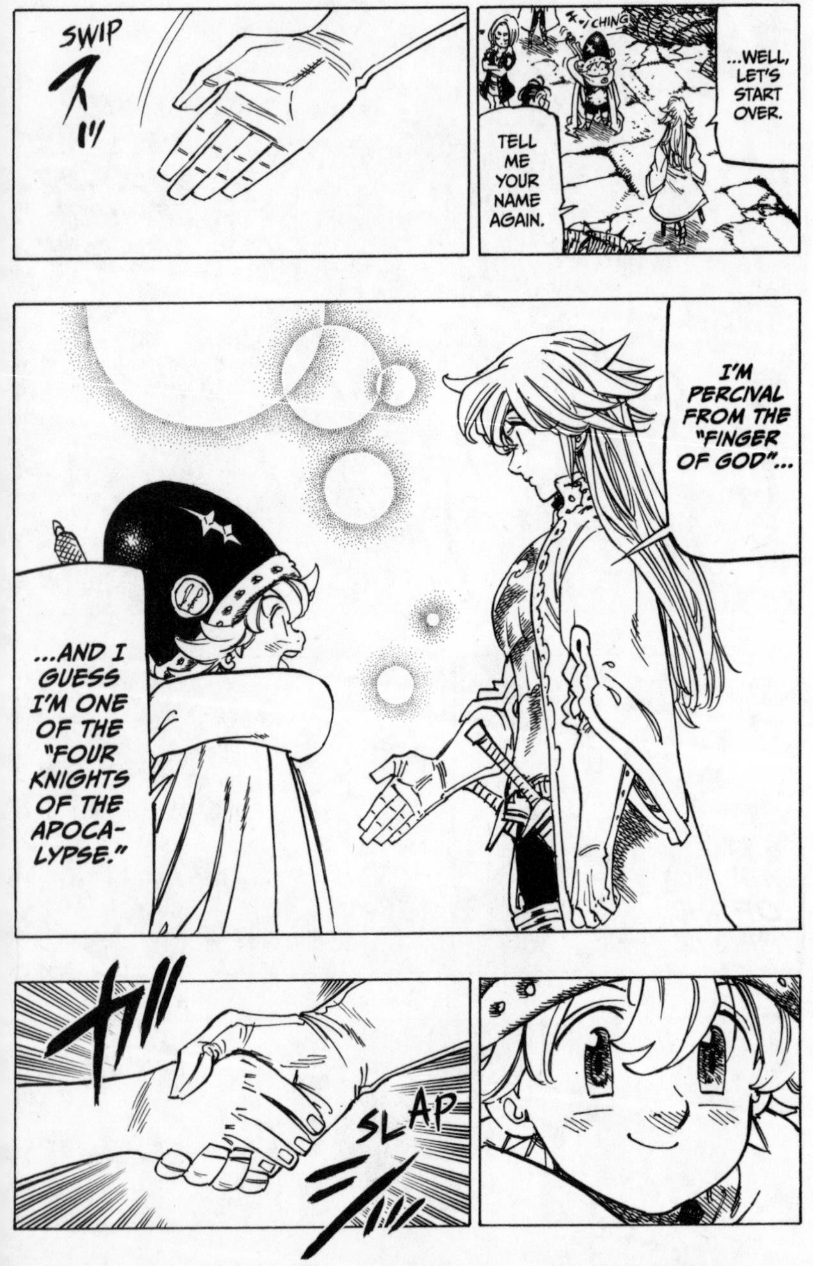
CHING
...WELL, LET'S START OVER.
TELL ME YOUR NAME AGAIN.
SWIP
I'M PERCIVAL FROM THE "FINGER OF GOD"...
...AND I GUESS I'M ONE OF THE "FOUR KNIGHTS OF THE APOCALYPSE."
SLAP

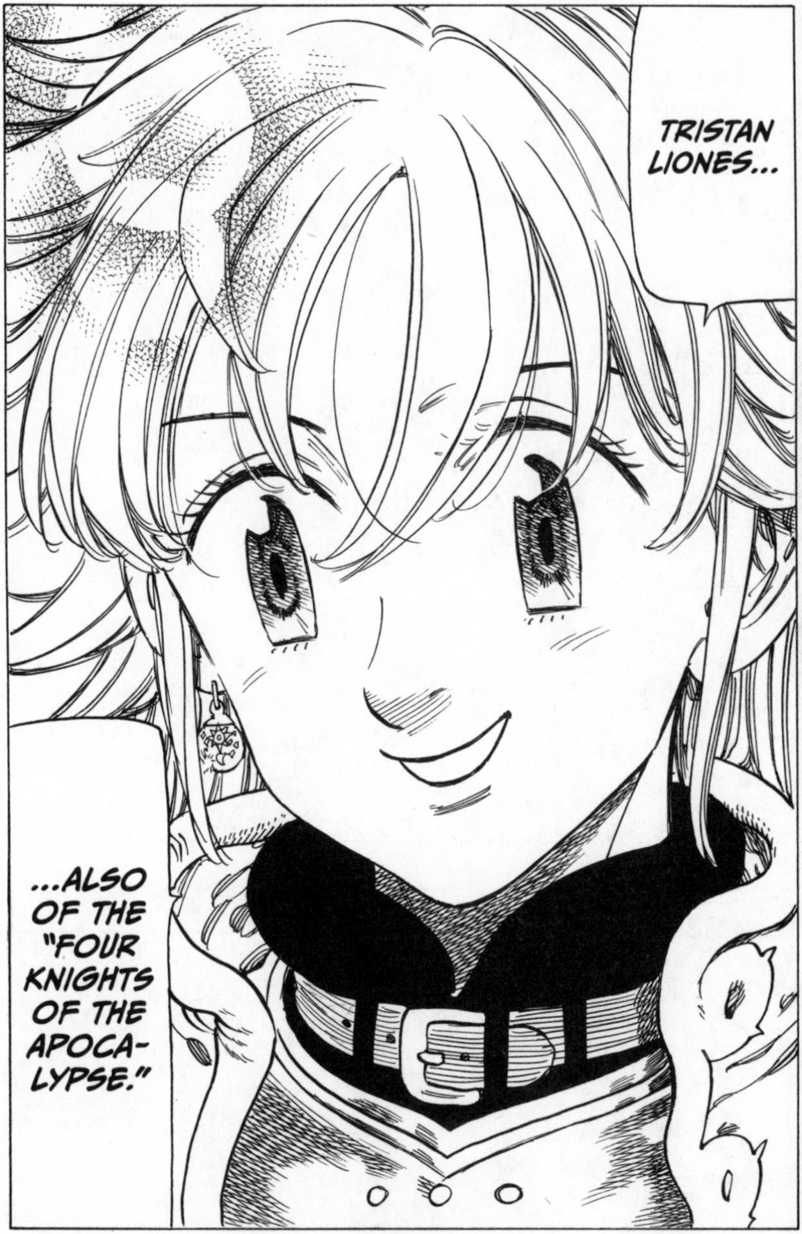
TRISTAN LIONES...
...ALSO OF THE "FOUR KNIGHTS OF THE APOCA-LYPSE."

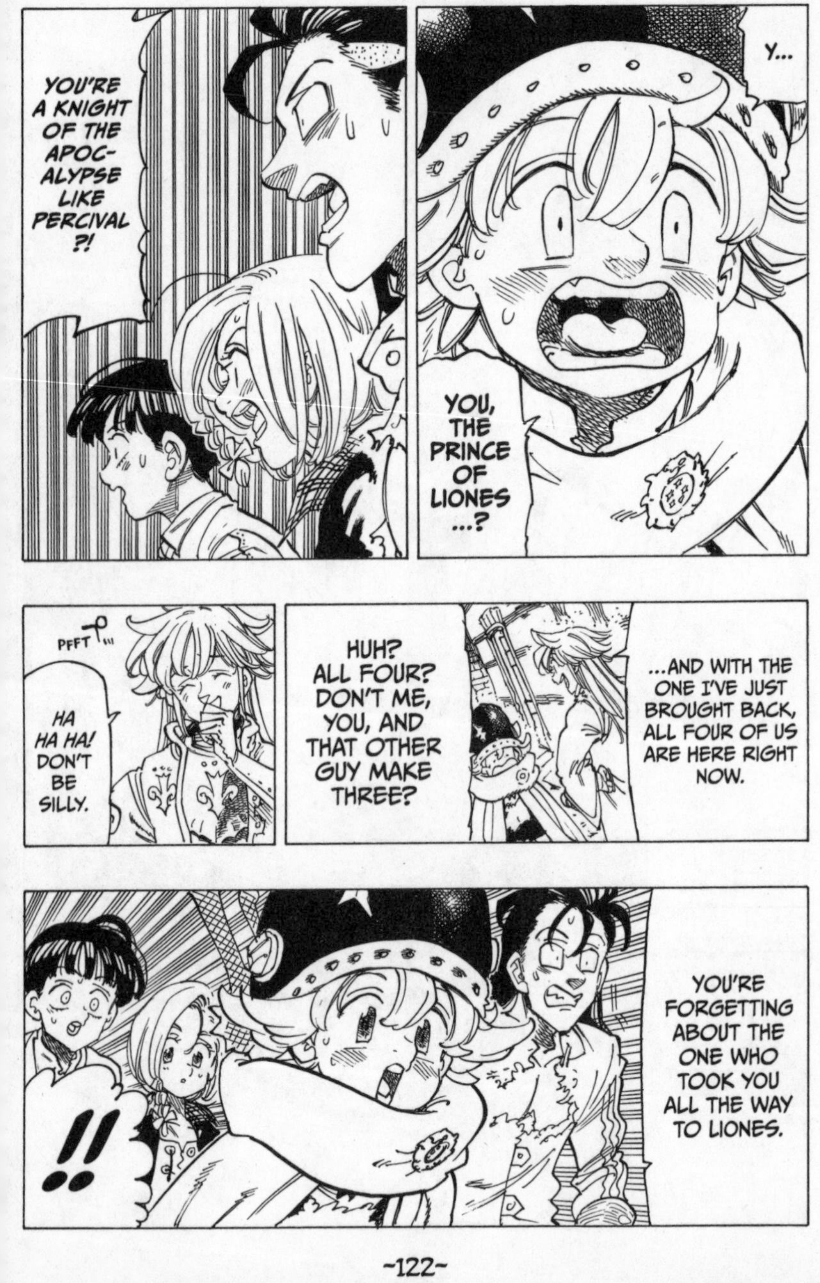
Y...
YOU, THE PRINCE OF LIONES ...?
YOU'RE A KNIGHT OF THE APOC-ALYPSE LIKE PERCIVAL ?!
...AND WITH THE ONE I'VE JUST BROUGHT BACK, ALL FOUR OF US ARE HERE RIGHT NOW.
HUH? ALL FOUR? DON'T ME, YOU, AND THAT OTHER GUY MAKE THREE?
PFFT
HA HA HA! DON'T BE SILLY.
YOU'RE FORGETTING ABOUT THE ONE WHO TOOK YOU ALL THE WAY TO LIONES.
!!

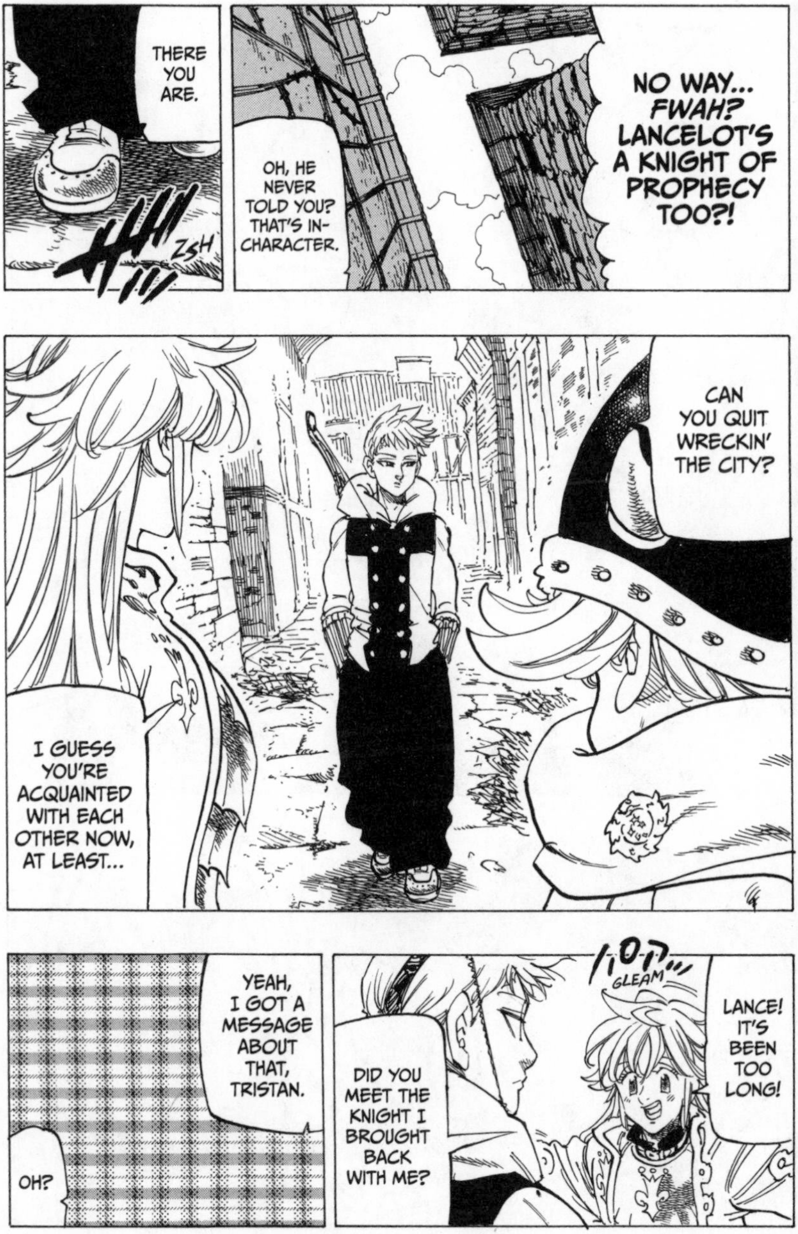
NO WAY... FWAH? LANCELOT'S A KNIGHT OF PROPHECY TOO?!
OH, HE NEVER TOLD YOU? THAT'S IN-CHARACTER.
THERE YOU ARE.
ZSH
CAN YOU QUIT WRECKIN' THE CITY?
I GUESS YOU'RE ACQUAINTED WITH EACH OTHER NOW, AT LEAST...
GLEAM
LANCE! IT'S BEEN TOO LONG!
DID YOU MEET THE KNIGHT I BROUGHT BACK WITH ME?
YEAH, I GOT A MESSAGE ABOUT THAT, TRISTAN.
OH?

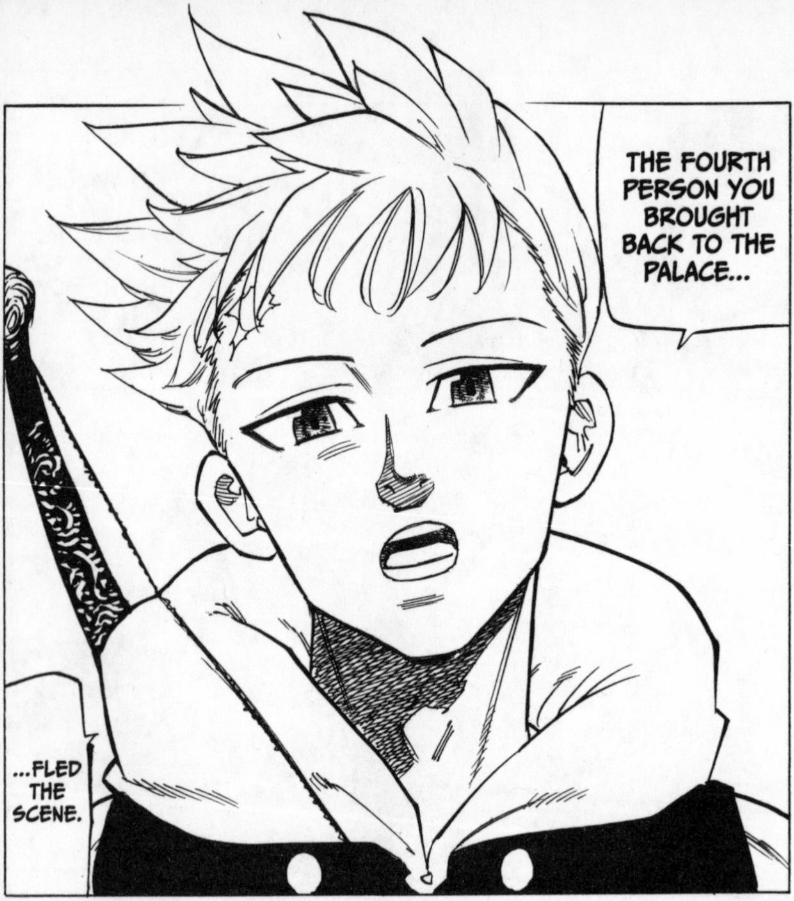
THE FOURTH PERSON YOU BROUGHT BACK TO THE PALACE...
...FLED THE SCENE.
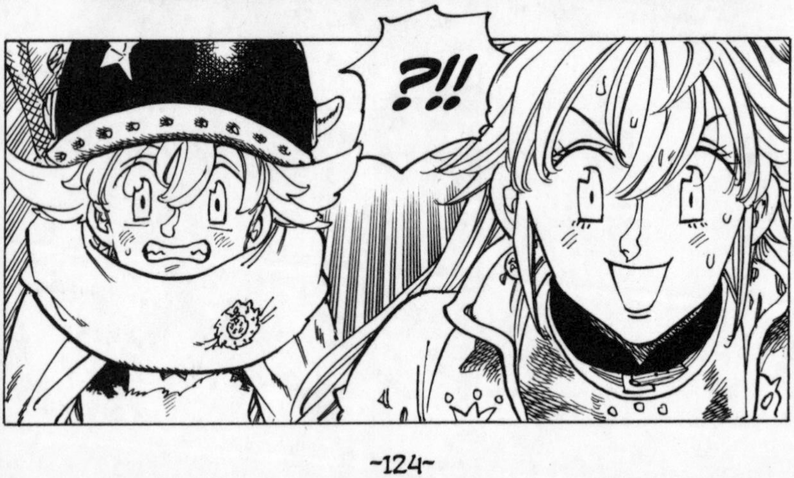
?!!

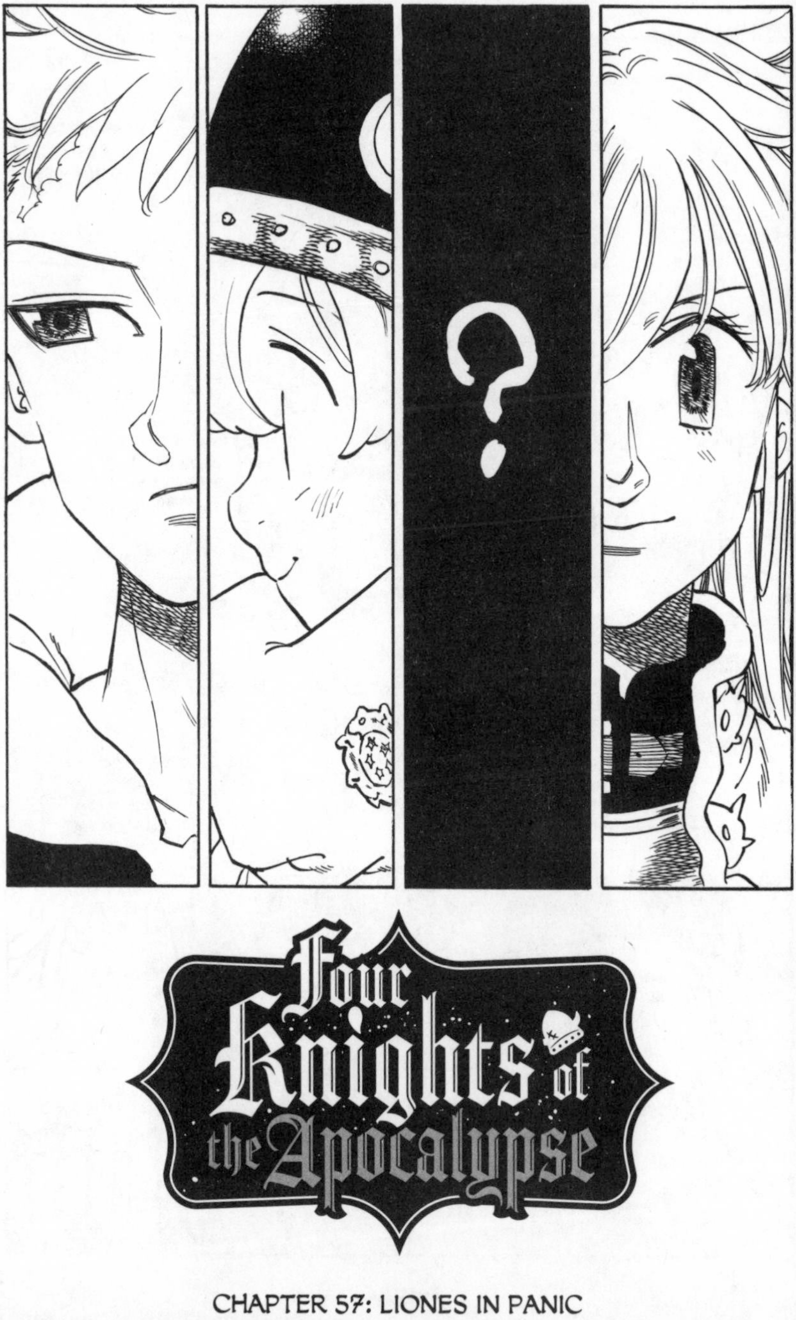

Four Knights of the Apocalypse

CHAPTER 57: LIONES IN PANIC

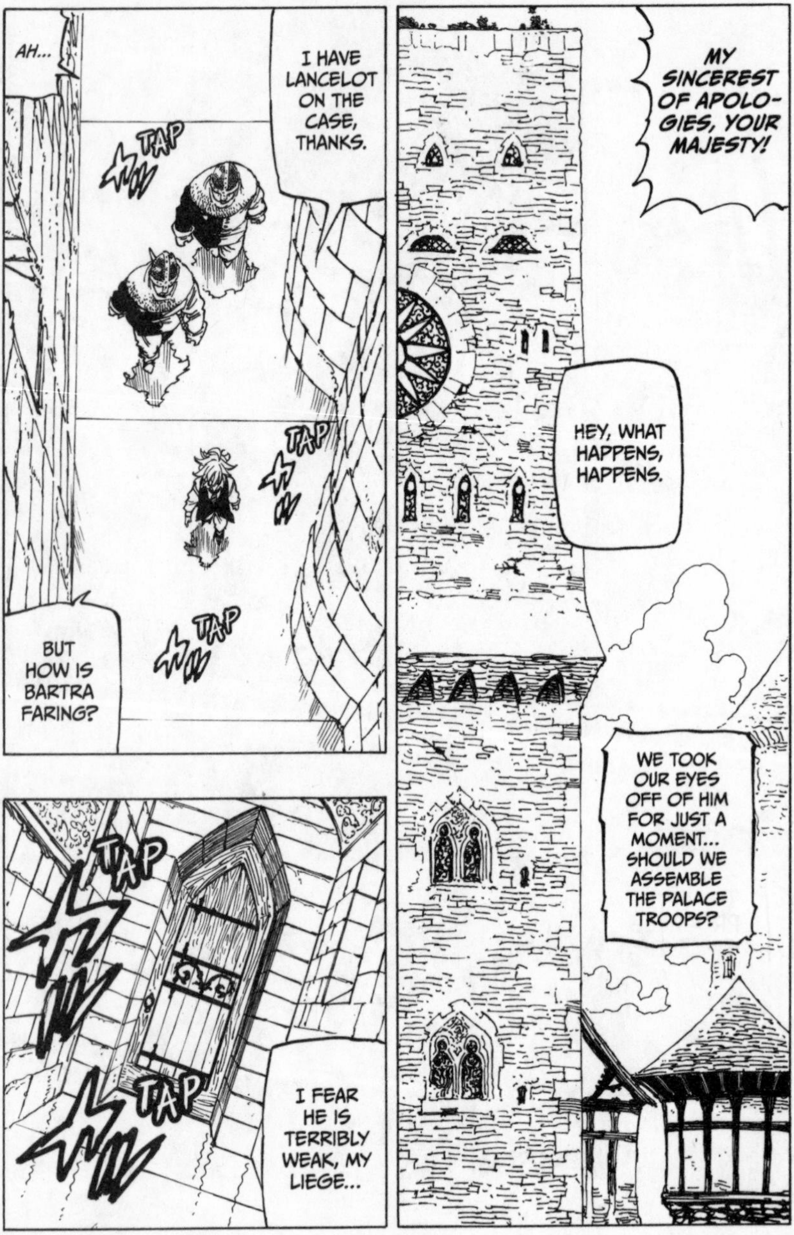
MY SINCEREST OF APOLOGIES, YOUR MAJESTY!
HEY, WHAT HAPPENS, HAPPENS.
WE TOOK OUR EYES OFF OF HIM FOR JUST A MOMENT... SHOULD WE ASSEMBLE THE PALACE TROOPS?
I HAVE LANCELOT ON THE CASE, THANKS.
AH...
TAP
TAP
TAP
BUT HOW IS BARTRA FARING?
TAP
TAP
I FEAR HE IS TERRIBLY WEAK, MY LIEGE...

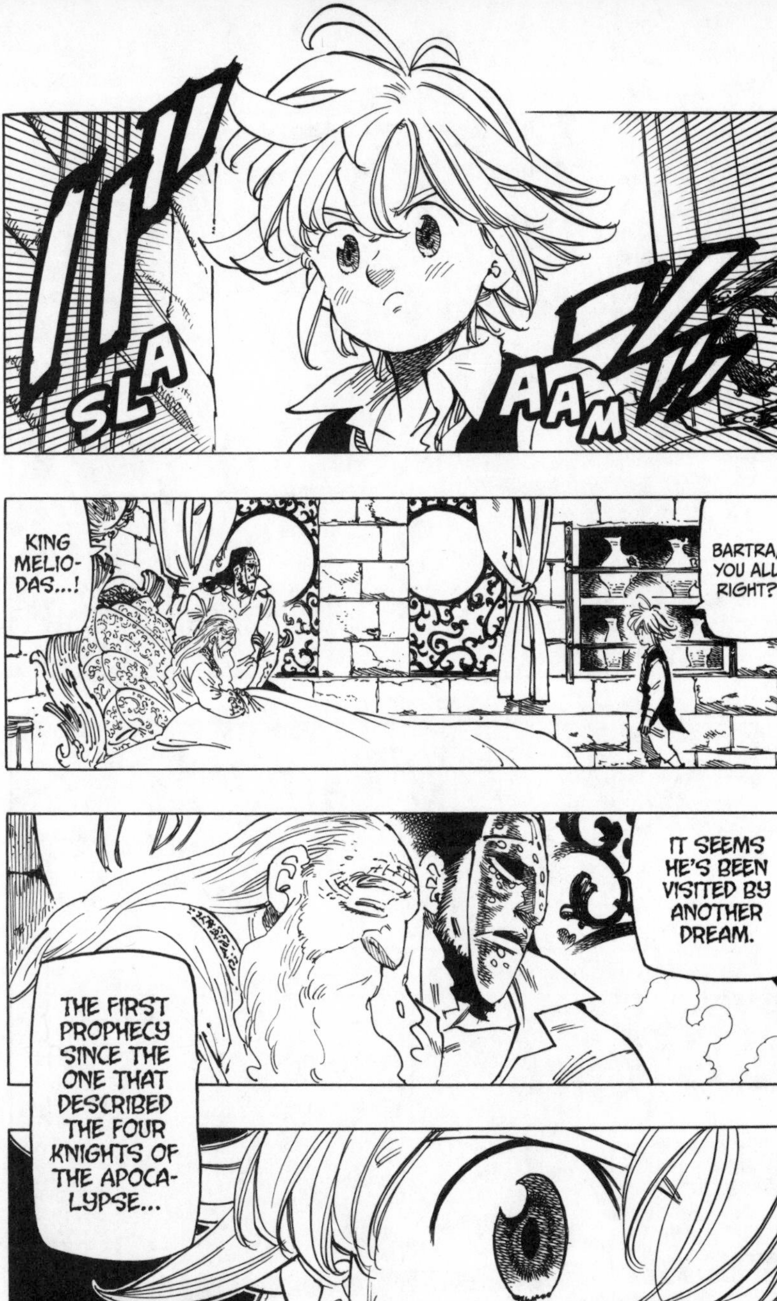
SLAAAM
BARTRA, YOU ALL RIGHT?
KING MELIO-DAS...!
IT SEEMS HE'S BEEN VISITED BY ANOTHER DREAM.
THE FIRST PROPHECY SINCE THE ONE THAT DESCRIBED THE FOUR KNIGHTS OF THE APOCA-LYPSE...

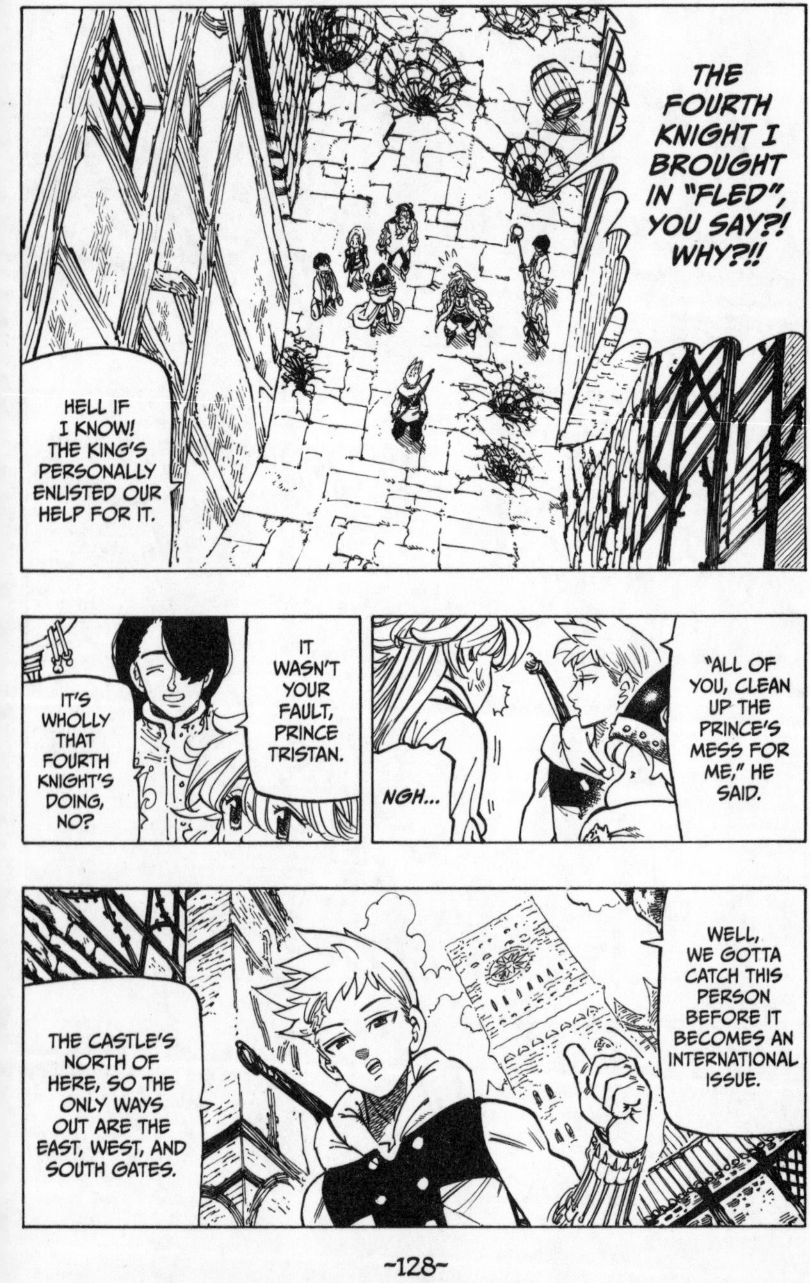
THE FOURTH KNIGHT I BROUGHT IN "FLED", YOU SAY?! WHY?!!
HELL IF I KNOW! THE KING'S PERSONALLY ENLISTED OUR HELP FOR IT.
"ALL OF YOU, CLEAN UP THE PRINCE'S MESS FOR ME," HE SAID.
NGH...
IT WASN'T YOUR FAULT, PRINCE TRISTAN.
IT'S WHOLLY THAT FOURTH KNIGHT'S DOING, NO?
WELL, WE GOTTA CATCH THIS PERSON BEFORE IT BECOMES AN INTERNATIONAL ISSUE.
THE CASTLE'S NORTH OF HERE, SO THE ONLY WAYS OUT ARE THE EAST, WEST, AND SOUTH GATES.

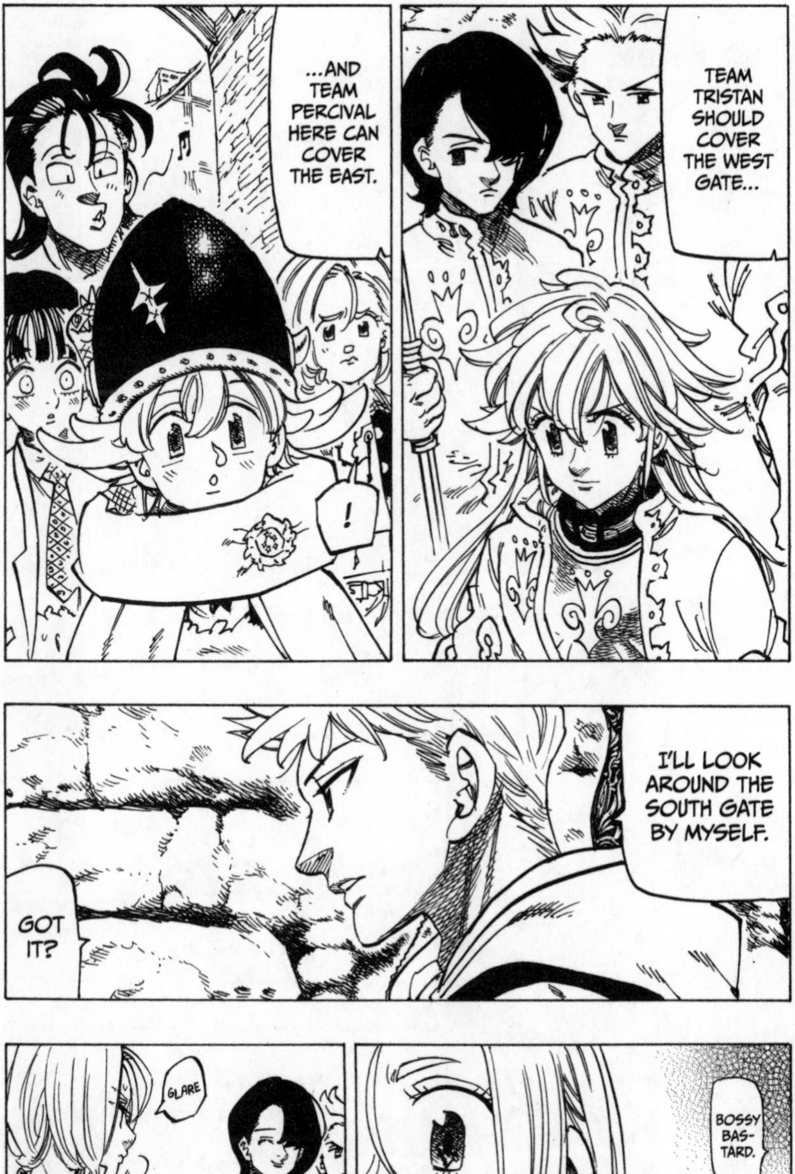
TEAM TRISTAN SHOULD COVER THE WEST GATE...
...AND TEAM PERCIVAL HERE CAN COVER THE EAST.
!
I'LL LOOK AROUND THE SOUTH GATE BY MYSELF.
GOT IT?
BOSSY BAS-TARD.
GLARE

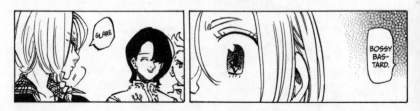

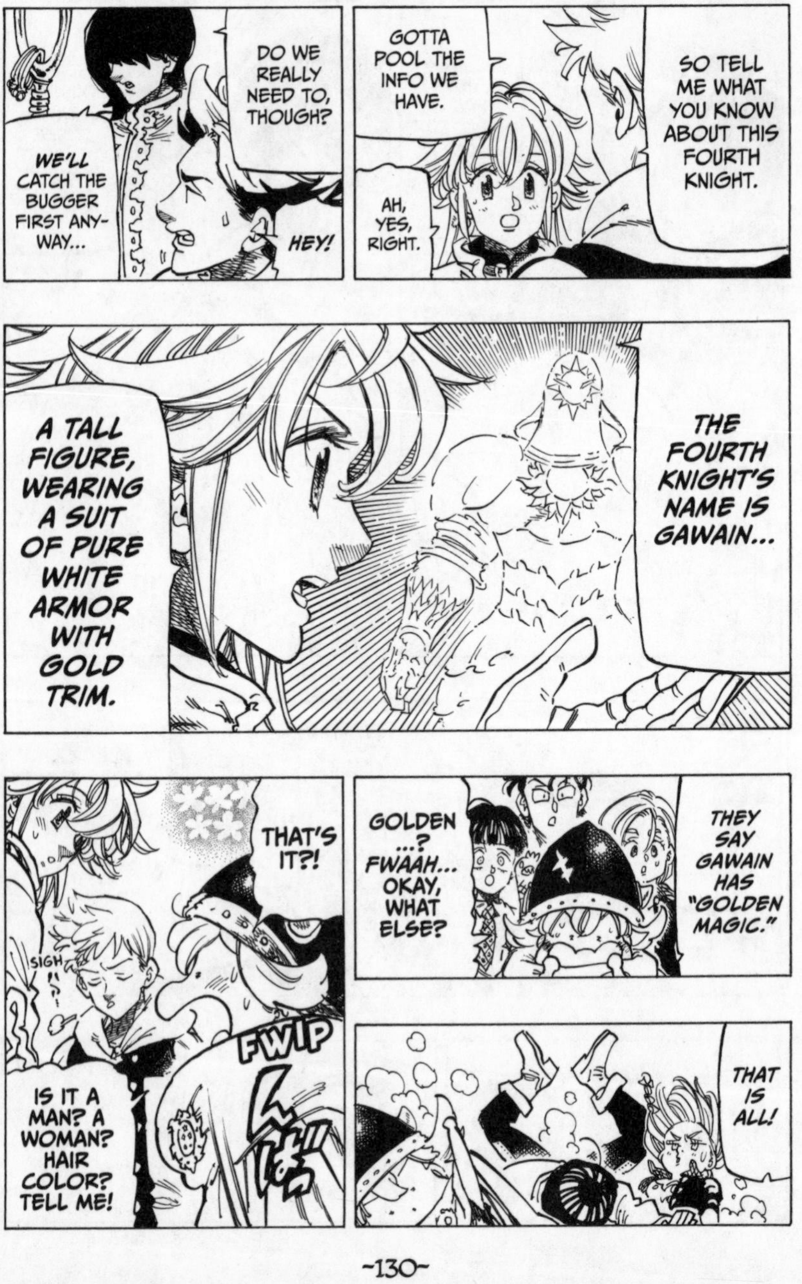
SO TELL ME WHAT YOU KNOW ABOUT THIS FOURTH KNIGHT.
GOTTA POOL THE INFO WE HAVE.
AH, YES, RIGHT.
DO WE REALLY NEED TO, THOUGH?
WE'LL CATCH THE BUGGER FIRST ANY-WAY...
HEY!
THE FOURTH KNIGHT'S NAME IS GAWAIN...
A TALL FIGURE, WEARING A SUIT OF PURE WHITE ARMOR WITH GOLD TRIM.
THEY SAY GAWAIN HAS "GOLDEN MAGIC."
GOLDEN ...? FWAAH... OKAY, WHAT ELSE?
THAT IS ALL!
THAT'S IT?!
SIGH
FWIP
IS IT A MAN? A WOMAN? HAIR COLOR? TELL ME!

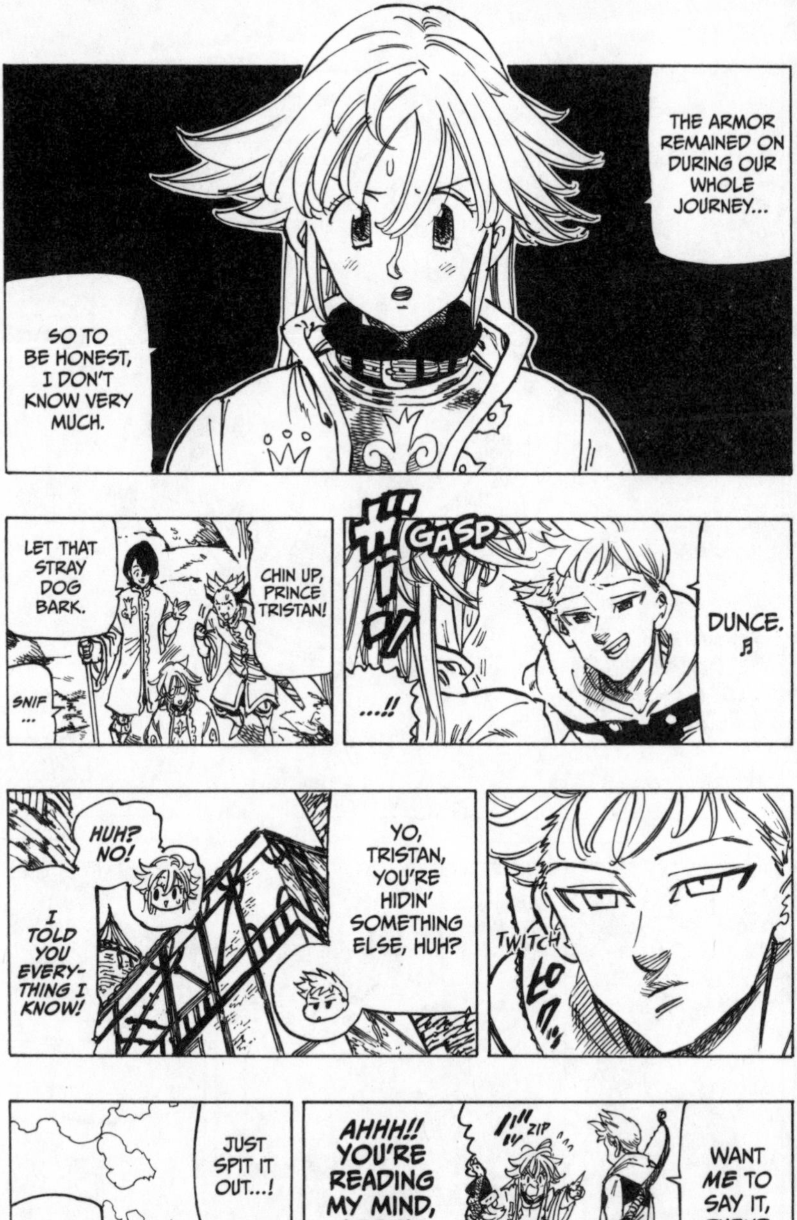
THE ARMOR REMAINED ON DURING OUR WHOLE JOURNEY...
SO TO BE HONEST, I DON'T KNOW VERY MUCH.
DUNCE. ♬
GASP
...!!
CHIN UP, PRINCE TRISTAN!
LET THAT STRAY DOG BARK.
SNIF...
TWITCH
YO, TRISTAN, YOU'RE HIDIN' SOMETHING ELSE, HUH?
HUH? NO!
I TOLD YOU EVERY-THING I KNOW!
WANT *ME* TO SAY IT, THEN?
ZIP
AHHH!! YOU'RE READING MY MIND, AREN'T YOU?!
JUST SPIT IT OUT...!
UGH...

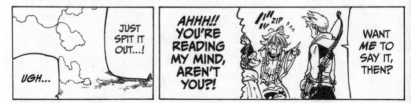

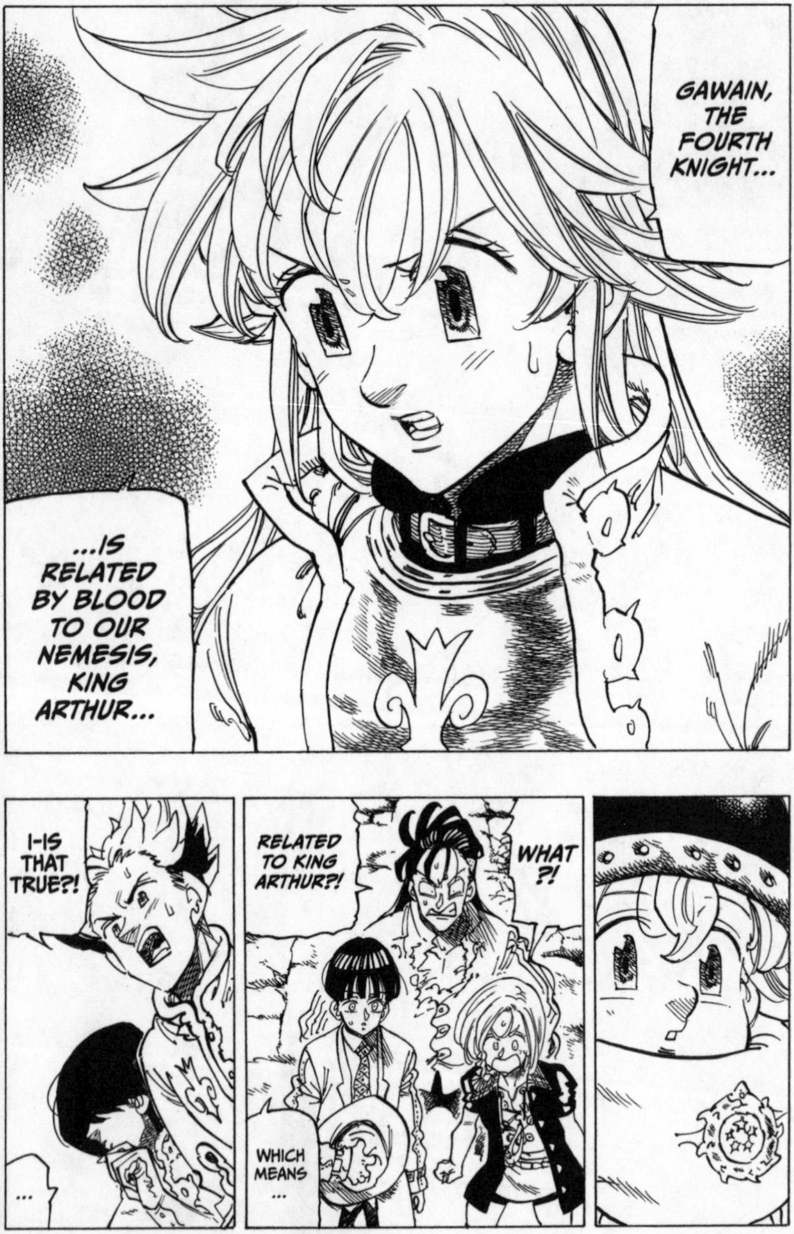
GAWAIN, THE FOURTH KNIGHT...
...IS RELATED BY BLOOD TO OUR NEMESIS, KING ARTHUR...
WHAT?!
RELATED TO KING ARTHUR?!
WHICH MEANS ...
I-IS THAT TRUE?!
...

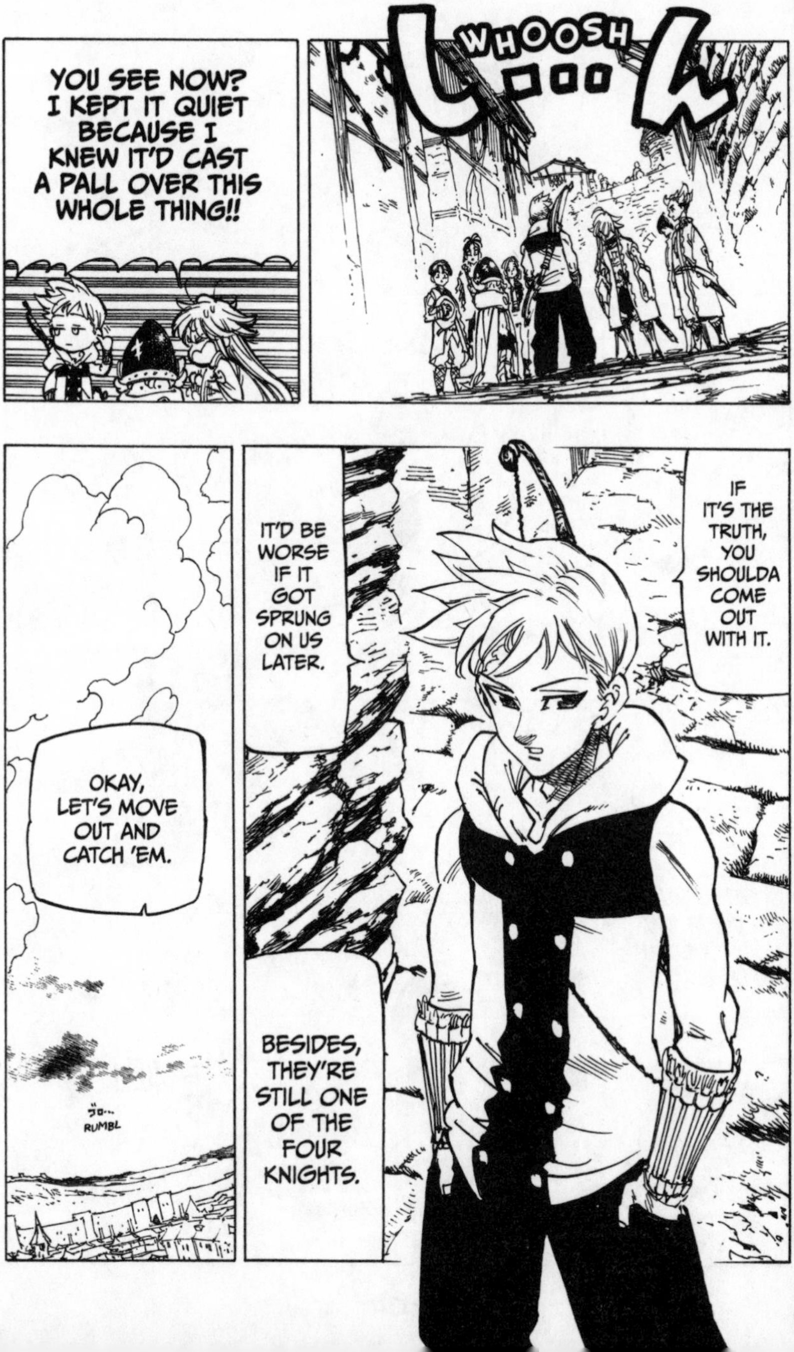
WHOOSH
YOU SEE NOW? I KEPT IT QUIET BECAUSE I KNEW IT'D CAST A PALL OVER THIS WHOLE THING!!
IF IT'S THE TRUTH, YOU SHOULDA COME OUT WITH IT.
IT'D BE WORSE IF IT GOT SPRUNG ON US LATER.
BESIDES, THEY'RE STILL ONE OF THE FOUR KNIGHTS.
OKAY, LET'S MOVE OUT AND CATCH 'EM.
RUMBL

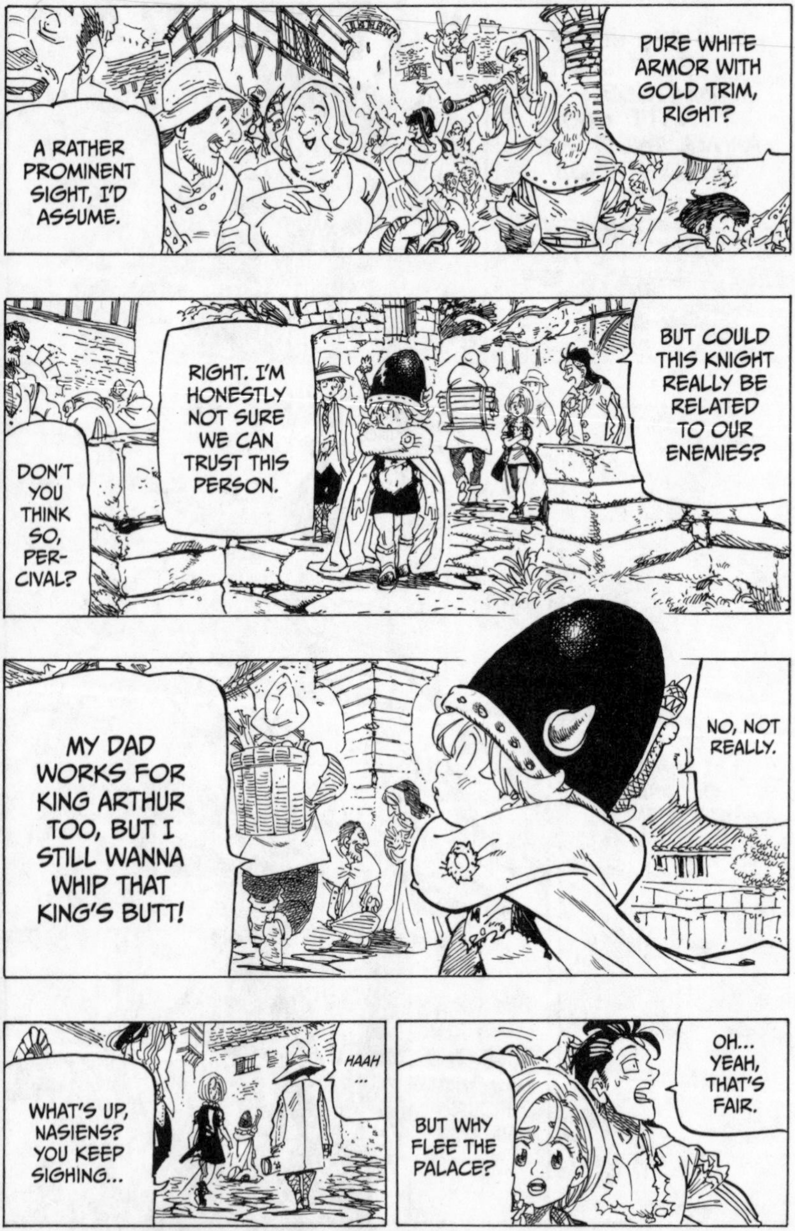
PURE WHITE ARMOR WITH GOLD TRIM, RIGHT?
A RATHER PROMINENT SIGHT, I'D ASSUME.
BUT COULD THIS KNIGHT REALLY BE RELATED TO OUR ENEMIES?
RIGHT. I'M HONESTLY NOT SURE WE CAN TRUST THIS PERSON.
DON'T YOU THINK SO, PER-CIVAL?
NO, NOT REALLY.
MY DAD WORKS FOR KING ARTHUR TOO, BUT I STILL WANNA WHIP THAT KING'S BUTT!
OH... YEAH, THAT'S FAIR.
BUT WHY FLEE THE PALACE?
HAAH ...
WHAT'S UP, NASIENS? YOU KEEP SIGHING...

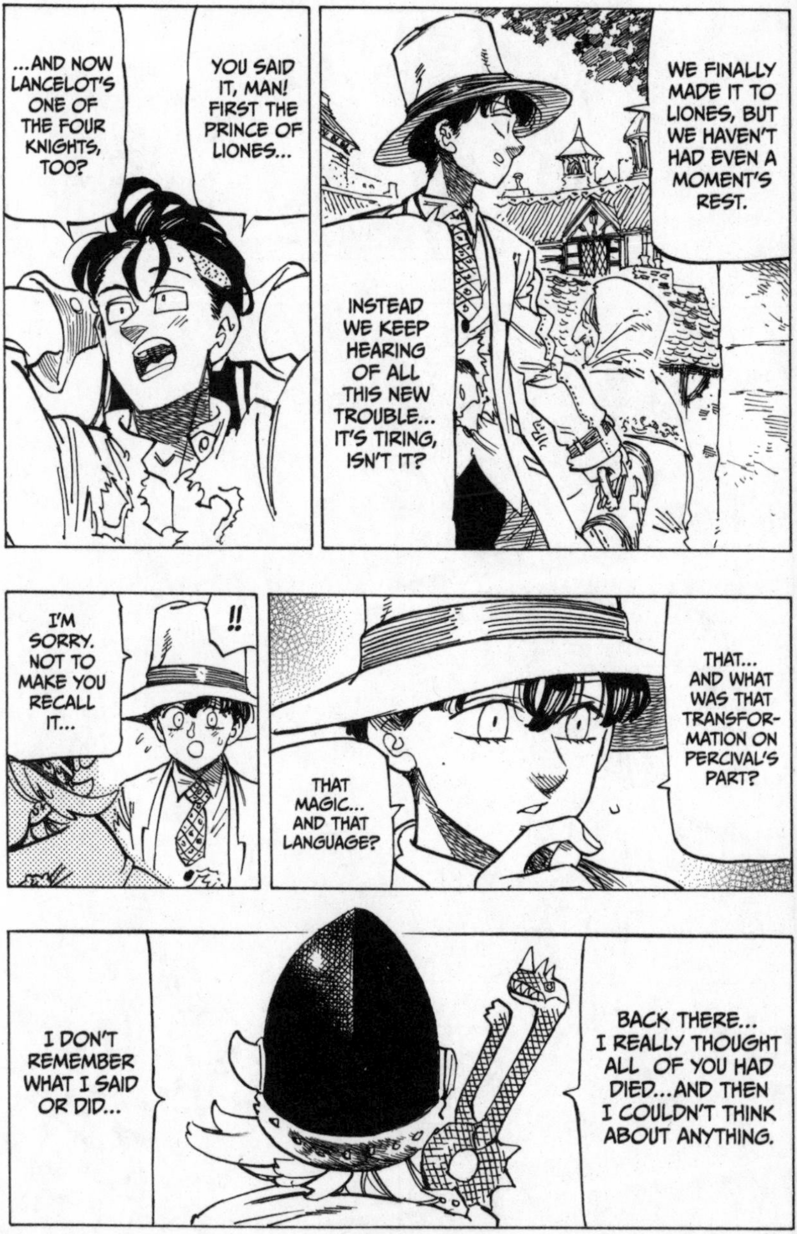

WE FINALLY MADE IT TO LIONES, BUT WE HAVEN'T HAD EVEN A MOMENT'S REST.
INSTEAD WE KEEP HEARING OF ALL THIS NEW TROUBLE... IT'S TIRING, ISN'T IT?
YOU SAID IT, MAN! FIRST THE PRINCE OF LIONES...
...AND NOW LANCELOT'S ONE OF THE FOUR KNIGHTS, TOO?
THAT... AND WHAT WAS THAT TRANSFORMATION ON PERCIVAL'S PART?
THAT MAGIC... AND THAT LANGUAGE?
!!
I'M SORRY. NOT TO MAKE YOU RECALL IT...
BACK THERE... I REALLY THOUGHT ALL OF YOU HAD DIED...AND THEN I COULDN'T THINK ABOUT ANYTHING.
I DON'T REMEMBER WHAT I SAID OR DID...

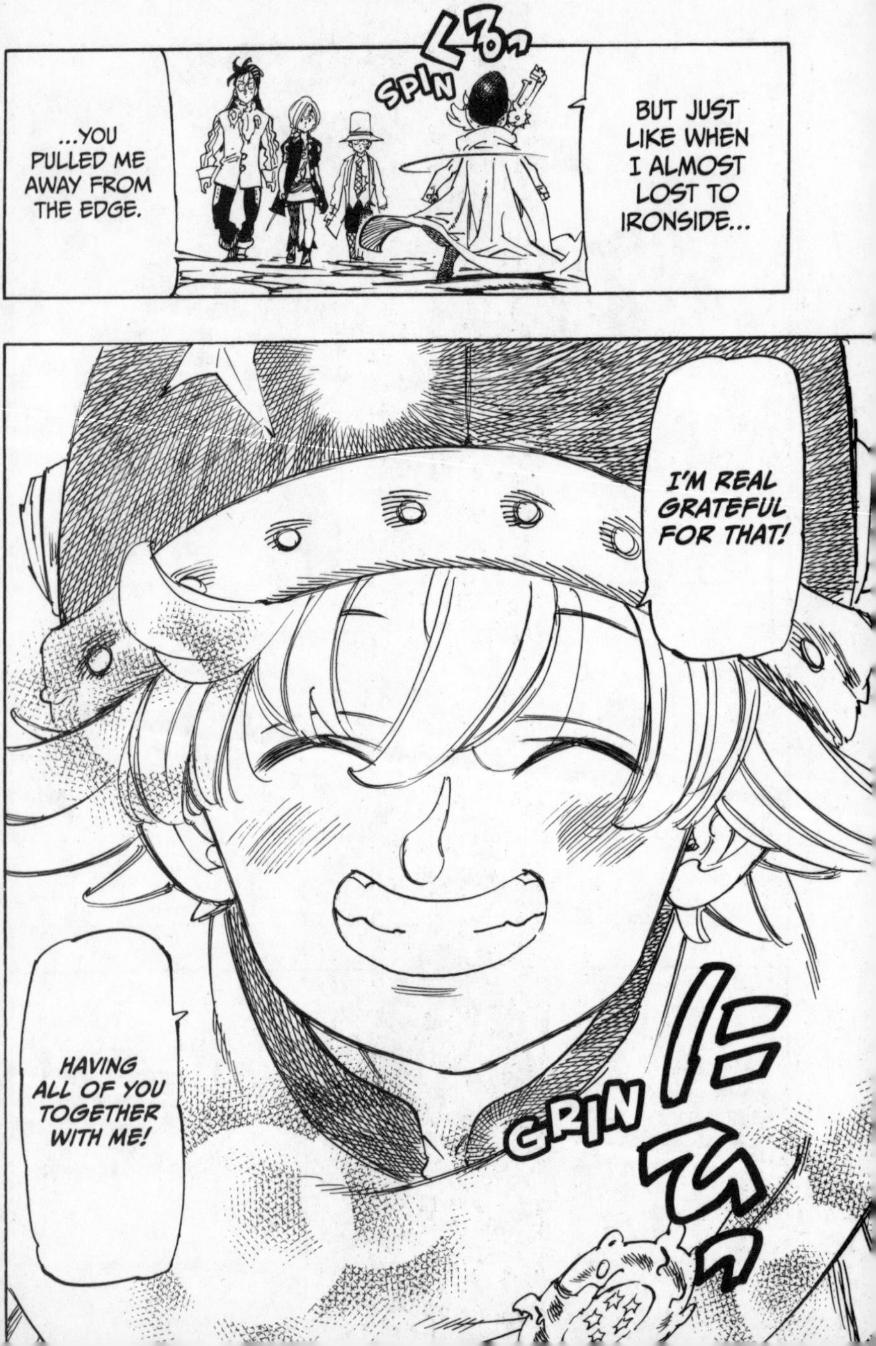
BUT JUST LIKE WHEN I ALMOST LOST TO IRONSIDE...
SPIN
...YOU PULLED ME AWAY FROM THE EDGE.
I'M REAL GRATEFUL FOR THAT!
GRIN
HAVING ALL OF YOU TOGETHER WITH ME!

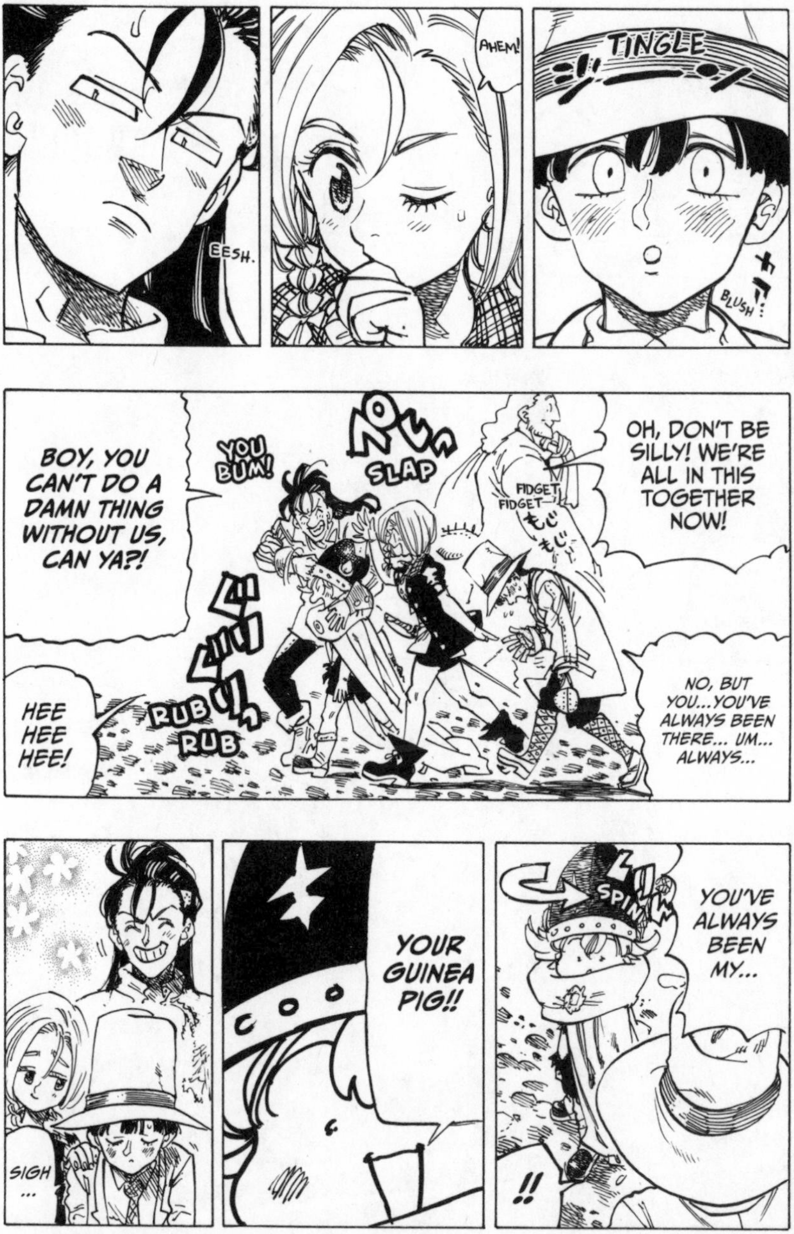
TINGLE
BLUSH
AHEM!
EESH.
OH, DON'T BE SILLY! WE'RE ALL IN THIS TOGETHER NOW!
FIDGET FIDGET
もじもじ
SLAP
YOU BUM!
BOY, YOU CAN'T DO A DAMN THING WITHOUT US, CAN YA?!
NO, BUT YOU...YOU'VE ALWAYS BEEN THERE... UM... ALWAYS...
RUB RUB
HEE HEE HEE!
YOU'VE ALWAYS BEEN MY...
SPIN
!!
YOUR GUINEA PIG!!
SIGH ...

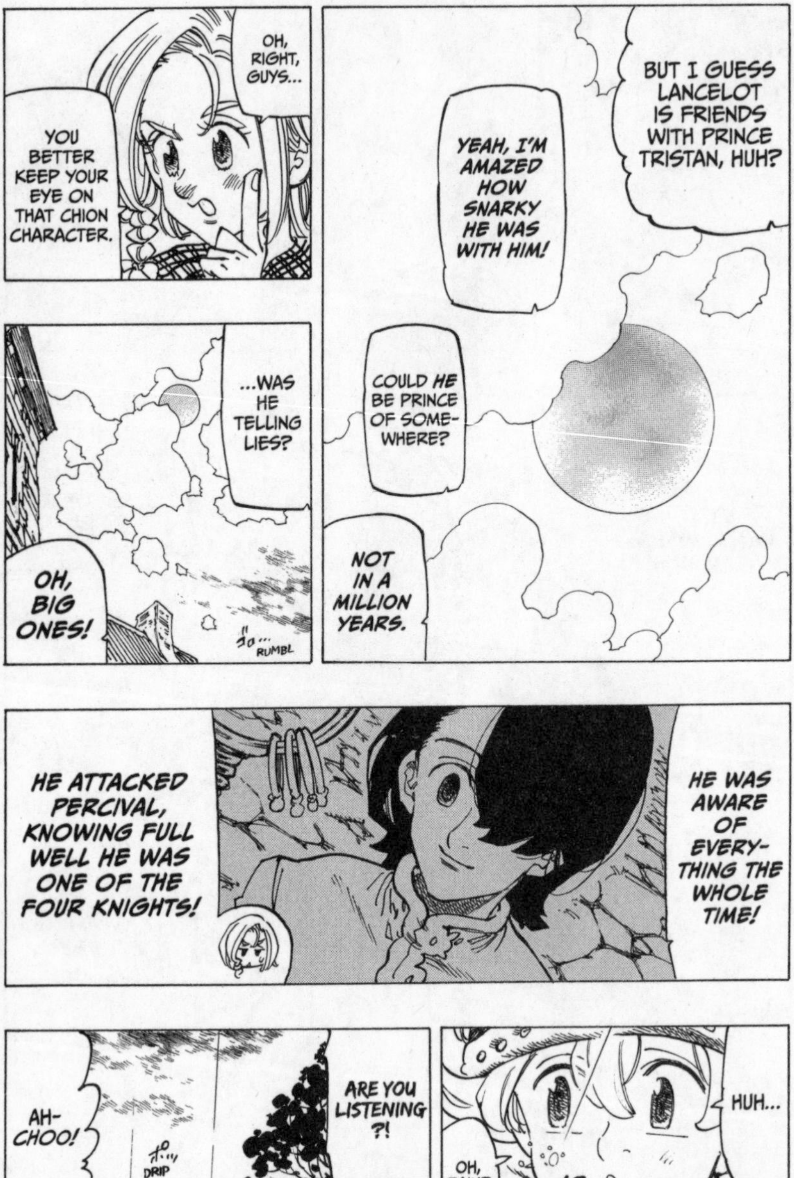

BUT I GUESS LANCELOT IS FRIENDS WITH PRINCE TRISTAN, HUH?
YEAH, I'M AMAZED HOW SNARKY HE WAS WITH HIM!
COULD HE BE PRINCE OF SOME-WHERE?
NOT IN A MILLION YEARS.
OH, RIGHT, GUYS...
YOU BETTER KEEP YOUR EYE ON THAT CHION CHARACTER.
...WAS HE TELLING LIES?
OH, BIG ONES!
ゴロ... RUMBL
HE WAS AWARE OF EVERYTHING THE WHOLE TIME!
HE ATTACKED PERCIVAL, KNOWING FULL WELL HE WAS ONE OF THE FOUR KNIGHTS!
HUH...
OH, RAIN?
ポッ PLINK
ARE YOU LISTENING?!
ポッ DRIP
AH-CHOO!

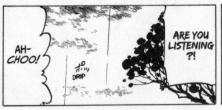

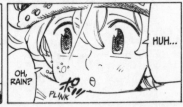

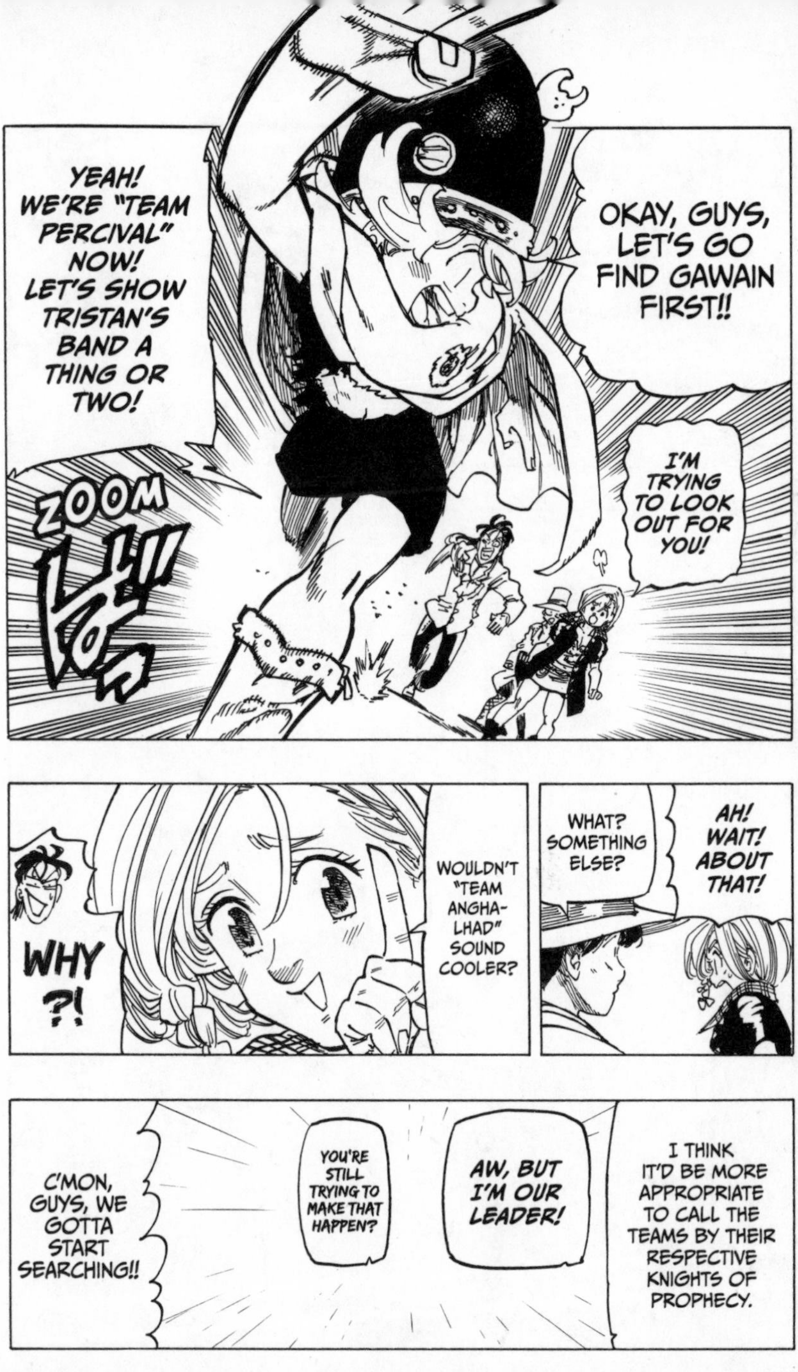
OKAY, GUYS, LET'S GO FIND GAWAIN FIRST!!
YEAH! WE'RE "TEAM PERCIVAL" NOW! LET'S SHOW TRISTAN'S BAND A THING OR TWO!
I'M TRYING TO LOOK OUT FOR YOU!
ZOOM
AH! WAIT! ABOUT THAT!
WHAT? SOMETHING ELSE?
WOULDN'T "TEAM ANGHA-LHAD" SOUND COOLER?
WHY ?!
I THINK IT'D BE MORE APPROPRIATE TO CALL THE TEAMS BY THEIR RESPECTIVE KNIGHTS OF PROPHECY.
AW, BUT I'M OUR LEADER!
YOU'RE STILL TRYING TO MAKE THAT HAPPEN?
C'MON, GUYS, WE GOTTA START SEARCHING!!

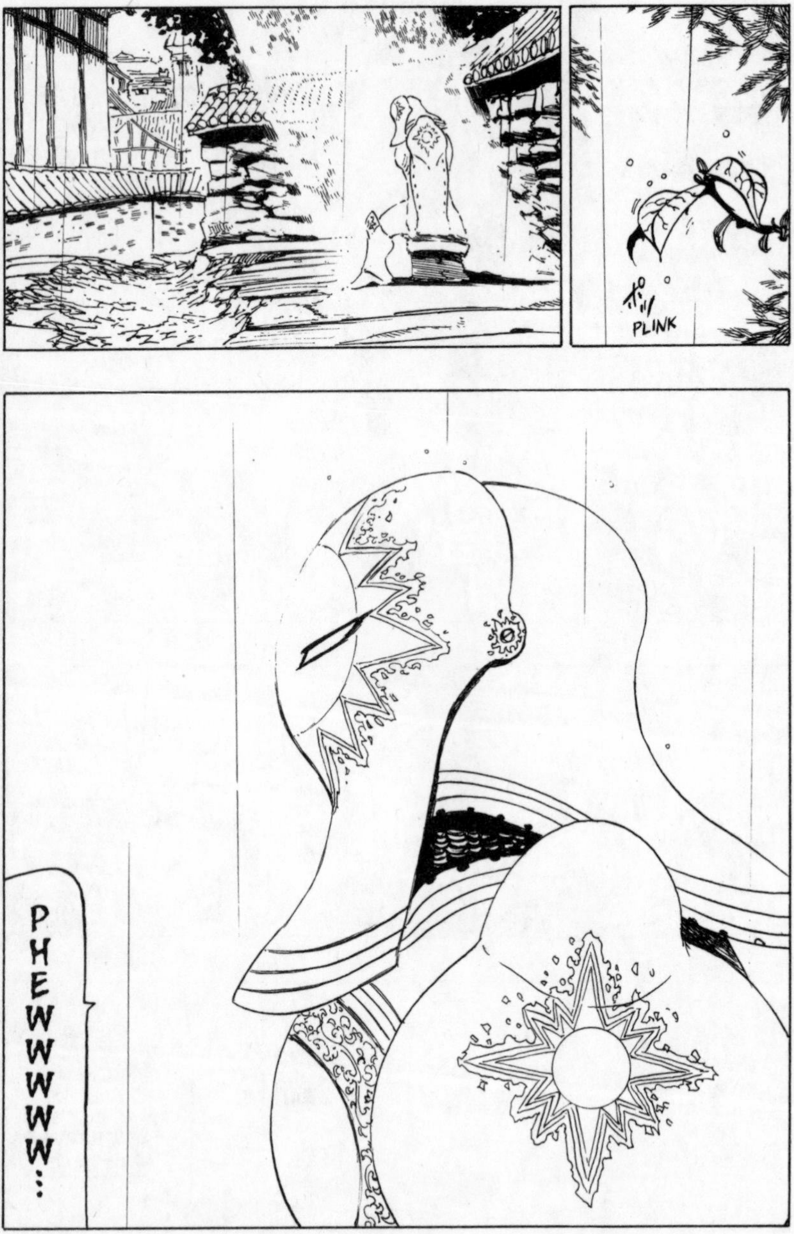
PLINK
PHEWWWWW..

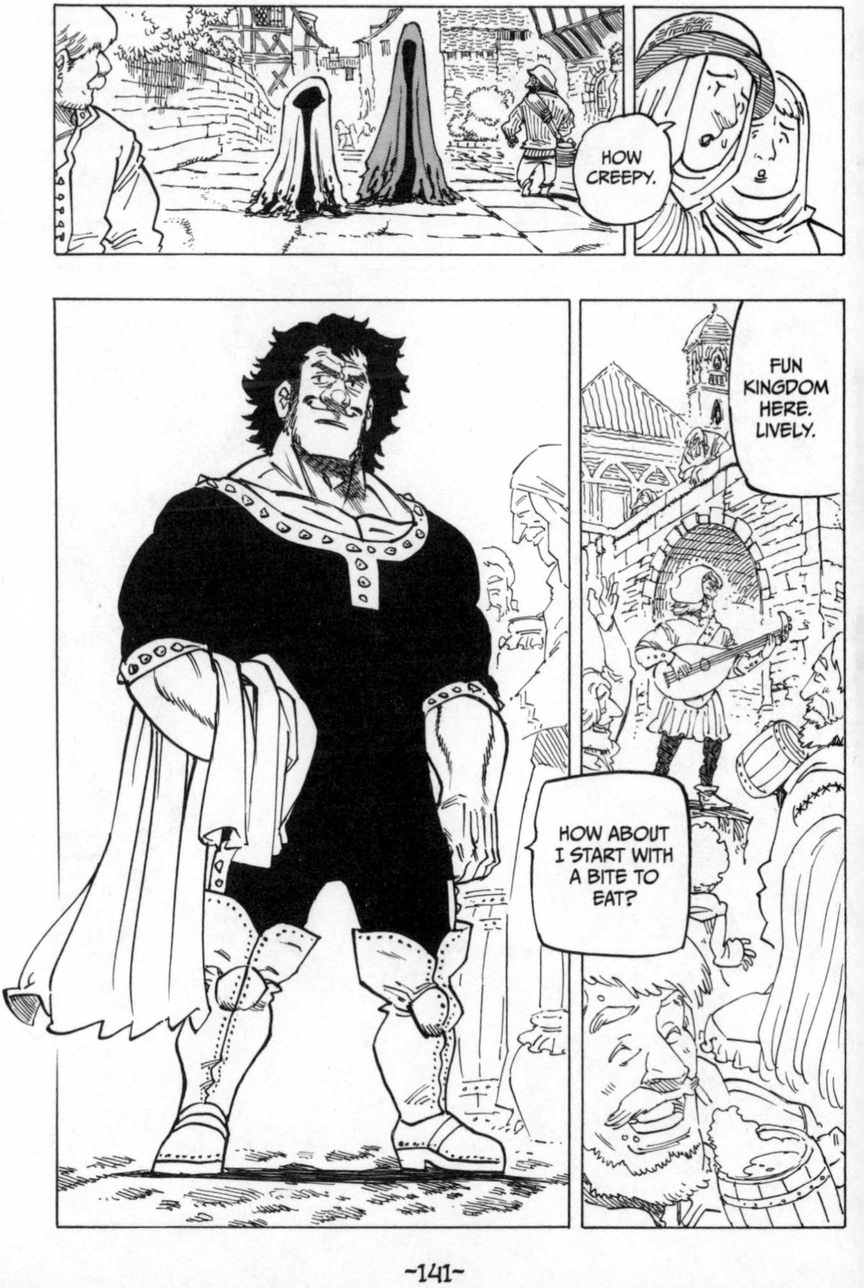
HOW CREEPY.
FUN KINGDOM HERE. LIVELY.
HOW ABOUT I START WITH A BITE TO EAT?

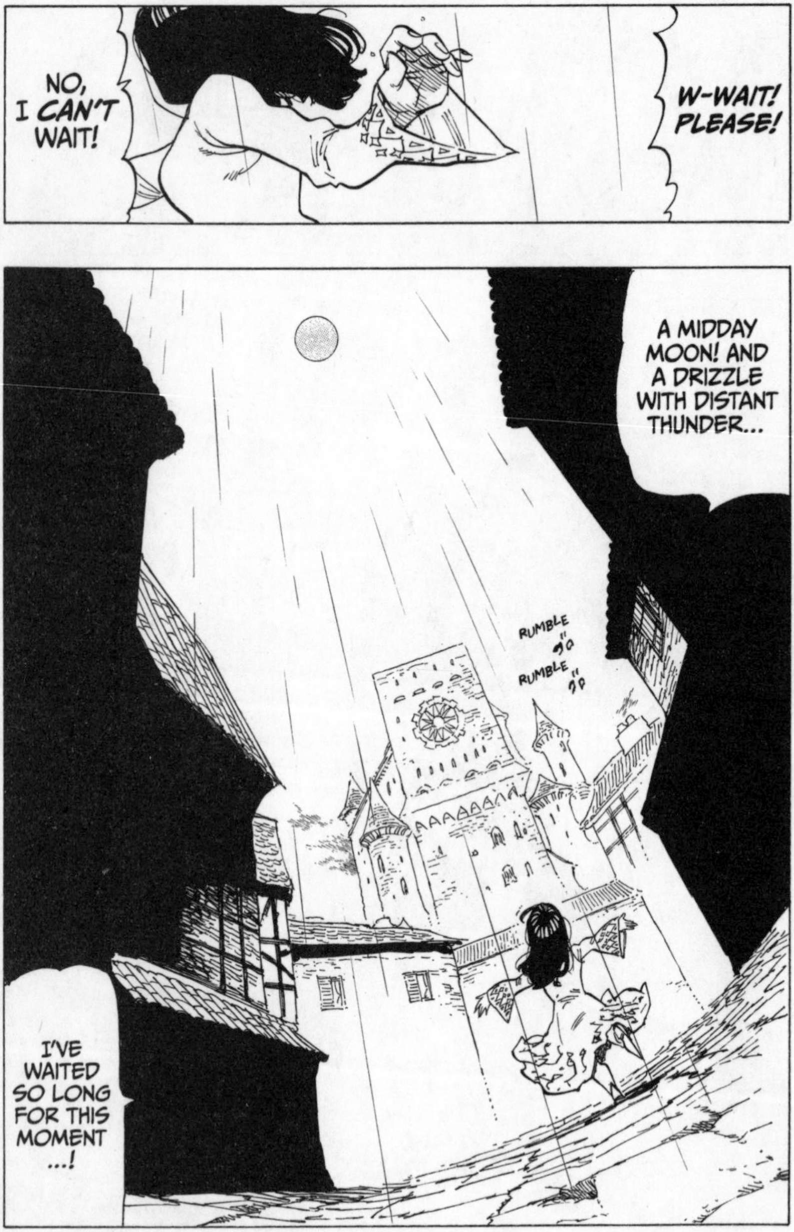
W-WAIT! PLEASE!
NO, I CAN'T WAIT!
A MIDDAY MOON! AND A DRIZZLE WITH DISTANT THUNDER...
RUMBLE
RUMBLE
I'VE WAITED SO LONG FOR THIS MOMENT ...!

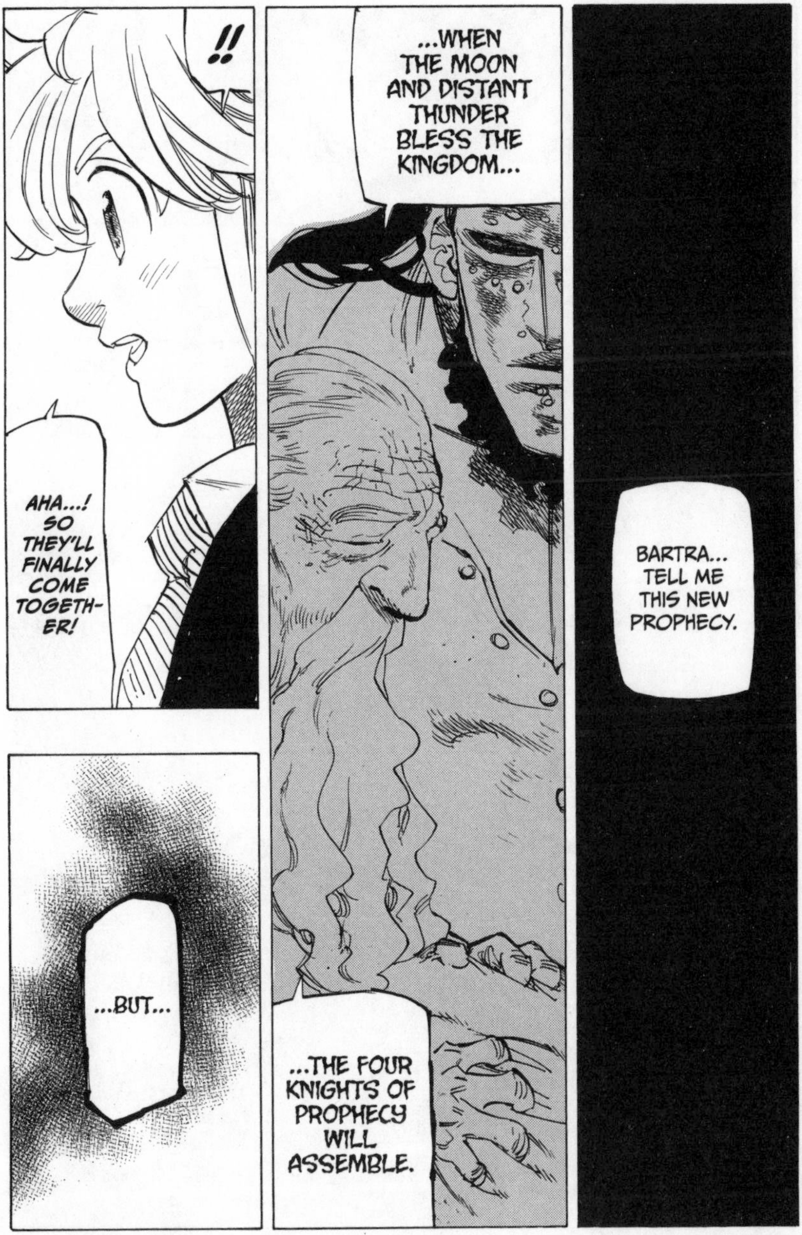
BARTRA... TELL ME THIS NEW PROPHECY.
...WHEN THE MOON AND DISTANT THUNDER BLESS THE KINGDOM...
...THE FOUR KNIGHTS OF PROPHECY WILL ASSEMBLE.
!!
AHA...! SO THEY'LL FINALLY COME TOGETH-ER!
...BUT...

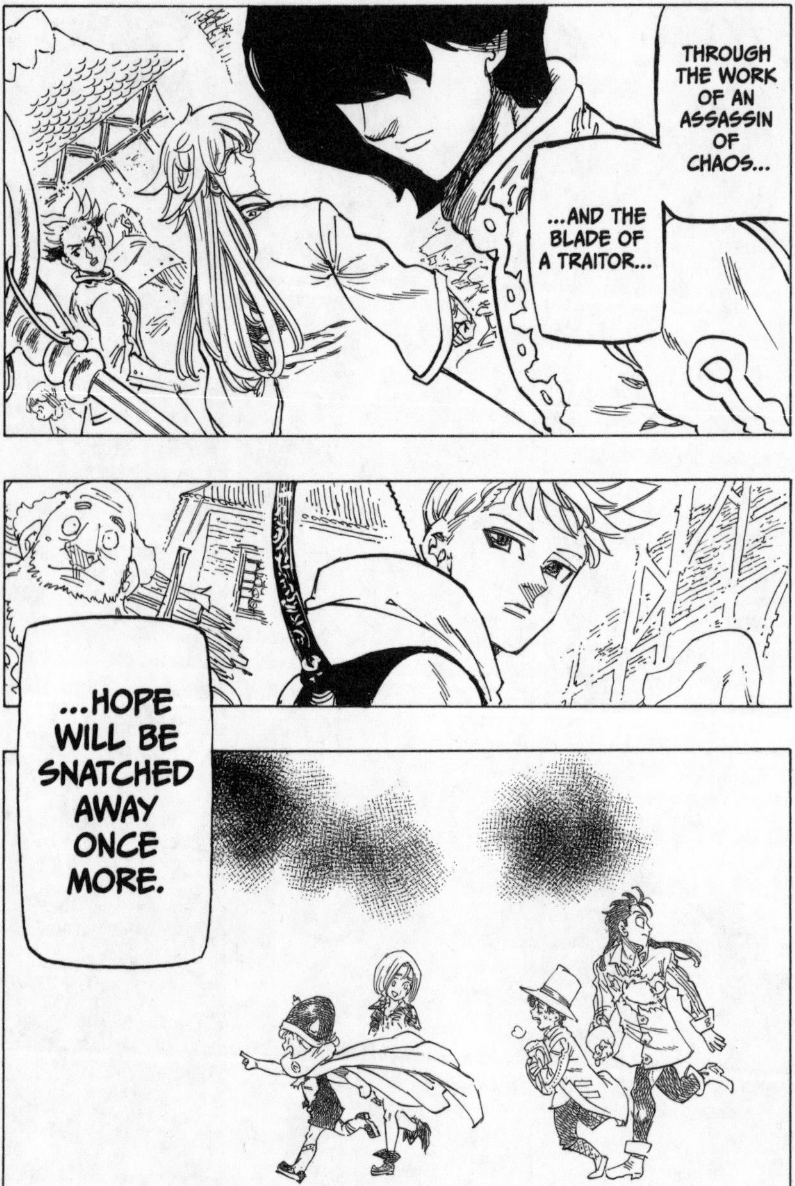
THROUGH THE WORK OF AN ASSASSIN OF CHAOS...
...AND THE BLADE OF A TRAITOR...
...HOPE WILL BE SNATCHED AWAY ONCE MORE.

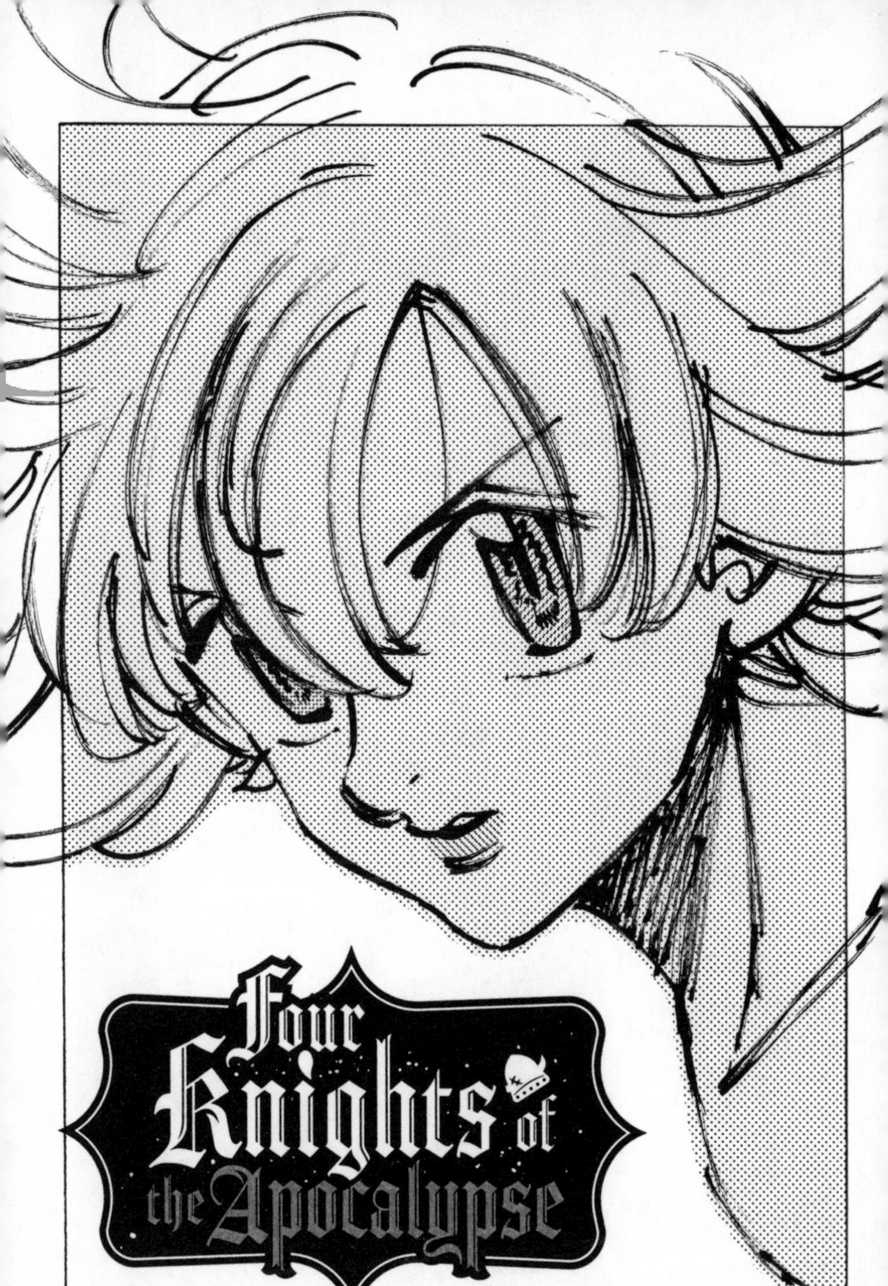
Four Knights of the Apocalypse

CHAPTER 58: CREEPING OMENS

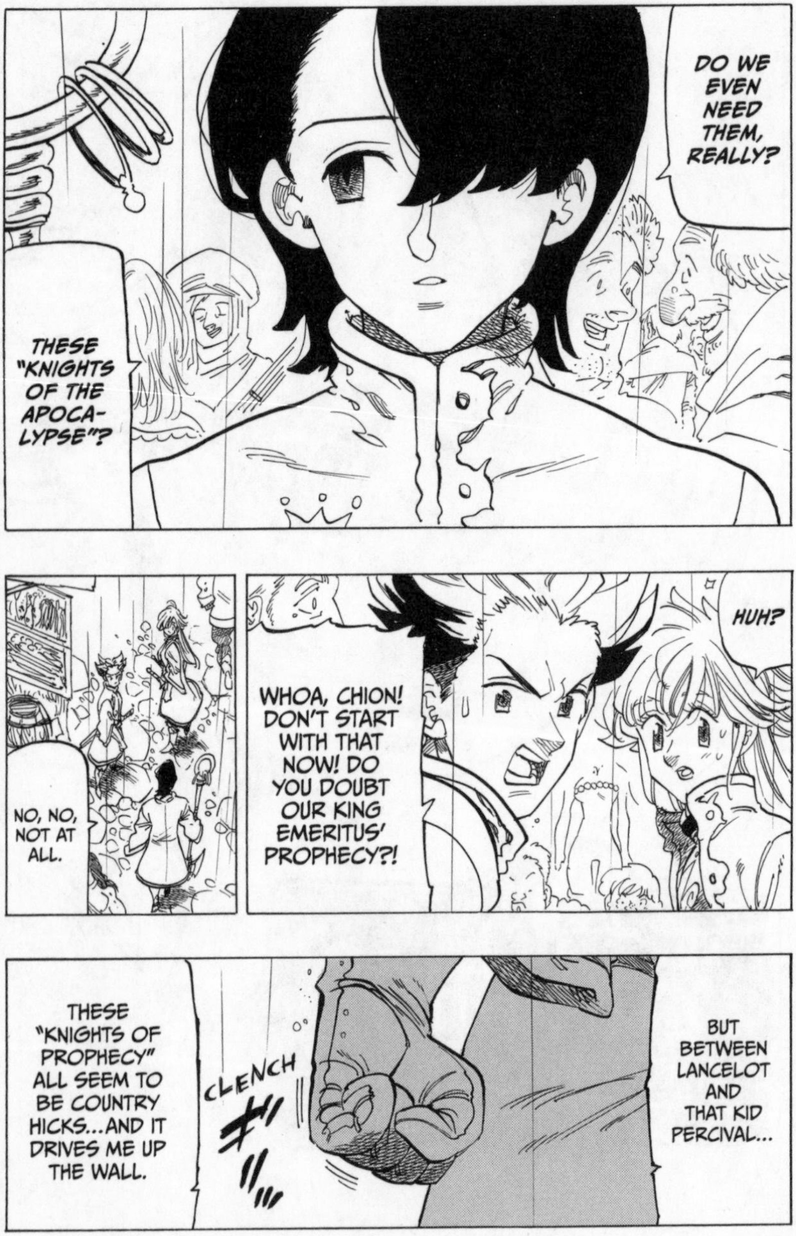
DO WE EVEN NEED THEM, REALLY?
THESE "KNIGHTS OF THE APOCA-LYPSE"?
HUH?
WHOA, CHION! DON'T START WITH THAT NOW! DO YOU DOUBT OUR KING EMERITUS' PROPHECY?!
NO, NO, NOT AT ALL.
BUT BETWEEN LANCELOT AND THAT KID PERCIVAL...
CLENCH
THESE "KNIGHTS OF PROPHECY" ALL SEEM TO BE COUNTRY HICKS...AND IT DRIVES ME UP THE WALL.

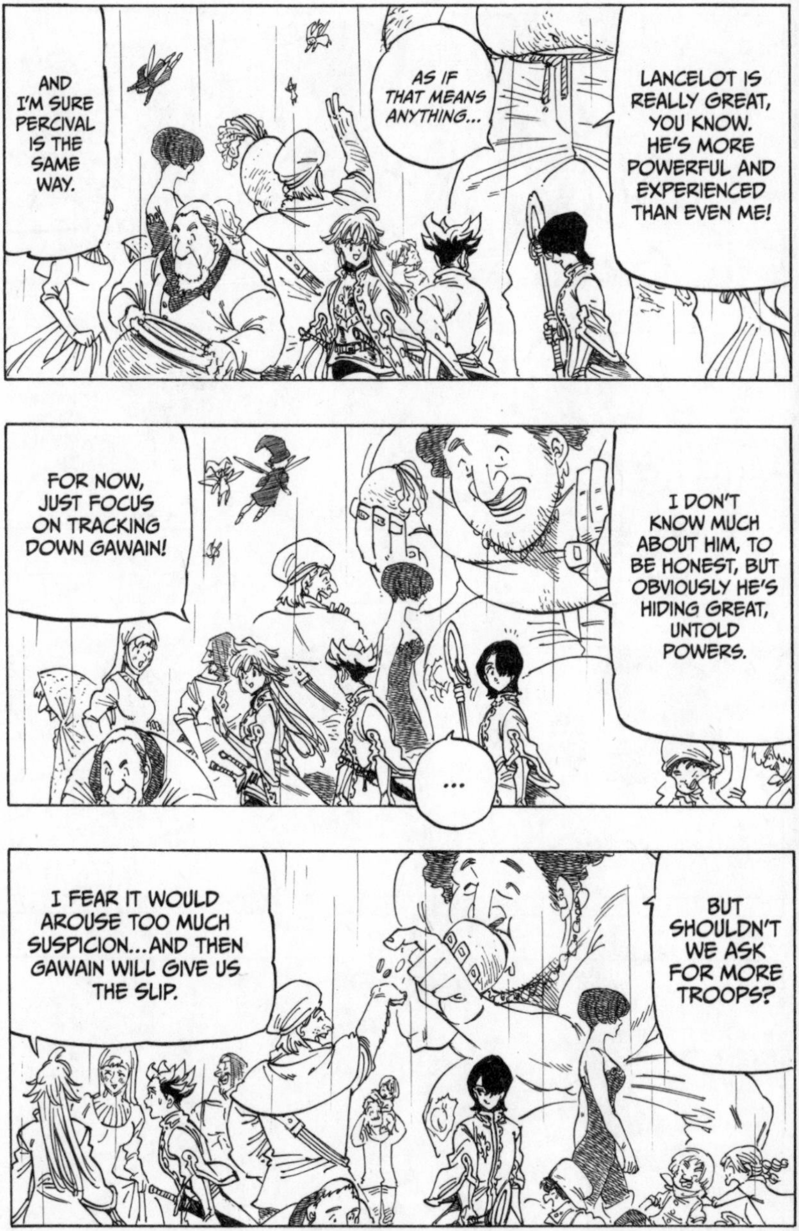
LANCELOT IS REALLY GREAT, YOU KNOW. HE'S MORE POWERFUL AND EXPERIENCED THAN EVEN ME!
AS IF THAT MEANS ANYTHING...
AND I'M SURE PERCIVAL IS THE SAME WAY.
I DON'T KNOW MUCH ABOUT HIM, TO BE HONEST, BUT OBVIOUSLY HE'S HIDING GREAT, UNTOLD POWERS.
...
FOR NOW, JUST FOCUS ON TRACKING DOWN GAWAIN!
BUT SHOULDN'T WE ASK FOR MORE TROOPS?
I FEAR IT WOULD AROUSE TOO MUCH SUSPICION...AND THEN GAWAIN WILL GIVE US THE SLIP.

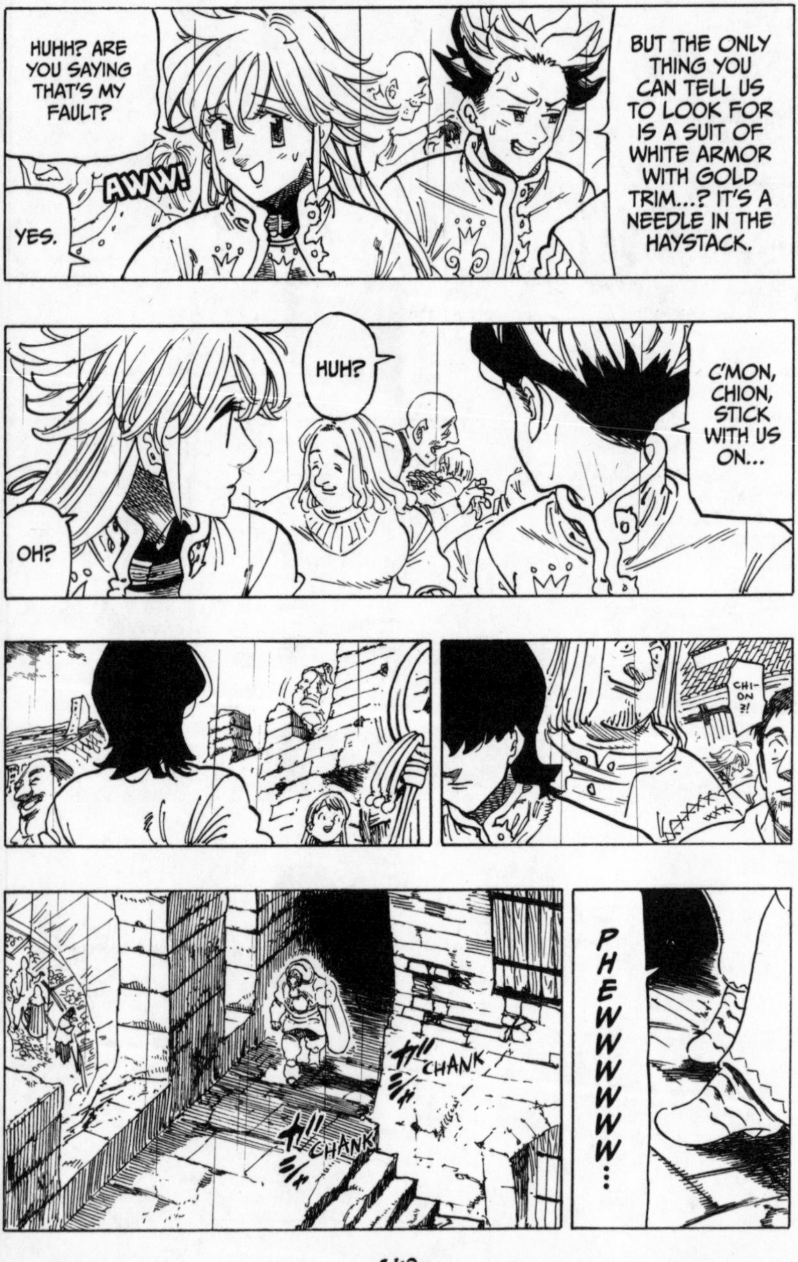
BUT THE ONLY THING YOU CAN TELL US TO LOOK FOR IS A SUIT OF WHITE ARMOR WITH GOLD TRIM...? IT'S A NEEDLE IN THE HAYSTACK.
HUHH? ARE YOU SAYING THAT'S MY FAULT?
AWW!
YES.
C'MON, CHION, STICK WITH US ON...
HUH?
OH?
CHION?!
PHEWWWWWWW...
CHANK
CHANK

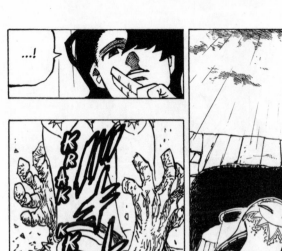

...!

KRAK

!!

GRAB

ONE MUST ALWAYS ASSUME THE WORST-CASE SCENARIO...

...AND YOUR "WORST CASE" IS HAPPENING RIGHT NOW.

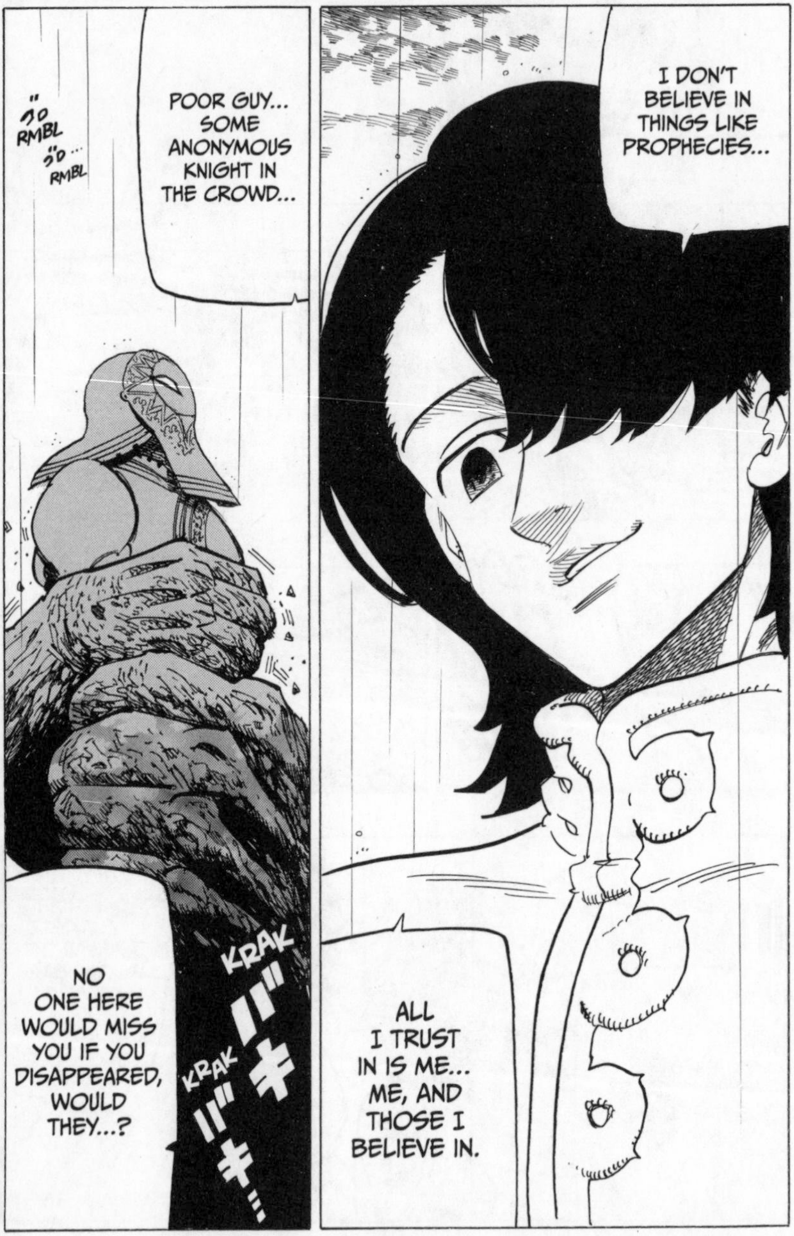
I DON'T BELIEVE IN THINGS LIKE PROPHECIES...
ALL I TRUST IN IS ME... ME, AND THOSE I BELIEVE IN.
POOR GUY... SOME ANONYMOUS KNIGHT IN THE CROWD...
RMBL RMBL
KRAK KRAK
NO ONE HERE WOULD MISS YOU IF YOU DISAPPEARED, WOULD THEY...?

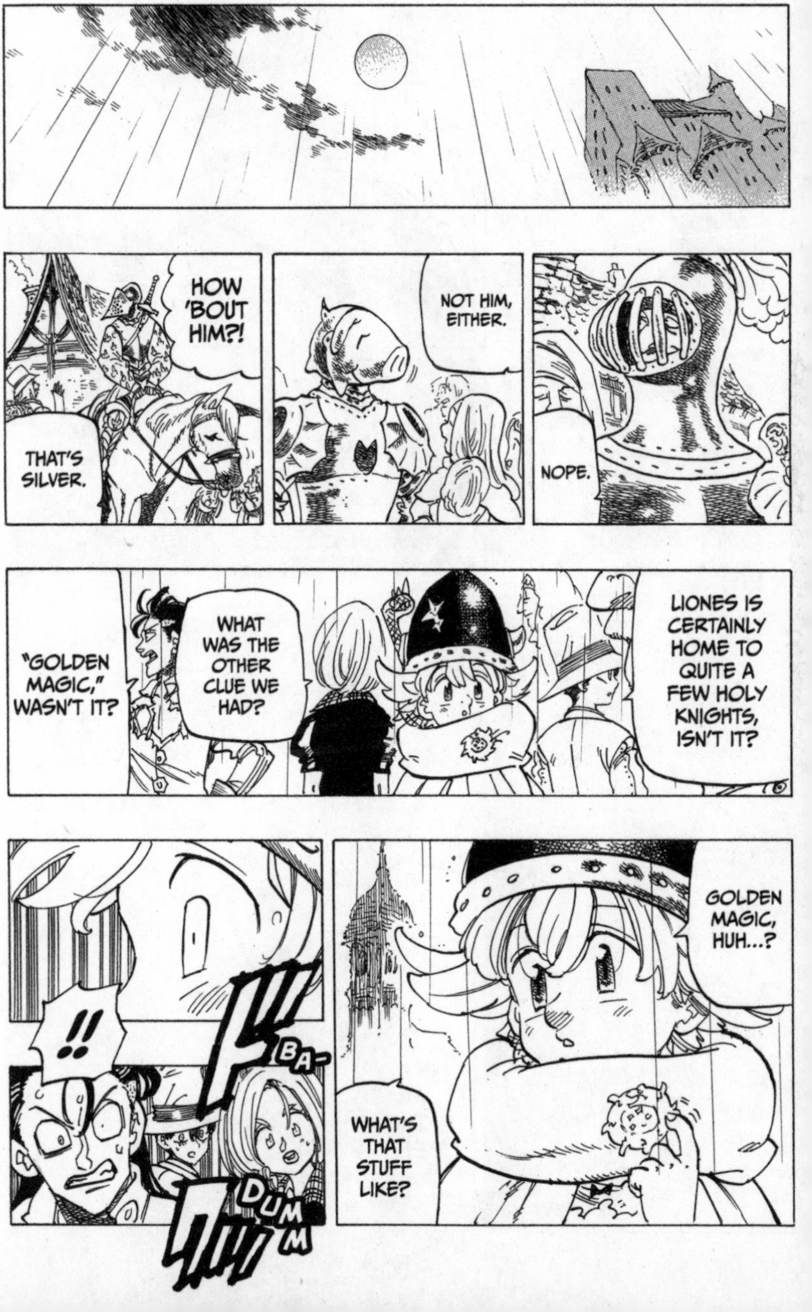
NOPE.
NOT HIM, EITHER.
HOW 'BOUT HIM?!
THAT'S SILVER.
LIONES IS CERTAINLY HOME TO QUITE A FEW HOLY KNIGHTS, ISN'T IT?
WHAT WAS THE OTHER CLUE WE HAD?
"GOLDEN MAGIC," WASN'T IT?
GOLDEN MAGIC, HUH...?
WHAT'S THAT STUFF LIKE?
!!
BA-
DUMM

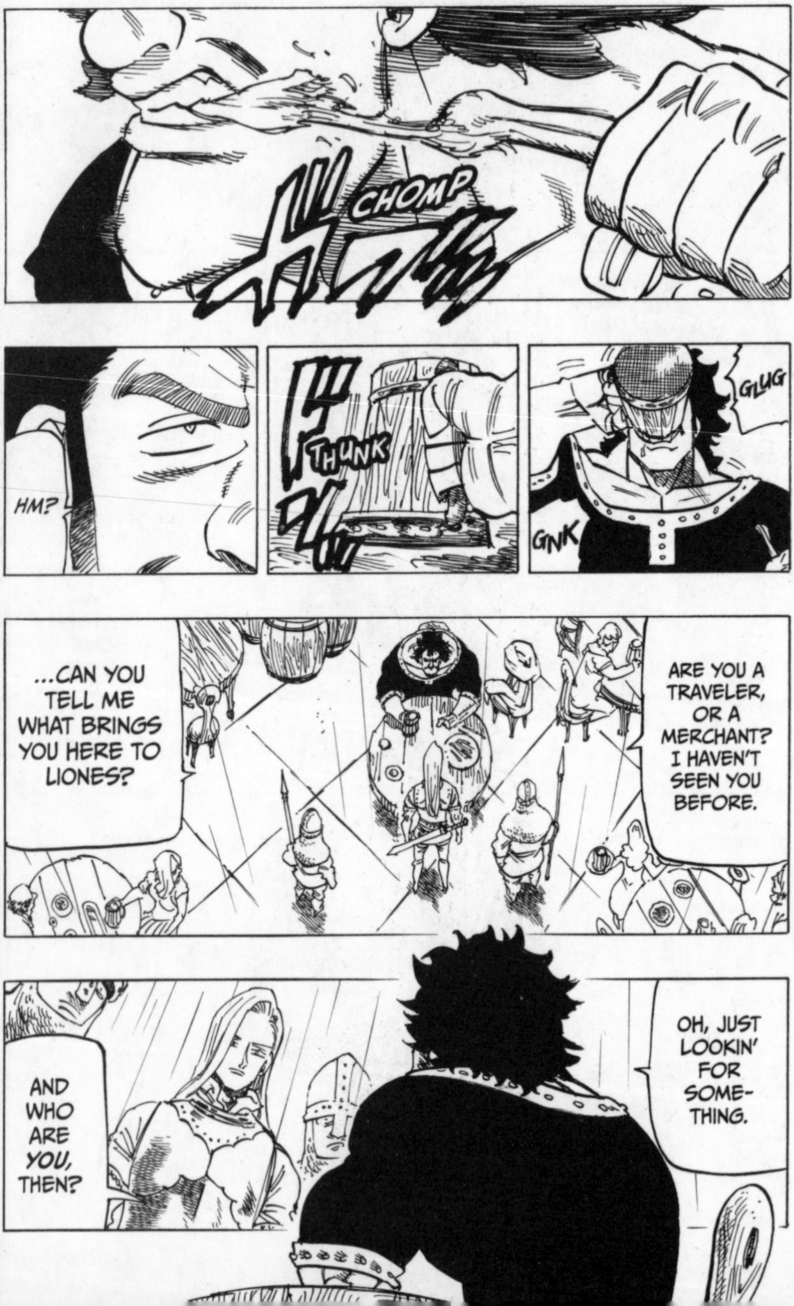
CHOMP
GLUG
GNK
THUNK
HM?
ARE YOU A TRAVELER, OR A MERCHANT? I HAVEN'T SEEN YOU BEFORE.
...CAN YOU TELL ME WHAT BRINGS YOU HERE TO LIONES?
OH, JUST LOOKIN' FOR SOME-THING.
AND WHO ARE *YOU*, THEN?

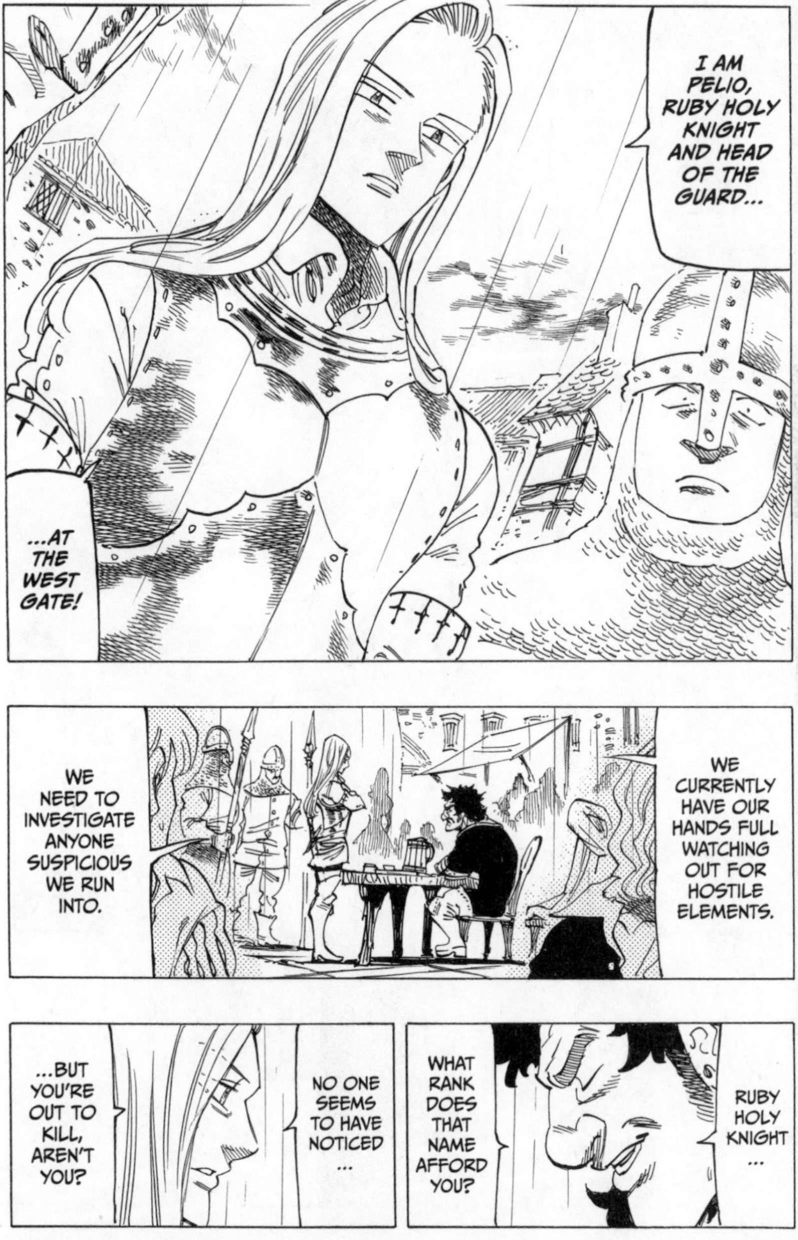
I AM PELIO, RUBY HOLY KNIGHT AND HEAD OF THE GUARD...
...AT THE WEST GATE!
WE CURRENTLY HAVE OUR HANDS FULL WATCHING OUT FOR HOSTILE ELEMENTS.
WE NEED TO INVESTIGATE ANYONE SUSPICIOUS WE RUN INTO.
RUBY HOLY KNIGHT ...
WHAT RANK DOES THAT NAME AFFORD YOU?
NO ONE SEEMS TO HAVE NOTICED ...
...BUT YOU'RE OUT TO KILL, AREN'T YOU?

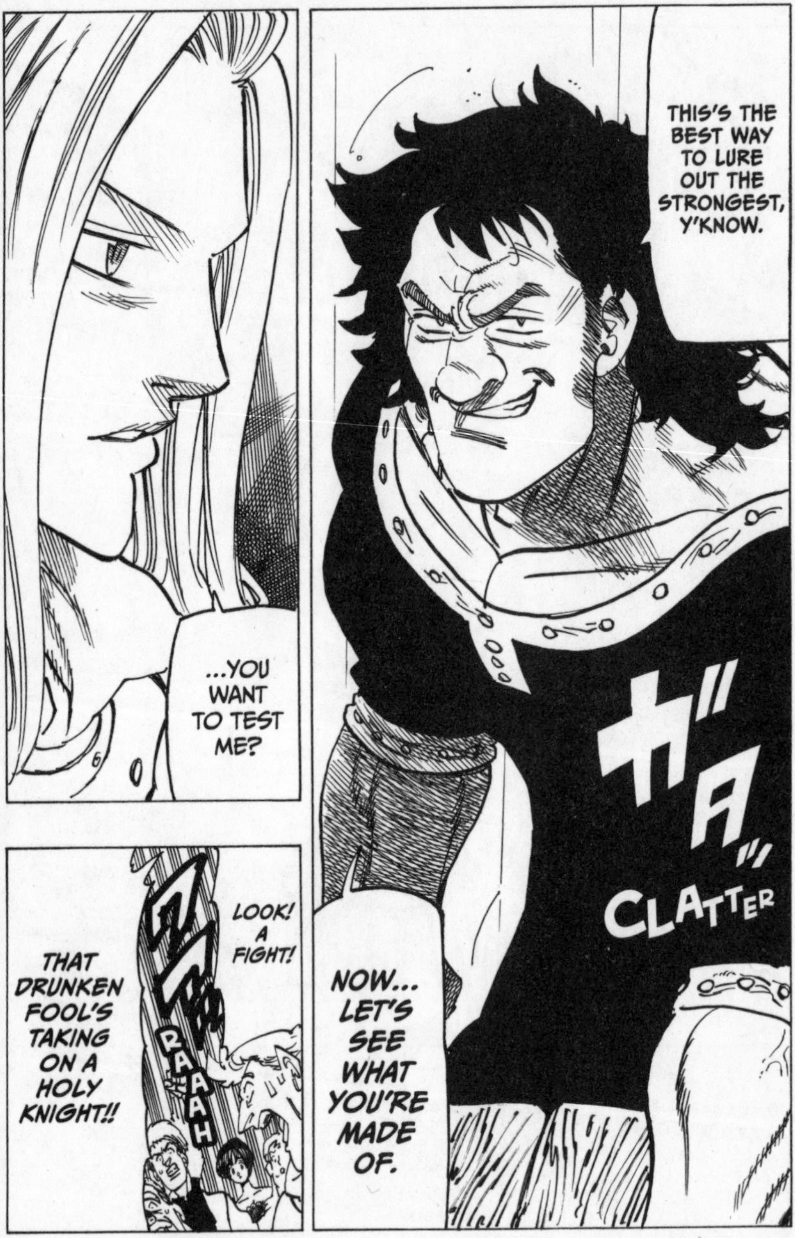

THIS'S THE BEST WAY TO LURE OUT THE STRONGEST, Y'KNOW.
CLATTER
NOW... LET'S SEE WHAT YOU'RE MADE OF.
...YOU WANT TO TEST ME?
LOOK! A FIGHT!
THAT DRUNKEN FOOL'S TAKING ON A HOLY KNIGHT!!
RAAAAH

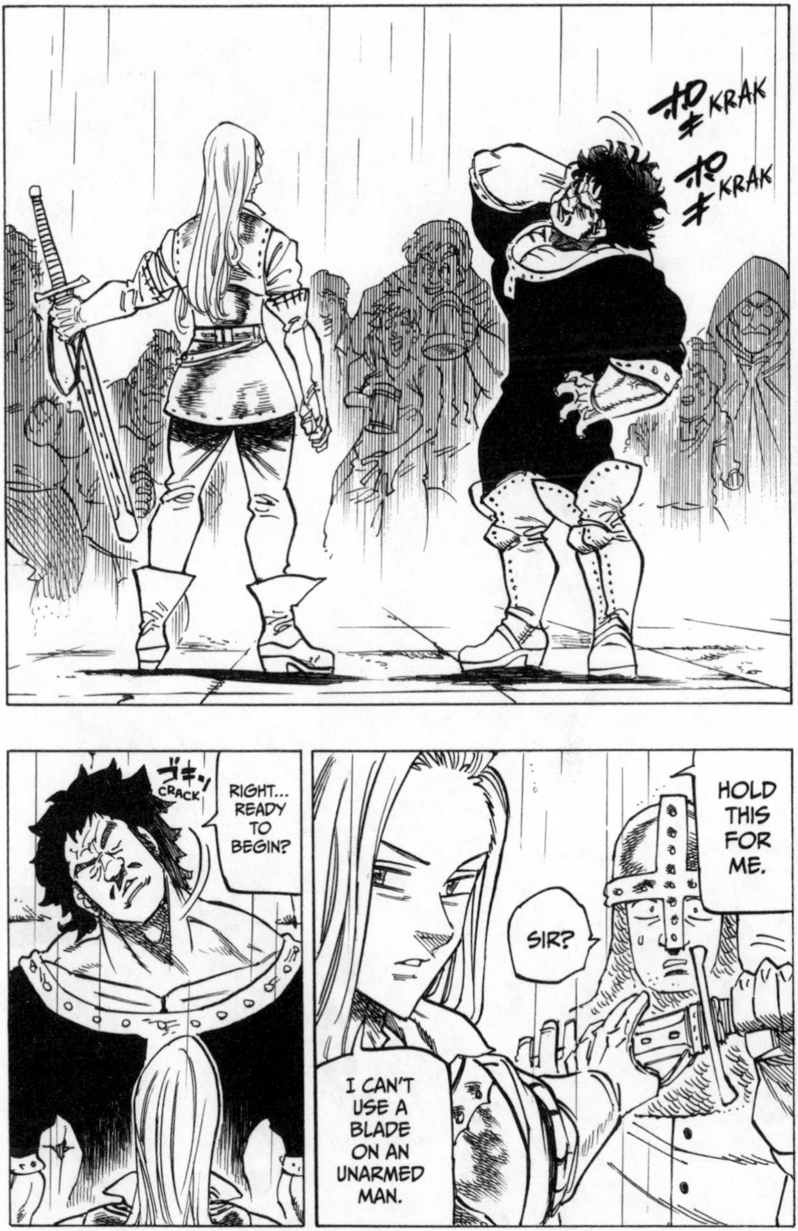
KRAK
KRAK
HOLD THIS FOR ME.
SIR?
I CAN'T USE A BLADE ON AN UNARMED MAN.
ゴキッ
CRACK
RIGHT... READY TO BEGIN?

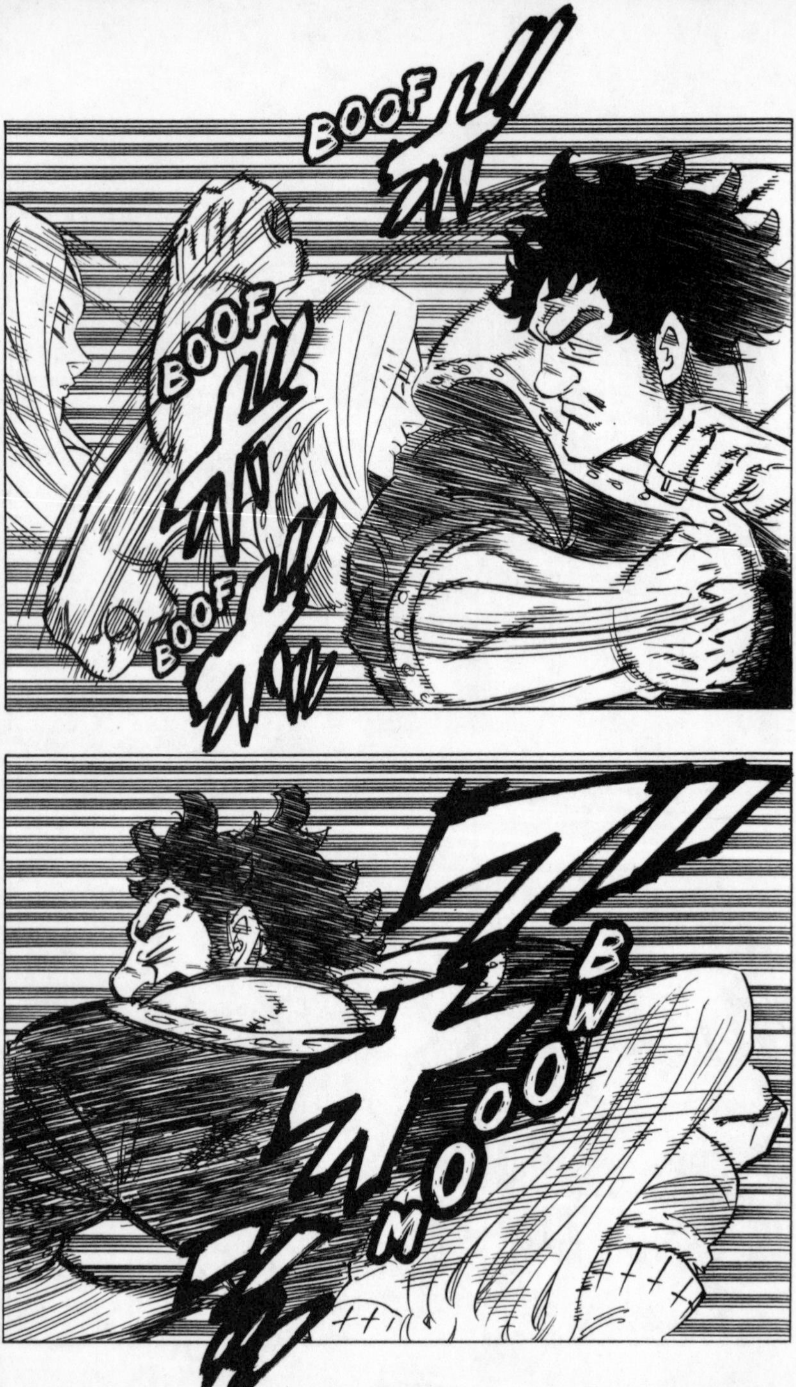
BOOF
BOOF
BOOF
BWOOOOM

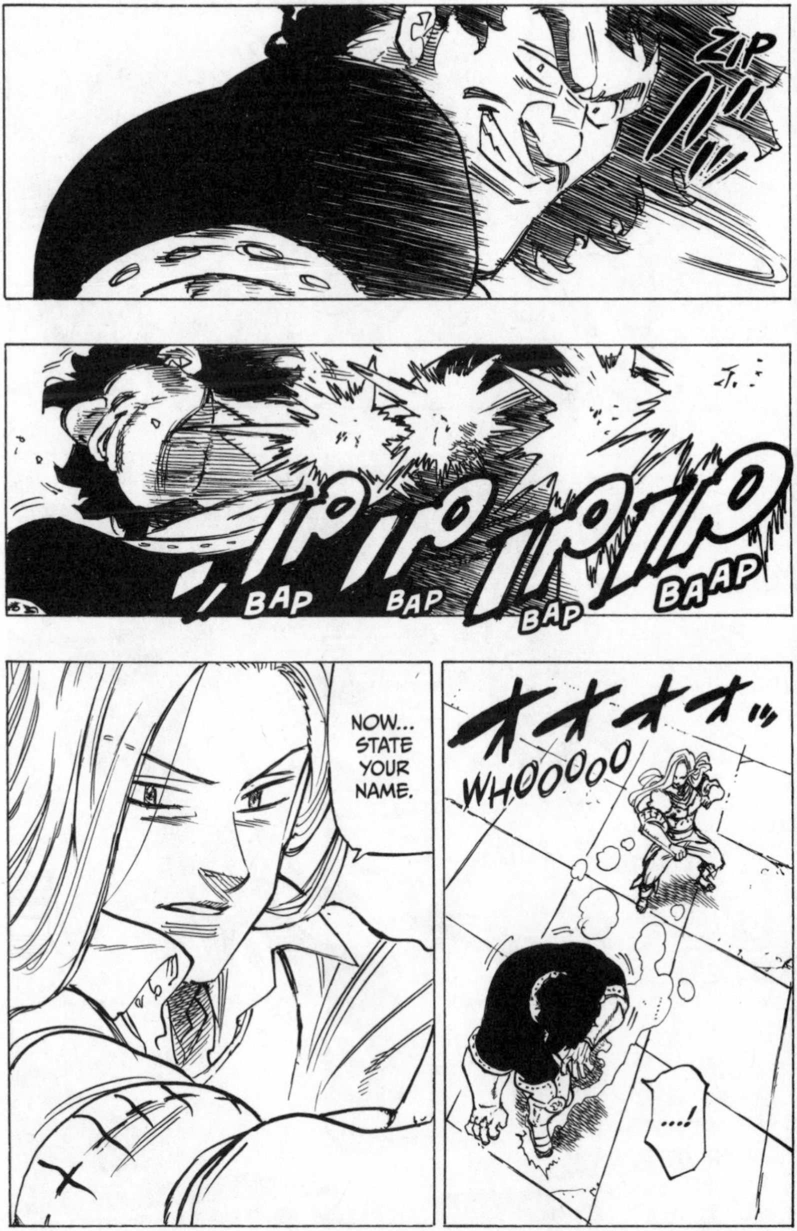
ZIP
BAP BAP BAP BAAP
オオオオオッ
WHOOOOO
...!
NOW... STATE YOUR NAME.

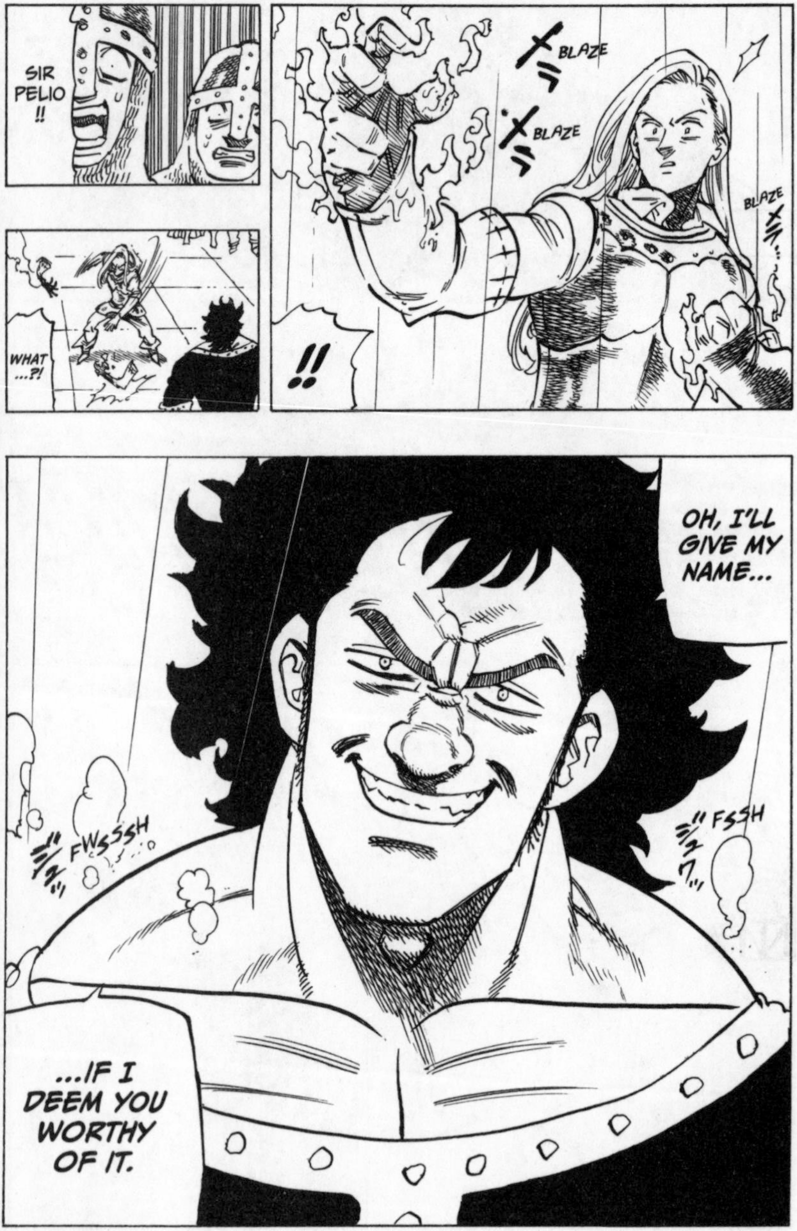

BLAZE
BLAZE
BLAZE
!!
SIR PELIO !!
WHAT ...?!
OH, I'LL GIVE MY NAME...
FSSH
FWSSSH
...IF I DEEM YOU WORTHY OF IT.

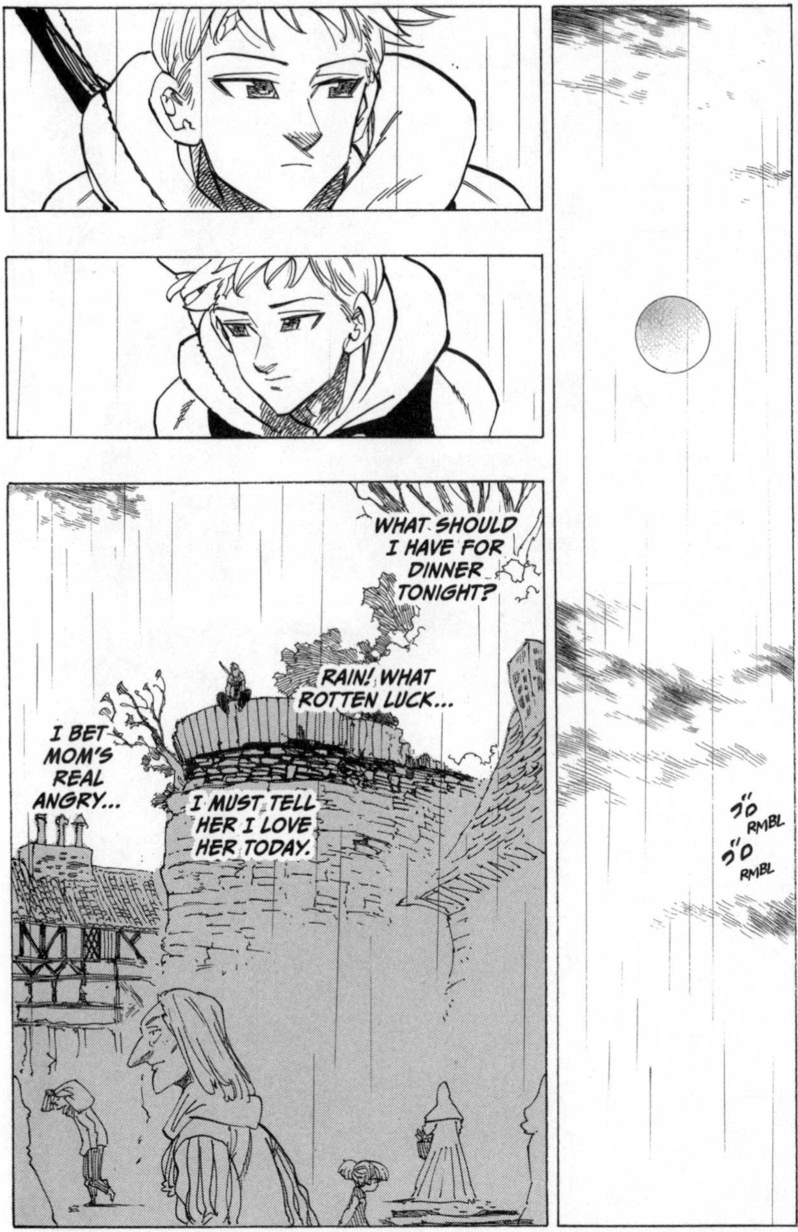
ゴロ
RMBL
ゴロ
RMBL
WHAT SHOULD I HAVE FOR DINNER TONIGHT?
RAIN! WHAT ROTTEN LUCK...
I MUST TELL HER I LOVE HER TODAY.
I BET MOM'S REAL ANGRY...

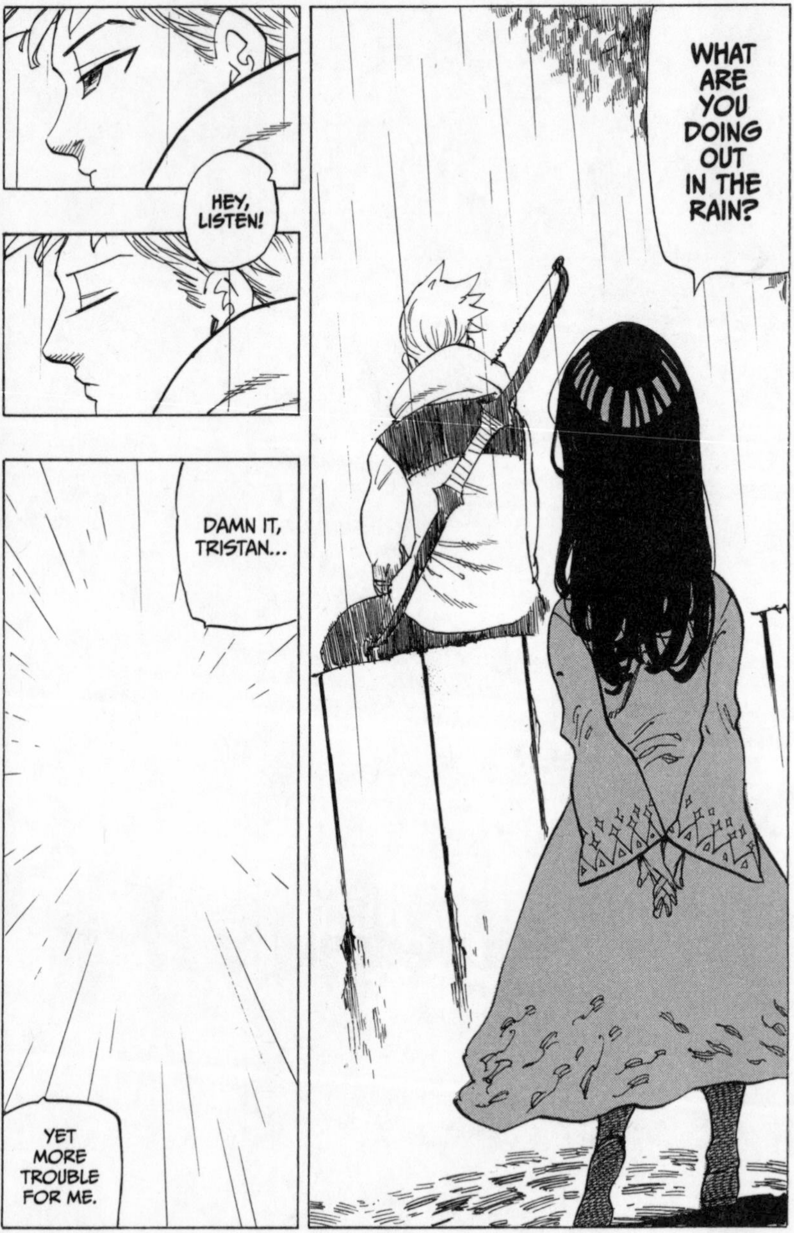
WHAT ARE YOU DOING OUT IN THE RAIN?
HEY, LISTEN!
DAMN IT, TRISTAN...
YET MORE TROUBLE FOR ME.

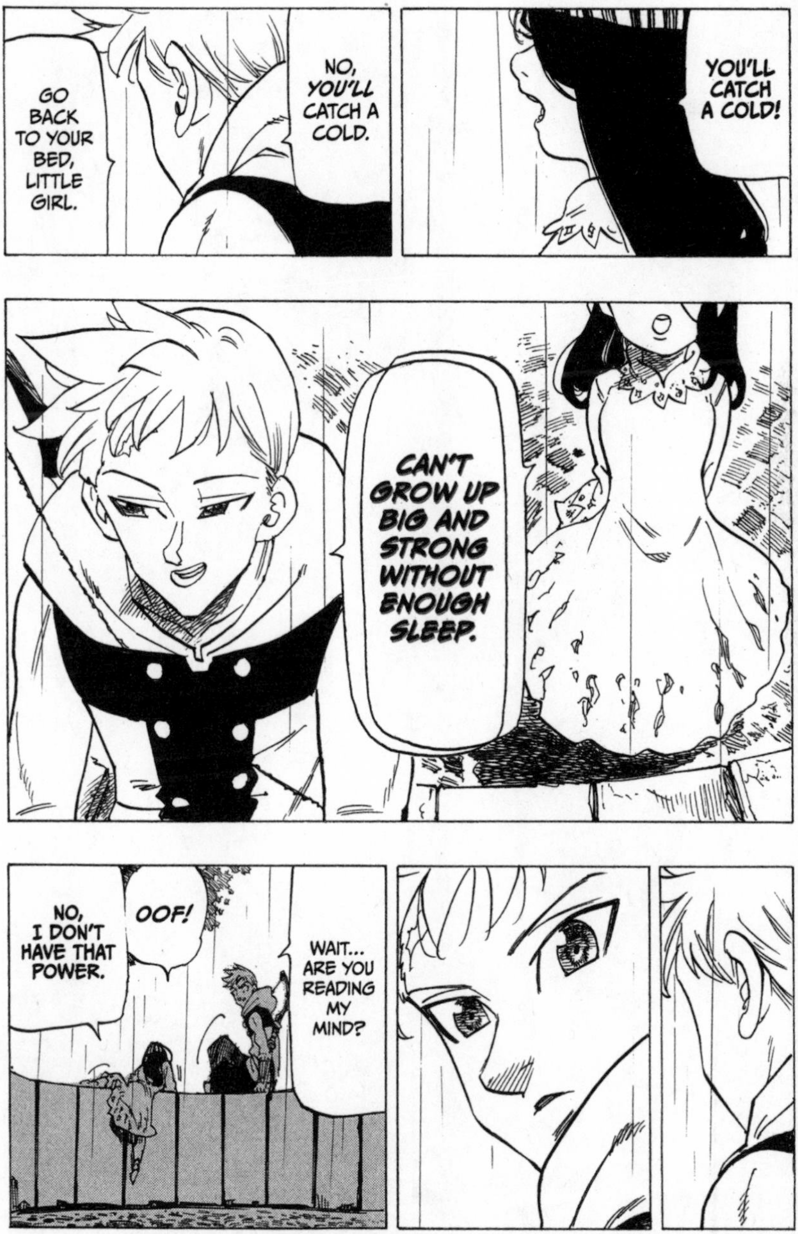
YOU'LL CATCH A COLD!
NO, YOU'LL CATCH A COLD.
GO BACK TO YOUR BED, LITTLE GIRL.
CAN'T GROW UP BIG AND STRONG WITHOUT ENOUGH SLEEP.
WAIT... ARE YOU READING MY MIND?
OOF!
NO, I DON'T HAVE THAT POWER.

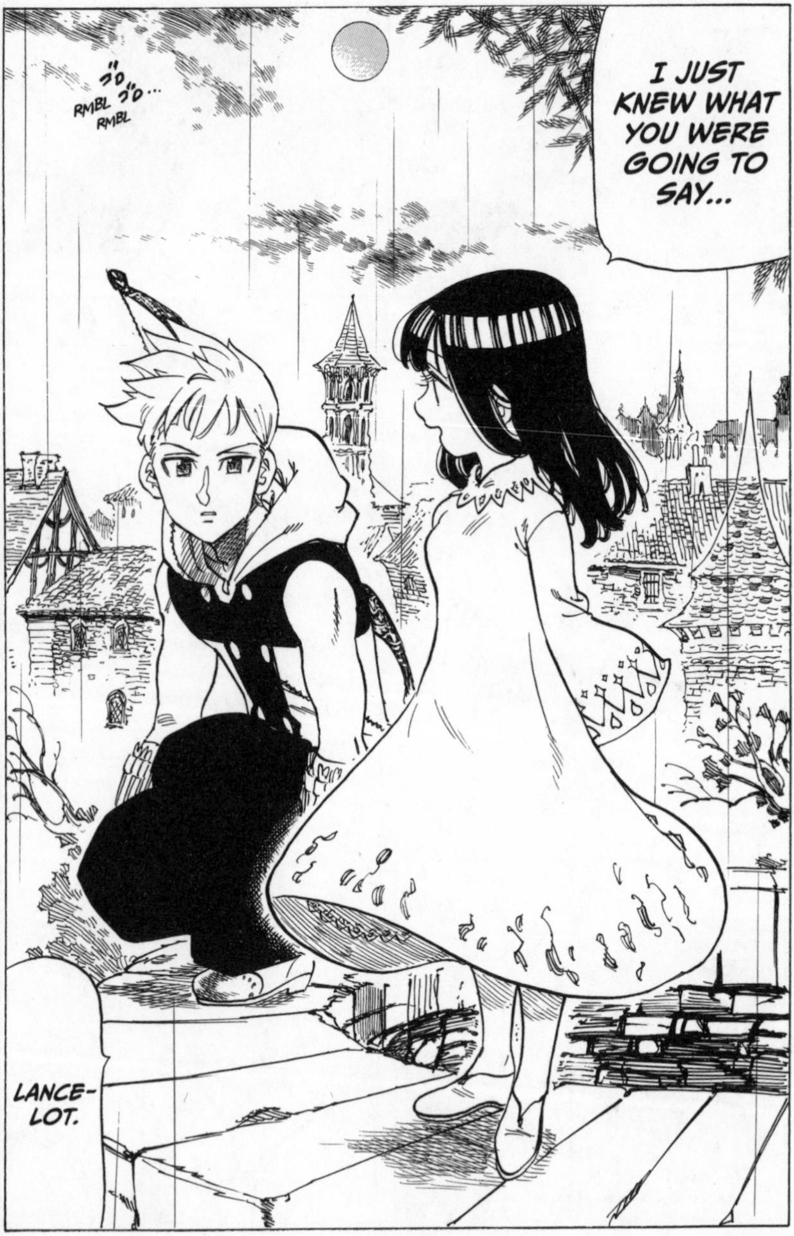

I JUST KNEW WHAT YOU WERE GOING TO SAY...
ゴロ RMBL ゴロ... RMBL
LANCE-LOT.

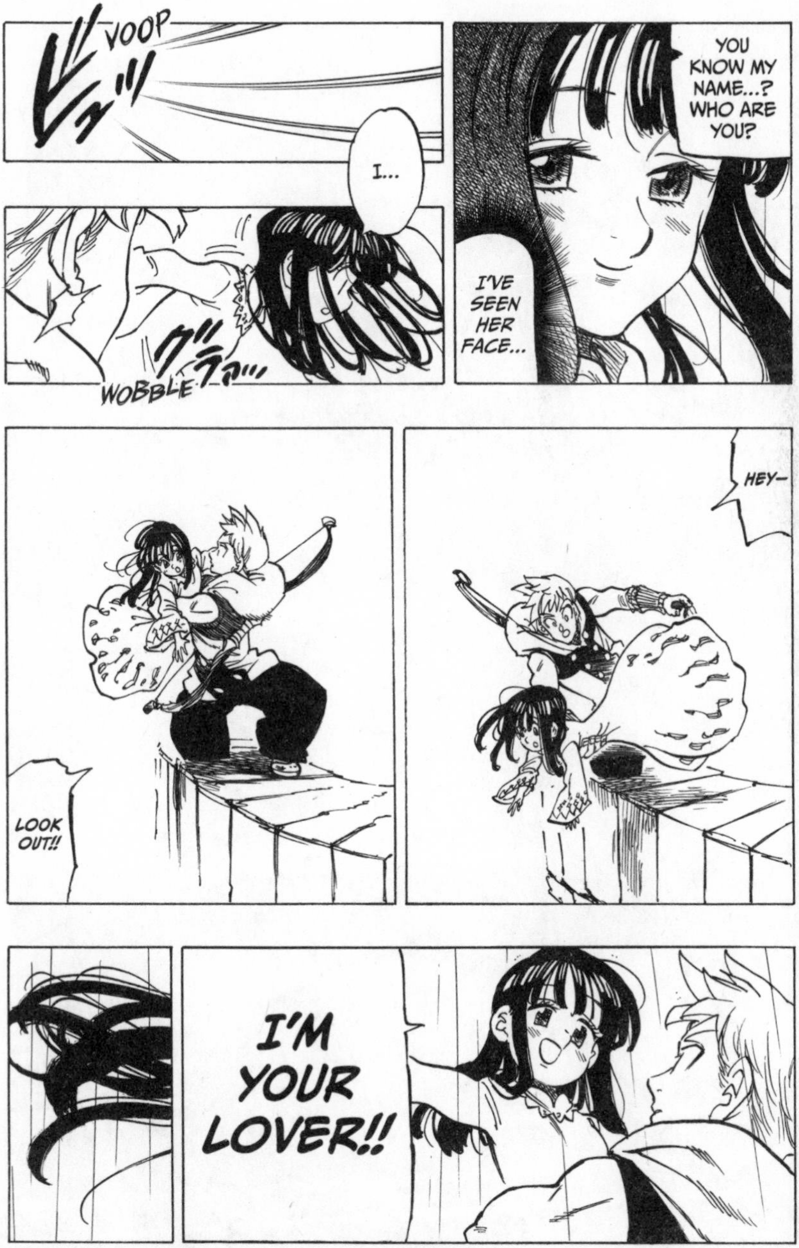
YOU KNOW MY NAME...? WHO ARE YOU?
I'VE SEEN HER FACE...
VOOP
I...
WOBBLE
HEY—
LOOK OUT!!
I'M YOUR LOVER!!

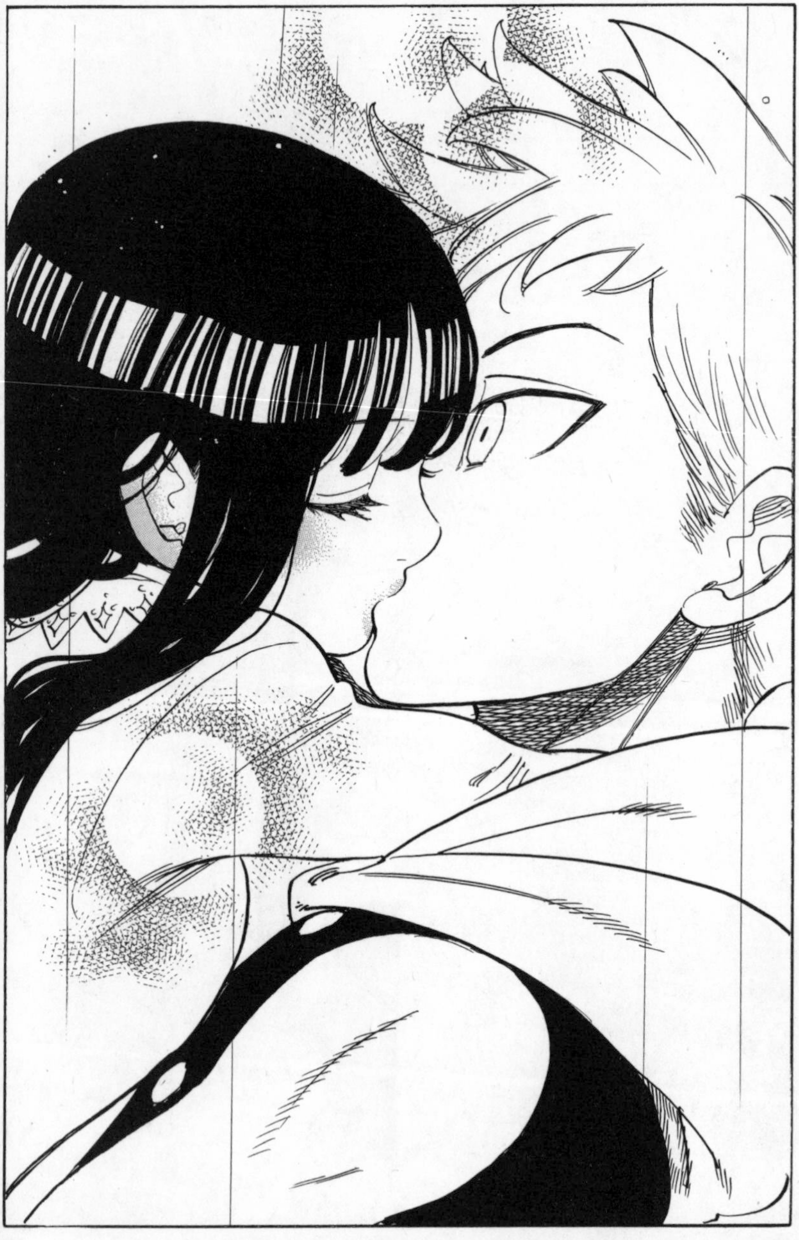

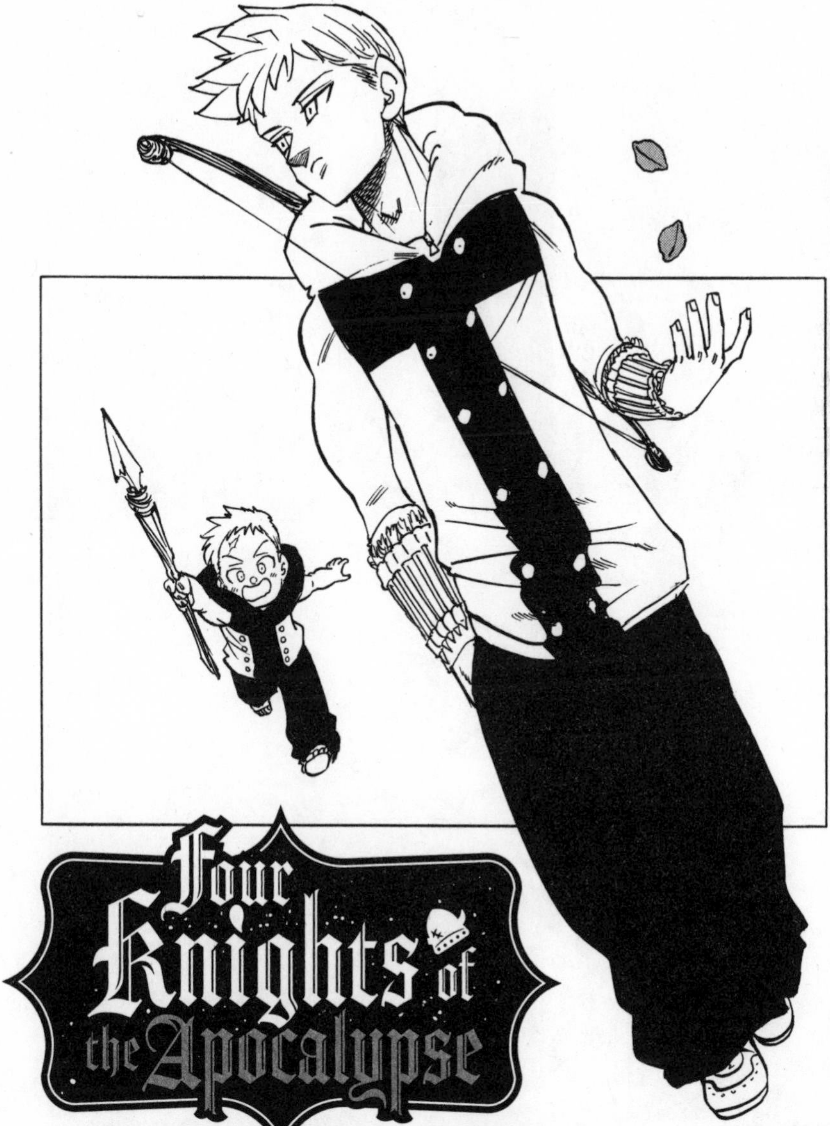
Four Knights of the Apocalypse

CHAPTER 59: LED BY THE NOSE

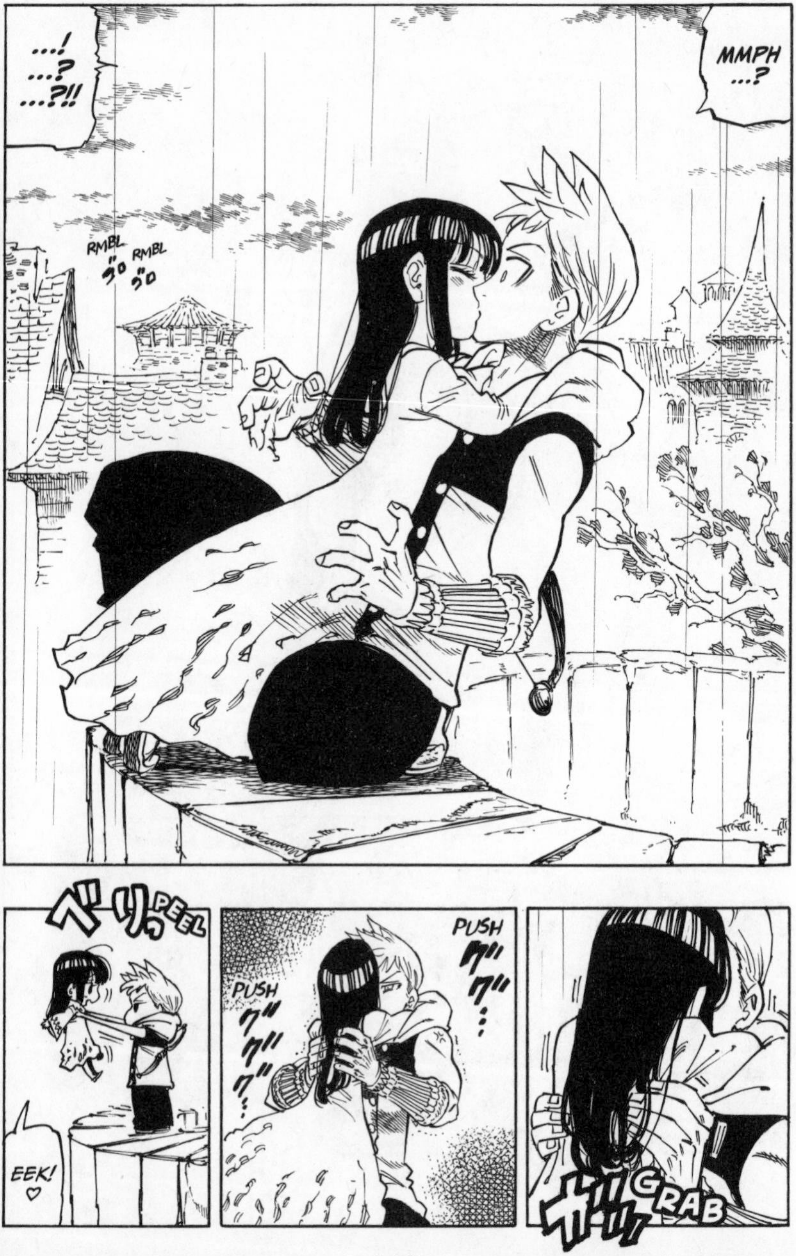
MMPH ...?
...! ...? ...?!!
RMBL ゴロ RMBL ゴロ
ガッ GRAB
PUSH グッグッ…
PUSH グッグッグッ…
ベリッ PEEL
EEK! ♡

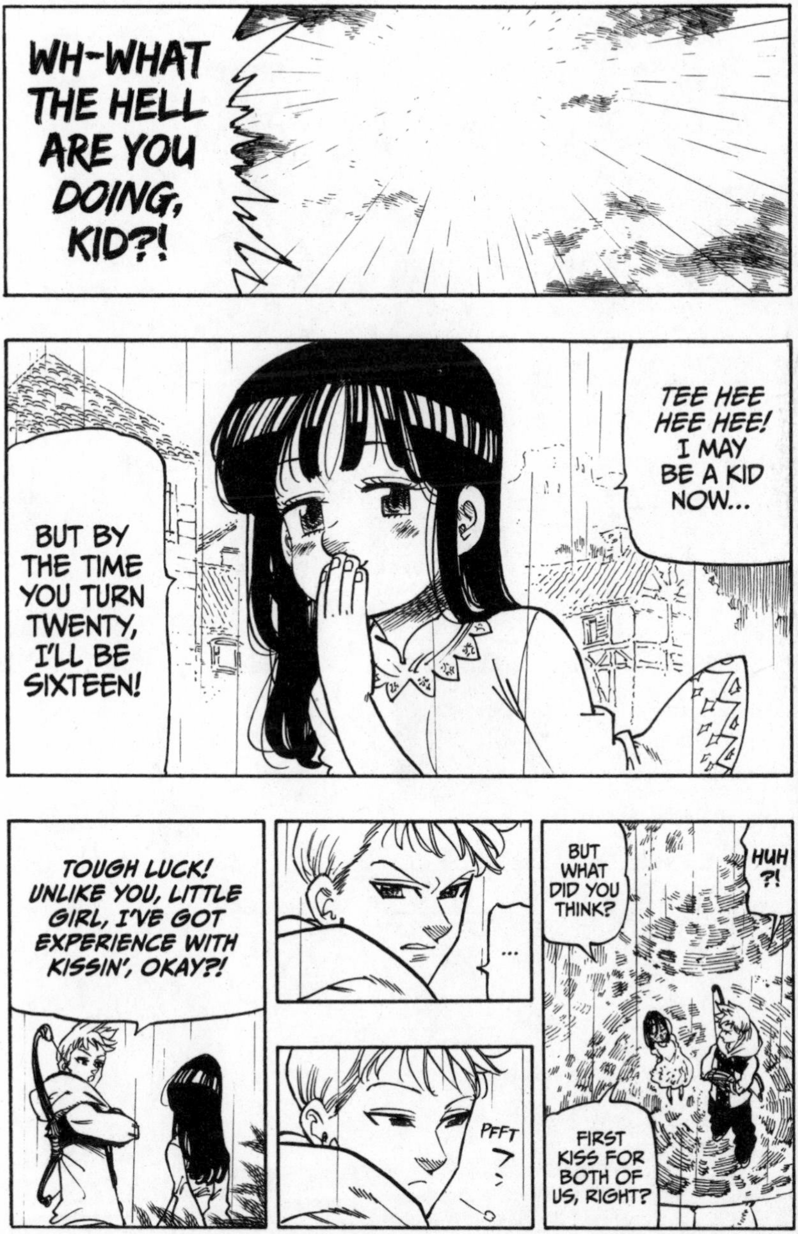
WH-WHAT THE HELL ARE YOU DOING, KID?!
TEE HEE HEE HEE! I MAY BE A KID NOW...
BUT BY THE TIME YOU TURN TWENTY, I'LL BE SIXTEEN!
HUH?!
BUT WHAT DID YOU THINK?
FIRST KISS FOR BOTH OF US, RIGHT?
...
PFFT
TOUGH LUCK! UNLIKE YOU, LITTLE GIRL, I'VE GOT EXPERIENCE WITH KISSIN', OKAY?!

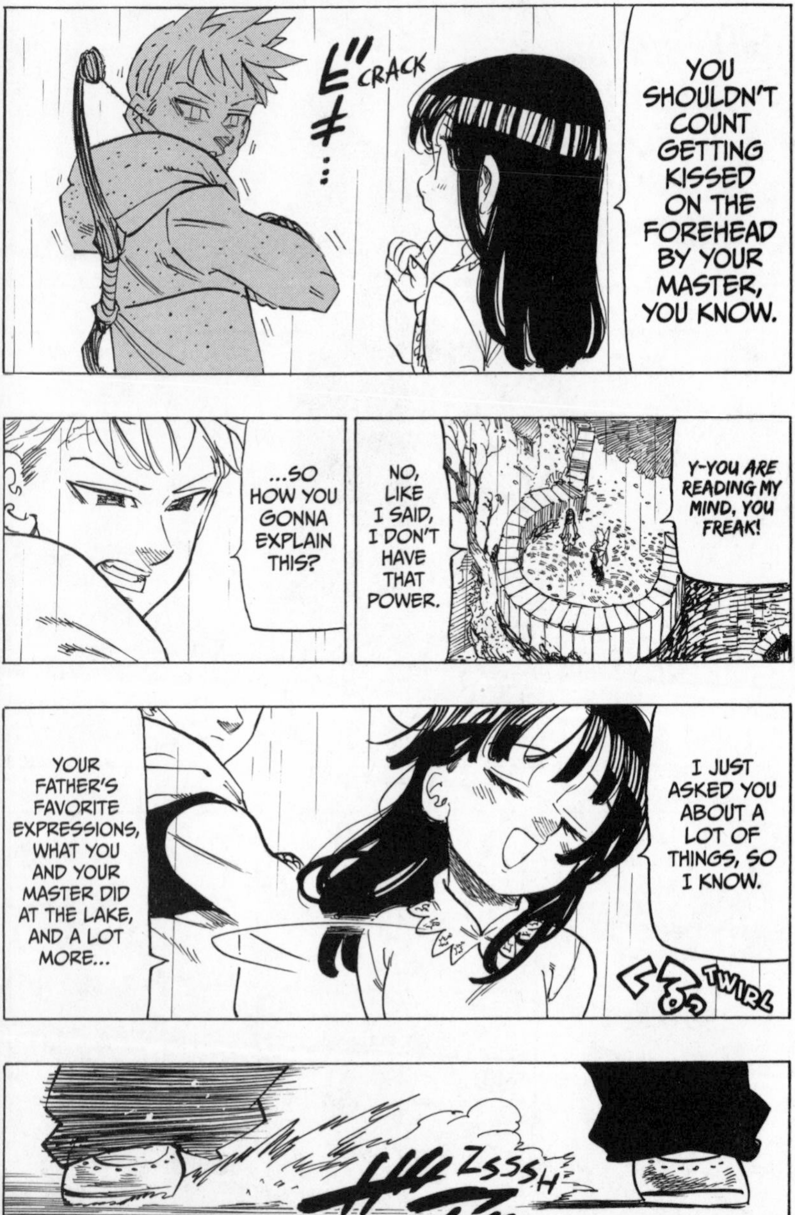
YOU SHOULDN'T COUNT GETTING KISSED ON THE FOREHEAD BY YOUR MASTER, YOU KNOW.
CRACK
Y-YOU ARE READING MY MIND, YOU FREAK!
NO, LIKE I SAID, I DON'T HAVE THAT POWER.
...SO HOW YOU GONNA EXPLAIN THIS?
I JUST ASKED YOU ABOUT A LOT OF THINGS, SO I KNOW.
YOUR FATHER'S FAVORITE EXPRESSIONS, WHAT YOU AND YOUR MASTER DID AT THE LAKE, AND A LOT MORE...
TWIRL
ZSSSH

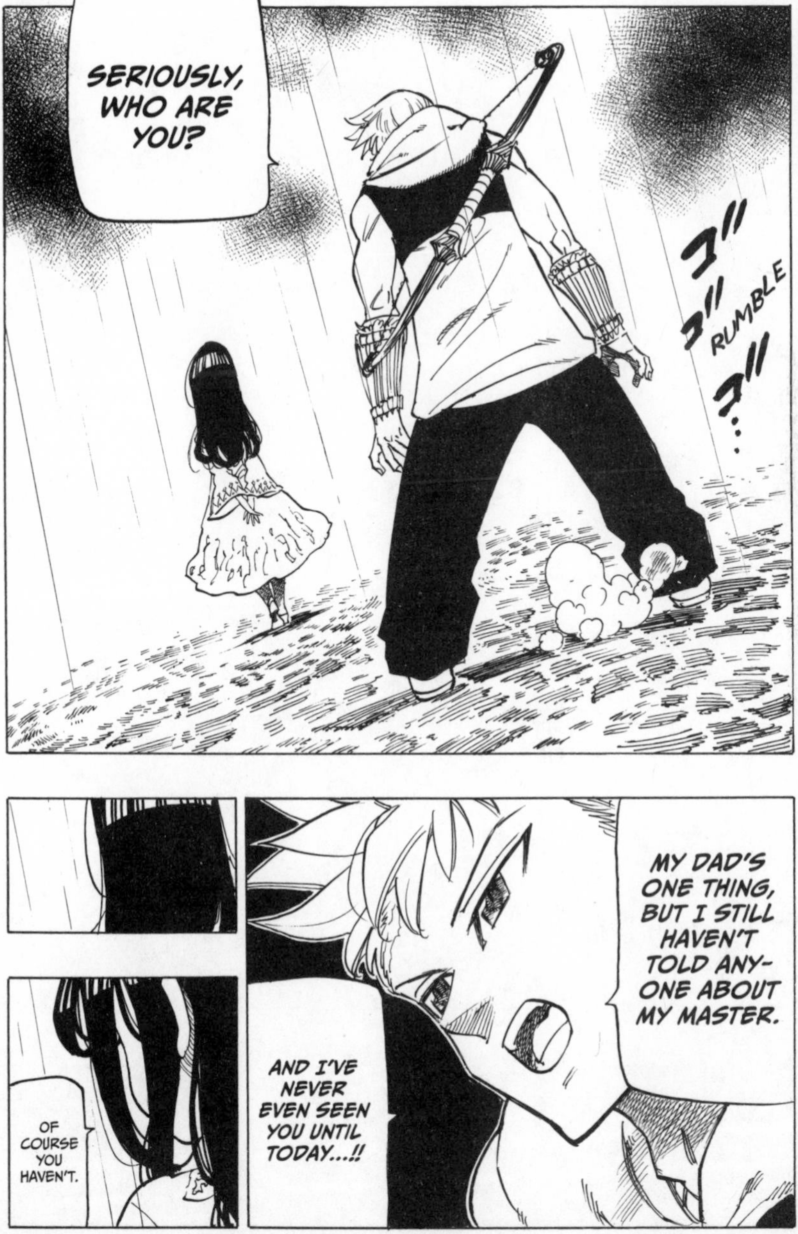
SERIOUSLY, WHO ARE YOU?
ゴゴゴゴ…
RUMBLE
MY DAD'S ONE THING, BUT I STILL HAVEN'T TOLD ANY-ONE ABOUT MY MASTER.
AND I'VE NEVER EVEN SEEN YOU UNTIL TODAY...!!
OF COURSE YOU HAVEN'T.

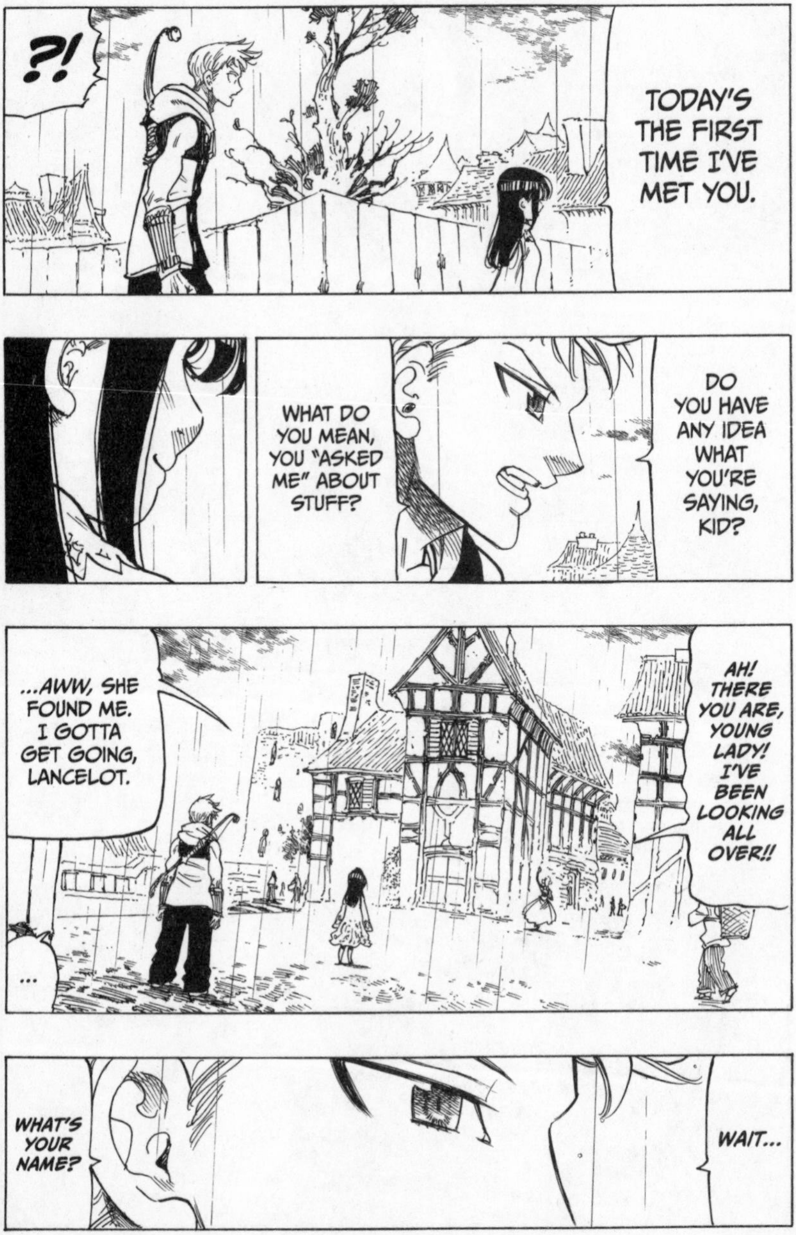
TODAY'S THE FIRST TIME I'VE MET YOU.
?!
DO YOU HAVE ANY IDEA WHAT YOU'RE SAYING, KID?
WHAT DO YOU MEAN, YOU "ASKED ME" ABOUT STUFF?
AH! THERE YOU ARE, YOUNG LADY! I'VE BEEN LOOKING ALL OVER!!
...AWW, SHE FOUND ME. I GOTTA GET GOING, LANCELOT.
...
WAIT...
WHAT'S YOUR NAME?

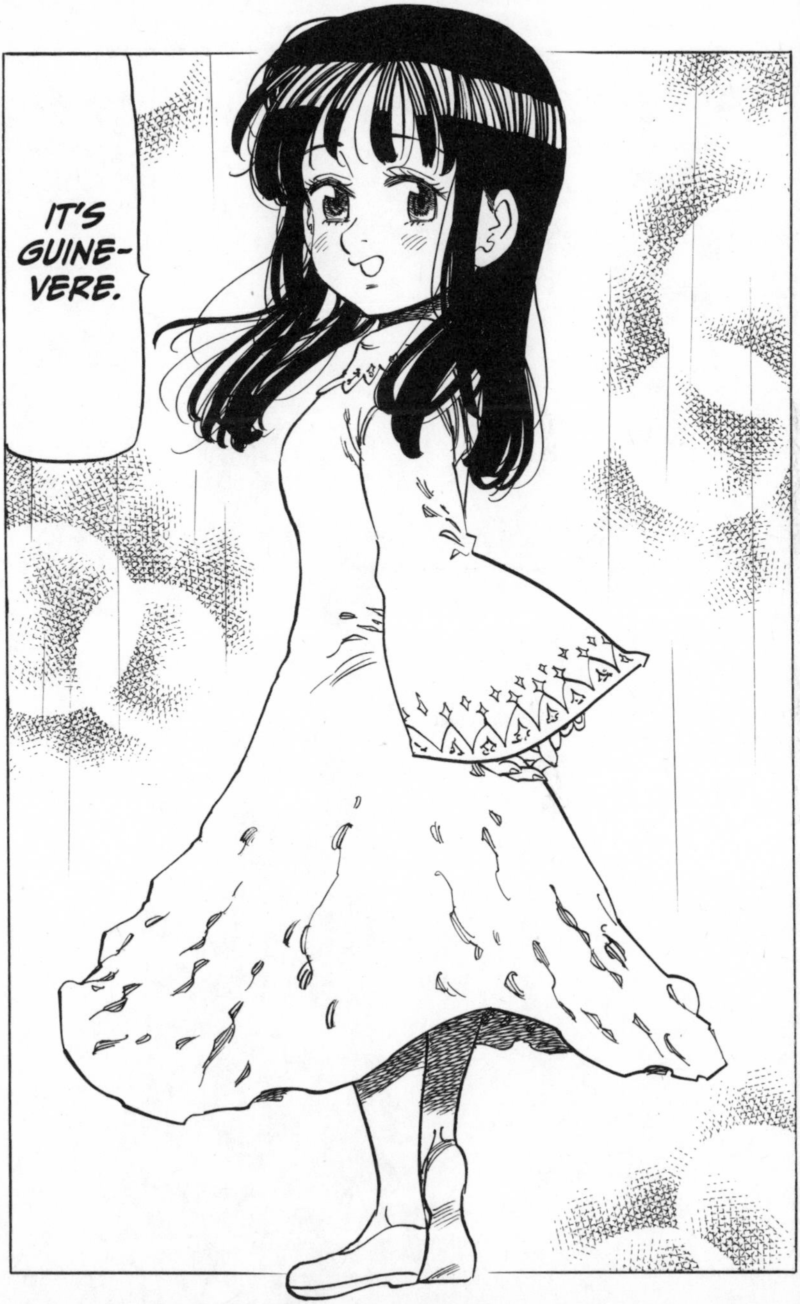
IT'S GUINE-VERE.

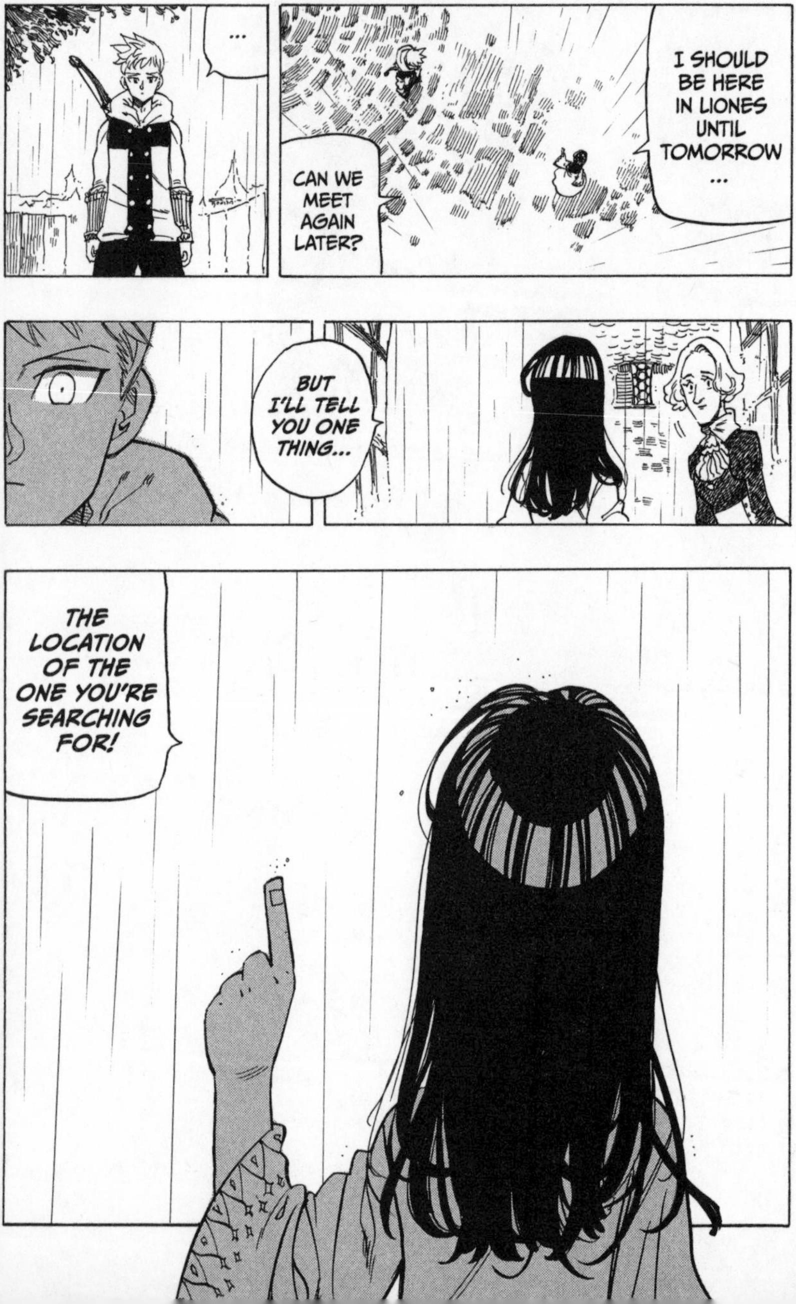
I SHOULD BE HERE IN LIONES UNTIL TOMORROW ...
CAN WE MEET AGAIN LATER?
...
BUT I'LL TELL YOU ONE THING...
THE LOCATION OF THE ONE YOU'RE SEARCHING FOR!

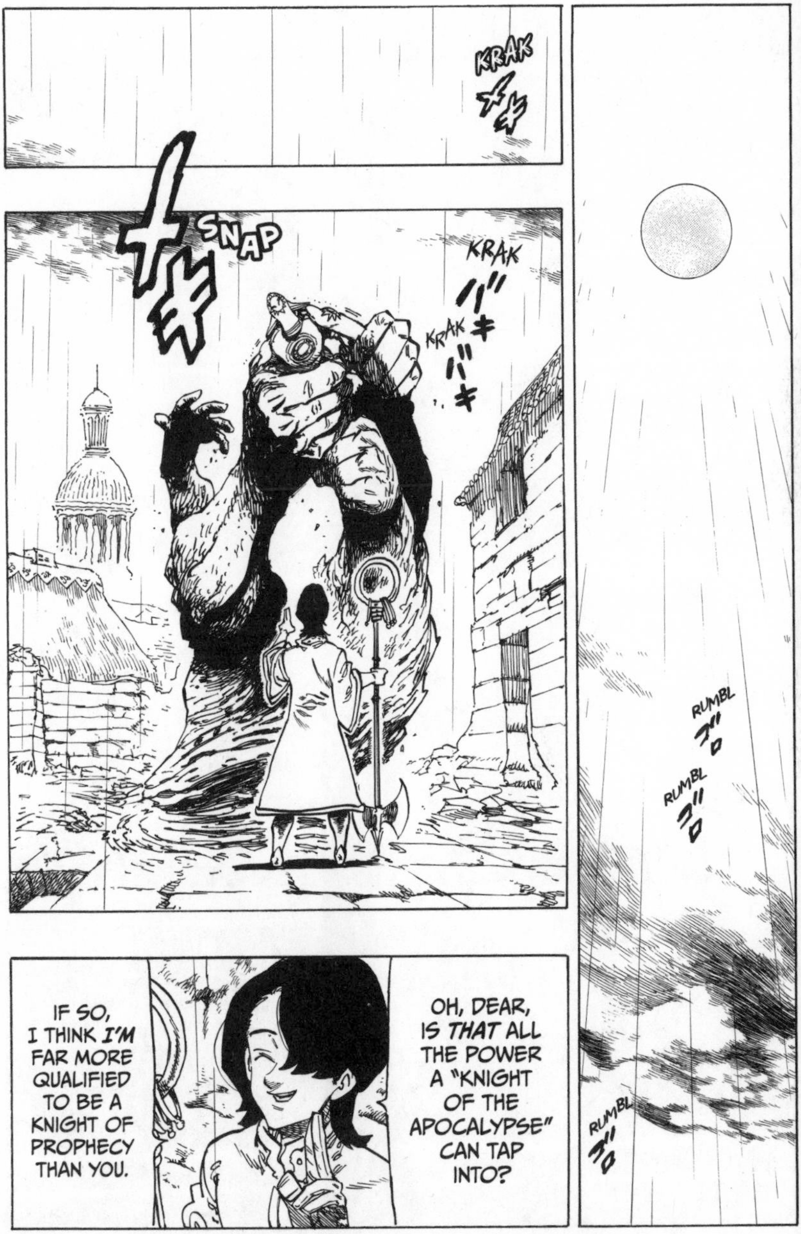
RUMBL
ゴロ
RUMBL
ゴロ
RUMBL
ゴロ
KRAK
メキ
SNAP
KRAK
バキ
KRAK
バキ
OH, DEAR, IS *THAT* ALL THE POWER A "KNIGHT OF THE APOCALYPSE" CAN TAP INTO?
IF SO, I THINK *I'M* FAR MORE QUALIFIED TO BE A KNIGHT OF PROPHECY THAN YOU.

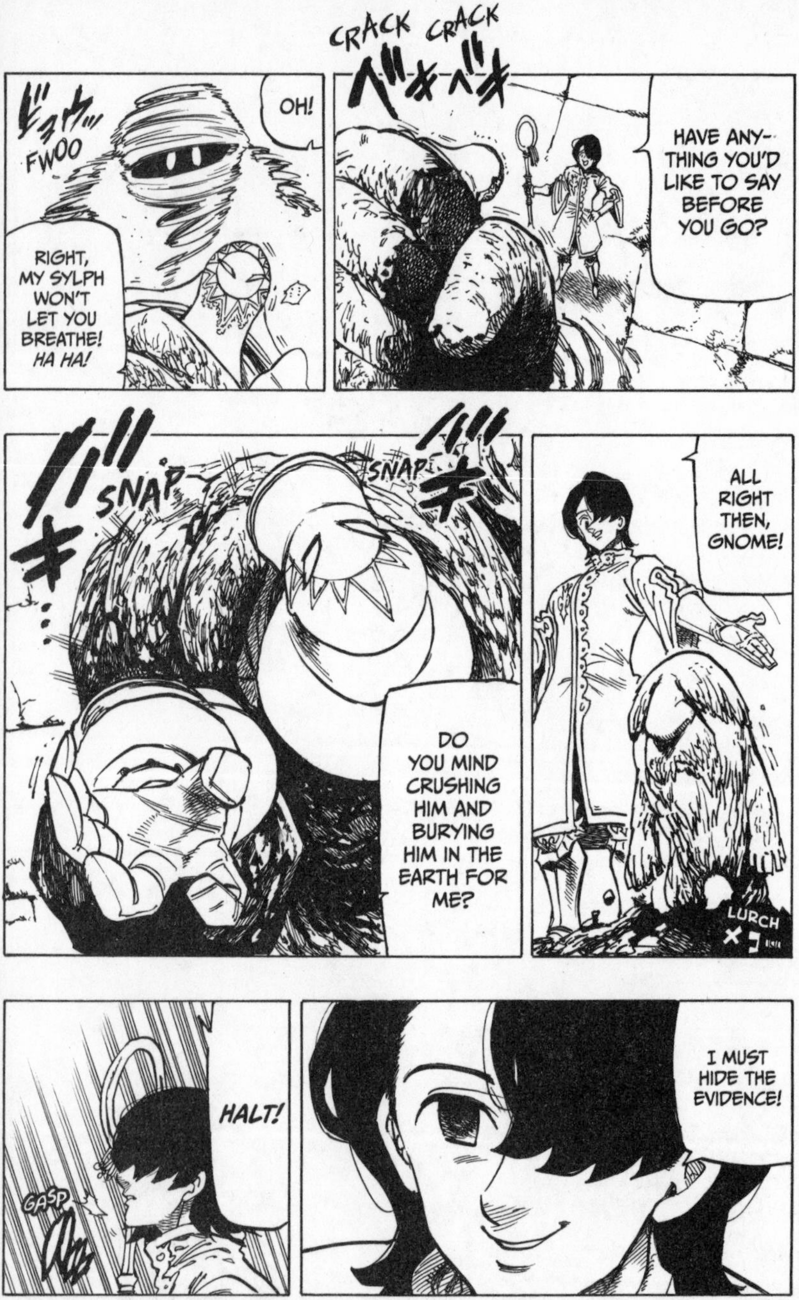
CRACK CRACK
HAVE ANY-THING YOU'D LIKE TO SAY BEFORE YOU GO?
OH!
FWOO
RIGHT, MY SYLPH WON'T LET YOU BREATHE! HA HA!
ALL RIGHT THEN, GNOME!
LURCH
SNAP
DO YOU MIND CRUSHING HIM AND BURYING HIM IN THE EARTH FOR ME?
SNAP
I MUST HIDE THE EVIDENCE!
HALT!
GASP

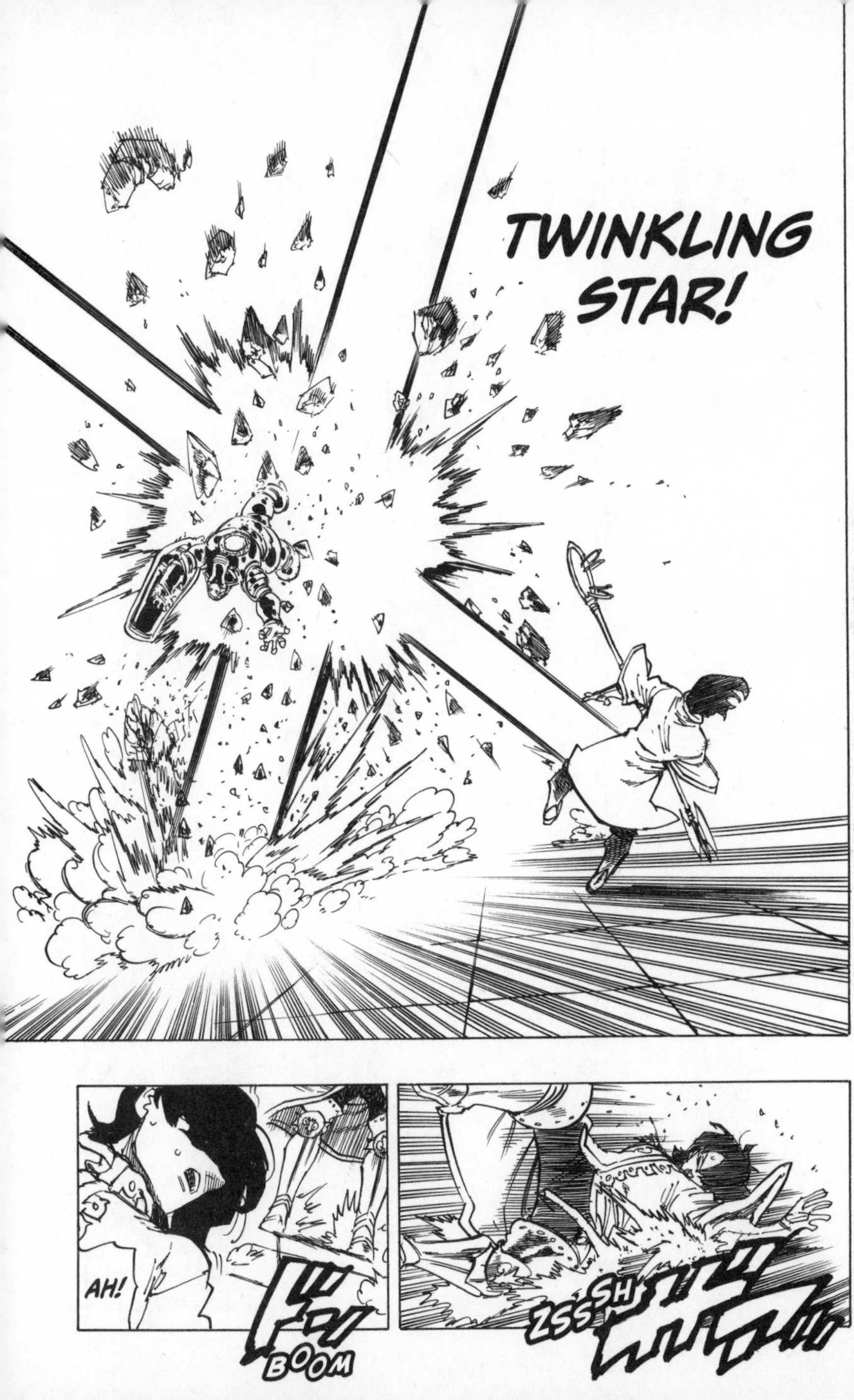
TWINKLING STAR!
ZSSSH
AH!
BOOM

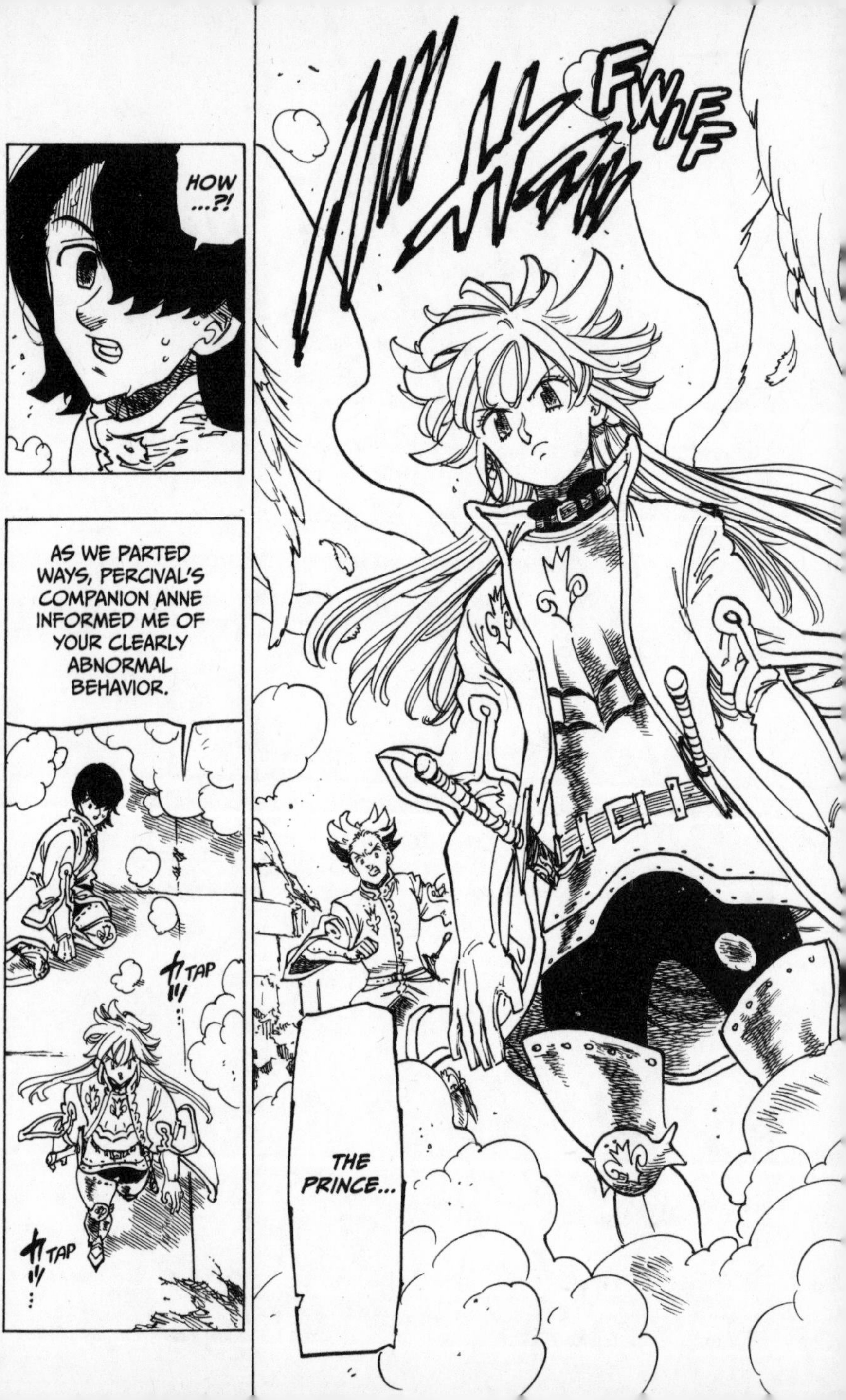
FWIF
THE PRINCE...
HOW ...?!
AS WE PARTED WAYS, PERCIVAL'S COMPANION ANNE INFORMED ME OF YOUR CLEARLY ABNORMAL BEHAVIOR.
TAP
TAP

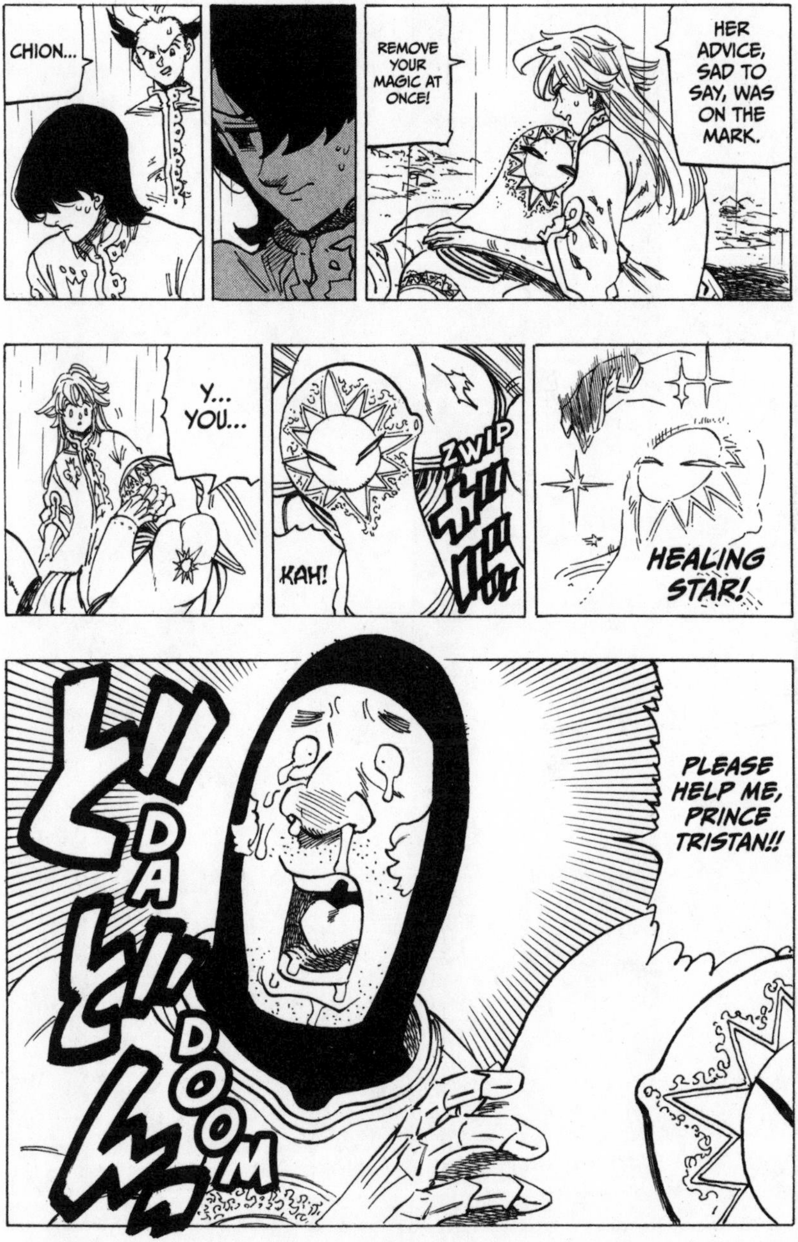
HER ADVICE, SAD TO SAY, WAS ON THE MARK.
REMOVE YOUR MAGIC AT ONCE!
CHION...
HEALING STAR!
ZWIP
KAH!
Y... YOU...
PLEASE HELP ME, PRINCE TRISTAN!!
DA DOOM

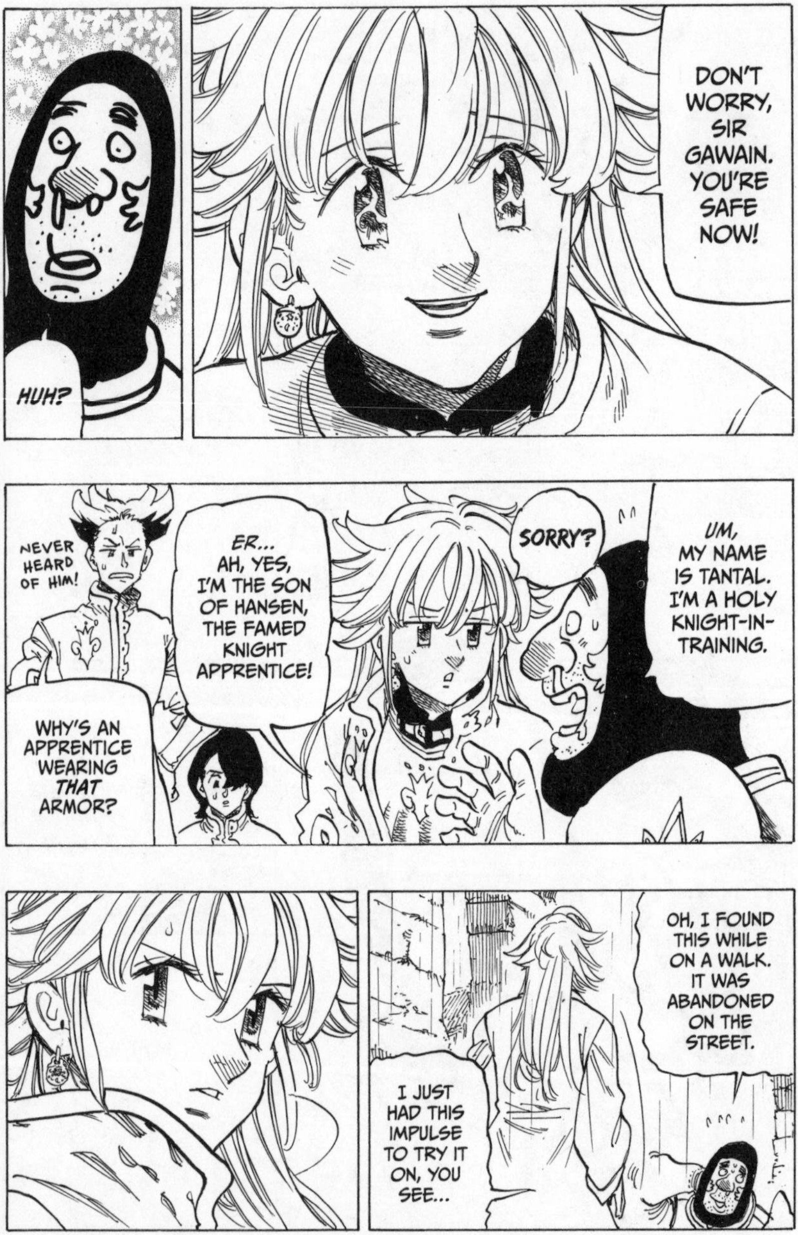
DON'T WORRY, SIR GAWAIN. YOU'RE SAFE NOW!
HUH?
UM, MY NAME IS TANTAL. I'M A HOLY KNIGHT-IN-TRAINING.
SORRY?
ER... AH, YES, I'M THE SON OF HANSEN, THE FAMED KNIGHT APPRENTICE!
NEVER HEARD OF HIM!
WHY'S AN APPRENTICE WEARING *THAT* ARMOR?
OH, I FOUND THIS WHILE ON A WALK. IT WAS ABANDONED ON THE STREET.
I JUST HAD THIS IMPULSE TO TRY IT ON, YOU SEE...

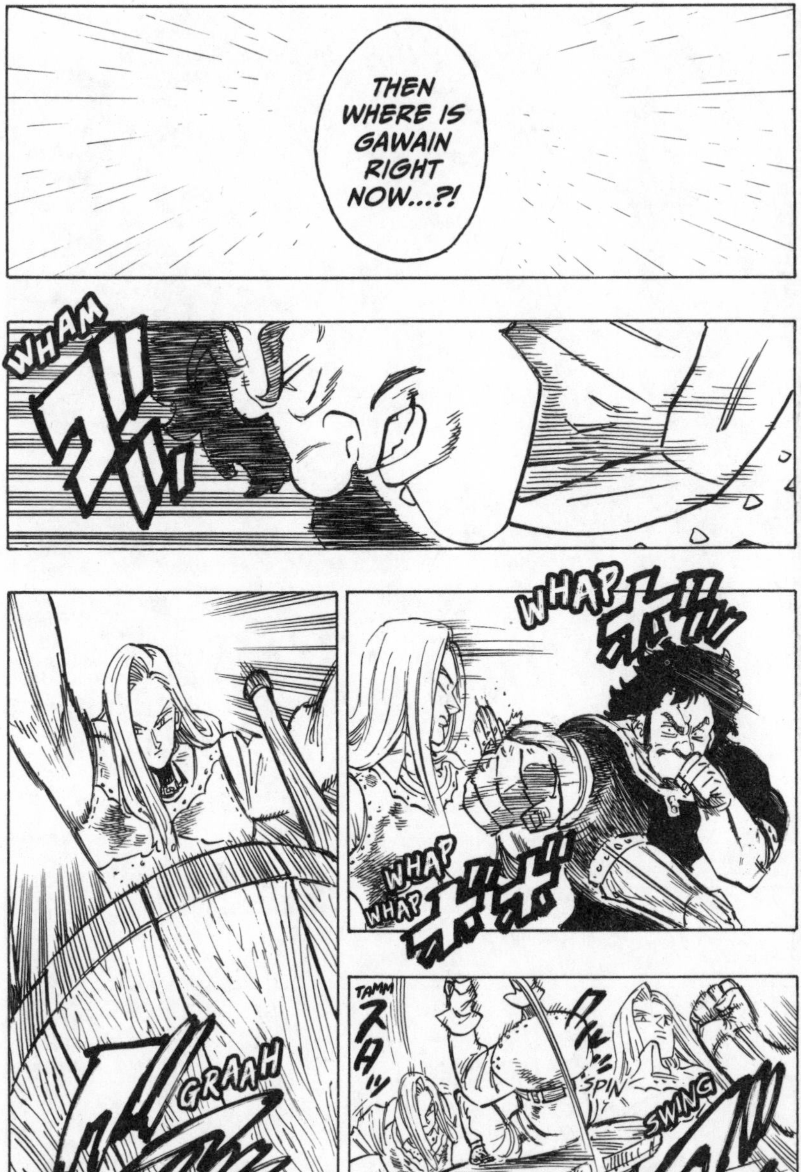
THEN WHERE IS GAWAIN RIGHT NOW...?!
WHAM
WHAP
WHAP WHAP
SWING
SPIN
TAMM
GRAAH

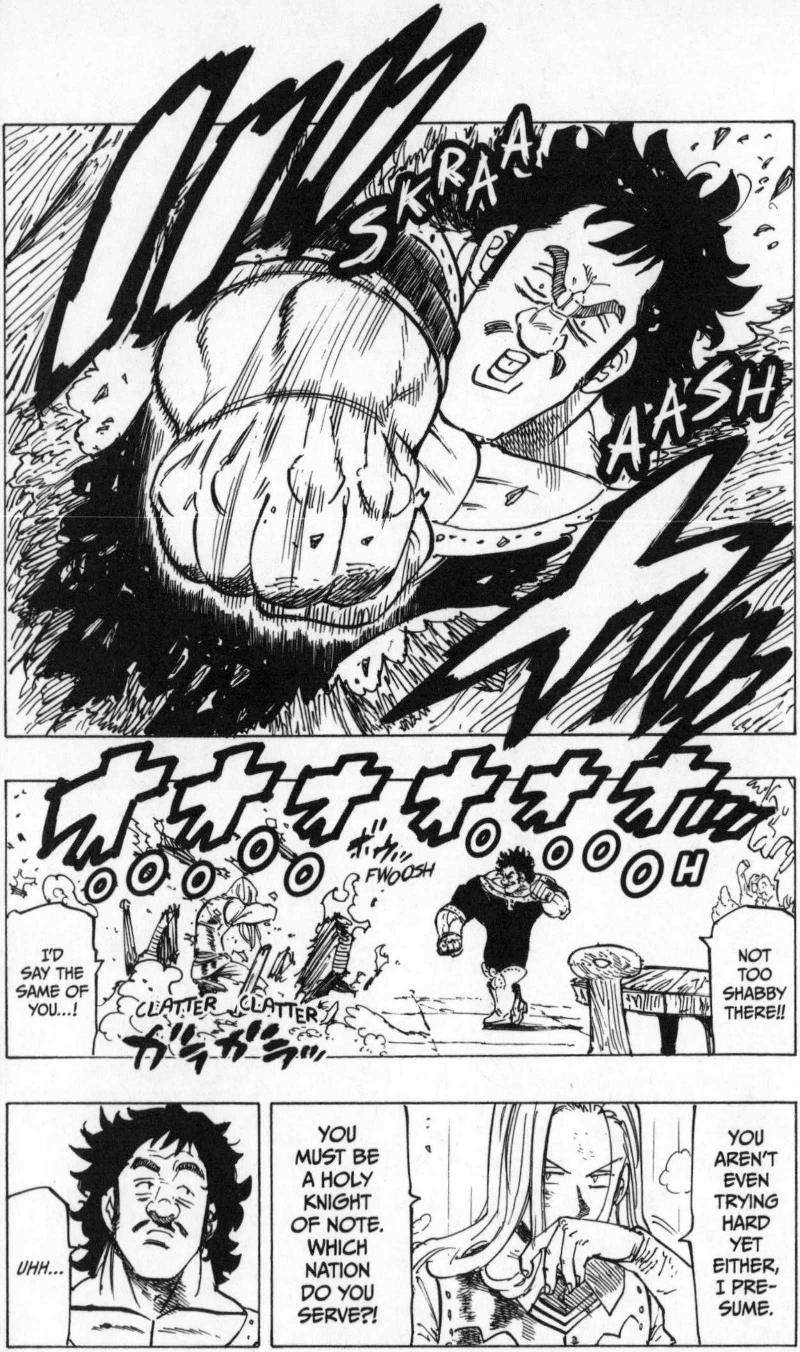
SKRAAAASH
NOT TOO SHABBY THERE!!
OOOOOOOOOH
FWOOSH
CLATTER CLATTER
I'D SAY THE SAME OF YOU...!
YOU AREN'T EVEN TRYING HARD YET EITHER, I PRESUME.
YOU MUST BE A HOLY KNIGHT OF NOTE. WHICH NATION DO YOU SERVE?!
UHH...

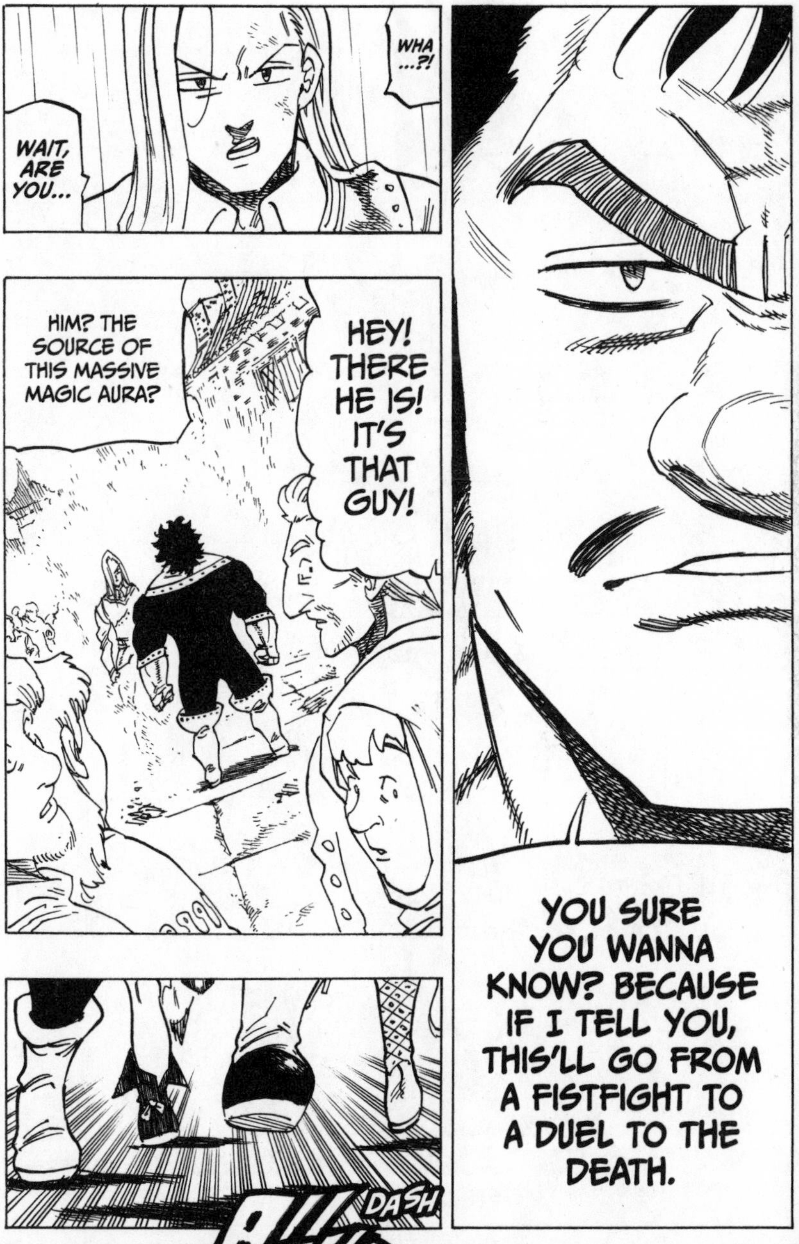
YOU SURE YOU WANNA KNOW? BECAUSE IF I TELL YOU, THIS'LL GO FROM A FISTFIGHT TO A DUEL TO THE DEATH.
WHA ...?!
WAIT, ARE YOU...
HEY! THERE HE IS! IT'S THAT GUY!
HIM? THE SOURCE OF THIS MASSIVE MAGIC AURA?
DASH

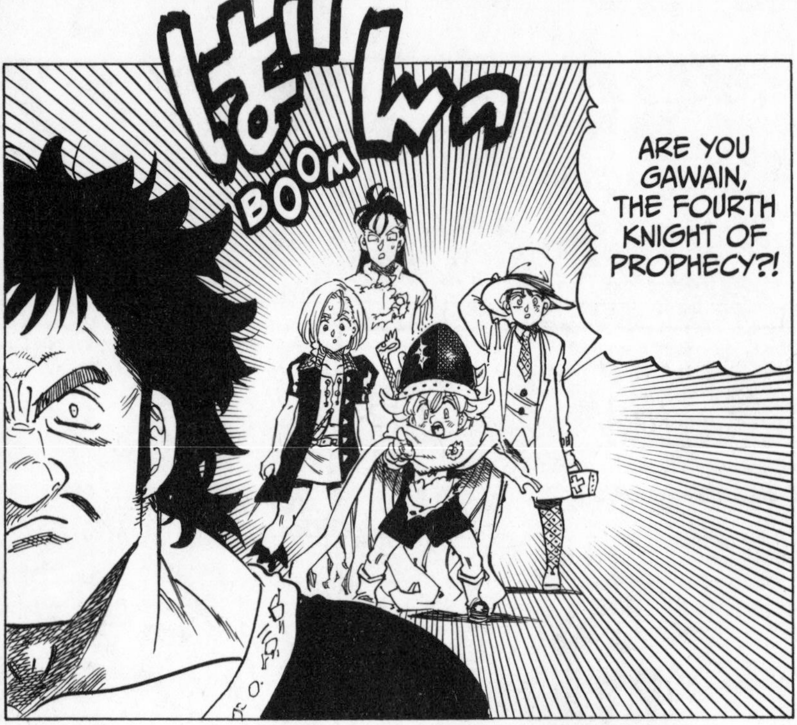
BOOM
ARE YOU GAWAIN, THE FOURTH KNIGHT OF PROPHECY?!
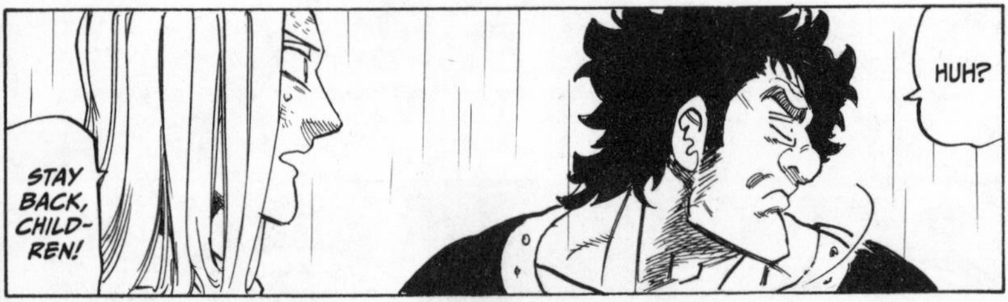
HUH?
STAY BACK, CHILD-REN!
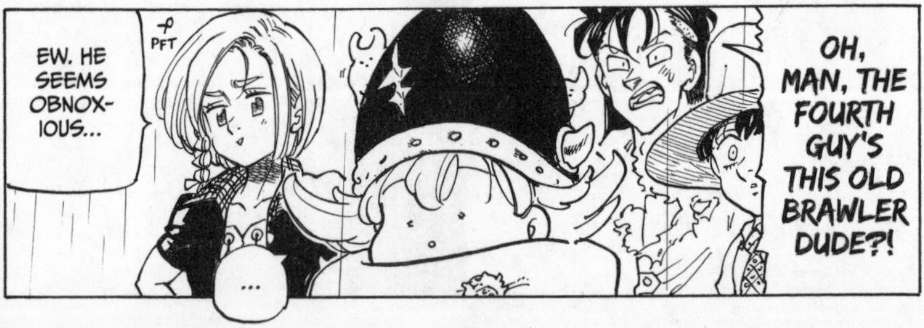
OH, MAN, THE FOURTH GUY'S THIS OLD BRAWLER DUDE?!
PFT
EW. HE SEEMS OBNOX-IOUS...
...

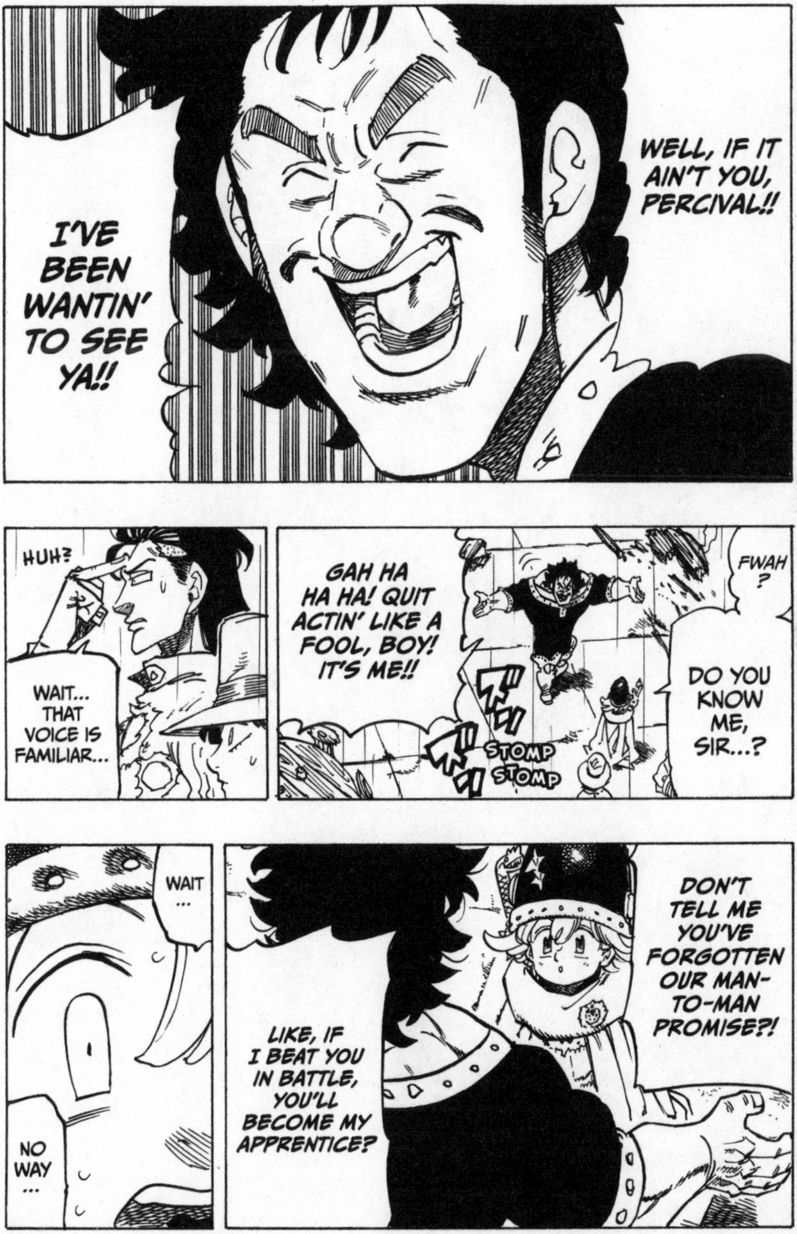
WELL, IF IT AIN'T YOU, PERCIVAL!!
I'VE BEEN WANTIN' TO SEE YA!!
FWAH?
DO YOU KNOW ME, SIR...?
GAH HA HA HA! QUIT ACTIN' LIKE A FOOL, BOY! IT'S ME!!
STOMP STOMP
HUH?
WAIT... THAT VOICE IS FAMILIAR...
DON'T TELL ME YOU'VE FORGOTTEN OUR MAN-TO-MAN PROMISE?!
LIKE, IF I BEAT YOU IN BATTLE, YOU'LL BECOME MY APPRENTICE?
WAIT ...
NO WAY ...

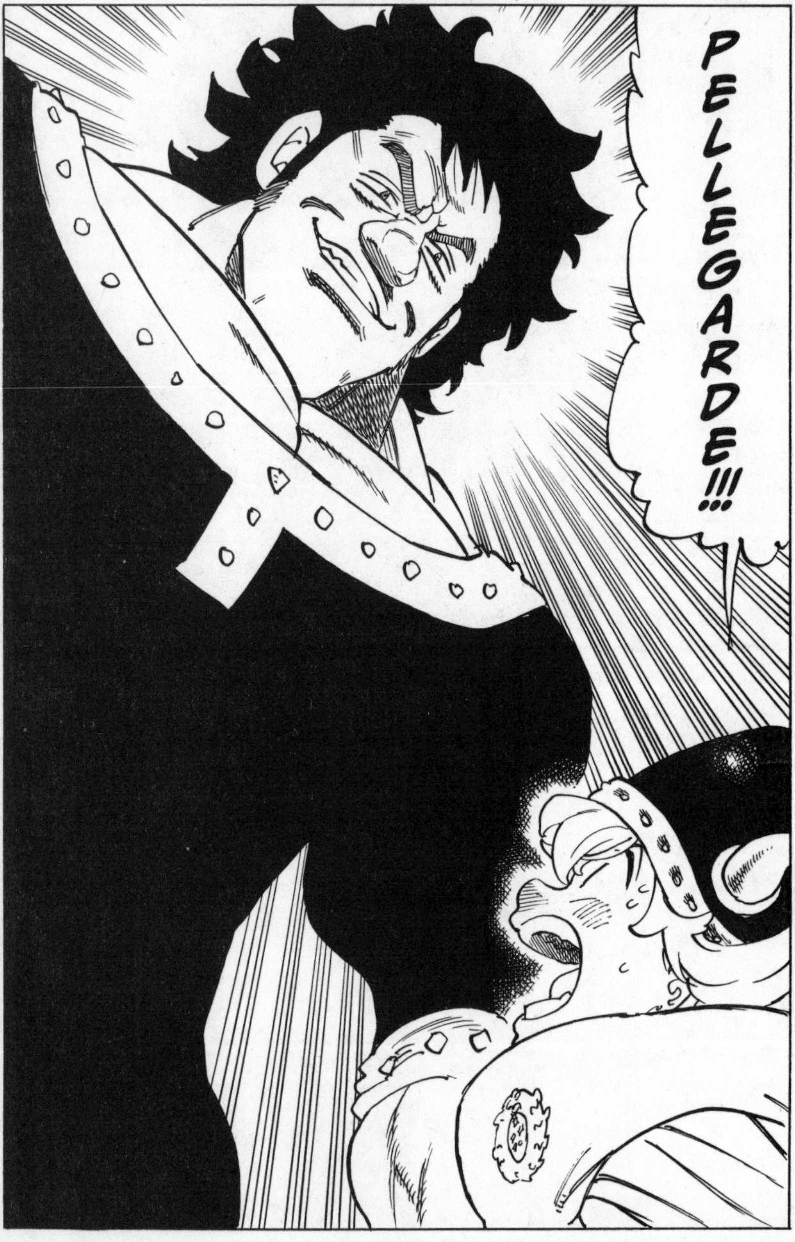
PELLEGARDE!!!

LANCELOT AND THE RED FOX

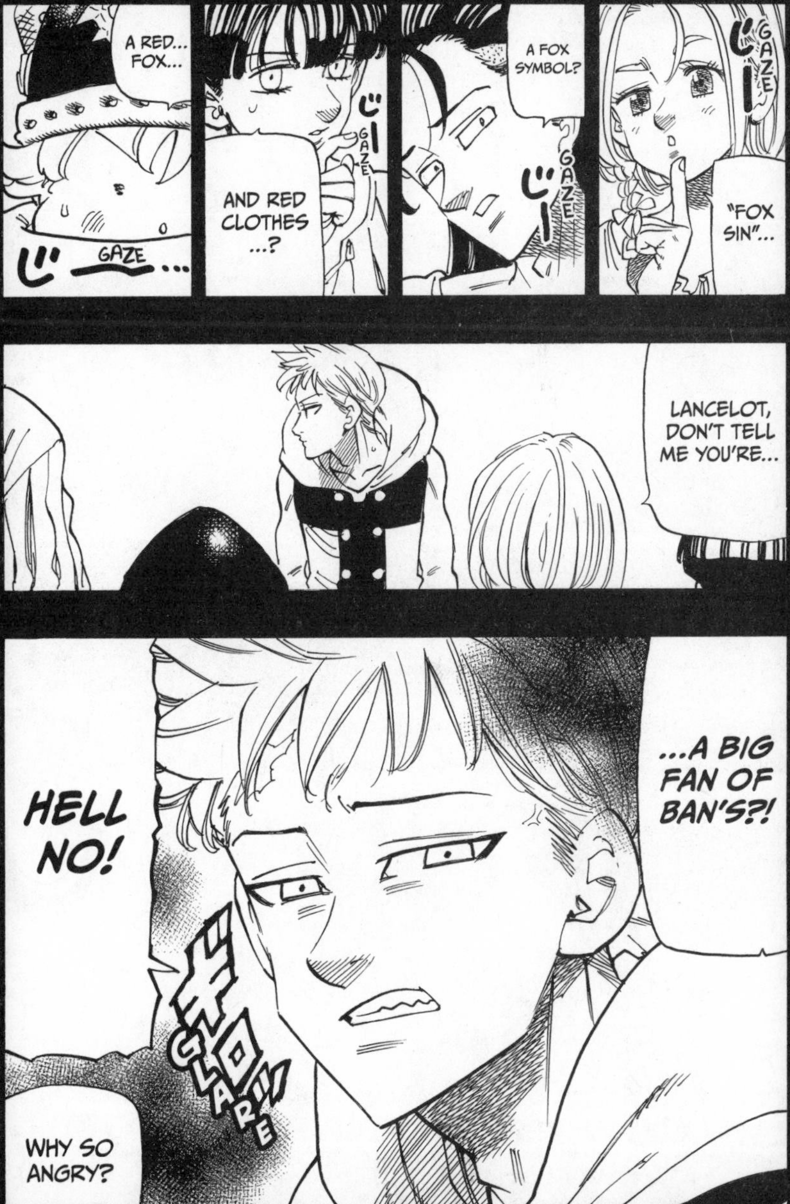

じー GAZE
"FOX SIN"...
A FOX SYMBOL?
じー GAZE
AND RED CLOTHES ...?
じー GAZE
A RED... FOX...
じー GAZE...
LANCELOT, DON'T TELL ME YOU'RE...
...A BIG FAN OF BAN'S?!
HELL NO!
GLARE
WHY SO ANGRY?

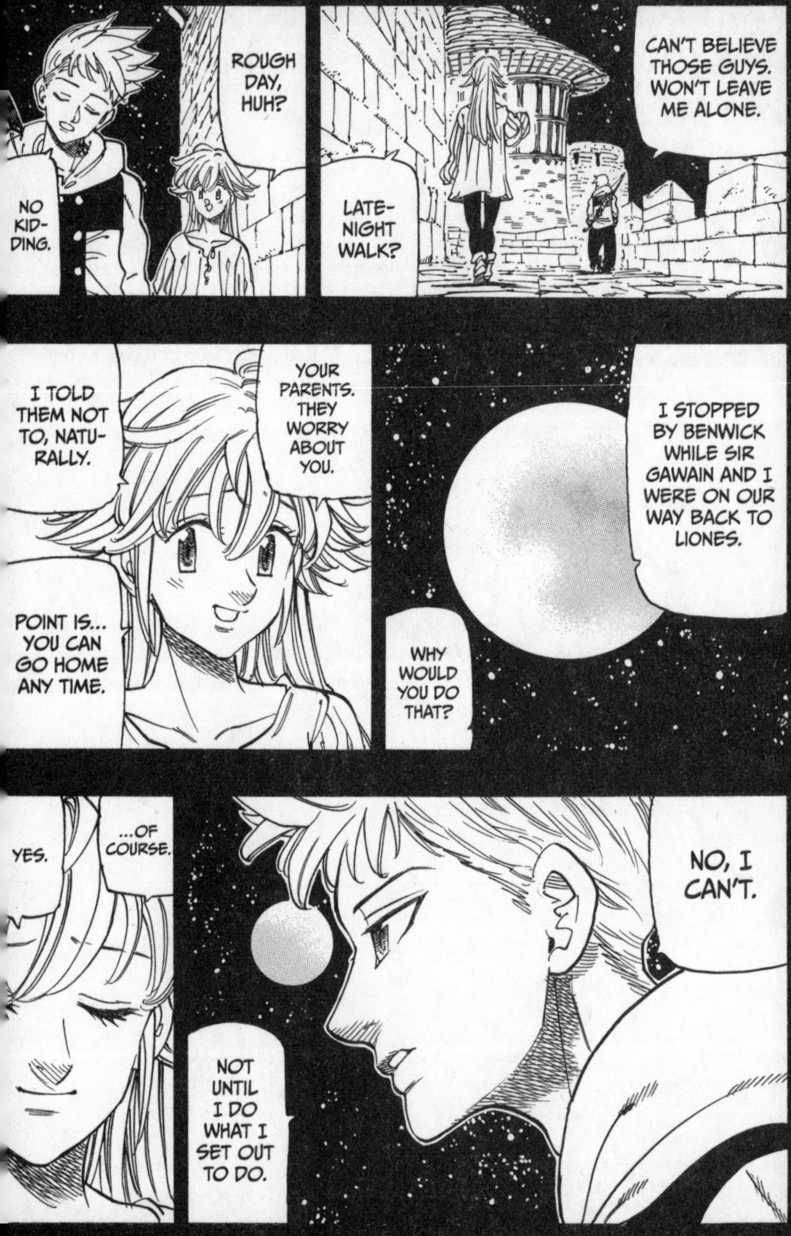
CAN'T BELIEVE THOSE GUYS. WON'T LEAVE ME ALONE.
LATE-NIGHT WALK?
ROUGH DAY, HUH?
NO KID-DING.
I STOPPED BY BENWICK WHILE SIR GAWAIN AND I WERE ON OUR WAY BACK TO LIONES.
WHY WOULD YOU DO THAT?
YOUR PARENTS. THEY WORRY ABOUT YOU.
I TOLD THEM NOT TO, NATU-RALLY.
POINT IS... YOU CAN GO HOME ANY TIME.
NO, I CAN'T.
NOT UNTIL I DO WHAT I SET OUT TO DO.
...OF COURSE.
YES.

Four Knights of the Apocalypse Art Corner

Artist Knights' Chamber

DON'T FORGET TO INCLUDE YOUR NAME AND ADDRESS ON YOUR POSTCARD!

P = D = S = A = L =

SPECIAL AWARD

YOU TWO GET ALONG SO WELL!

HA HA! DON'T BE MAD. OR SHY.

I'M NOT YOUR TOY!

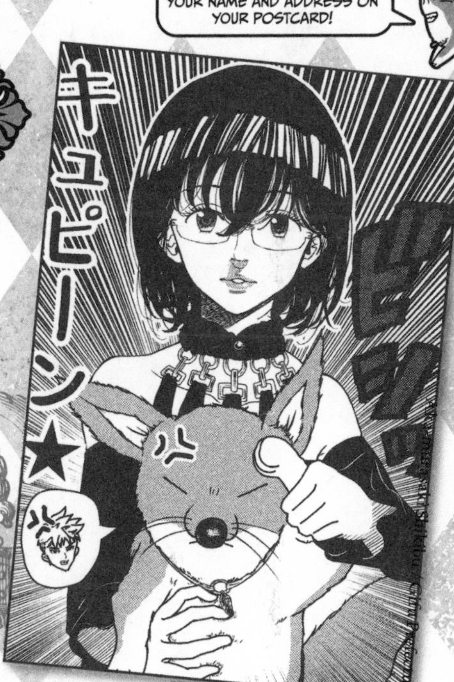

キューピーン★

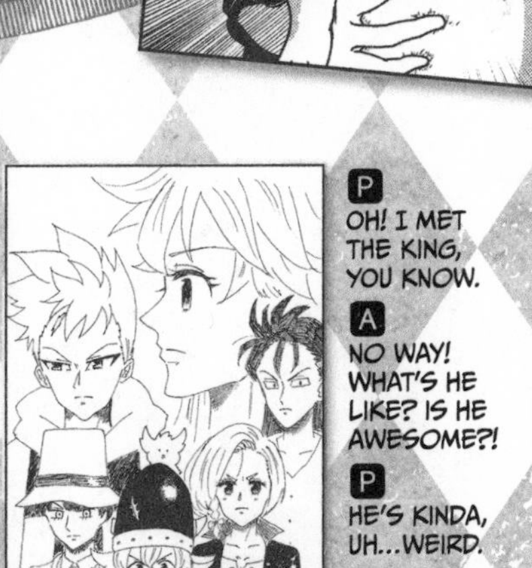

D
CAN'T BELIEVE WE GOT THREE KNIGHTS OF THE PROPHECY AT ONCE!

N
I'M WORRIED ABOUT THE LAST ONE, THOUGH...

Katsumi Kabuki / Shizuoka Prefecture

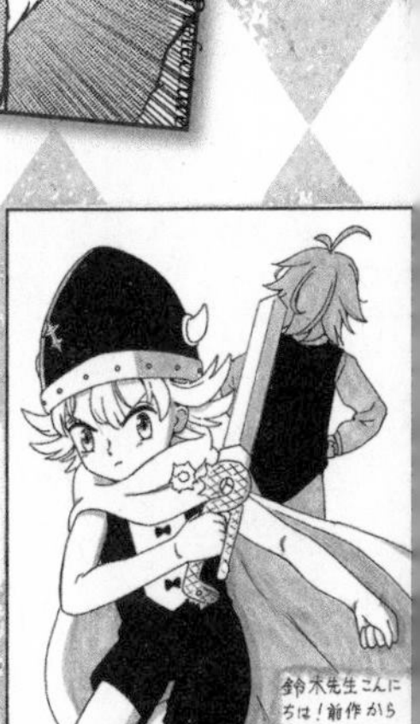

鈴木先生こんにちは！前作から楽しく読ませてもらっています！これからもがんばってください！

P
OH! I MET THE KING, YOU KNOW.

A
NO WAY! WHAT'S HE LIKE? IS HE AWESOME?!

P
HE'S KINDA, UH...WEIRD.

A
HUH?

Kazu-chan / Ehime Prefecture

N
I'D LIKE A MINI-PERCIVAL ALL TO MYSELF.

D
TO ADMIRE? OR EXPERIMENT ON?

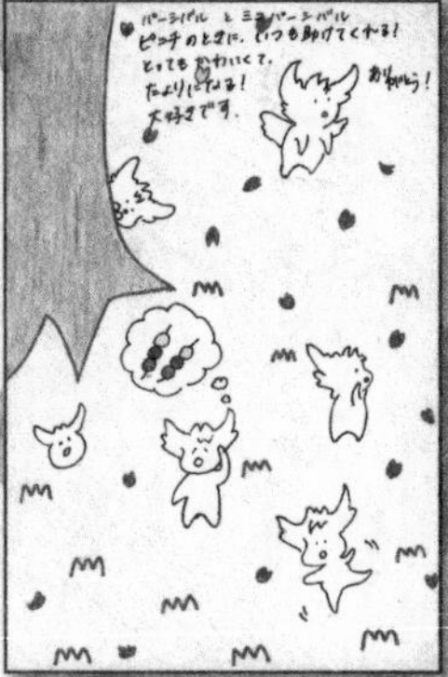

パーシバル と ミニパーシバル
ピンチのときに、いつも助けてくれる!
とってもかわいくて、
たよりになる!
大好きです。
かわいい!

Macchan / Nagano Prefecture

D
ALL THE LADIES WHO SHOW UP HAVE SOME SORT OF WEIRD QUIRK...

A
BUT NOT ME, RIGHT?!

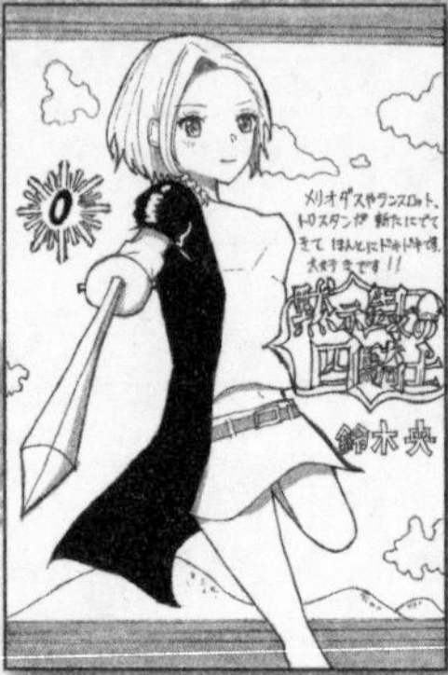

メリオダスやランスロット、
大好きです!!
黙示録の四騎士
鈴木央

Kurena / Tottori Prefecture

D
ALL THE WHAT'S THIS, CUTE BY CONTRAST?! YOU AGREE I'VE GOT THE BETTER FACE, RIGHT? RIGHT??

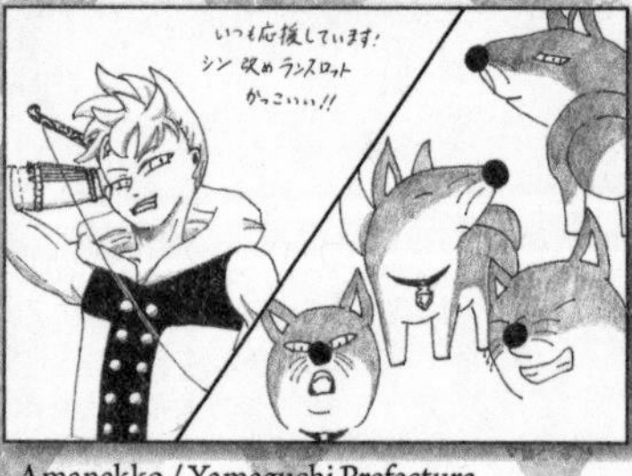

いつも応援しています!
シン 改め ランスロット
かっこいい!!

Amanekko / Yamaguchi Prefecture

P
HOW CAN I GET THAT STRONG?!

N
DON'T BOTHER. THAT GUY'S INHUMAN.

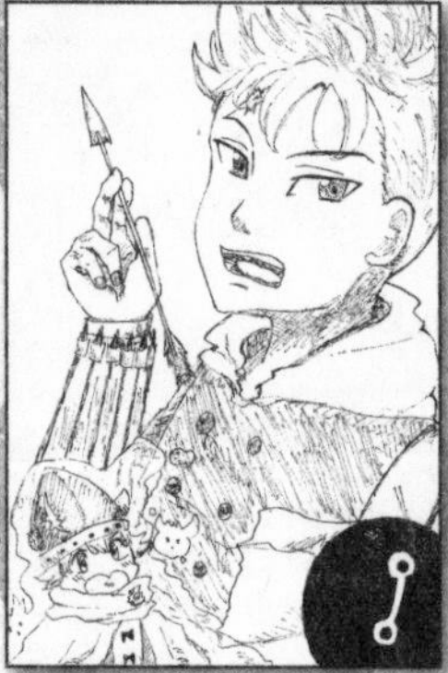
suzu / Hokkaido

D
LANCELOT ALWAYS GIVES THE MOST SPOT-ON ADVICE!

P
YEAH! HE'S AMAZING!

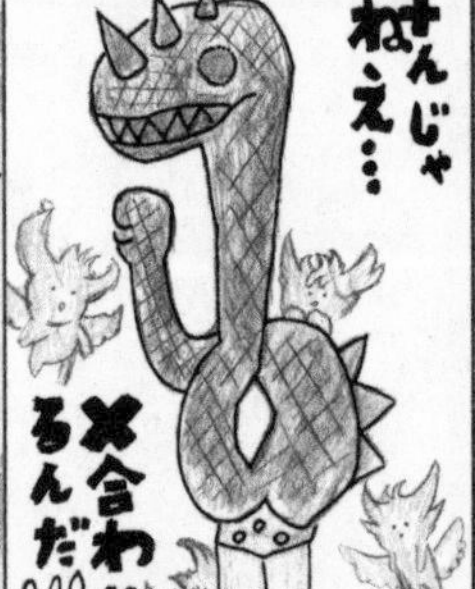

せんじゃねえ…
合わせるんだ!!!

Mango Yellow / Gunma Prefecture

D
THINK YOU CAN MAKE MINIS OF US WITH YOUR MAGIC, TOO, PERCIVAL?

P
WON'T KNOW UNLESS WE TRY!

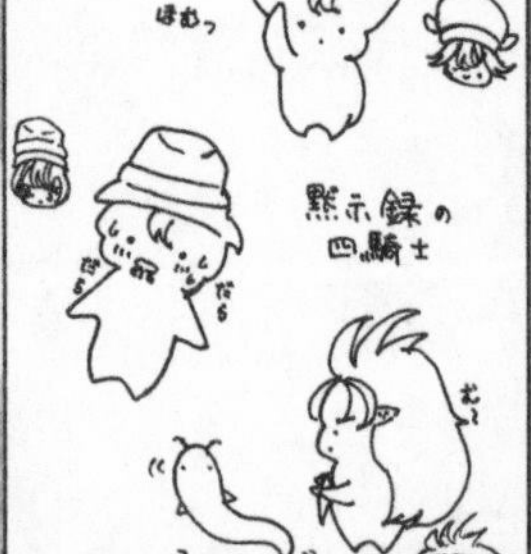

ほむっ
黙示録の四騎士
ふよよ〜
P.N.リディアーヌ

Lydianne / Kumamoto Prefecture

YOU'RE OBVIOUSLY TRYING TOO HARD TO SHOW OFF FOR SOME PRETTY YOUNG THING.

HRK! K-KEEP IT TO YOURSELF!

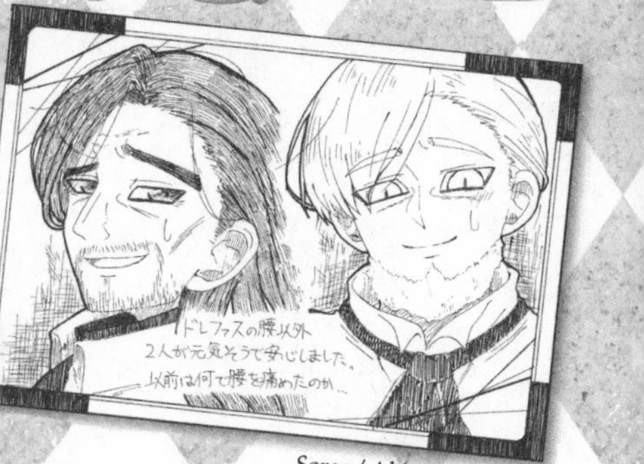

ドレファスの腰以外
2人が元気そうで安心しました。
以前は何で腰を痛めたのか…

Sorae / Akita Prefecture

N THAT'S *CLEARLY* A FAERIE POWER...

D YOU THINK? I THINK HE LOOKS HUMAN...

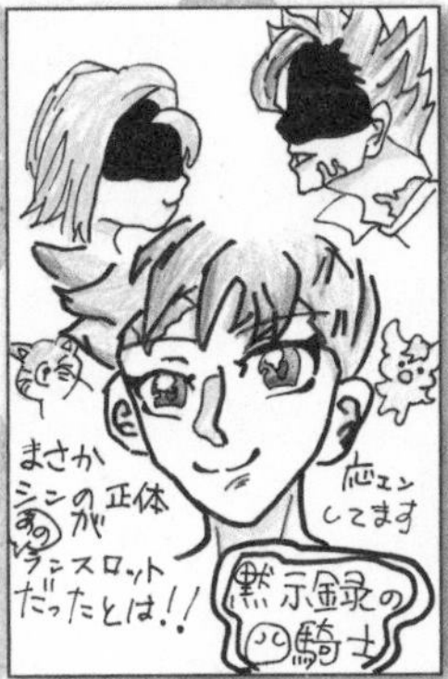

まさか
シンの正体があのランスロットだったとは!!
応エンしてます
黙示録の四騎士

Mei Tamamura / Osaka Prefecture

A I WISH I COULD BE A PART OF TEAM ANGHALHAD! HAI! HAI! HAAAAI!

D DOING THE WHOLE CHEER ON YOUR OWN?

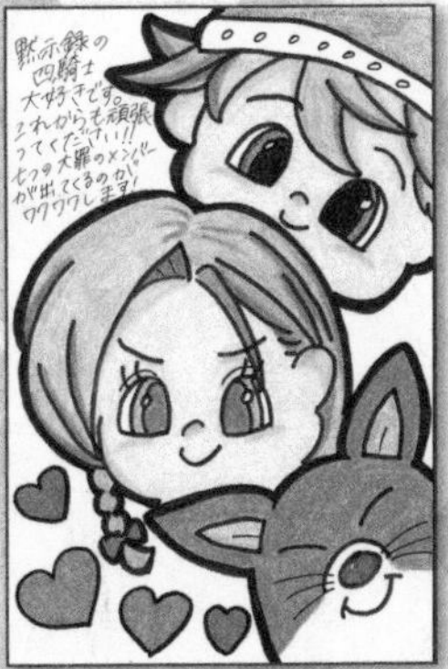

黙示録の四騎士大好きです。
これからも頑張ってください!!
七つの大罪のメンバーが出てくるのがワクワクします!

Mimomo Shibata / Aomori Prefecture

Submit Your Drawing!

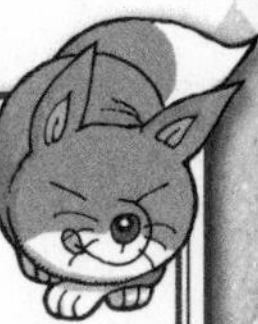

- ART MUST BE ON A POSTCARD OR POSTCARD-SIZED PAPER.
- WRITE YOUR NAME AND ADDRESS ON THE BACK OF YOUR PICTURE! YOU CAN INCLUDE COMMENTS IF YOU WANT. ALL ART WILL BE PRINTED IN BLACK AND WHITE, EVEN IF YOU SUBMIT IT IN COLOR.
- COPYING NAKABA SUZUKI'S ART STYLE IS FINE, OF COURSE, BUT COPYING PICTURES DRAWN BY OTHER FANS IS DEFINITELY NOT OKAY.

IF YOUR PIECE IS PRINTED, YOU'LL GET SPECIAL MERCH!
THE BEST PIECE IN EACH VOLUME WILL RECEIVE THE "SPECIAL AWARD" AND AN AUTOGRAPH!

SEND SUBMISSIONS TO:
KODANSHA WEEKLY SHONEN MAGAZINE
ATTN: FOUR KNIGHTS OF THE APOCALYPSE ART TROOP
2-12-21 OTOWA, BUNKYO WARD, TOKYO PREFECTURE 112-8001

NOTE: SUBMISSIONS WILL BE GIVEN TO THE ARTIST. PLEASE UNDERSTAND THAT THIS INCLUDES ANY ADDRESS, NAME, OR OTHER PERSONAL INFORMATION WRITTEN ON SAID SUBMISSIONS.

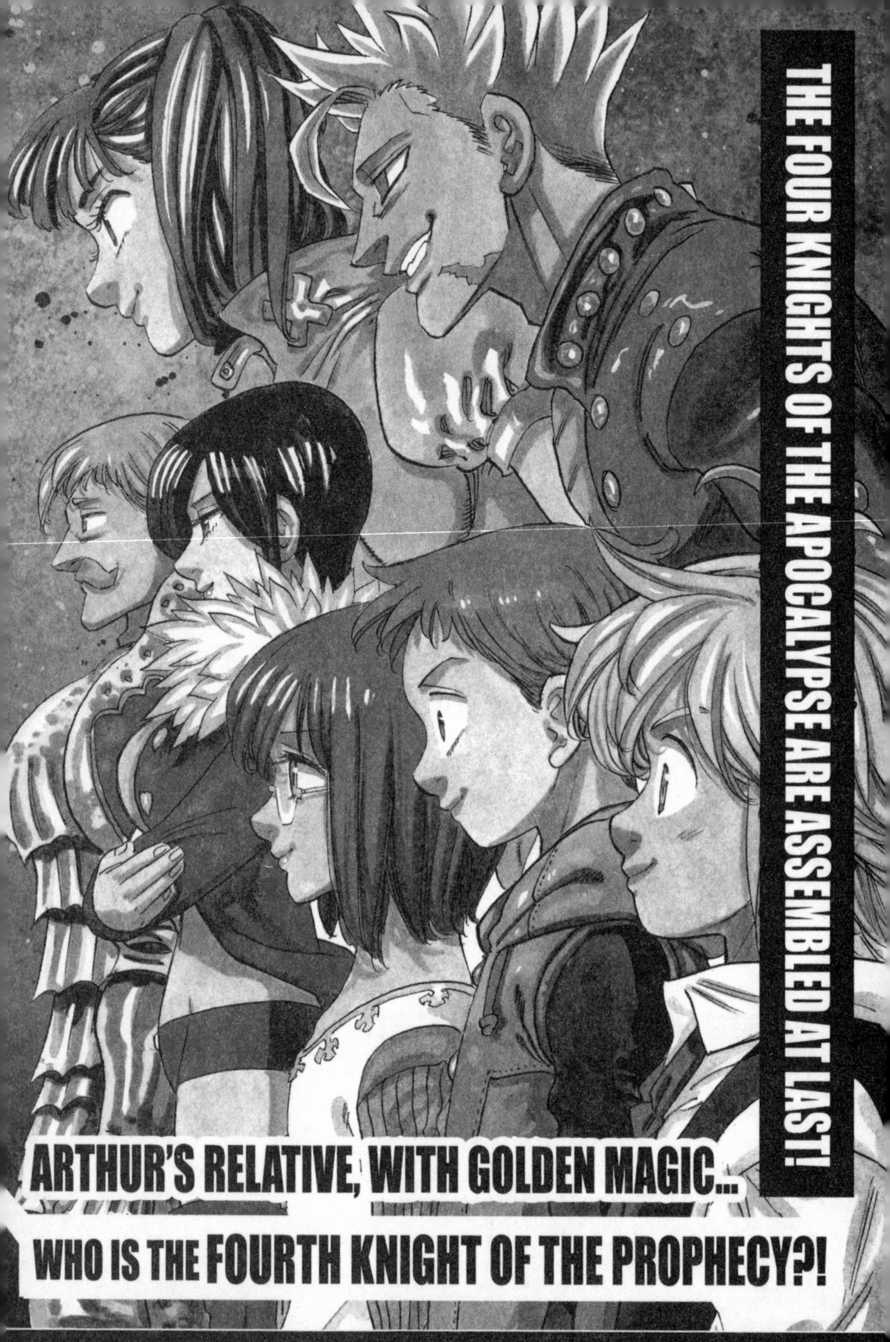
THE FOUR KNIGHTS OF THE APOCALYPSE ARE ASSEMBLED AT LAST!
ARTHUR'S RELATIVE, WITH GOLDEN MAGIC...
WHO IS THE FOURTH KNIGHT OF THE PROPHECY?!

TO THE WORLD'S DESTRUCTION?!

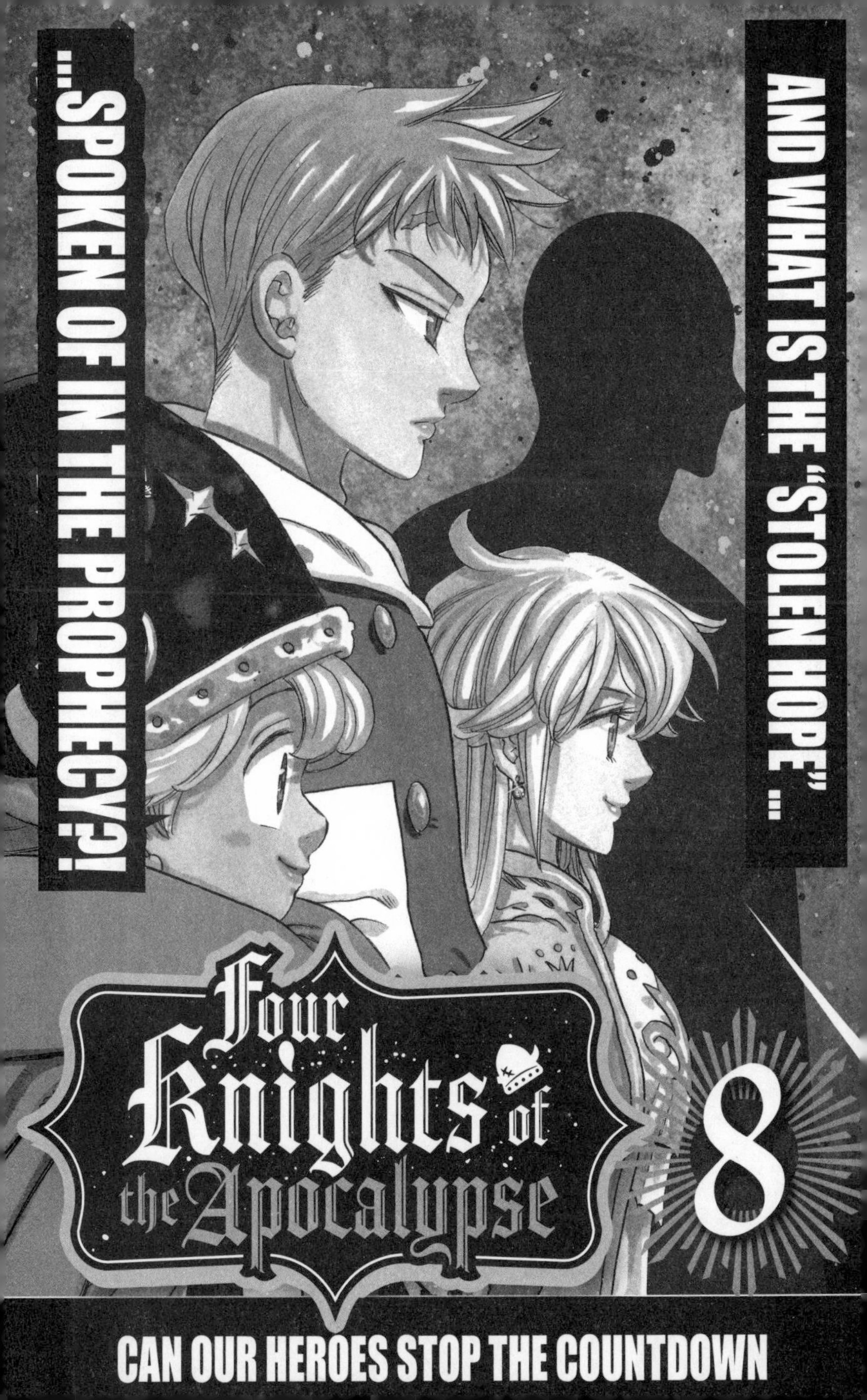
CAN OUR HEROES STOP THE COUNTDOWN
...SPOKEN OF IN THE PROPHECY?!
AND WHAT IS THE "STOLEN HOPE"...
Four Knights of the Apocalypse
8

A Kodansha Trade Paperback Original

The Seven Deadly Sins: Four Knights of the Apocalypse 7 copyright © 2022 Nakaba Suzuki
English translation copyright © 2023 Nakaba Suzuki

Published in the United States by
Kodansha USA Publishing, LLC, New York.

Publication rights for this English edition arranged through
Kodansha Ltd., Tokyo.

First published in Japan in 2022 by Kodansha Ltd., Tokyo
as *Mokushiroku no Yonkishi 7*.

ISBN 978-1-64651-728-2

Printed in the United States of America.

9 8 7 6 5 4 3 2 1

Original Digital Edition Translation: Kevin Gifford
Original Digital Edition Lettering: Darren Smith
Print Edition Translation: Kevin Steinbach
Print Edition Lettering and Layout: EK Weaver
Print Edition Editing: Aimee Zink
YKS Services LLC/SKY Japan, Inc.
Kodansha USA Publishing edition cover design by Matthew Akuginow

Publisher: Kiichiro Sugawara

Director of Publishing Services: Ben Applegate
Director of Publishing Operations: Dave Barrett
Publishing Services Managing Editors: Alanna Ruse, Madison Salters,
with Grace Chen
Production Manager: Emi Lotto

KODANSHA.US

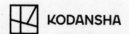

KODANSHA